Research Methods for Social Psychology

For my friend, David Raves, whose heart is also in the work

Research Methods for Social Psychology

Dana S. Dunn

WILEY-BLACKWELL

A John Wiley & Sons, Ltd., Publication

This edition first published 2009
© 2009 Dana S. Dunn

Blackwell Publishing was acquired by John Wiley & Sons in February 2007. Blackwell's publishing program has been merged with Wiley's global Scientific, Technical, and Medical business to form Wiley-Blackwell.

Registered Office
John Wiley & Sons Ltd, The Atrium, Southern Gate, Chichester, West Sussex, PO19 8SQ, United Kingdom

Editorial Offices
350 Main Street, Malden, MA 02148-5020, USA
9600 Garsington Road, Oxford, OX4 2DQ, UK
The Atrium, Southern Gate, Chichester, West Sussex, PO19 8SQ, UK

For details of our global editorial offices, for customer services, and for information about how to apply for permission to reuse the copyright material in this book please see our website at www.wiley.com/wiley-blackwell.

The right of Dana S. Dunn to be identified as the author of this work has been asserted in accordance with the Copyright, Designs and Patents Act 1988.

Wiley also publishes its books in a variety of electronic formats. Some content that appears in print may not be available in electronic books.

Designations used by companies to distinguish their products are often claimed as trademarks. All brand names and product names used in this book are trade names, service marks, trademarks or registered trademarks of their respective owners. The publisher is not associated with any product or vendor mentioned in this book. This publication is designed to provide accurate and authoritative information in regard to the subject matter covered. It is sold on the understanding that the publisher is not engaged in rendering professional services. If professional advice or other expert assistance is required, the services of a competent professional should be sought.

Library of Congress Cataloging-in-Publication Data

Dunn, Dana.
  Research methods for social psychology / Dana S. Dunn.
      p.   cm.
  Includes bibliographical references and index.
  ISBN 978-1-4051-4980-8 (hardcover : alk. paper)   1. Social psychology–Research–Methodology.   I. Title.
  HM1033.D86 2008
  302.072–dc22

                                        2008003442

A catalogue record for this book is available from the British Library.

Set in 10.5 on 13 pt Minion by SNP Best-set Typesetter Ltd., Hong Kong
Printed in Singapore by Fabulous Pte Ltd

1   2009

Brief Table of Contents

Detailed Table of Contents

List of 34 Active Learning Exercises for Doing Social Psychological Research

Preface

"It is with something akin to despair that one contemplates the piffling, trivial, superficial, damnably unimportant topics that some social scientists investigate with agony and sweat" (Carl Murchison in the Preface of *A Handbook of Social Psychology*, 1935, p. ix).

If Professor Murchison were alive today, I believe he would draw a very different conclusion about the social sciences in general and social psychology in particular. As a discipline, social psychology has hit its stride: courses, books, and journals on the subject, not to mention researchers who conduct it, abound. And then there are the students who are eager to learn about the latest findings concerning social behavior—findings that are not "piffling, trivial, [or] superficial" but are, to the contrary, highly important, touching on matters of the head, the heart, and how people relate to one another. Prejudice, emotion, conflict, cooperation, aggression, love, are all fascinating social psychological topics—and are all part and parcel of our social lives. Once they are exposed to social psychology, many students do not only want to learn more about the discipline, they want to contribute to it.

Undergraduate psychology students—most of whom will be majors at the sophomore level or higher—constitute the primary audience for this book. Some beginning graduate students in social or personality psychology (and their graduate instructors) may benefit from the book as well. The book will work nicely as a main text in social psychological courses that have a research or laboratory component. Such courses include Research Methods in Social Psychology, Research Methods in Personality, or an Advanced Seminar in Social Psychology. However, it also could be used as a supplemental text in a seminar in social psychology. For example, an instructor teaching a seminar on some specific topic (e.g., altruism and prosocial behavior) could assign the book so that students could learn to design and execute research projects dealing with when and why people choose to help others.

I wrote *Research Methods for Social Psychology* with two guiding pedagogical principles in mind: Social psychology is not a spectator sport, and students learn best by doing. Social psychologists are trained observers of social behavior who study people in controlled settings (the proverbial lab) or out in the field. To do so effectively, they have developed a variety of research methods—practical tools for practicing their craft—designed to tease cause and effect apart in social settings. These tools promote clarity and reduce opportunities for various biases to cloud interpretation.

A Focus on Students

I wrote *Research Methods for Social Psychology* so that students can learn to use the discipline's tools to conduct empirical research in social psychology. This book is designed to teach students to think like experimental social psychologists, that is, to use or develop explanatory theories and to manipulate and measure variables in order to explain the origin or purpose of some aspect of social life. Students will learn to perform research projects on human social behavior from start to finish, from selecting a research topic, to collecting and analyzing data, to writing up and reporting the results using the American Psychological Association's required format (i.e., APA style). Along the way, they will learn about the particular ethical issues social psychologists face, the logic of experimental design, sorting accuracy from error in research, and how to present their findings orally, among other issues. My hope, of course, is that students will actually get to conduct some empirical project, either one of their own design, a collaboration with a peer or peers, or perhaps a group-based project guided by their course instructor.

A Focus on Doing Social Psychology

My book is distinct from other research methods books in social psychology because each chapter contains classic as well up-to-date scholarship. I routinely present seminal research examples (e.g., social facilitation, obedience, and conformity) as well as con-temporary ones (e.g., stereotype threat, culture, and personal agency) to illustrate key concepts and illuminate how social psychologists study social behavior. Indeed, studies with people are the cornerstone of social psychology, so each chapter opens with a representative piece of research related to the chapter's topic. Reviewing research allows students to appreciate the elegance of clever theories and the simplicity of good research designs, and they will learn from as well as being inspired by social psychol-ogy's great experimenter-teachers.

One of social psychology's founders, Kurt Lewin, famously claimed that "there is nothing so practical as a good theory." We might safely add that there is nothing as practical as research practice-oriented "how to" topics that other texts often exclude (e.g., how to perform random assignment; how to recruit people to take part in research; how to write an experimental script so student-experimenters know what to say and do, and when to do both; how to plan data analyses before a study begins).

Additionally, each chapter has one or more specially designed Active Learning Exercises. These activities bring chapter topics to life by helping students apply key concepts when designing and executing their own research projects. In chapter 3, for example, the Active Learning Exercises focus on ethical issues, so that students learn to create their own in-class Internal Review Board (IRB) as well as to complete a standard IRB questionnaire and to write an informed consent form. In chapters 7 and 8, which deal with independent and dependent variables respectively, students learn to develop and manipulate independent variables, craft manipulation checks, and to adapt dependent variables from the literature or to design their own (the 34 *Active Learning Activities* appear in **boldface print** in the detailed table of contents and in a complete list on pages xv–xvi). Finally, each chapter concludes with optional exercises that extend or apply chapter concepts.

A Focus on Currency

Research Methods for Social Psychology discusses a variety of important current topics that other texts might exclude. For example, I discuss the problems associated with labeling, explaining in detail why the active term "participants" is now preferred over the passive, objectifying term "subjects." An entire chapter (Chapter 5) is devoted to research alternatives social psychologists use when experiments are not possible or appropriate, including observational and correlational research, quasi-experimental research, experiencing sampling methods (ESM) and diary approaches, Internet research and online data collection, and archival research and meta-analysis. In lieu of conducting a traditional experiment, many students prefer to do a survey. To help them conceive and write clear questions, as well as avoid common pitfalls (e.g., "double-barreled" questions, context effects, social desirability), an entire chapter (chapter 6) is devoted to developing high quality questionnaires and surveys.

A Focus on Sharing Social Psychological Knowledge with Others

As a discipline and a pursuit, social psychology is about expanding what we know about social behavior. This book is meant to encourage students to be producers of knowledge, not just consumers. To help students write scholarly research summaries, detailed guidance is provided in chapter 12 and in an annotated student research paper provided in Appendix C. Further, chapter 12 contains detailed guidance on delivering oral presentations (and using visual aids properly) in class or at conferences, as well as how to create poster displays of research summaries, which are now common features of many academic settings.

Acknowledgments

I cut my academic teeth in social psychology at Carnegie Mellon University and then learned the rigors and pleasures of research at the University of Virginia. I am grateful to the social psychology faculty at both institutions, but am understandably most thankful for the guidance provided by my mentor, Tim Wilson. I left Virginia years ago, but his scholarly example, creativity, and commitment to social psychology guide me still.

Books take time to plan, to write, and to pull together. My exceptional editor at Blackwell, Christine Cardone, was both patient and supportive, and gave terrific editorial advice throughout the project. Thanks, Chris. I am very grateful to Sarah Coleman for her meticulous attention to detail and her quick answers to my many (no doubt often tiring) questions. More recently, I appreciate the help and organizational skills of Kelly Basner. I thank the copyediting and production staff at Blackwell, especially Jenny Roberts, who guided the project through the last stages.

The content of the book was improved by the critical and constructive comments of peer reviewers. I thank Kevin Apple (James Madison University), Jeffrey Berman (University of Memphis), Marianne Miserandino (Arcadia University), and Joel Wade (Bucknell University) for their detailed suggestions and recommendations. Any remaining missteps in the text are my own.

I thank Bonnie Falla, Dorothy Glew, Wendy Juniper, and Beth Fuchs of Moravian's Reeves Library for their helpful comments on chapter 2. The Department of Psychology at Moravian College continues to be a congenial place for a social psychologist like me to teach, think, and write. I thank my colleagues for their support. Jackie Giaquinto deserves special credit once more for helping me attend to details great and small associated with this project. As always, I thank my loving family—Sarah, Jake, and Hannah—for their unstinting support of my writing activities.

I would be delighted to hear from readers. Please let me know what you liked about *Research Methods for Social Psychology*, as well as what topics you feel can be improved for a second edition.

Dana S. Dunn
Bethlehem, PA
dunn@moravian.edu

The author and publisher gratefully acknowledge the permission granted to reproduce the copyright material in this book:

Mitchell, J., © 1972 (Renewed). "You turn me on, I'm a radio," On *For the Roses*. Crazy Crow Music. All Rights Administered by Sony/ATV Music Publishing, 8 Music Square West, Nashville, TN 37203. All Rights Reserved. Used by Permission of Alfred Publishing Co., Inc.

"Dewey Defeats Truman," From the St. Louis Globe-Democrat Archives of the St. Louis Mercantile library at the University of Missouri-St. Louis.

The Rand Corporation, *A Million Random Digits with 100,000 Normal Deviates*, Glencoe, IL: Free Press (1955), pp. 3

Chapter 1

Studying Social Psychology

Back in the early 1930s, a professor took several sightseeing tours back and forth across the United States and up and down California's Pacific Coast. A young couple, a husband and wife, accompanied him. The couple happened to be Chinese; the professor, Richard LaPiere, was White. During the trip, the three stayed at many hotels, guesthouses, and campgrounds, and ate at numerous restaurants. After trying 251 establishments, only *once* were they denied service, which was highly unusual given the amount of prejudice and discrimination aimed at Asians in America at that time. In fact, before embarking on the trip, LaPiere had worried that he and his friends would not be well treated during their travels (LaPiere, 1934).

What makes this otherwise happily uneventful tale extraordinary is what happened later. The isolated prejudice experienced during the trip puzzled LaPiere, so he resolved to explore people's social reactions further. Six months after visiting each establishment, the professor sent a questionnaire asking whether "members of the Chinese race" were welcome as guests. Of the many replies he received, over 90% said no, they would not offer service to such guests. All the others were uncertain ("depends upon the circumstances") except for a *single* reply indicating that Chinese guests were welcome. In other words, apparently prevailing attitudes did not predict behavior.

Take a few minutes and think about this story. With that one exception, why do you believe that the travelers did not experience any overt signs of prejudice during their trip? Why did the prejudice appear later, and only in writing? Why did the establishments so dramatically change their previous policies, rejecting the same sort of guests they readily entertained, face-to-face, only a short time before? How certain are you of your conclusions?

Introducing and Defining Social Psychology

In answering these and other questions about LaPiere's experience, you are doing something that you do each and every day: You are thinking about people and speculating about the reasons for their behavior. Like most people, you probably spend much of your waking hours trying to explain why the people you encounter—your family, your friends, even the strangers you pass on the street—do what they do. You also think about people you do not actually encounter, people you read or hear about, like LaPiere, his traveling companions, and the individuals they encountered so long ago. Of course, you don't just think about other people; you also wonder about yourself and what motivates your own social behavior.

By thinking about yourself in relation to other people, you are doing social psychology. Indeed, you have always been one sort of social psychologist—a curious observer. My goal throughout this book is to help you move from casual observation to active intervention, to enable you to design and create events—especially experiments—that mimic everyday experience so that you can examine and explain intriguing social behavior like that witnessed by LaPiere and his friends. But I am getting ahead of myself. What exactly is *social psychology*?

Various definitions for social psychology exist; however, they all tend to identify a similar set of concerns. Social psychology is the scientific study of everyday social behavior—how the thoughts, feelings, and actions of individuals are influenced by situations, the individuals themselves, and other people, whether real or imagined (Allport, 1985). This classic definition of the field is readily applicable to our historic example. How did the people the travelers encountered—innkeepers, waiters, and so on—think and feel about them? Were their thoughts and feelings positive or negative? What role, if any, did the context—asking and paying for services—play? What about race? In the case of our three travelers, their real physical presence led to almost no prejudiced behavior, although a White male accompanied the Chinese couple. Did that matter? Later, simply the imagined presence of "members of the Chinese race" appears to have triggered antisocial responses. Explanatory possibilities abound, but no one knows what specific factors caused the discrepancy between the reactions during and after the trip. We can only speculate.

Although LaPiere's (1934) study is a classic, provocative piece of research in social psychology, it is fundamentally flawed. Perhaps you have already identified the main problem: LaPiere could not pinpoint what factors caused the warm in-person reception at one point in time and the later cold rejection on paper. Because he lacked control over who participated at the two different points in time, LaPiere could not determine if the people who answered his follow-up questionnaire were the same ones who originally greeted and seated them or gave them a room. Can you think of any other problems with his study?

To combat such flaws and to explain the underlying causes of social behavior, social psychologists rely on *research methods*. Research methods are tools for observing, measuring, manipulating, and controlling what takes place in social psychological investigations. This book will teach you how to use the research methods social psychologists use. This broad collection of tools allows social psychologists to scientifically determine cause and effect in social situations. I asked you above how confident you were in your ability to explain why attitudes did not predict behavior in LaPiere's (1934) study. Now that you have thought about LaPiere's lack of control in the study, are you less confident that you know what caused the attitude–behavior breakdown?

As you will see throughout this book, careful and thoughtful application of research methods allows social psychologists an opportunity to be reasonably confident when it comes to explaining social behavior, especially what factors cause the behavior to occur.

By using various research methods, social psychologists systematically examine situational and personal *variables*—influential, measurable factors that can take on different values—whose change can affect social perception, judgment, and interaction when people think about one another or gather together. Variables vary in value, which allows social psychologists the opportunity to introduce the presence of a variable in one setting to see how people react and to then compare the effects of its absence on other people in a similar setting.

Situational variables are literally outside people, often in the environment, serving as tangible (e.g., rules, physical boundaries), intangible (e.g., roles, cultural norms, expectations), and even transient (e.g., crowding, temperature, deadlines) influences. In contrast, personal variables include people's physical (e.g., race, gender, height, weight) and dispositional (e.g., a shy or outgoing personality) characteristics, their affective states (i.e., emotions, such as happiness or sadness), and whether they are perceivers (the judges) or being perceived (the judged) by others. On occasion, social psychologists study groups and group processes, how the thought and behavior of individuals is affected by collections of people who share some common quality or interest.

Despite limitations, LaPiere's (1934) pioneering study led to a great deal of subsequent research on how, why, and when attitudes do or do not predict behavior (e.g., Albarracin, Johnson, & Zanna, 2005; Wicker, 1969). To his credit, LaPiere used two research methods—observation and questionnaires—in a real life situation which revealed some interesting findings but did not allow him to determine why a given establishment's attitudes did not predict the behavior of its employees. Both these research methods are considered later in this book (in chapters 5 and 6, respectively). What could LaPiere have done to better determine what caused the lack of consistency between attitudes and behavior?

Establishing causality: The importance of experimentation in social psychology

Determining causality—what event led to what outcome—seems simple enough. For centuries, scientists argued that a presumed cause must precede any observed effect. Further, a cause must be demonstrated to occur before an effect in such a way that alternative accounts for the effect are unlikely to be true. These simple statements summarize the basic goal of controlled experiments, which are often easier to describe than to satisfactorily craft and carry out. An *experiment* is a trial or test designed to prove that one explanation for what causes some behavior is superior to others. To do so, key aspects of the phenomena under study are systematically varied in order to determine how their presence or absence affects behavior.

LaPiere (1934) could have relied on a more experimental approach to learn why almost no prejudice or discrimination occurred during the actual trip but a considerable amount was disclosed on paper, in the returned questionnaires. Experimental research in social psychology starts with a specific *hypothesis* indicating how one variable causes a change in another variable. The causal variable is called the *independent variable* and the effected variable is labeled the *dependent variable*. Social psychologists create a situation in which to test whether a given independent variable causes change in a given dependent variable. The researcher manipulates the independent variable by creating two or more *conditions*, distinct experiences corresponding to different qualities of that variable. Unlike other research approaches, experiments possess one defining feature: Participants are assigned at random to one and only one condition, and each person has the same chance as all the others of ending up in any of the conditions.

Let's leave the LaPiere (1934) study's causal uncertainty for a bit and review a recent study on a different topic, an aggression experiment illustrating clear causal connections among a hypothesis, an independent variable, and a dependent variable. Klinesmith, Kasser, and McAndrew (2006) hypothesized that men who hold guns experience a hormonal reaction that primes them to behave aggressively. A group of men gave saliva samples from which their testosterone levels were measured. Working alone, each man was seated at a table with paper and either a big handgun or the children's board game Mouse Trap. They were told to take apart the gun or the game and to write directions for disassembly and assembly on the paper.

After 15 minutes, the men's saliva was again collected, revealing that testosterone levels spiked in those who handled the gun but remained the same in those taking apart the game. Aggressiveness was measured in the last part of the experiment, where the men's "taste sensitivity" was examined. Specifically, they were asked to evaluate the taste of a glass of water with a drop of hot sauce in it. They were asked to make a similar drink for the next person in the study, using as much or as little hot sauce as they wished.

What did Klinesmith and colleagues (2006) find? The men who held the gun added three times as much hot sauce to the water for the next person—an aggressive act—compared to those who worked with the game. In other words, higher levels of testosterone caused more hot sauce to be added to the drink to be given to another person.

What were the variables in this study? How did they relate to the hypothesis? The independent variable—the observable cause of the aggression—was the object the men took apart and put back together, and it had two conditions: the gun and the game. By chance, each man either ended up with the gun or the game. Touching the gun was expected to heighten the hormone levels, whereas handling the game was not. The dependent variable was the relative amount of hot sauce put in the glass of water; more sauce (hence, more aggression) was dropped by the high testosterone men who had held the gun.

Klinesmith and colleagues (2006) used the first samples of saliva to demonstrate that all the men had similar levels of testosterone prior to handling the gun or the game, but not after. Thus they ruled out a major alternative explanation for the results, namely that the men had different levels of hormones before the experiment began. The second saliva sample demonstrated that only those men who worked with the gun subsequently displayed higher levels of testosterone. The researchers also made certain that all the men had similar experiences in the same setting. The only thing that ever differed was whether a man was given the gun or the game.

Now that you understand the importance of experiments in social psychology, can you see the problem in determining cause and effect in the now historic attitude study reported by LaPiere (1934)? Although it is still an important milestone report in the study of attitudes, LaPiere's study was not an experiment. His research lacked the causal clarity associated with experiments like the one reported by Klinesmith and colleagues (2006). LaPiere did not manipulate and measure any variables, nor did he have a working hypothesis that he tried to test. Unfortunately, we know what happened but not necessarily why; put another way, we cannot clearly identity the root cause of why little prejudiced behavior occurred on the cross-country trip although a considerable amount of prejudiced attitudes were revealed following the trip. Note that we are not criticizing LaPiere's work; rather, we are highlighting the fact that social psychologists prefer to use experiments rather than simple observations or other approaches to form coherent, compelling explanations for the occurrence (or absence) of prejudice and discriminatory behavior (e.g., Whitley & Kite, 2006). Experiments represent an ideal (Wilson, 2005), one that sometimes cannot be met due to particular circumstances, the availability of resources, time constraints, or even ethical issues.

Thus far we have considered a definition for social psychology and reviewed some illustrative research. Besides defining what social psychology *is*, we also need to know what it is *not*; that is, we need to compare its research focus with some of the other branches of psychology and the social sciences.

Levels of Explanation: Social Psychology's Relation to Other Fields of Inquiry

Social psychology is one field of scientific inquiry. Whether within or outside of psychology, different fields rely on different *levels of explanation* (see Table 1.1). Different levels of explanation tell us different things about people's behavior. Table 1.1 lists several fields of inquiry ranging from those with a more *collective* focus (a larger group or groups) to the more *individual* (solitary person or process) level of analysis. By moving downward in Table 1.1, the focus becomes narrower and the phenomena of interest become more internal and distinct to individuals. Moving upward in the table, the research emphasis becomes broader and more inclusive, increasingly involving

Table 1.1 Explaining Behavior: Selected Fields and Their Levels of Scientific Explanation

Field of inquiry	Level of explanation for behavior
	More collective focus
Anthropology	Cultural features and differences of past and present
Sociology	Societal social structures and customs of groups
Social psychology	Individual affect, cognition, behavior influencing interactions with other people, groups
Personality	Personal psychological processes, individual differences between people
Developmental psychology	Ages, stages, and life span issues in individuals and groups
Cognitive psychology	Individual mental structures, cognitive processes
Neuroscience	Individual electrochemical processes
	More individual focus

both individuals and their relations to groups, as well as within- and between-group processes.

Social psychologists are generally interested in the experience of people as individuals, notably how real or imagined others influence them in terms of affect (emotions, feelings), cognition (thoughts, beliefs), and behavior (actions, intentions). After learning about LaPiere's work, for example, most people are curious to know about the nature of the interactions between the travelers and the people they met. What, for example, were the innkeepers and waiters thinking and feeling when they served the travelers? Similarly, we would like to know the thoughts and feelings of the respondents who later indicated on paper that Chinese guests were unwelcome.

By comparison, psychologists interested in the emerging areas of neuroscience would want to examine the electrochemical activity in the brain during social encounters with minority group members or when thinking about minority groups (see the bottom of Table 1.1). Neuroscientists study neurochemical processes and how these processes affect the cognitive and behavioral responses of individuals. In contrast, a cognitive psychologist would be curious about a slightly higher level of analysis than a neuroscientist. What is the nature of the mental structures, for example, that leads someone to categorize a person as a member of a minority rather than a majority group? Developmental psychologists, in turn, examine social, cognitive, and emotional changes that occur at different ages and stages of development (see Table 1.1).

Sociologists are often interested in some of the same issues that attract the attention of social psychologists. Yet sociologists would be likely to take a different, more collective approach, one involving a search for the general laws of behavior that are based on the nature of social structures and groups. In the context of LaPiere's research, instead of focusing on the experience of individual service providers, a sociologist would be interested in the nature of relations between different racial or ethnic groups, the effects of socioeconomic class, and possibly in the ways that owner-managers as a group held different beliefs than hired workers (see Table 1.1). Thus sociology's level of analysis is more societal, aimed at the effect of social institutions and customs on groups of people rather than individuals (see, e.g., Burke, 2006). Finally, an anthropologist would want to examine the origins and the physical, cultural, and social development of groups of people. In our current example, an anthropologist could examine how perceived differences between racial groups originated and influenced social interaction across time.

Not all academic fields relevant to social psychology are represented in Table 1.1, of course. Instead, my purpose here is to identify social psychology's unique place as a bridge between individual and collective levels of explanation. Thus social psychological research examines individual processes that people have in common with others, and how those processes regulate a person's interactions with other people, including groups. But what about processes unique to each person—in other words, how does social psychology relate to the discipline of personality psychology?

Personality psychology's relation to social psychology

Earlier, I noted that people's dispositions, their personalities, were often considered by social psychologists. That is true, and social psychologists often consider the role of personality in their work. Personality psychologists often work closely with social psychologists; indeed, many researchers identify themselves as "social-personality psychologists" and many academic organizations and journals (see Appendix A) serve as common resources for both types of researchers.

Still, personality psychology adopts a somewhat different level of analysis than social psychology. Personality psychologists are interested in the private psychological functions of individuals and how these functions lead to differences between individuals (see Table 1.1). The term "individual differences" refers to those qualities found in one person's personality that causes him or her to be different than other people. One personality psychologist might want to know which of the people LaPiere and his friends encountered were naturally more helpful than the others; another personality researcher would be interested in knowing who among the people who answered LaPiere's (1934) survey had a truly prejudiced personality. In contrast, a social psychologist is focused on the common experience of all the individuals who encountered the travelers, as well as the shared qualities of those who returned the surveys. In short, what led *most* people to offer LaPiere and the couple a place to stay, what led *most* survey respondents to later say Chinese guests were unwelcome?

You may be thinking, "Now wait a minute, isn't it the case that your personality determines whether your prejudiced feelings lead to a discriminatory action, like denying a couple a place to stay or eat because of their race?" Sometimes, yes; but not always. Social psychologists believe that situations often matter much more when it comes to causing behavior than do people's personalities, especially at a common level of analysis.

This view may initially seem hard to believe. Yet ample research demonstrates that the power of situations often overrides the effects or role of personality. Indeed, in everyday life, people are repeatedly found to overestimate the influence of personality while underemphasizing the effects of situations as the causes of behavior (see Gilbert, 1998; Malle, 2004; Ross, 1977; Ross & Nisbett, 1991). Whether they possessed any number of personality types linked with prejudiced feelings, such as authoritarianism (Adorno, Frenkel-Brunswik, Levinson, & Sanford, 1950) or social dominance (Pratto, Sidanius, Stallworth, & Malle, 1994; Sidanius & Pratto, 1999), for example, the business owners may not have turned away the travelers for sheer economic reasons—money was to be made by housing or feeding them at that moment in time. Alternatively, perhaps the hotel restaurant workers simply did not have the authority to deny anyone service, thus their personalities, prejudiced or otherwise, had no role in guiding their actions. (Remember, we do not know if the persons who actually met LaPiere and his friends were the same ones who answered the later surveys.) Again, we will never really know what the actual causal factors involved were because LaPiere's (1934) study was not an experiment.

Whether an investigation is an experiment or another approach to research, the social psychologist doing the research is apt to follow an established procedure. This procedure is generally known as the scientific method, the topic of the next section.

The Scientific Method: Doing Social Psychology

In daily life, we try to make sense out of people's actions and intentions in order to make sense out of our social experiences, whether past, present, or future. In this way, we all share the interest of professional social psychologists, individuals who spend their careers trying to understand, explain, and predict the behavior of people in all kinds of social situations. Social psychologists do virtually the same thing you do, with one big exception. Besides formulating questions, they use a variety of formal tools to test whether their assumptions about the causes of behavior are accurate.

How do social psychologists go about conducting scientific research that explains human social behavior? In the first place, there is not one set approach—there are many, so that what works to study one social phenomenon may be ill-suited to another. Social psychologists are flexible and creative when it comes to examining and explaining the nature and consequences of people's affect, cognition, and behavior. Generally, one shared principle does guide social psychologists: Whenever possible, they rely on the scientific method.

The *scientific method* is a relatively formalized way of formulating and stating a research question, selecting a research approach and designing a study, collecting data, analyzing the data and drawing conclusions, and sharing the results. The goal of using the scientific method is to systematically identify and argue for one explanation for the behavior of interest over other possible accounts. LaPiere (1934) relied on the scientific method as a framework for his investigation of prejudiced attitudes and

Table 1.2 The Scientific Method: Five Steps for Doing Social Psychological Research

Step 1	Formulating a testable hypothesis
Step 2	Selecting a research approach
Step 3	Data collection
Step 4	Analyzing the data and drawing conclusions
Step 5	Sharing the results with the scientific community; return to Step 1 and begin again with a new or related hypothesis

behaviors. Let's quickly review his research in terms of the scientific method's five steps, which are listed in Table 1.2.

Step 1: Formulating a testable hypothesis. Social psychologists often develop research questions based upon their own experiences, as when something socially interesting or puzzling occurs to them or to other people. Alternatively, they already have an established interest in a research topic or they may decide to study some social phenomenon that has already received a great deal of attention. LaPiere (1934), for example, was already interested in the relationship between people's social attitudes toward others and their subsequent actions. Based on some early experiences traveling with the Chinese couple, he hypothesized that despite the pervasive prejudicial attitudes towards minority groups, actual discriminatory behavior toward minority group members might not occur. A *hypothesis* is a testable question, an educated assumption or guess that allows an investigator to predict what outcome will occur under what situation. LaPiere guessed that in spite of prejudiced attitudes, the various workers he and the couple encountered would not turn them away.

Step 2: Selecting a research approach. As you will learn throughout this book, social psychologists have a variety of research approaches and designs at their disposal. The main approaches to research used by many social psychologists are listed in Table 1.3. Selecting which one to use depends upon the nature of the hypothesis, of course, as well as the research topic and a host of practical questions. LaPiere's (1934) study was occurring with real people out in the real world, which meant that his ability to control the situation was quite low. But he did something clever. Instead of relying on only one research approach, he actually used two complementary approaches. First, LaPiere adopted the research approach known as *observation* (see Table 1.3). Observational research can be conducted in a variety of ways, but it generally involves an investigator carefully watching some social event take place. Simply put, during their trips, LaPiere planned to observe how his friends were received.

What about the second research approach? Remember that besides collecting observations, once the trips were over, LaPiere (1934) sent each establishment a questionnaire to find out whether Chinese guests were welcome. Similar to observational research, *questionnaire research* embraces a straightforward conclusion: If you want to

Table 1.3 Some Research Approaches in Social Psychology

Experimental approaches
    Laboratory-based experiments
    Some field-based experiments

Nonexperimental approaches
    Observational research
    Correlational research
    Quasi-experiments
    Experience sampling methods
    Diary research
    Internet-based research
    Archival research
    Meta-analytic research

Self-report-based approaches
    Surveys
    Questionnaires

know what people think or feel, why not ask them directly? You are used to answering questions all the time—some are verbal, but many are written. Like LaPiere, social psychologists use questionnaires to find out people's opinions towards a wide variety of social issues. Such questionnaires usually contain a number of questions that focus on the same topic.

A distinction should be drawn between *survey research* and questionnaire research (see Table 1.3). A survey is a questionnaire that is given to a carefully selected sample of people in order to estimate how the larger population from which they were drawn feels about a given social issue. LaPiere (1934) used a questionnaire to assess the attitudes towards Asians only at the places he and his friends visited—he did not attempt to measure the general attitudes of all the workers at the hotels and restaurants in the states they crossed, let alone the entire United States.

Could LaPiere (1934) have adopted a different research approach? Of course. If he did so, LaPiere probably would have had to redesign the whole study because he took advantage of the fact that he was traveling repeatedly across the country with his friends. Table 1.3 contains other approaches that social psychologists use to explore social behavior. For example, he could have relied on another nonexperimental approach by using archival data (see the middle section of Table 1.3). By doing so, he could have read and categorized newspaper accounts of prejudiced or discriminatory behavior aimed at minority group members, especially those of Asian descent. Or, do you think that LaPiere chose well under the circumstances?

Step 3: Data collection. The third step in the scientific method is data collection. The word "data" refers to information that is gathered to test the hypothesis. You already know what LaPiere (1934) did. He observed: Whenever the Chinese couple were checking into a hotel or asking for a table in a dining room, LaPiere hung back a bit and watched how they were received. In fact, he took detailed notes—observations—about each and every encounter, but he was not obvious about it. Later, he sent out the questionnaires to all the sites they visited and waited for the responses in the return mail.

Step 4: Analyzing the data and drawing conclusions. Once the data were collected, LaPiere (1934) performed his analyses. As you already know, the nature of the data he collected—the number of times he and his friends were accepted versus turned away, the number of returned questionnaires that indicated that Chinese guests were welcome—were relatively easy to track and tally. They were turned away once and only one of the returned responses said minority group guests were welcome. Although LaPiere's study used refreshingly basic analyses, most social psychological investigations use more complex and sophisticated analytic methods. In fact, social psychologists, like most other research psychologists, rely on statistical analyses to tease apart cause and effect relationships within the data sets they collect in the course of doing research. A statistic is a piece of information that is described in numerical form. A *statistical analysis* is a mathematically based technique used to answer a specific question or to search for a pattern within some data. You will learn about planning and selecting basic statistical analyses later, in chapter 11 of this book.

What conclusions did LaPiere (1934) draw based upon his analyses? He observed that for whatever reason—personal, social, or economic, among other possibilities—hotel and restaurant workers were unlikely to behave in a prejudiced manner in face-to-face encounters. However, the same establishments were quite willing to discriminate on paper, to say that they would turn away potential guests who were of Asian descent. As predicted by the hypothesis, people's actual behavior did not correspond to their expressed attitudes toward minorities. We will return to the implications and short-comings of LaPiere's research in the next section of this chapter. Before doing so, however, we need to consider the last step of the scientific method.

Step 5: Sharing the results with the scientific community. Once some research is complete, what happens? Ideally, social psychologists will share what they learned with other social psychologists. Such sharing can occur in many ways. Results can be shared with students in a classroom setting, for example, or a researcher might be invited to deliver a talk, to speak about the findings at a college or university or during a professional conference (see chapter 12). The most appropriate way to share the results, however, is to summarize them in the form of a journal article. Journals are specialized publications found in all scientific disciplines. There are hundreds, possibly thousands, of journals in psychology that publish research on countless specialized questions and topics. Appendix A lists various journals that publish social psychological research.

Journal articles in psychology follow a set of guidelines for presenting research in a concise, clear, and required format (see chapter 12). Quality journals are peer reviewed, that is, before an article is published it is carefully and thoroughly reviewed by a panel of experts who are knowledgeable about the topic under examination (for discussion of scholarly reviews, see Sternberg, 2006). Peer review is a cornerstone of publication in social psychology, and reviewers carefully screen every article to be certain that its contents are innovative, convincing, and truly noteworthy. An article will not be published until a group of (usually) anonymous expert judges that an author scrupulously followed the scientific method and that his or her conclusions are valid. Rejection is common; most high quality journals accept and publish fewer than 20% of all submissions. Thus peer-reviewed journals are deemed to be the reliable and "authoritative sources of information in their field" (Orne, 1981, p. 3). Without the quality control created by the peer review process, social psychology could not progress because its findings could not be trusted to appropriately shape future research efforts. As with all sciences, progress in social psychology is incremental.

Why? Social Psychology is Social

Why bother studying social psychology? Why do social psychological research? The answer is perhaps obvious in the definition I offered earlier: to learn how individuals think or feel about, influence, or interact with real or imagined others. Besides this connection to others, people are affected by situation, circumstance, and custom. The discipline of social psychology explores behavior by pursuing three related lines of inquiry: social thought, social influence, and social connections.

Social thought

When people read the term "social thought," they usually think of philosophy or political science. Social psychologists use the term rather literally: how we think about ourselves and other people. The disciplinary label for this area of study is *social cognition*. The study of social thinking entails a critical evaluation of the origins and functions of people's attitudes, inferences, and beliefs. Consider some major questions posed by social cognitive researchers: Are your first impressions of other people usually accurate? Are your social judgments prone to predictable errors and biases? How well do you know yourself? Do you have access to privileged self-knowledge that someone who knows you well or meets you for the first time does not?

Social influence

Social thinking occurs mostly inside our heads but it does have profound consequences for our behavior. When social thought gets outside the head, it often affects how we interact with and relate to one another. One of the great lessons of social psychology—a lesson you observed when learning about the LaPiere (1934) study—is that humans are often very concerned with the opinions of others or what others will think of them.

The second major area of social psychological inquiry aims to understand the nature and power of such social influence. Think about social influence this way: How often do you look to other people to determine what you should do or how you should behave? Simply put, we are influenced by the other people around us. They affect how we think, feel, and act. Social influence is the invisible force that allows us to be persuaded by others to do some things and not others. Of course, we also affect other people's behavior, leading them toward performing some actions and away from others. Social psychological research on social influence concerns gender relations and roles, persuasion processes and attitude or belief change, and effects of group and group membership on behavior, among other topics.

Social connections

Social thought and social influence point to the third line of disciplinary inquiry: the social connections we form with other people. Most of us do not live in isolation, and the essence of social life is engaging in activities or relationships with others. In a real sense, however, social connections represent the best and worst in humanity. We want and need to connect with others, but real and serious problems sometimes arise when we do so. Some connections are positive and constructive, as is the case when we help other people or form close relationships with them. Other connections are negative and problematic, such as harboring a prejudice towards a group and engaging in discriminatory activities. The study of social connections reminds us that conflict between individuals or among groups is a regrettable but real aspect of human experience. The beneficial connections we do form with others remind us how much others contribute to our well-being.

Whether you are interested in studying social thought, social influence, or social connections, note that the social psychological processes in each area all involve some degree of thinking, feeling, and behaving. In the same way, the real or imagined presence of other people also affects how we think, influence, or connect with others. Let's turn to the venues where social psychological research is conducted.

Where? The Lab and the Field

The bulk of social psychological research relies on experimentation (e.g., Higbee, Millard, & Folkman, 1982), and two-thirds of all experimental studies occur in the lab (e.g., Adair, Dushenko, & Lindsay, 1985). Social psychologists often speak of working "in the lab" or "in the field." What do these phrases mean? Or, more importantly, where is the *lab* versus the *field*?

The lab

When social psychologists refer to the lab or laboratory, they do not usually mean a space inhabited by scientific equipment, test tubes, and the like. Rather, the term is used to refer to any place or space—often a room or suite of rooms—that allows psychological research to be carried out in a highly controlled manner. The *control* is necessary so that everyone taking part in an experiment, for example, experiences the same thing, that no distractions or extraneous variables (e.g., noise) detract from the impact of the independent variable or cloud the intent of the dependent variable. Most social psychological research is conducted in a room with a few chairs and a table (recall the description of the Klinesmith et al., 2006, aggression experiment, for example). By relying on such spare spaces, social psychologists hope to maximize cause and effect relations by minimizing all other influences.

The focus on control is a strength but it also highlights a pitfall of rigorous experimentation: dissimilarity from everyday experience. Lab settings can seem artificial, less natural, even somewhat removed from people's normal experiences. Critics of social psychological experiments correctly raise an important concern: How can researchers be sure that people's social behavior in the lab is anything like the behavior they display out in the hectic pace of the real world? As an antidote to this problem, many social psychologists replicate—that is, repeat and verify—lab-based efforts out in the field.

The field

The "field," as in field research or field studies, is social psychological research that occurs in settings that lack the control associated with the lab. Field settings not only have a high degree of naturalism in that they mimic everyday life, they often take place during everyday life in everyday settings. Field settings can be in classrooms, offices, shops or malls, on campus, at concerts, in parks—really, anyplace that by its nature reduces the amount of control a researcher can exercise. For this reason, perhaps, field research is sometimes called *naturalistic research* in that settings are "real" and the behavior occurring within them is presumed to be more natural than that associated with the lab. Sometimes independent variables can be manipulated and measured in field settings, other times interesting results are obtained—again, LaPiere's (1934) results are still provocative even after 70 years—but causal conclusions cannot be drawn from them. Field research can be difficult to do precisely because control is an issue.

On the other hand, field studies often display a quality that some controlled experiments lack: *generalizability*. The findings from field research are often thought to be more generalizable, that is, descriptive of behavior performed by other people at other times and in other places, than those based on lab research. Ironically, social psychologists know the behavior observed in field settings is usually natural and therefore comparable to what we might observe in countless similar settings (e.g., any restaurants or hotels LaPiere or others could have visited elsewhere in the US of the 1930s), but they remain unable to offer causal explanations about it.

Thus there is a fundamental trade-off between social psychological research conducted in the lab or the field. As shown in the top of Figure 1.1, the increasing control associated with the lab provides us with empirical certainty, much more than can ever be found in field settings. The trade-off, however, is shown in the bottom of Figure 1.1: The ability to generalize from one setting to another increases out in the field while it decreases in the lab. The hard truth is that there is no ideal research setting where both control and generalizability can be maximized. Either control must be sacrificed

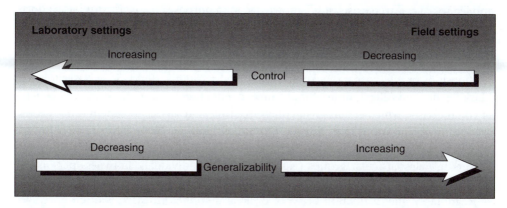

Figure 1.1. The trade-off between control and generalizability in lab and field research. Adapted from Figure 7.1 in Dunn (1999, p. 219)

to obtain more naturalism or generalizability must be reduced so that greater control can be exercised for greater inferential clarity. These issues are revisited in chapter 9.

How do social psychologists deal with the problems posed by the trade-off shown in Figure 1.1? They acknowledge it by doing programmatic research using both lab and field settings (Aronson, Wilson, & Brewer, 1998). Novel hypotheses concerning social behavior are usually first developed and tested in lab settings. As the researchers become more comfortable in making obtained effects "behave," they design subsequent studies that gradually move out into the field. Findings discovered in the lab are replicated and extended in the field, boundary conditions or limits are identified, and the developing theory is refined. By the same token, interesting and novel observations uncovered in the field are subjected to the rigor of the lab. Such "give-and-take" between the lab and field is essential to the process of advancing knowledge in social psychology.

One more distinction: Basic and applied research

Whether to work in the lab or the field is not the only distinction that social psychologists must consider. There is also the matter of whether their research is considered to be basic or applied. *Basic* social psychological research is conducted out of pure intellectual interest. The goal of basic research is scientific: to expand the available knowledge base concerning human social behavior. This is the search for "knowledge for its own sake." Most basic research efforts, especially experiments, are designed to answer a single question (e.g., Why does physical anonymity increase the incidence of antisocial behavior?; Diener, 1976; Zimbardo, 1969). The results from basic research efforts are pored over by researchers who are looking to discover the presence of statistically significant effects (Bickman, 1981; Hedrick, Bickman, & Rog, 1993). Once verified, the results are used to further develop social psychological theory and to design the next round of experiments so that the search for new knowledge can continue.

Applied research in social psychology is typically conducted for a specific purpose, most often to understand or address some socially relevant problem. If a maxim for applied social research exists, it is "knowledge for a purpose." As is true for basic efforts, applied research relies on careful methodological practices and statistical analyses. The goals of applied research differ, however. Most applied projects aim to answer multiple questions and the search for statistical significance is often sacrificed for finding practical relationships or effects (e.g., Bickman, 1981; Hedrick et al., 1993). Social psychologists Mark Snyder and Allen Omoto, for example, conduct research on the costs and benefits of volunteerism, which entails giving one's free time and service to benefit other people, groups, or organizations (e.g., Snyder, Omoto, & Lindsay, 2004). The practical knowledge gained from such applied research can be invaluable when it comes recruiting volunteers to help particular groups (e.g., AIDS/HIV+ individuals, homeless persons) in need (e.g., Clary, Snyder, Ridge, Miene, & Haugen, 1994; Omoto & Snyder, 1993).

Regrettably, the distinction between basic and applied research is often portrayed as somewhat adversarial, as if one approach is somehow superior to the other (e.g., "basic research is real science," "applied research improves people's lives"). As I am sure you can imagine, a similar sort of tension is often cited as existing between lab and field research. The distinction between basic and applied research is not absolute and really more a matter of degrees; one social psychologist's basic research is seen by another as applied (or vice versa). As one of my teachers once put it, the distinction is more apparent than real and, in any case, both approaches contribute to our understanding of social behavior. As Aronson, Wilson, and Brewer (1998, p. 135) put it, "If the distinctive contribution of experimental social psychology to the general body of knowledge is ever to be realized, an optimal integration of theory-oriented laboratory research with applied field experimentation will be required." These are wise words to keep in mind as you learn to conduct research in social psychology.

Social Psychologists Today

As you've learned in this chapter, social psychology is about people being interested in other people. What better way for you to learn more about the discipline than by researching the people who work in it? And here is an interesting and related fact: Social psychology is a very young discipline, having largely developed following World War II, so that its coming of age as a distinct discipline was in the 1950s. Thus most of the social psychologists you will learn about in this book or whose work you will encounter in introductory social psychology texts are alive and hard at work. In fact, one of the best ways to get a sense of what social psychology is all about is by becoming familiar with the research program of a social psychologist. What follows is an exercise that will help you come to know the background, professional life, theoretical perspective, and publications of one or more professionals.

Because social psychology is an academic field, most social psychologists are employed in college and university settings, and they can be found in psychology or other social science departments. Some social psychologists, however, work for the government or in private industry. Don't unduly limit your search to academic settings.

ACTIVE LEARNING EXERCISE   1A

Learning About Active Social Psychologists

Each chapter in this book contains one or more active learning exercises designed to provide you with some hands-on research experience. Before you begin to develop your own research topic, however, you should learn about existing research and some of the researchers who conduct it. Here are three related Internet-based activities you can do to learn about the life and work of contemporary social psychologists.

Web site activity. One of the best available web sites dealing with social psychology is the Social Psychology Network, developed and maintained by Professor Scott Plous of Wesleyan University. The site is located at: http://www.socialpsychology.org. This site provides a wealth of information about social psychology— everything from specific research topics to online studies and demonstrations. One of the site's best features, however, is its listing of over 1,000 profiles of social psychologists. These profiles can be searched by researchers' names or key words, browsed by research topics (e.g., close relationship, emotions, health, gender), or reviewed alphabetically. Most profiles contain contact information, institutional affiliation, a photo, a short biographical sketch, some description of research and teaching interests, and a list of selected publications, such as recent journal articles and books.

Go to the Social Psychology Network web site and select one or two profiles to read. You might search for a psychologist whose name is familiar, a topic that interests you, or for fun, simply select a profile at random. Read the individual's profile carefully to learn what you can. Do you see any indication regarding how this person became interested in social psychology? Print out or write down the references for one or two of the researcher's publications and then go to the library. Look up the references and read them carefully. What makes the research an example of social psychology? What prompted the researcher's interest in the topic?

Web search activity. Instead of searching the profiles at the Social Psychology Network, you can select a social psychologist to learn more about by examining the lists of references found at the back of this book or by looking through virtually any introductory text in social psychology. Once you have a researcher's name, use one of the traditional Internet search engines, such as google.com or yahoo.com. Type in the individual's name and see what materials are found in cyberspace. Depending upon the person, you may receive a list of links to his or her publications, professional appearances at psychology conferences, a home page address,

Continued

and information about his or her place of employment. Follow the suggestions above in the *web site activity* and learn what you can about your researcher's interests.

Home page activity. A third alternative for learning about the work of contemporary social psychologists involves visiting their *home pages*. Some home pages will be accessible through either of the above activities (the Social Psychology Network profiles often provide links) or by simply visiting the researcher's institution's web site. Most psychology departments, for example, maintain faculty profiles with links to the colleagues' home pages (social psychologists who teach at your institution are fair game, as well!). Go to one and see what you can learn about your chosen social psychologist. Does the home page reveal anything else about the researcher's current interests in social psychology, including publications?

Learning Research Methods for Social Psychology

The goal of this book is a straightforward one: to teach you research methods so that you can actually *do* social psychology—conduct social psychological research—and not merely read about it. In subsequent chapters, you will learn:

- To move from casual speculation to expressing focused questions;
- To search the social psychological literature for relevant theory or research pertaining to topics of interest;
- To turn questions and supporting research into specific hypotheses;
- To design experiments to test competing hypotheses in the search for the best explanation for some social behavior;
- To conduct a social psychology project from conception to completion;
- To select alternative approaches to social psychological research when experiments are not appropriate;
- To share research results with others, either in written or spoken form;
- To add your point of view to our growing knowledge regarding the origins, description, and function of social behavior.

Although you will learn these and other techniques as you read subsequent chapters in this book, it is never too early to begin planning your own research. With this goal in mind, this first chapter closes with a practical, helpful active learning exercise that you can return to again and again as your work proceeds.

ACTIVE LEARNING EXERCISE   1B

Planning a Research Project in Social Psychology

Doing research takes time and effort: Both these qualities determine a project's likelihood of success. Whenever you plan a research project in social psychology, consider what activities need to be accomplished in light of the time available. Less or more time will affect what you choose to do and often how you will go about doing it. I urge you to keep in mind a maxim a wise psychologist I know relies on where research and writing are concerned: "Things always take longer than they do."

You may not be ready to actually do this exercise yet, especially if you are just finishing this first chapter. Nonetheless, you should become familiar with what you will need to learn to do. Before you proceed further in this book, then, you should have a clear sense of what must be done in order to bring a research project from conception to fruition. Table 1.4 lists the main activities common to most social psychological investigations. As you can see, this table identifies the activity and where it can be found in this book. Additionally, there is space in Table 1.4 for you to estimate how long each activity will take to complete.

Table 1.4   Research Activities for Doing Social Psychological Research

Activity	Chapter location	Estimated time to complete
Identifying a research topic	2	_____ day(s)
Searching the literature	2	_____ day(s)
Reading the literature	2	_____ day(s)
Completing an IRB form	3	_____ day(s)
Choosing an approach and performing research:		
Experimental research	4 and 10	_____ day(s)
Nonexperimental research	5	_____ day(s)
Questionnaire/survey research	6	_____ day(s)
Writing operational definitions	4	_____ day(s)
Creating independent variables	7	_____ day(s)
Creating dependent variables	8	_____ day(s)
Recruiting participants	10	_____ day(s)
Verifying validity and reliability	9	_____ day(s)
Summarizing and analyzing project data	11	_____ day(s)
Writing or presenting research results	12	_____ day(s)

Exercises

1   Obtain a copy of LaPiere's (1934) article and read it carefully. If you had been there with LaPiere, what changes would you have made to the study? How would you redesign it? What other variables would you consider examining?
2   What do you think would happen if you were to repeat LaPiere's (1934) study today? Instead of using a Chinese couple as the contact minority, what do you think would happen if you used an African-American couple, a Hispanic or Latino couple, or a gay or lesbian couple? Would prevalent attitudes today predict behavior—why or why not?
3   Generate a list of three or more topics that you would like to examine using research methods from social psychology.

Chapter 2

Developing Research Topics in Social Psychology

Where do social psychologists get ideas for their research? The real answer is deceptively simple: all around them. I am not trying to be flip or clever here; rather, I am actually identifying one of the main sources of research ideas. Many social psychologists develop research topics by witnessing something that causes them to wonder about the underpinnings of social behavior. Here are my goals for this chapter. First, I will teach you a variety of strategies for identifying and developing researchable topics in social psychology. I will then explain how to successfully search the social psychological literature, both online and by checking the resources available in your institution's library. After you gather some sources, I will offer advice on how to critically read and review them so that you use the most relevant information for your research project. The chapter also contains a few active learning exercises designed to help you develop research topics, organize a bibliography, and to properly use material from existing research in social psychology.

Consider a straightforward experiment that came into being precisely because an investigator was promoted to "look around" after noticing an intriguing, anomalous pattern in some data. The experiment I am referring to happens to be the first one ever conducted in social psychology. In the late 19th century, Norman Triplett, a professor at Indiana University, noticed something while poring over bicycle racing times (Triplett, 1898). The records revealed that cyclists who were competing against one another in races achieved speeds that were around 20% faster than solo cyclists racing against the clock.

Triplett wondered what factors would cause cyclists to race faster in the presence of others than when riding alone. While doing so, he identified a variety of possible factors that might lead to speedier times when more than one cyclist is present. If you watch bicycle races like the Tour de France, for example, you can probably think of one related to physics. Cyclists often ride closely behind one another so that a lead rider acts as a windbreak for those behind him—while he pedals hard and fast, his "followers" pick up speed but exert less energy.

Though such physical accounts are interesting in their own right, Triplett was not satisfied by them. Instead, he believed that something more psychological was actually behind the results. What social psychological factors do you think operate in cycling

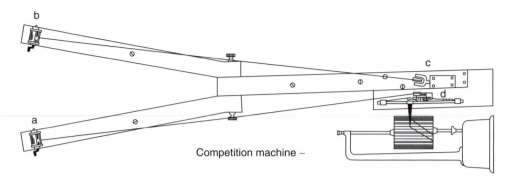

Figure 2.1.   A diagram of Triplett's competition machine. *Source:* Triplett (1898, p. 519)

competitions or, more generally, when people are performing the same behaviors side by side rather than alone? Triplett hypothesized that the mere presence of another person arouses a competitive instinct within each of us.

To test his hypothesis in a more controlled and careful manner, he left the velodrome and created a clever device that measured how quickly a person could turn the crank on a fishing reel (see Figure 2.1). He then had children perform the reel-cranking task alone or competing against other kids. Triplett found that children reeled much faster when they competed against a "coactor" than when reeling by themselves. A general principle resulted: Social influence in the guise of interpersonal competition improves performance when people perform relatively easy behaviors.

So far, so good, but did Triplett's original experiment spawn additional, related research? Did his casual observation and subsequent experiment have any lasting effect in social psychology? Absolutely. Triplett's experiment was the first in a long line of studies examining a social psychological phenomenon now known as social facilitation (but see Strube, 2005, for another view on Triplett's contribution to social psychology's history). Social facilitation involves the effects of whether the presence of other people helps or hinders an individual's performance. In general, having others present improves our performance on easy tasks (as is the case for pedaling a bike or reeling in a fishing line) but impairs our performance on more difficult tasks (e.g., solving a puzzle or problem; Baron, Moore, & Sanders, 1978; Bond & Titus, 1983; Zajonc, 1965). Although it is quite interesting, social facilitation is but one topic within a wide range of topics currently studied by social psychologists.

The Scope of Social Psychology

Let's turn to a more pressing set of questions: What social psychological topic would you like to study? What sort of social psychological research do you want to conduct? How can you identify and develop a research topic in social psychology?

Table 2.1   The Scope of Social Psychology: Some Sample Topics

Social thought

    Self and self-perception

    Beliefs about and perceptions of others

    Attitudes and behavior

    Affective forecasting

Social influence

    Genetic influences (nature)

    Gender

    Culture (nurture)

    Conformity, compliance, and obedience

    Persuasion and attitude change

    Social facilitation

    Groups and group processes

Social connections

    Stereotypes, prejudice, and discrimination

    Aggression

    Close relationship: attraction, liking, and love

    Helping and cooperating

    Conflict and negotiation

    Begin by thinking about the scope of social psychology. Social psychology is a broad field that covers a wide variety of social behavior involving the experiences and interactions of individuals. Think about your own daily experiences. What social processes comprise the bulk of your experience? Daily life is filled with social behaviors and processes that receive a great deal of scientific scrutiny from social psychologists. Table 2.1 categorizes some representative examples under the three headings introduced in chapter 1: *social thought* (how we think about other people and ourselves), *social influence* (how we affect and are effected by others), and *social connections* (how our encounters with others shape the social world and how we navigate within it). You will notice that social facilitation, the subfield spawned by Triplett's (1898) research of long ago, is categorized as an example of social influence.

    One way to begin thinking about what research topic or topics interests you is by examining the contents of Table 2.1. You may already have an interest in a particular subtopic, perhaps one that you remember studying in the section on social behavior in introductory psychology or in an introductory social psychology course. If you are unfamiliar with specific subtopics, consider focusing on which of the three organizing themes in social psychology most intrigues you. Are you interested in how we interpret the actions or intentions of others, how other people sometimes sway our opinions or actions, or the social bonds that tie us together? Table 2.1 is by no means exhaustive;

as a discipline, social psychology has spawned more subtopics than can be easily listed here. Still, this list is a good starting point.

Traditional topics and new avenues for research

Another method for identifying a topic that interests you is to review established research. I think a good approach is to learn about a traditional—what we might even call "classic"—topic as well as a new area of inquiry. If you look at Table 2.1 again, you will notice that two subtopics are italicized: affective forecasting and helping and cooperating. The former is relatively new, whereas the latter has drawn interest from researchers for several decades. For purposes of example, let's review each subtopic and consider the kinds of research questions that could be asked in order to extend what is already known.

We will consider the traditional topic, helping behavior, first. The study of what factors motivate people to help others, which is often referred to as prosocial behavior, is not new. Since ancient times moral philosophers have attempted to identify the nature of the "good" in people as well as what acts should be performed in the interests of social welfare and collective well-being. Social psychologists' explicit interest in helping, however, began in earnest in the 1960s and 1970s and focused on factors that impede people's willingness to offer aid to others. Some sample research questions concerning helping and prosocial behavior are shown in the top half of Table 2.2.

Table 2.2   Some Sample Research Questions within the Research Areas of Helping and Affective Forecasting

Helping
Why do people help others (or fail to do so)?
When will people offer help?
Does altruism (selfless help) exist?
Do people possess a motivation to help others?
What personal qualities (e.g., personality, religiosity) promote helping?
How do recipients react to being helped?
How can we increase the likelihood that people will offer help when it is needed?

Affective forecasting
How well do people predict the valence (directional strength) of their future feelings?
How does current mood influence judgments about future feelings or emotions?
Are individuals able to predict specific emotions regarding future events?
Do people accurately assess how long future feelings or emotions will last?
How well do individuals estimate the intensity of future emotions?
What errors and biases do people unknowingly rely on when forecasting their anticipated future feelings?

A classic series of social psychological studies were conducted by John Darley and Bibb Latané (1968; Latané & Darley, 1968, 1970), who puzzled over the causes of an awful public event: the failure of witnesses to prevent a young woman's murder. Late on the night of March 13, 1964, Kitty Genovese was attacked and stabbed to death while 38 of her neighbors in the Kew Gardens section of Queens listened to her anguished cries for help. Her neighbors recognized that she was being attacked—her assailant brutalized her for quite some time. They recognized, too, that the situation was an emergency, that someone should do something. As the neighbors looked out their lighted windows into the darkness, they even sensed one another's presence. Yet no one went out to help the young woman or to scare her attacker away; no one even bothered to call the police until it was too late to be of any use (for a different view of this event, see Manning, Levine, & Collins, 2007).

Why didn't anyone come to Kitty Genovese's aid? Did her neighbors fear for their own safety? Did they not want to "get involved"? Were they terrible people who were so indifferent to the sufferings of another human that they simply ignored the crime? The media aired these and other explanations, most of which were grounded in the idea that Americans were becoming increasingly alienated from one another, more concerned about themselves rather than their fellow citizens.

In a series of groundbreaking studies, however, Latané and Darley offered an intriguing alternative explanation that ran counter to the public's assumptions about why people don't help those in need. The presence of other people—fellow witnesses to an emergency—can actually hinder any individual's decision to offer help. How so? Emergencies can often appear ambiguous to us. Although it may seem implausible, some of Kitty Genovese's neighbors may have assumed that she was involved in a lover's spat, for example, rather than a fight for her life.

The researchers created a model (Darley & Latané, 1968; Latané & Darley, 1970), arguing that a bystander must make several decisions before offering help. Initially, a person must determine that a real need for help exists; then the person must decide that it is his or her responsibility to take action; and finally, the person has to conclude that there is some concrete thing he or she can do to help. Each of these decisions must be in an affirming direction. The presence of other people actually complicates people's decision making and is the root cause for inhibiting aid. If no one else appears alarmed by an event, everyone present is likely to conclude that no emergency exists, so no action will be taken. The apparent absence of concern is termed *pluralistic ignorance* (Miller & McFarland, 1987), indicating that if no other bystander appears worried or upset, then people assume that there must not be anything wrong, and help is withheld.

When do we offer help? The short answer is when a situation is an unambiguous emergency (e.g., Clark & Word, 1972). Latané and Darley (1968) did find that people were apt to offer aid when no other bystanders were present—in other words, when the responsibility to respond fell squarely on them. When others were present, people looked for cues from one another about what to do and whether to take action (Darley, Teger, & Lewis, 1973; Ross & Braband, 1973). If no one acts as if anything is wrong—

even when smoke is pouring into a room (Latané & Darley, 1970) or a crash in a neighboring room is followed by cries of pain (Latané & Rodin, 1969)—help is less likely to follow.

The study of prosocial behavior developed in a variety of ways since these powerful, early efforts. The study of help-giving moved from consideration of situational variables (e.g., the presence of other people, the number of people present, time pressure) to examining social norms, the effects of emotion, and whether humans are motivated to act by empathy or altruism (e.g., Batson, 1987, 1991, 1995). The role of personality, if any, in prompting helping has drawn research interest (e.g., Penner, 2002). Other work addresses whether people's religiosity increases the likelihood of caring for the needs of others (e.g., Hansen, Vandenberg, & Patterson, 1995). Finally, some social psychologists concern themselves with the effects of education: Making others aware of what factors inhibit helping actually appears to enhance the chances that audience members will offer aid when needed in the future (Beaman, Barnes, Klentz, & McQuirk, 1978). The plethora of service learning opportunities now appearing on college and university campuses would seem to provide an interesting backdrop for contemporary studies of helping behavior—perhaps yours?

Unlike the study of helping, which connects us to others, the newer topic identified in Tables 2.1 and 2.2, affective forecasting, is inwardly focused. Affective forecasting concerns how people anticipate they will feel in the future. How will I feel if I win the lottery, for example, or am offered the job of my dreams? Will a vacation in Barbados be more or less satisfying than one in upstate New York? If you move to Nebraska, will you be less happy living there than in Georgia? How will you feel once you finish reading this chapter?

Our answer to such self-predictions—how we anticipate what we will feel in the future—is a form of social cognition, the experimental study of the consequences of how people think about themselves and others. We may know how we expect to feel under well-defined circumstances, such as doing well on an exam (we are happy), cleaning the bathroom (we are not happy but resigned to the necessity of the job), or raking leaves (bored). Under other circumstances, however, we miss the mark and "mispredict" how we actually feel after a dissolved romance (life actually continues) or guessing that life is better in sunny California than in America's heartland (happily, perhaps, it's not; Schkade & Kahneman, 1998).

How far off are people's predictions? In a study of women's anticipated responses to sexually harassing questions during a job interview, for example, Woodzicka and LaFrance (2001) found that many candidates expected to feel angry. Under the actual conditions of being asked harassing questions, however, women tend to report more fear than anger. Does this mean that our response to negative events is often incorrect? Possibly, but in a very interesting way: We tend to assume that bad things will affect us for a much longer time than they actually do, a phenomenon labeled the *impact bias* (Gilbert, Pinel, Wilson, Blumberg, & Wheatley, 1998).

Consider a career-oriented example of this impact bias. Gilbert and colleagues (1998) asked university faculty to predict their happiness after earning or being denied academic tenure. Most participants in the study claimed that loss of an academic post would be a terrible event for their career aspirations as well as their personal happiness. Yet a few years after the event, both those who received or did not receive tenure reported relatively the same level of happiness. Thus our overfocus on events and their presumed long-term effects, whether good or bad, is misplaced; our actual feelings are not going to be what we expect (Brickman, Coates, & Janoff-Bulman, 1978; Schkade & Kahneman, 1998; see also Gilbert, 2006).

People seem to be quite biased when it comes to accurately assessing the intensity and duration of their feelings regarding some future event (Wilson & Gilbert, 2003, 2005). We are generally, then, not very good affective forecasters. Other research questions concerning this new area of social psychological inquiry are shown in the bottom half of Table 2.2.

Extending earlier research

Tackling unanswered questions identified by previous researchers is a final way to think about the scope of social psychological research. Look to guidance, insights, and suggestions offered in published works, especially textbooks and the conclusions of journal articles. In spite of the best efforts of editors and peer reviewers, many authors still close topical discussions by writing variations on the theme that "future research on *x* should address. . . ." Ironically, such clichéd closings can be a boon for students or researchers looking to extend work on an established topic.

Finding a Research Question

Relying on standard and established topics in social psychology is not the only way to develop a research idea. Recall that I said at the outset of this chapter that many investigators begin, like Triplett, by looking around. Let's review some sources of ideas that are readily available to you right now.

Self-reflection

Plato wrote that his teacher, Socrates, advised that it is a hard but worthy goal to "Know thyself." How well do you know yourself? Put another way, what is happening in your life, right now, that might make an interesting social psychology project? Quite a bit of social psychological scholarship in the last 20 to 30 years has focused on the self (see Table 2.1). Have you ever wondered what factors outside you influence your self-esteem? Perhaps you frequently take on more work than you know you can reasonably accomplish in the time available. Or you may suffer from procrastination, a problem shared by many students. Any one of these topics or another one that comes to mind based on your own experiences could be developed into a project that examines how people like you generally respond to such situations.

Explore but verify hindsight

One of the typical complaints aimed at social psychology and the social sciences more generally is that research reveals obvious findings, the sorts of things that "we all know intuitively, anyway." In other words, social psychology only proves what is usually already recognized by collective common sense. What if I told you that social psychologists have confirmed the proverb that "absence makes the heart grow fonder"? Does this surprise you? Perhaps you can think of various scenarios where separated lovers remain faithful to one another despite great distances or demands upon their time. Consider your likely response if I had posed that social psychological research instead finds that the adage "out of sight, out of mind" hits the romantic mark more closely. In other words (with apologies to Crosby, Stills, & Nash), we are more likely to "love the one we are with" than to remain faithful to our absent others. Wouldn't you be able to think of supporting examples just as quickly?

Various authors (Fischoff, 1975, 1982; Lazarsfeld, 1949; Myers, 2005; Slovic & Fischhoff, 1977) point out that our apparent certainty in the face of possible inconsistency is evidence for a *hindsight bias* (also sometimes known as the "I-knew-it-all-along effect"; see Myers, 2005, pp. 18–19). This inferential bias occurs any time we inflate our ability to have predicted some result in advance, but only *after* learning the actual result. Our sense that some outcome was inevitable becomes a pronounced feeling of certainty—to call upon another maxim, our "hindsight is 20:20"—but only after we know what happened.

How can the troublesome side of our intuitive hindsights help you develop a social psychological research topic? Think of some of the everyday conclusions based on folk wisdom and then look to see whether there is any psychological research verifying their accuracy. Voltaire, the French *philosophe*, once remarked that "common sense is not so common." Why not prove him right (or wrong) by exploring whether people's social behavior actually adheres to the supposedly tried and true maxims that easily confirm people's beliefs about the actions of others.

Your campus

What is occurring on your campus these days? Are there issues of concern facing the student body, the faculty, or the administration? Consider the extremes, for instance: What unites your peers when it comes to complaints or unrestricted praise? Take a moment and think about what people have been talking about lately. Typical discussion topics on most college campuses include the rising cost of tuition, the institution's perceived ranking in various college guides, the lack of parking spaces, grade inflation, the quality of the cafeteria's food, and how well (or badly) the favored athletic team is doing. Do any of these topics look familiar to you?

Instead of exploring one of these surface problems, I suggest you think about something psychologically deeper yet common—if only in perception—to most college

campuses today: student apathy. Faculty, administrators, and often students themselves will often make the claim that the student body is not interested or emotionally
engaged in important issues of the day. The observation is often made that relatively
few students attend the performances of concerts or plays, or that the turnout for visiting speakers to campus is often low. (Curiously, the same observation often holds true
for participation of faculty members at such events, but this fact is either overlooked
or conveniently forgotten.) When I enter into discussions of student apathy like this
one, I always wonder what evidence actually exists to concretely demonstrate apathy.
How many students should be at a given event, for example? Are the events actually
timed to fit students' schedules? Do many students on the campus hold down jobs, a
reality that might preclude their attendance? What sort of intervention, if any, might
motivate more people to attend community events? These and other questions could
make for an interesting exploration of real or apparent apathy on many campuses.

Of course, social apathy may not interest you (note that I am not suggesting that
you are apathetic). I have no doubt that there is some equally challenging and socially
relevant issue worth studying on your campus—you need only identify it. If campus
conditions do not spark any ideas, then expand your search to the local community.

Your community

As I wrote this chapter, the city where I live was wrestling with whether to allow legal-
ized gambling in the form of slot machines. The community is deeply divided over
the issue. Newspaper stories and letters to the editor, both pro and con, have been
appearing for months. Some people argue that gambling dollars will bring much
needed revenue to the town, as well as many jobs and new businesses. Other citizens
claim that the availability of gambling will adversely affect the most vulnerable members
of the community—low-income people who can ill afford to lose their hard-earned
income to slot machines. A fascinating study could be conducted on the origins of the
community's attitudes toward gambling or whether those attitudes lead to particular
public responses—either organized protest or enthusiastic endorsement. Many front
yards, for example, now sport pro or con signs proclaiming the homeowners' allegiance, and I cannot recall when my community has been so passionately split down
the middle when it comes to defining the public good.

Controversial issues like this one happen in every community at one time or
another. What is happening in your town or city that is dividing people's loyalties and
opinions? Can you turn the controversy into a researchable topic in social psychology?
If there is no event or public policy shift that affects the entire community, is there a
smaller scale issue that will touch the lives of one segment of the community?

Look to the media

A good source—really, multiple sources—of ideas are the local and national
media. Newspapers are an excellent source of research ideas. Do you read your local

newspaper? If the answer is no, you might want to develop the habit. Alternatively, national news stories that are featured in the headlines of major newspapers may spark your creativity. While I wrote this chapter, for instance, both local and national headlines were dominated by controversy concerning the teaching of "intelligent design" alongside evolutionary theory in public schools.

Instead of following the newspaper, you could watch the local or national news on television. Feature stories, those accounts of unusual or interesting people and events, are often good sources of ideas. Each evening these days, one of the national networks displays the picture and a brief biography of one American soldier who has been killed in the war in Iraq. I am always moved by the loss, which is made all the more poignant by a few details about the soldier's family and life. When I watch these brief accounts, I wonder what effect they have on the moods of all the other people watching the news—do they become sad, momentarily reflective, or do these losses trigger a sense of patriotism? How do these biographies make the viewers feel about loss and conflict, for example? I have no doubt that television can be a source of interesting research possibilities about the human condition and social behavior.

Finally, of course, there is the Internet, where you can surf into an endless array of web pages that mix the latest breaking news with tales of human interest. Many of these web pages will send you to numerous links providing detailed background about the breaking story. My only caution here is to remind you that not all sites on the Internet are reliable ones. Be sure that the source for your news is trustworthy (Dunn, 2008, chapter 3).

The wider world

You can look well beyond your immediate experience to find good social psychological questions. While I was writing this chapter, the United States was still reeling from the effects of two natural disasters—the hurricanes Katrina and Rita, which severely damaged the Gulf Coast of the southern part of the nation, especially the city of New Orleans. Questions abound when people face and cope with calamities (e.g., Lazarus & Folkman, 1984) or learn about those who do (e.g., Peterson & Seligman, 2003). As our fellow citizens tried to cope with flooding, displacement, and loss of homes, possessions, and many lives and livelihoods—all unimaginably terrible events—I wondered what effects the disaster reports had on other people as they watched, heard, or read about what happened. Did these stories make people more generous, for example? Many people immediately donated money to charities and relief efforts. Did the stories and images make people more compassionate about others around them (Cassell, 2002; see also Batson, Ahmad, Lishner, & Tsang, 2002)? For example, did people far removed from the devastation nonetheless become more aware of the needs of strangers—what we might call public courtesy, such as holding doors open for others, greeting and smiling, even saying "thank you," "please," or "excuse me" more often than usual. Human beings are often surprisingly resilient in the face of trauma (e.g.,

Frankl, 1985; Janoff-Bulman, 1992; Taylor, 1983); thus I think it is quite likely that such inspirational examples have consequences on those of us who observe an event from far away.

With luck, no natural disasters or other calamities are taking place while you read this book. Yet I am sure that somewhere some large-scale event is taking place and drawing national or international attention. Is there something about this event that puzzles you, startles you, or suggests an interesting set of questions about social psychology? If the answer is "yes," then you may well be on to a solid topic for your research efforts.

Ask an expert

One of the best sources of project ideas is likely to be the person who is teaching the class for which you are reading this book. Your instructor is either a social psychologist or someone who knows quite a bit about the field. Ask your teacher how he or she became interested in social psychology. No doubt your teacher will mention his or her research interests, including past research and current directions. If the topic interests you, then you might be able to pursue a question that your teacher suggests. Thus you can help your instructor and yourself—imagine how much you can learn about a topic when you have immediate access to an expert in that area, someone who can guide your investigation of a topic.

Alternatively, take advantage of your teacher's general knowledge in social psychology. What does your teacher believe is the current hot topic dominating the field? What area of inquiry does he or she believe is emerging as an important focus? Another approach is to select a topic from one of those listed in Table 2.1 or from an introductory textbook in social psychology. Tell your teacher about the topic that interests you and ask if he or she is aware of what issues pertaining to it remain to be addressed. The wonderful thing about the research process is that virtually no social psychological topic is ever exhausted—there is always a new question to ask and something else to learn. Perhaps your resident expert, your class instructor, can suggest some fruitful avenues for further investigation regarding the topic you choose.

The World Wide Web

One of chapter 1's active learning exercise recommended that you learn about the research efforts of a working social psychologist by reading his or her profile on the Social Psychology Network (SPN) (www.socialpsychology.org). This particular website is loaded with lots of other information about social psychology, including an e-forum (online discussion) for students, online psychology studies you can participate in, and a lengthy list of social psychology topics with links to related sites on the web. To search the SPN web site, you need only enter key words or search terms drawn from whatever topic interests you (of course, you can also do such a search using any major search engine).

Watch other people

We have come full circle in our topic search. You need only to look around you—literally—by watching what other people do. People are endlessly fascinating. We all know this is true because we spend so much of our daily lives wondering about what causes their quirks or their kindness. Whenever I am having difficulty thinking of a research topic or deciding on the best way to approach one I have already selected, I will usually seek a change of scene. My usual habit is to leave my office and building for a few minutes. I walk to a shaded bench and watch the members of my campus community changing classes. And then I think for a while, pausing occasionally when I recognize a former or current student, or when some article of clothing or hairstyle draws my curiosity. This activity may sound very arbitrary, but social psychologist Robert Cialdini and his colleagues (1976), for example, found that students often "BIRG" ("bask in reflected glory") by wearing apparel (sweatshirts, t-shirts, hats) emblazoned with their college or university's logo on the Monday after a winning weekend for the football team. (Of course, less loyal students also "CORF"—"cut off reflected failure"—when the home team loses; see Cialdini & Richardson, 1980.) Is there some place on your campus where you go or can go to do some people watching?

Other sources for research ideas

Table 2.3 includes some other sources for developing or identifying research projects in social psychology.

Table 2.3   Other Sources for Research Project Topics in Social Psychology

1   Look in the index of any social psychology book to find key words or terms that point to possible topics.
2   Search for book reviews of new titles published online in PsycCRITIQUES—*Contemporary Psychology: APA Review of Books*—this online journal might be accessible in your library.
3   Attend a lecture delivered by a social psychologist—listen or look for issues that surprise, puzzle, or make you want to learn more about the topic.
4   Check the references section of an article or book dealing with social psychology—search there for interesting titles, topics, or frequently cited authors.
5   Recruit some friends and try the active learning exercise on "brainstorming" (Active Learning Exercise 2A) presented in this chapter.

ACTIVE LEARNING EXERCISE   **2A**

Developing Topic Ideas by Brainstorming

Ideas for research projects or paper topics can also be developed using a creative technique called "brainstorming." Brainstorming is often used to identify radical or unusual solutions to questions or problems, but it can also be used to pinpoint topics in social psychology. The instructions are simple: Try to identify an area of interest from social psychology (e.g., aggression) and then write down as many things that come to your mind as possible. This is the idea generation phase (Hayes, 1981, pp. 204–206). The ideas may be zany, ridiculous, or outlandish—but so what? The purpose at this point is to generate as many leads as you can and without your usual inclination to self-censorship (e.g., "That's too hard" or "How dull—that's been done so many times before"). Your initial goal is to open yourself to possibilities that you have not recognized previously or to look at an idea from a fresh perspective. Once you have a list of potential topics, review them in the idea evaluation phase and see which ones might be worth developing into a topic (Hayes, 1981).

Group brainstorming. Individual brainstorming is a great way to quickly produce many possible topics, but it suffers from one drawback—there is no one else to rely upon during the evaluation phase. An alternative approach to solo-brainstorming is to involve a few other people (this is a very useful exercise if you are doing a group research project). Two group members serve distinct roles—one is the *leader* and the other is the *recorder* (Hayes, 1981). The leader keeps the group "on task" by making sure the discussion flows and that everyone gets a chance to share ideas (in some groups, for example, turn taking is imposed to ensure everyone gets the opportunity to contribute). The leader also reminds everyone that unduly editing or eliminating suggestions comes later; however, group members are encouraged to combine or expand upon the suggestions of others. Meanwhile, the recorder writes down all the ideas as they are stated (doing group brainstorming in a room with a blackboard or some other large writing surface is a good idea, especially when the ideas come at a fast and furious pace). There is one important guideline for the first part of group brainstorming—do not pursue one line of thinking for too long—move on to a new one.

Once topic generation is over, the group evaluates each of the suggestions one at a time. Friendly criticism and editing are now the rule: some ideas are changed, others dropped, and the list is winnowed down to a few possibilities. An important aspect of group brainstorming is that the majority rules; that is, if most people are in favor of keeping an idea, it is retained; if not, it is discarded (of course, the recorder still has an intact record of all entries). This process continues until the group (ideally) reaches a unanimous conclusion about which research topic is worth doing. The search for supporting research from the social psychology literature then begins in earnest.

ACTIVE LEARNING EXERCISE   2B

Keeping a Social Psychology Log

Social psychologists are keen observers of the interactions between people, but they do need a system for keeping track of their ideas. As research ideas come to mind, you will need to have some way to keep track of them before you forget or misplace them. I recommend that you start a social psychology log right now. A social psychology log is simply a notebook, a dedicated repository for your ideas, stray thoughts, observations, or really anything that has to do with your thoughts about human social behavior. Besides containing your comments, it might also hold suggestive clippings from magazines or newspapers, as well as pages photo-copied from social psychology journals. The notebook need not be anything fancy or elegant—ideally, it will be used frequently. Compared to a neat and tidy note-book, a battered or tattered one usually indicates that its owner consults it often. Many professional social psychologists always keep such a notebook handy so that fleeting insights are not lost in the busyness of daily life—they later flesh out and improve upon these quick jottings when time and schedule allow.

A social psychology log should contain dated entries describing:

- paper ideas;
- detailed observations of social behavior that surprise or puzzle you;
- interesting findings about behavior drawn from lectures, class discussion, or periodicals;
- random thoughts and musings about people;
- responses to readings you do for class or after doing library research;
- book titles and journal references you want to remember.

In lieu of carrying around a notebook, you may prefer to summarize your thoughts in a file in your computer—especially if you carry a laptop with you—or even in a personal digital assistant (PDA). I will caution you about waiting too long to record your thoughts, however. In my experience, good ideas that are not written down are like the vivid dreams we sometimes remember upon waking—their details fade all too quickly from memory. Thus even the smallest logbook may have a decided edge over many high-tech devices.

Alternative social psychology log exercise. In lieu of a standard log of ideas, you could instead maintain a dialectical social psychology log. The term "dialectic" refers to a careful examination of reasoning processes achieved through thorough, critical discussion. Dialectical analyses often involve an exploration of the tensions identified between opposing ideas or points of view. To maintain a dialectical log, follow the directions provided above and record your observations on the left-hand pages in the notebook. The right-hand page in each pair is reserved for your self-reflections, questions, and interpretations that occur to you later, after an original entry is made. Although left page entries can be made any time something occurs to you, a specific time should be reserved (say, every three days) for making dialectical entries. By revisiting and rethinking what you wrote in passing—in a sense, conducting a conversation with yourself on paper—you may discover another approach to defining a possible topic.

The dialectical alternative for the social psychology log is not just for developing topic ideas. The notebook provides an opportunity for you to think about a research project as it develops, especially those aspects that need to be completed, pose problems, or need to be worked through further. A dialectical notebook is a good place to jot down questions or ideas that seem to be idle speculations for now—later you may be able to use them for another purpose.

Searching the Social Psychological Literature

"There is no new thing under the sun" (Ecclesiastes 1:9).

Once you select a research topic, you will need to familiarize yourself with the existing research related to it. Newcomers to the discipline are often surprised by the availability of research already done on many of the questions they think of. More surprising still is the sheer amount of citations that are available. I issue this gentle warning because my students are often taken aback that their "original" idea turns out to not be so original. Where many (not all) research questions are concerned, there is rarely anything new under the sun.

Do not be put off by this fact, however. Just because a topic has been studied before is no reason to assume that you will not bring a fresh perspective and clever insights to it. Social psychologists reresearch or, if you prefer, recycle topics all the time, and with great success. Remember, Triplett's (1898) early work on co-active social influence anticipated Zajonc's (1965) later work on social facilitation; existing knowledge is often the foundation for deeper understanding of social phenomena. Before you begin your project, however, it is essential that you become familiar with what has been done before, what was found, and how the research was conducted. To do that, you must search the social psychological literature.

When referring to the social psychological literature, we note distinctions among three kinds of sources: primary, secondary, and tertiary.

- *Primary source*—Original reports of research, especially journal articles, books, chapters, and empirical summaries. For example, articles appearing in the *Journal of Personality and Social Psychology* or *Personality and Social Psychology Bulletin* are primary sources. A researcher's report of his or her original work is a primary source. An interview with or a personal communication from a social psychologist would also be a primary source.

- *Secondary source*—Summaries of or commentaries on the existing literature pertaining to a topic. Articles appearing in journals like the *Review of Personality and Social Psychology*, *Psychological Review*, and *Psychological Bulletin* are secondary sources. Such sources may or may not be authored by the researchers whose work is described therein.
- *Tertiary source*—Usually contains information drawn from secondary sources rather than primary sources, and is designed to inform a general or popular audience about some topic, rather than professional researchers or students. Tertiary sources share information but do not critique or expand upon what is already known. An encyclopedia entry defining cognitive dissonance or an article appearing in *Psychology Today* on the same topic would be tertiary sources.

The first two types of sources are particularly appropriate for doing a research project in social psychology (see also Appendix A), including writing a paper describing what was found (see chapter 12). Although they are interesting to read in their own right and may be a good source of ideas (recall, for example, our earlier discussion of the media as sources for ideas), tertiary sources are not generally used in research reports describing social psychological findings. Neither do such sources represent good additions to student research projects, APA-style lab reports, or other term papers.

What is the best way to begin a search? Before you do anything, you need to have the steps in a typical search laid out before you. Table 2.4 identifies the basic steps in most searches of the social psychological literature. As you can see in Table 2.4, I identify six discrete stages for the search—depending on your topic, there may be more or fewer and, of course, any stage may also have a few steps associated with it. Still, we will follow the stages outlined in Table 2.4 in order to identify appropriate sources for your project. We will focus on two ways to search the social psychological literature—using online sources and looking in your library's holdings. As you gain experience, you may develop shortcuts that allow you to effectively search for sources.

Table 2.4   Searching the Social Psychological Literature

Stage 1	Write a sentence or two defining your thesis, hypothesis, or research topic.
Stage 2	Using search terms and key words, search online databases (e.g., *PsycINFO*) for references (see also Table 2.6's list of databases).
Stage 3	Obtain copies of journal articles from library holdings, downloadable sources, or interlibrary loan.
Stage 4	Check the references sections in the sources you have for additional references; go back to Stage 3 as needed.
Stage 5	Using search terms (see Stage 2) and subject headings, search the library's catalog for books and book chapters; check appropriate works out of the library and look for new references cited in them. Go back to earlier stages as needed.
Stage 6	Maintain a working bibliography (see Table 2.7).

Before you begin any search, however, you need to have your research question, your thesis, hypothesis, or topic—whichever term you prefer—firmly in your mind and clearly stated on paper (see Stage 1 in Table 2.4). In fact, this clear and concise statement (it may be a few sentences) needs to be with you throughout the search process. First, be sure that your topic is not too broad. Deciding that you are interested in doing a project on "interpersonal attraction" (recall Table 2.1), for example, is much too broad. What *particular* aspect of attraction between people interests you? Do you want to study friendships (liking) or romance (love)? If the latter, are you interested in what physical qualities, situational factors, or personality traits lead to love or promote passionate connections?

Refining a topic requires that you continually narrow your focus until you can state your research question in a sentence or two. Here are two possible examples dealing with close relationships, one concerning self-disclosure (e.g., Derlega, Metts, Petronio, & Margulis, 1993) and the other equity (e.g., Clark & Mills, 1993):

Example 1: As close relationships grow, do people disclose more intimate aspects of themselves to others?
Example 2: Do people involved in short-term relationships expect greater equity (exchange of rewards) than those in long-term relationships?

Perhaps you can already state your project question in a similar manner. If so, you can head to the next section and begin an online search. If not, how can you narrow your topical focus and craft a statement or two like those shown above? Try completing one or more of these sentence fragments in order to refine your topic. Once you are satisfied with the result, head on to the next section.

My social psychology project examines _____ .
I am interested in demonstrating how _____ causes a change in _____.
I wonder why _____ .

If you are extending prior research, then try completing these statements:

Research on _____ found that _____. I intend to continue this line of research by demonstrating that _____.

Searching for sources online

To search the social psychological literature, you will need to use the various databases that are available (see Stage 2 in Table 2.4). Many of these databases are held by most college and university libraries, either in printed form or accessible online. If at all possible, I recommend that you search for social psychology references online (if your library lacks online databases, consult a reference librarian about how to search through printed versions of databases). What online databases should you consult? If available, the primary online database for social psychology (in fact, all areas of the discipline) is *PsycINFO*, which is updated and maintained by the American Psychological Association (APA). *PsycINFO* contains an extensive list of citations and abstracts from journals, books, book chapters, and book reviews in psychology (from 1887 to the present), as well as similar sources in education, psychiatry, nursing, and sociology. Another APA database, *PsycARTICLES*, allows users to access the full text of articles previously published in APA journals.

For purposes of illustration, I will focus on how to do a search using *PsycINFO*, the broader of these two databases. In order to effectively search this database, you need to rely on search terms, that is, key words that are associated with research published on a given topic. If you used particular terms or key words when crafting your research question (recall the stem completion exercise presented above), begin your search with those words (for future reference, be sure to record these and all other search terms in your social psychology log; see *Active Learning Exercise 2B*). Another easy way to identify search terms related to your topic is to consult an introductory textbook in social psychology. If you are interested in interpersonal attraction, turn to the appropriate chapter in the book and examine headings and subheadings that organize the text (e.g., attachment, passionate love, companionate love, similarity, physical attractiveness). Write down terms and key words appearing in these headings, and then look in the text under the headings for other words and phrases appearing in boldface or italics (McCarthy & Pusateri, 2006).

Alternatively, you might consult an encyclopedia of psychology and draw search terms from entries in this reference work. Table 2.5 lists a few of these encyclopedias. Be sure to check your library's reference area for others.

Once you have a working list of terms from a social psychology text or an encyclopedia, try using other index terms that are conveniently accessible through the *PsycINFO* database. Once you are in the database, look for a way to access the online

Table 2.5 Searching for Search Terms: Some Encyclopedias in Psychology

Corsini, R. J. (Ed.) (2001). *The Corsini encyclopedia of psychology and human behavior* (3rd ed., Vols. 1–4). New York: Wiley.

Eysenck, H. J., Arnold, W., & Meili, R. (Eds.) (1979). *Encyclopedia of psychology*. New York: The Seabury Press.

Goldenson, R. M. (1970). *Encyclopedia of human behavior* (Vols. 1–2). New York: Doubleday.

Harré, R., & Lamb, R. (Eds.) (1983). *Encyclopedic dictionary of psychology*. Oxford: Basil Blackwell.

Kazdin, A. (Ed.) (2000). *Encyclopedia of psychology* (Vols. 1–8). Washington, DC: American Psychological Association.

Ramachandran, V. S. (Ed.) (1994). *Encyclopedia of human behavior* (Vols. 1–4). San Diego, CA: Academic Press.

Wolman, B. B. (Ed.) (1977). *International encyclopedia of psychiatry, psychology, psychoanalysis, and neurology* (Vols. 1–12). New York: Van Nostrand Reinhold Company.

Table 2.6   Other Helpful Databases for Literature Searches in Social Psychology

Current Contents
Educational Resources Information Center (ERIC)
Sociological Abstracts
Social Sciences Index (SSI)
Social Science Citation Index (SSCI)

thesaurus of psychological index terms (see also APA, 2004). You should be able to click on this option using your mouse (if you cannot locate this online thesaurus, ask a reference librarian to help you locate it). Besides *PsycINFO*, you might also search through one or more of the databases listed in Table 2.6.

Online searches using computers have dramatically changed the way interested readers find existing research—literally, in a few seconds, you can identify practically every available publication on a given topic or even everything written by a particular social psychologist. The ability to access so much so quickly is both a blessing and a curse: Everything you need is suddenly there, in front of you—the problem becomes one of properly selecting which references are best suited to your work. A general rule of thumb is to rely on the most recent publications dealing with your topic.

Once you determine which references will best suit your needs, you should immediately obtain copies of them (see Stage 3 in Table 2.4). With luck, the journal articles you need will either be in your library's collection or downloadable from some online source. If the former, then you need only go to the periodicals section and then to a copy machine. If the latter, a librarian can help you print what you need if you do not already know how to do so yourself. What happens if a reference is not available in your library? You will either have to make a special trip to another college or university library, or rely on interlibrary loan. An interlibrary loan service can be a great way to obtain articles and even books, but there is a distinct drawback: time. You may not receive what you need for several days or even weeks. So do not put off beginning your search for information for your research project—start immediately in case you must wait for some sources to arrive.

A word to the wise: Use one reference to find others. Experienced researchers know that one of the most reliable ways to learn about the available literature on a topic is by examining the reference sections of the works already found (Dunn, 2008; McCarthy & Pusateri, 2006). Use the references you have to locate other references (see Stage 4 in Table 2.4). Unless a work is listed as unpublished, under review, or in press, such references lists can only point you toward materials that are already published and available. Still, a reference list in a journal article will quickly identify the main researchers associated with a topic, as well as some of the key references. For example, you can do a further search of the literature using an author's name to locate all of the publications he or she published on the topic. You can also search for articles appearing in a specific journal, during a period of time (a year or years), and by other search terms you uncover.

One final suggestion: Helpful references can often be found in the reference sections of review articles appearing in journals such as *American Psychologist, Psychological Bulletin,* and *Psychological Review.* Alternatively, consult review chapters dealing with social psychological topics that occasionally appear in the *Annual Review of Psychology.* Finally, you might look in the two-volume *Handbook of Social Psychology* (Gilbert, Fiske, & Lindzey, 1998) to see if any of the chapters covering content areas contain helpful references.

Searching your library

The content of your school's library catalog is also probably searchable online—that is, it is likely to have an online catalog, one that you may be able to access from your dorm, home, or some other remote location. When you search an online catalog, you are looking for books or book chapters pertaining to some topic (see Stage 5 in Table 2.4). The best way to begin is by searching for books written by the same authors whose journal article publications you found previously (see Stages 3 and 4 in Table 2.4). After searching by author names, try searching by book titles and key words, relying on terms that you used earlier (recall Stage 2).

To further refine your search (see Stage 5 in Table 2.4), you should identify relevant subject headings by finding your topic as it is listed in the Library of Congress Subject Headings (LCSH; Library of Congress, 1995). The LCSH is a five-volume, A-to-Z guide that will usually be found next to the main online catalog in a library. Once you find the alphabetical listing of a topic or term, the LCSH will point you to related as well as more specific terms you use to search the library catalog. As you locate books in the catalog, write down their call numbers in your social psychology log or print out the reference information for future use. Finally, head to the stacks, locate the books, and determine whether their content is appropriate for your work.

Seeking help: Speak to reference professionals

Every library employs a group of reference librarians, experts whose purpose is to help people use a library's resources to the fullest extent possible. If you cannot find information on a topic or question, do not assume that the library lacks materials pertaining to the topic. Instead, assume that you have not done a complete search of the available resources or used them to their best advantage. Go to the reference area and ask a librarian for help. Share the search terms you are using, tell the librarian about the databases you used as well as any problems encountered, and describe the purpose of your research project. It is very likely that the librarian will help you find some material that you missed. If nothing else, be sure to consult a reference librarian if you are having difficulty navigating an online database—there is no substitute for the reassurance and knowledge a librarian can bring to research questions.

ACTIVE LEARNING EXERCISE   2C

Maintaining a Bibliography and Organizing Sources

Online searches of the psychological literature or a library's holdings simplify the researcher's task—many references can quickly be located. Such searches also create a predicament, however: How will you keep track of all of the books, chapters, journal articles, and websites you collect? Computer printouts, scraps of paper with the call numbers of books, a photocopy of a page from a journal—all of these stray pieces of paper will begin to accumulate as you research a topic. As time passes, you may forget where and when you found some fact, reference, or idea, which will pose a real problem when you are trying to finish a project or write a paper referencing all the sources you consulted.

As you begin to collect research sources you will need to start—and more importantly, maintain—a working bibliography (see Stage 6 in Table 2.4). A bibliography is a list of works related to some topic. When you need to consult a reference for information pertaining to your project, the bibliography will tell you where the work can be found. If you need to cite a research reference in a paper, the correct information can be found in the bibliography.

Table 2.7 contains the sort of information you should maintain about sources in a bibliography. You should get into the habit of recording the relevant information concerning a source as you determine that it is relevant for your social psychology project. Later, if you decide that you need to consult the resource again for more information, for example, your working bibliography will tell you where it can be found. Having such detail available at your fingertips will save you much time, stress, and heartache.

Table 2.7   Keeping Track of Social Psychological Resources in a Working Bibliography

---

Author(s) last names, first and middle initials
Editor(s) last names, first and middle initials
Complete title of source (including any subtitle)
Call numbers of library books
Complete journal title
Edition number of a book (e.g., 3rd edition)
Volume number and issue number of a journal
Volume number of a book in a series
Publisher of book or book chapter
Place of publication (usually a city) for book or book chapter
Year of publication
All page numbers for journal articles and book chapters
Date and place of a presentation, colloquium, or poster session.

Continued

Here are four suggestions for maintaining a working bibliography:

- If you use *PsycINFO* or another online database, get in the habit of printing out a copy of the page containing all of the reference information. If you obtain a copy of an article, staple the reference information page to it.
- Write down complete citations in your social psychology log (Active Learning Exercise 2B). You can put the citations in alphabetical order later, when it is time to write a paper incorporating them.
- When you go to the library or search an online database, keep a stack of blank note cards with you. When you find a useful source, record the details on one of the cards. Alphabetize the cards at the end of every search session.
- Rely on your computer for keeping a working bibliography. There are various software packages available that will keep track of the information for you—you just need to remember to enter it with some regularity.

Reading Social Psychology Research

Once you have sources in hand, you must read them and evaluate whether their content will help you with your research project. Many of your sources will be social psychology journal articles. Unless you have read professional journal articles before, these sources can sometimes be a bit daunting. To help you learn to read—and to learn from—journal articles, turn to Appendix B, which specifically discusses how to read one from beginning to end.

The advice on reading I offer here is meant to be more general, as journal articles are probably not the only sources you will find in the course of your search. Be sure to consider books as well as chapters from edited books. First, you need to set aside a meaningful amount of time to read your sources. Many will be dense, technical, and detailed, which means that you should read them in a quiet place free of distractions, including people, music, and phones (including your cell phone). Table 2.8 offers guidance for reading any primary or secondary source.

As you can see, there are three stages involved in approaching a reading: prereading, reading, and postreading (see Table 2.8). Each stage has suggested steps to help you draw and retain information from a reading. If you are already familiar with the general topic or literature related to it, then prereading may be less important. If the topic is new to you, then beginning with prereading and working your way through all three stages and their individual steps will help you master it.

A note on note taking. Where reading is about finding meaning in what you read, note taking is about making meaning from what you read. To begin with, you should always take notes on what you read. Such notes need not be exhaustive—after all, the

Table 2.8 Drawing Meaning from a Primary or Secondary Source

Prereading

1 Examine the title: What does it mean? What does the title suggest will be the reading's focus?

2 Preview the reading: How long is it? How is it sub-divided (e.g., chapters, sections)? How do the sub-divisions relate to one another?

3 What is your purpose for doing this reading (e.g., background research, research design ideas, identifying potential independent or dependent variables)?

4 Do you need any other sources to help you do this reading (e.g., dictionary, other sources by the same author)?

Reading

1 Make frequent predictions about where the author is heading. Are you accurate? Make new predictions accordingly.

2 Take notes by paraphrasing—restate the reading's meaning in different words—as you read. If a reading is difficult, you may need to obtain the "gist" of it by skimming ahead and then coming back to the section where you got stuck.

3 Identify and write explanations for any key quotes, terms, or ideas you come across.

4 Is the supporting evidence convincing—why or why not? Write down what else you think you need to know that is not provided in the reading.

5 Be on the look out for new sources, jotting down any bibliographic information while you read (see Table 2.7).

Postreading

1 Write down the most important idea(s) from the reading. Do you agree with the hypotheses or findings? Did anything surprise you? How will this idea(s) help you with your research project or paper?

2 Re-read any difficult passages in the reading: Do they reveal anything new to you? What else do you need to know from the reading? Does the reading send you to other sources or necessitate a new literature search?

3 What questions do you still have about the reading and the research described within it?

Source: Adapted from the Moravian College Committee for the Advancement of Teaching, October 18, 2005.

reading should still be accessible to you. Your goal is to pull various issues and elements together, to synthesize them into a meaningful whole. The point is that you should be able to summarize the general idea or specific purpose of any article, chapter, or even a book in a few sentences or even a paragraph. If you need more detailed information, you can always consult the source itself. Some suggestions for ways to take helpful and effective notes on what you read are provided in Table 2.9.

As you take notes, be sure to paraphrase—that is, put down ideas into your own words. Doing so will help you retain the information and integrate it with what you already know. Thus note taking is ideally an active exercise that helps you think through research issues while you read and draw information from resources. If you

Table 2.9   Suggestions for Note Taking on Readings

Never take notes when you are tired or sleepy.

Only take notes on issues that you believe are relevant to your research project or paper.

Use notes to record key arguments, questions, explanations, definitions, and facts drawn from readings.

Write short, focused statements that identify or explain main points or concepts (e.g., hypotheses, research findings). Notes are not exhaustive summaries—you can always return to the reference.

Use your note taking as a way to interpret what you read and to draw conclusions as you read.

When reading a book, take the bulk of your notes on the first and last chapters, as those are the places an author is likely to explain key themes and pull main ideas together.

When pressed for time, read a journal article's abstract to get a sense of the work, then skim through it to take notes on the hypothesis, method, and results. You can carefully reread the article before you need it for a project or paper.

Whenever possible, use or create concrete examples to illustrate concepts in your notes. Such examples will refresh your memory later and give life to your project or paper.

---

treat is as a mechanical exercise, you will begin to copy information word for word from what you are reading. Then, when the time to draft and write a paper or lab report comes, you will run the risk of plagiarizing the ideas of already published authors.

I do not need to tell you that plagiarism is the worst sin that any writer, student, or social psychologist can commit—stealing the ideas of others without proper citation is as bad as fabricating research results. If you do locate a quotation that is essential to your work, be sure that if you copy it down you also record the necessary bibliographic information (see Table 2.7) and that you clearly label it as a "quotation" in your notes (Dunn, 2008, p. 52).

Borrowing ideas from published social psychology experiments

"If I have seen further it is by standing upon the shoulders of giants" (Isaac Newton, 1675, Letter to Robert Hooke).

You should never feel uncomfortable or constrained about borrowing ideas from the social psychological literature. Virtually every journal article, for example, cites or uses techniques, variables, research designs, terms, or findings from previously published work. The science underlying social psychological phenomena is incremental: Researchers build upon the foundation of other researchers' ideas. Even truly new ideas—and they are rare—tend to be legitimized by the "scaffolding" that established social psychological findings or perspectives provide. In fact, by using and citing existing research you are behaving like any good and thorough scholar in the discipline.

Just be sure to provide proper credit to the original research and the researcher who conceived it.

Exercises

1   Select a recent article from the *Journal of Personality and Social Psychology* or the *Journal of Experimental Social Psychology*. Turn to the references section of the article and, using publication dates, identify the earliest reference(s) the author(s) cites. Did the author "borrow" ideas from early publications? Are the linkages between the current research and the past research direct (same topic) or indirect (the topic evolved)?

2   Using the two entries shown in Table 2.2 as examples, identify a series of questions—subtopics—associated with your intended research area.

3   Create a "Reader's Guide" for your research topic (see Henderson, 2000), a synopsis that provides (1) a content outline (e.g., historical background, theoretical and methodological issues, major issues and research areas); (2) theorists and contributors (a list of the main workers in an area, accompanied by brief, three-sentence characterizations explaining their role and importance); (3) central concepts (a list of the essential 10 or so concepts in an area); (4) hot or current topics (what topics recur, which ones cause debate); (5) major resources (important handbooks, chapters—including those in the *Annual Review of Psychology*, main journals, Internet sources).

Chapter 3

Ethical Issues in Social Psychological Research

Imagine yourself in this situation: Having agreed to participate in a psychology experiment on visual perception, you are the last person seated around a large table. The experimenter shows you and six fellow students a simple chart with three vertical lines on it labeled 1, 2, and 3. You are then shown a second chart with a single line on it, which the experimenter refers to as the "standard line." The judgment task is simple and straightforward: Taking turns, you and your peers announce aloud which of the three comparison lines is the same length as the standard line. A group of sample lines is shown in Figure 3.1. As you can see, it is quite obvious which line (number 2) is the same as the standard line. The task is almost too easy, you believe, and in fact, it is: Each of your peers says "line 2" and then it's your turn. You give the same answer.

So far, so good. A few minutes and a second set of charts pass; you are becoming slightly bored with the task. What's the big deal? On to the third set of charts. Suddenly, the first peer seated at the head of the table chooses "line 1." You are taken aback because the right answer has to be "line 3." What's wrong with the first guy's eyes, you wonder. But then the second student also says "line 1." So does the third, fourth, fifth, and sixth student. Uh-oh! You're number seven. Do you say what you think—no, what you *know*—is true ("line 3") or do you give the same answer as your peers ("line 1")?

I have just described social psychologist Solomon Asch's (1956) classic study on conformity and social influence. What happened? Surprisingly, 76% of the participants fell prey to the pressure of their peers by knowingly giving wrong answers. There were 12 trials altogether and, on average, individual participants tended to conform on a third of them. Based on their behavior and what they subsequently disclosed to Asch, we know that the participants feared standing out by being the solo dissenter from the group in spite of the fact that the peers were complete strangers. This study is an elegant and clear portrayal of the power of conformity pressures.

Yet our purpose in this chapter is not to discuss the conformity literature per se, but instead to explore ethics and to examine a quality present in the Asch (1956) study and a few other social psychological experiments we will discuss: deception. In social psychological research, the term *deception* refers to intentionally withholding key information from a research participant in an attempt to observe or measure how the

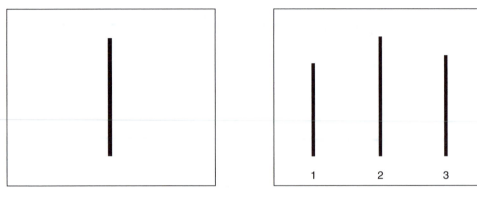

Figure 3.1.   Sample stimuli used in the Asch (1956) line judgment task

participant would react in a similar, real life setting. Is this or any deception acceptable and necessary when it comes to studying social behavior? Most of us may not make many line judgments in daily life, but we are all familiar with peer pressures of various types, just as all of us have at one time or another been pitted against the dominant opinion of some group—whether it involved choosing toppings for a pizza ("Well, I guess mushrooms are okay if everybody else likes them") or disclosing how we really feel about a controversial social or political issue (e.g., gay marriage or abortion).

If you took part in Asch's (1956) study, how do think you would feel afterwards knowing that everyone in the room was deceiving you by intentionally giving incorrect answers to see how you would react? How would you feel knowing that you had been told the research involved perceptual judgments when it was really aimed at seeing whether a single person—you, in this case—would be swayed by a group of six peers who were following a script and collaborating with the experimenter? Would you feel misled? Lied to? Or would you conclude that the research was interesting and worthwhile because it reveals how people respond when faced with subtle conformity pressures? Further, would your answer to any of these or any related questions be dependent upon whether, and the degree to which, you fell prey to conformity pressures?

This chapter is about ethics in social psychological research, that is, the use and applications of moral principles and practices in the context of studying people's thoughts and behavior. Social psychologists bear a great responsibility to treat human research participants ethically. Concern for the welfare of human research participants developed following the disclosure of atrocities committed on people who were held in prison or concentration camps during World War II. Innocent men, women, and children were subjected to unspeakable horrors in the name of "science" or "medical research." These individuals had no choice but to take part in Nazi experiments. Many died, others were maimed mentally or physically for the remainder of their days.

Following World War II, the Nuremberg Code (Beals, Sebring, & Crawford, 1946–1949) was created to protect all human beings who participate in medical and scientific research, whether minor or major. The Code articulates principles such as acquiring voluntary consent, full disclosure of the purpose of research, the risks involved and protection against them, the need for qualified researchers, the right of participants to withdraw from a project at any point in time, and the termination of a project whenever people's welfare is threatened. These principles helped shape the ethical guidelines we will review in this chapter. Before we do so, however, let's consider another social psychological study that is often mentioned in the same breath as Asch's (1956) conformity work.

Milgram's Obedience Research

Many readers—and you may be one of them—probably concluded that the Asch (1956) experiment was tame. After all, were any of the participants really upset about learning the study's true purpose or that all of the other "participants" were helping the experimenter? Like you, I will hazard a guess that the majority of participants were more intrigued than upset by the truth and, in any case, they were thoroughly debriefed by Asch once the 12th set of stimuli were shown.

Hold on for a moment, however. Let's consider another, more emotionally arousing experiment dealing with a stronger form of social influence: obedience to authority. Can we be compelled by others, notably authority figures, to perform acts that go against our beliefs? What are the social and moral consequences of following orders we know will harm others? What ethical concerns arise when social psychologists explore these questions in settings that intentionally create distress in participants?

Imagine yourself in this setting: You answer an ad to take part in an experiment at Yale University on the effects of punishment on learning. You meet a dour experimenter in a gray lab coat who introduces you to a fellow participant, a genial middle-aged man. You and this person draw slips of paper from a hat. Your slip is inscribed "teacher"; the other participant reports that his slip says "learner." The experimenter explains both roles. As teacher, you will read a list of word pairs to the learner (e.g., "wild–duck") once and then test the learner by seeing whether he can correctly recall the second word in each pair. Here's the catch: For every wrong answer the learner makes, you are required to press a switch which delivers an electric shock to him. Here's the problem: As his errors mount, the shocks get progressively stronger.

The shock-generating machine delivers shocks ranging from 15 volts to 450 volts (levels were labeled with descriptions starting with "Slight Shock" to the last levels, "Danger: Severe Shock" and the ominous "XXX"). To put these voltage levels in proper perspective, a standard wall plug in the United States carries 115 volts. To give you a real sense of what the learner will face, the experimenter gives you a mild electric jolt. Before you sit down in front of the shock generator to begin the experiment, you watch the experimenter strap the learner into a chair in an adjacent room. Before the door is closed, you see an electrode attached to his arm. You are now ready to begin. Do you think you would feel anxious or nervous about shocking a stranger, even in the hallowed halls at Yale and under what you believe is professional supervision?

Many people who hear about this experiment for the first time believe they would stop right here, before any harm was done. Yet no one did. Let me summarize what happened next and tell you what was really going on. Of course, no real shocks were delivered and the learner was a confederate. On cue, however, the learner made intentional errors, which forced the teacher to "shock" him. The pressing of each button on the shock generator caused a buzzing sound. Whenever necessary, the experimenter told the teacher to increase the shock. And when a teacher wavered, expressing concern about the learner's welfare or threatening to stop the study, the experimenter used specific "prods" designed to encourage obedient reactions:

Prod 1: Please continue, *or*, Please go on.
Prod 2: The experiment requires that you continue.
Prod 3: It is absolutely essential that you continue.
Prod 4: You have no other choice, you *must* go on.

These were delivered in a firm but never rude manner. The experiment ended only if the participant refused to continue after hearing the fourth prod.

The results were unequivocal: Despite cries of help (also scripted—at 150 volts the learner yelled, "Experimenter, get me out of here! I won't be in the experiment anymore! I refuse to go on!" and at 330 volts noises from him ceased) and the teachers' own experienced upset, most participants—nearly two-thirds of them—continued to the highest levels of shock (see Figure 3.2). The sobering reality is that these people were no different than you or me. Take a good look at Figure 3.2 because without a doubt, most of us would behave the same way.

Over 1,000 people took part in variations of the basic experimental paradigm (for a discussion of all the variations, see Milgram, 1974). By reviewing this classic example of social psychology, our purpose is to consider the ethical issues involved. Did participants really and truly believe they were shocking the innocent learner? Did they become emotionally or physically upset by doing so? Was the deception too great? Did Milgram (1963) overstep legitimate research boundaries by conducting this study? Many of the "teachers" did become very upset by what they sincerely believed was really happening—*what they were doing*—to the learner. Reflecting on what became all-too-typical reactions, one observer of Milgram's study commented that:

I observed a mature and initially poised businessman enter the laboratory smiling and confident. Within 20 minutes he was reduced to a twitching, stuttering wreck, who was rapidly approaching a point of nervous collapse. He constantly pulled on his earlobe, and twisted his hands. At one point he pushed his fist into his forehead and muttered "Oh God, let's stop it." And yet he continued to respond to every word of the experimenter, and obeyed to the very end. (Milgram, 1974, p. 377)

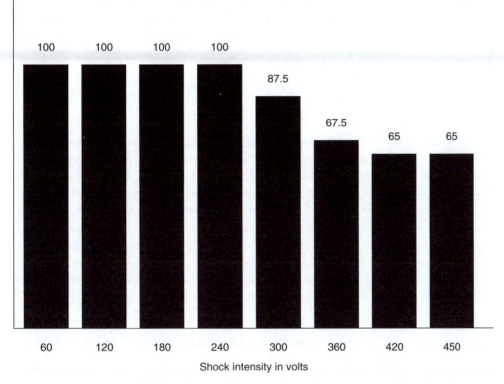

Figure 3.2. Percentage of the Milgram (1963) Study's "Teachers" Obeying an Authority Figure's Instructions to Shock the "Learner" by the Level of Shock Intensity. Based on data from Milgram (1963); adapted from Figure 21.2 in Abelson, Frey, and Gregg (2004)

Here are some of the ethical issues to consider regarding this work:

- Participants genuinely believed they were hurting another person, just as they genuinely believed they had to do so in the interest of the "experiment."
- The participants were not told in advance what was going to happen or their role in the proceedings (doing so would have biased their responses).
- Many learned something unsettling about themselves, that they were entirely capable of obeying authority, of "hurting" someone despite his protests.
- Others, a minority, learned they were capable of disobeying an authority figure in order to avoid harming another person.

Generations of students and fellow social psychologists were moved to ask whether Milgram's (1963) methods were justified and justifiable. Was the knowledge about behavioral responses to obedience worth it? Did Milgram treat his participants fairly?

These and related issues were debated once his controversial work appeared. Milgram had defenders (e.g., Blass, 2004) and critics (e.g., Baumrind, 1964, 1985; Orne & Holland, 1968), and he spent considerable efforts dealing with reactions to the obedience paradigm (Milgram, 1964, 1972, 1977). The debate regarding the obedience studies continues (see Blass, 2000; Miller, 2004).

Other ethically challenging examples

The Milgram (1963) experiment is but one example of social psychological research that raises ethical questions and concerns. Depending upon who is drawing up the list, one critic's ethically problematic study is another's classic effort. Opinions vary. Table 3.1 lists an example from sociology and another from social psychology. Where concern about Milgram's efforts focused on the perils of creating undue stress in participants, the original works and critics' responses shown in Table 3.1 focus on matters of privacy and deceptive invasion of personal space. Identifying when personal space is private, not public, and when behavior can or cannot be examined there, is difficult (Diener & Crandall, 1978). We must further explore the use of deception and whether it has a proper role, if any, in social psychological research.

Table 3.1   Some Ethically Challenging Studies on Privacy Invasions: Research, Researchers, and Critics

---

From sociology: Observing gay sexual encounters in public restrooms

Original work
Humphreys, L. (1975). *Tearoom trade: Impersonal sex in public places* (2nd ed.). Chicago: Aldine.

Responses
Sieber, J. E. (Ed.). (1982). *The ethics of social research: Surveys and experiments*. New York: Springer-Verlag (see chapter 1).
Warwick, D. P. (1973). Tearoom trade: Means and ends in social research. *Hastings Center Studies, 1*, 27–38.

From social psychology: Crowding and bathroom behavior

Original work
Middlemist, R. D., Knowles, E. S., & Matter, C. (1976). Personal space invasions in the lavatory: Suggestive evidence for arousal. *Journal of Personality and Social Psychology, 33*, 541–546.

Responses
Koocher, G. P. (1977). Bathroom behavior and human dignity. *Journal of Personality and Social Psychology, 35*, 120–121.
Middlemist, R. D., Knowles, E. S., & Matter, C. F. (1977). What to do and what to report: A reply to Koocher. *Journal of Personality and Social Psychology, 35*, 122–124.

The Problem of Deception in Social Psychology Experiments: Balancing Benefits and Costs

Deception is the planned withholding of certain information from human participants in some research experience, most often a social psychology experiment. There are two main categories of deception: active deception and passive deception (Rosnow & Rosenthal, 1996, p. 53). *Active deception* occurs when participants are intentionally misinformed about the true state of affairs in a study. The role and behavior of confederates in both the Asch (1956) and Milgram (1963) studies represent examples of active deception. The withholding of truth or some relevant information occurs when *passive deception* is employed. In the first few minutes after a study begins, social psychologists often ask participants to complete personality measures or other questionnaires with no explanation whatsoever. The scores on these instruments are then used to assign participants to particular conditions or groups in the study. Whether active or passive, the use of deception is not fully disclosed to participants until their role ends.

There was a time when the majority of social psychology experiments being performed and then published relied on some form of deception. Estimates vary, but some authors contend that deception studies appearing in the *Journal of Personality and Social Psychology* increased from around 20% in 1960 up to almost 70% in the mid-1970s (e.g., Adair, Dushenko, & Lindsay, 1985). Deception became popular and perhaps much too easy to employ in research efforts. Has social psychology's reliance on deception changed? Generally, yes, there is much less deception in the average empirical investigation (Nicks, Korn, & Mainieri, 1997; Vitelli, 1988), but we must keep in mind that the presence of deception is more a matter of degree than whether it is present or absent.

Critics can rightly charge that *any* psychology experiment—not just those performed by social psychologists—employs *some* degree of deception. How can that be? Consider the fact that no amount of disclosure about the nature of a study given before someone takes part in it can really do justice to the experience. Hearing about what will happen, whether the study involves completing a survey of political attitudes or looking at random shapes in a perception study, is a far cry from actually writing answers on a survey form or watching stimuli parade across a computer screen. Such differences may be minor, but they are real and constitute a mild form of unintentional deception—but it is deception nonetheless. Intentionally avoiding disclosing the true purpose of a study on conformity or obedience until its conclusion, of course, represents a more obvious, higher level of deception.

If you look at Table 3.2 you will see where and when some form of deception occurs in the typical social psychology experiment. For each entry, I indicated the relative level of deception found within the usual three phases of any social psychology experiment. These deception estimates will vary depending upon the nature of the investigation or the author (in this case, me) evaluating them. Determining whether the level

Table 3.2   Sample Forms of Deception Found During the Usual Phases of Social Psychology Experiments

Recruiting participants
Observing participants in the field without their consent (mild)
Coercing participation with inducements (e.g., money, course credit) (medium)
Researcher's name withheld at research sign-up (mild)
Title of experiment misleading (mild)
True purpose of research not revealed prior to participation (medium)

During experiment
Not revealing true purpose of research during participation (medium)
Giving untrue or misleading information about procedure, questionnaires, and other
   aspects of the project (medium)
Giving a participant false feedback (high)
Employing confederates (high)
Holding back information (medium)
Using hidden measures or cameras (high)

During debriefing and after the research ends
Giving false feedback during debriefing (high)
Not explaining research results in full depth or detail for fear of biasing future participants
   (medium)
Using participant's responses that were "discarded" during the procedure (high)
Reporting a participant's verbatim response in a publication (high)

Note: General relative levels of deception—mild, medium, or high—are noted parenthetically behind each action. Given levels associated with actions will vary depending upon the nature of the experiment.

of deception involved is mild, medium, or high generally depends on the information involved. Is some information being intentionally withheld from the participants or are they being given false information in order to elicit certain predicted behavioral reactions? Withholding the name of a researcher at the research sign-up is a failure to disclose information, but that information is not likely to have much effect on participants' decision to take part in the study or their subsequent behavior, hence it represents a mild form of deception (see the top section of Table 3.2). In any case, many psychology departments require that the name of the lead researcher should always appear on a sign-up form. Yet how many participants do you suppose pay attention to such information when deciding whether to take part in a given study? I will guess very few.

   In contrast, intentionally withholding the true purpose of a project until it ends represents a medium rather than mild level of deception (see the middle section of Table 3.2). Why? Researchers want participants' reactions to mimic real life behaviors—those reactions that occur outside the lab in response to similar circumstances— as much as possible. At a study's outset, if participants knew that a project was on racial stereotyping, they might screen their thoughts and behaviors much more carefully than is usually the case to avoid giving any prejudiced response. That is, accurate knowledge about a project's purpose would taint or change a participant's usual or likely reactions. Employing deception regarding the study's purpose is more likely to obtain a true measure of a participant's behavior (or, more to the point, an accurate assessment of all the participants' typical reactions, not that of any one person; recall chapter 1's discussion of social psychology studying collective rather than individual social behavior).

The highest level of deception is reserved for portions of a study that intentionally mislead the participants, often by providing them with false information or not revealing some crucial information. The use of confederates in both the Asch (1956) and Milgram (1963) studies, for example, represent this highest level of deception. Participants in both studies believed that the other participants were no different than themselves; they had no idea that the others taking part were following an established script in collaboration with the experimenter (see the middle section of Table 3.2). Similarly, giving participants "false feedback," that is, an untrue message designed to affect their subsequent behavior in the study (e.g., "You performed worse on the intelligence test than all but 10% of those who have ever taken it"), is deception at its highest. One of the dangers of delivering false feedback is that even when participants are explicitly told the information is bogus, many later persist in believing its validity (e.g., Ross, Lepper, & Hubbard, 1975). Such belief perseverance in the face of accurate information is one reason that high levels of deception are problematic and should be used rarely, if ever. In fact, many social psychologists will try to develop a less deceptive approach to obtain and examine the same behavioral reaction without resorting to relying on false feedback. Of course, nondeception alternatives are not always feasible and there are arguments to be made that support the use of deception in research.

Arguments for using deception: Some benefits

Given all these cautions, is deception ever justified? I think there are compelling reasons to argue that the adequate study of various social phenomena could not be done without resorting to some deceptive practices. If people knew in advance that some situation in an experiment was not "real" (i.e., an experimenter staged a minor accident), for example, they might not take it seriously, would feel self-conscious or even foolish for trying to help, or might simply weigh their reactions much more carefully than usual. Any or all of these responses are different than the spontaneity associated with routine offers of assistance associated with daily social life. In other words, the participants would fail to behave as they normally do in similar circumstances. As social psychologists, we want participants to be actively involved in our studies. Sometimes, deceiving them with plausible "cover stories" or contrived events is necessary to insure they are fully engaged in the experiment.

It makes sense at this point to introduce two terms associated with participants' level of involvement in experiments. Social psychologists typically distinguish between experimental realism and mundane realism (Aronson, Brewer, & Carlsmith, 1985; Aronson, Ellsworth, Carlsmith, & Gonzales, 1990; Aronson, Wilson, & Brewer, 1998). *Experimental realism* refers to how much the experiment absorbs the participants' attention. The more absorbed they are, the more seriously they will perform whatever activities are called for. In the Milgram (1963) study, for example, the participants did not just "go through the motions" in response to the authoritarian experimenter's demands; they were not play-acting. Rather, their emotional and behavioral responses implicated psychological processes linked to authority and obedience. Though high in experimental realism, the Milgram study certainly did not reflect a situation associated with everyday life, but it did simulate qualities associated with many such situations. You will likely agree that you have met people who display rigid, even dictatorial behavior when interacting with others. Sadly, too, human history amply illustrates that people are all too willing to harm one another when coerced by others, including governments, to do so.

The degree to which an experiment imitates real life or an everyday setting is called *mundane realism*. No laboratory situation will ever achieve the qualities of a real life situation, especially because the participants knowingly agreed to take part in an experiment, but *similarity* to everyday life encourages active engagement. Observing someone drop something, say, a file full of documents, is an everyday event, and such staged mishaps aimed at studying helping behavior are quite high in mundane realism (e.g., Isen & Levin, 1972). We will discuss experimental realism, mundane realism, and trade-offs between the two in more detail in chapter 9.

Realism aside, we should also consider whether the usual deception found in social psychology experiments offers any benefits. Table 3.3 lists benefits associated with the

Table 3.3   Some Benefits Associated with Using Deception in Social Psychology Experiments

Benefits for participants

Learning important things about themselves, perhaps gain some self-insight
Behaviors and responses are spontaneous and genuine, not biased, planned, or rehearsed.
Knowing they are directly contributing to the growth of scientific knowledge.
Learning about social psychological research by experiencing it, not just reading or hearing about it.

Benefits for culture

Collective knowledge about importance of prosocial (e.g., altruism, helping) and antisocial (e.g., prejudice, stereotyping, discrimination) behavior grows.
Science of social psychology advances so that theories and predictions become more precise.
Research findings can be used to improve human welfare.
Investigations of some topics may be (or will become) unnecessary (e.g., obedience to authority).

use of use of deception where participants and our wider culture are concerned, respectively. The fact is that few participants ever complain about being deceived. Even when the experiments create some degree of stress or upset, as is the case in studies on whether bystanders will offer help to the "victims" of staged accidents, most participants claim the research is educational as well as ethical (Schwartz & Gottlieb, 1981; see also Christensen, 1988; Sharp, Adair, & Roese, 1992; Smith & Richardson, 1983). Similarly, 84% percent of the "teachers" who took part in the Milgram (1963) study reported they were "glad to have been in the experiment" (Milgram, 1974, p. 195). Of the remaining 16%, less than 2% reported they had any negative feelings about the experience (Milgram, 1974, p. 195). Furthermore, taking part in research is beneficial educationally. Short of conducting your own research (skills you are acquiring right now), there is no better way to learn about social psychology than to take part in a study. Unless, like some critics, you worry that awareness of social psychological results undermines and nullifies them (e.g., Gergen, 1973, 1976, 1982; but see Schlenker, 1974, 1976), simply reading or hearing about an experiment in class is no substitute for taking part and directly contributing to the scientific enterprise (see the entries in the top half of Table 3.3).

How can deception benefit our culture? As shown by the entries in the bottom half of Table 3.3, knowledge regarding constructive and destructive social psychological processes can grow. As our knowledge regarding human social behavior grows, our theories and predictions should become more specific. Eventually, perhaps, such knowledge can be used to promote human well-being while combating destructive behavior. With effort and luck, some of this knowledge will be used to shape social and educational policies, inform lawmakers, and to generally shape society in beneficial ways. Finally, investigating some topics may become unnecessary or obsolete. Ethical principles in psychology would likely prevent anyone from replicating the Milgram (1963) study or conducting a project similar to it. On the other hand, the findings regarding the negative power of obedience are so definitive that there is little need to revisit the topic.

Arguments against using deception: The costs

Of course, we must balance arguments for deception with those against using it in social psychological research. The main argument against using deception in social psychology experiments (or at least reducing its use as much as possible) is the social cost involved. By social cost, I refer to the losses in good will incurred by research participants and by our larger society (see the upper entries in Table 3.4). When a social psychologist deceives a single participant in the course of a study, for example, that researcher may embarrass or upset the individual for that moment in time. Such discomfort seems small and, as noted earlier, what we learn about human behavior through occasional acts of deception may, on balance, be worth it. Yet attention must be paid to a related issue: Are social psychologists justified in forcing participants to

Table 3.4 Some Social Costs Incurred by Participants and the Culture When Deception is Employed in Social Psychological Research

Social costs to participants
  Potential embarrassment or upset at being intentionally deceived ("lied to") by researchers.
  Being forced to learn sometimes upsetting, troubling, or surprising things about oneself in the course of an experiment
  Less favorable view of science
  Distrust or suspicion of other people, especially former role models (e.g., researchers, teachers).

Social costs to culture
  Science and its practitioners are viewed with doubt or skepticism (e.g., "Why do they have to lie to people in order to learn about them?")
  Increased sense of generalized suspicion (e.g., "Are my actions being watched? How do I know this isn't a social psychology experiment?").
  False rumors about the intentions or effects of social psychological research (e.g., wrong belief that the Milgram obedience study used actual electric shocks on actual victims).

learn upsetting or troubling things about themselves (e.g., one's willingness to obey authority) in the course of an experiment?

What happens if that single participant subsequently develops a mistrust of researchers and less appreciation for scientific work in general? Is the knowledge gained by the use of deception still worth it? Views of scientific research, those who conduct it or share it with others, may suffer in the process.

As you mull over your answers to these questions, consider some of the other individual and social costs we incur when we use deception (see Table 3.4). Such questions are difficult to address adequately and I am not suggesting that social psychology students and researchers abandon the practice immediately. Rather, I am urging you to think carefully—long and hard—before you consider using anything above the milder forms of deception identified in Table 3.2.

The special role of confederates

Experimenters often need assistance when running an experiment. Most of that help, as well as a good deal of deception in social psychological research, depends upon the willing participation of confederates. A *confederate* is a "stooge," an inside helper of the experimenter. Confederates usually appear to be fellow participants taking part in an experiment. In practice, confederates are often college students (or they appear to be college students) because most of the people who take part in social psychological research are college students (e.g., Dawes, 1991; Schultz, 1969; Sears, 1986). The confederates in the Asch (1956) conformity study were students, for example. If the participants are members of a community, as was the case for the men in the Milgram

(1963) study, then the confederate will appear to have the same background (Milgram's confederate was a friendly, 47-year-old accountant).

Although the social psychologist designs whatever deceptions are used in an experiment, it is up to the confederate (or confederates) to perform the actual deception. Confederates do have a special role—really, a responsibility—in social psychological research, one that should not be approached lightly. The task of purposefully misleading participants when interacting with them, providing false information or feedback on some task, behaving brusquely or rudely, or whatever the legitimate research demand, must be approached professionally.

In fact, as aids to the researcher or experimenter, confederates should be carefully trained in research ethics. Confederates are especially bound by privacy rules where participants are concerned. In research contexts, *privacy* refers to what information (physical behavior, self-reports) research participants share in the course of taking part in any research. Confederates cannot disclose anything to anyone about what any individual participant did. They cannot, for example, carry entertaining tales about human foibles beyond the lab. They must respect the participants and, given the demands of any experimental situation, empathize with them.

Confederates, then, should learn that their role, while essential to the scientific enterprise, should be approached with a high degree of caution. If you rely on confederates for your project, make certain they have an opportunity to meet and speak with each participant once the experiment ends and after the postexperimental interview is over (see chapter 10). This friendly opportunity for closure is doubly important if participants taking part in your project encounter anything more than mild deception.

Labels Do Matter: Participants, Not Subjects

How should we refer to the people who take part in social psychological research? What should we call them? Traditionally, individuals who took part in any psychology experiment were called "subjects," as their behavior was the "subject" under an experimenter's scrutiny. Interestingly, the first edition of the APA Publication manual urged authors to provide information about "subjects, observers or reactors" (Peerenboom et al., 1929, p. 59). Relatively recently, the term *subjects* fell into disfavor in the context of any research involving human beings (see, e.g., Gillis, 1976). Instead, the American Psychological Association (APA) requires that researchers, students, or anyone else who writes about psychological research involving humans refer to them as "participants." Why the change?

In the first place, the term *participants* denotes what is actually going on in research, especially social psychological research: People are participating in it—they are doing something, for example, filling out a questionnaire, being observed, performing an act or a series of behaviors. They are not simply *subject* to what happens in an experiment, rather, they *react to* what is happening—hence, they are participants. By participating, they are sharing a part of themselves—often a very private part of themselves—with an experimenter who, in turn, will share what the participants did (usually in an aggregated form to preserve any individual's anonymity) with many other people, most often readers of psychology journals and books. People who take part in psychological research usually agree to do so, especially when their participation is voluntary or when they do so to fulfill a course requirement, which is common at many colleges and universities.

When referring to people, there is a second, arguably more socially compelling, reason for using the more active term *participants* instead of the more passive term *subjects*. How we label people, what we call them when we describe them to others, matters a great deal. Labels have a certain power in that they can define people by drawing attention to them, their skills as well as abilities, or demean them by reducing or even eliminating their unique qualities or contributions (e.g., Dunn & Elliott, 2005; Wright, 1983, 1991; see also Wright & Lopez, 2002). After all, people are not things.

Think about this example: In a study on self-identity following a diagnosis of serious health threats, is there a difference between referring to a single participant as "an AIDS patient" or "a person with AIDS"? Although it is subtle, an important distinction exists. If you refer to someone as "an AIDS patient," you are putting the condition ahead of the individual, thereby highlighting it as more important than the person experiencing the condition. In contrast, referring to someone as "a person with AIDS" retains the importance of the individual who is being identified while also acknowledging his or her health condition.

Some researchers bristle at having to worry about how to properly refer to research participants (e.g., Roediger, 2004; see also Observer Forum, 2004), including the arguably modest move away from using the label "subjects." Yet language has a profound, even powerful, effect when it comes to influencing how we think and feel about others (Caplan, 1995; Sapir, 1951; Whorf, 1964). Indeed, labels provide a compelling form of social influence that can have positive or negative effects on perceivers and the perceived (Rosenthal & Jacobson, 1968). Whenever possible in social psychological research, then, the goal is to use inclusive language when describing people and what they did behaviorally. The same guideline for inclusive language holds true when it comes to referring to groups. If you were conducting a project concerning social networks among residents in an assisted living facility, would you identify the participants in your paper as "the elderly," "elderly people," or "elderly residents"? In general, the goal is to avoid monolithic labels like "the elderly" while also trying to remain scientifically precise and socially sensitive. In this example, "elderly residents" is more accurate than "elderly people" (for further examples, see Dunn, 2008; APA, 2001). Invoking a golden rule is appropriate here: You should label people, in writing or discussion, what they prefer to be called.

Given that you are more likely to involve fellow students in your own research than the members of any other group, are there issues that should concern you? Absolutely. Your chief concern will probably involve how to refer to gender and sex. Let me explain. Psychologically speaking, the term *gender* refers to how people think about themselves. In contrast, *sex* is reserved for an individual's biological identity; that is, does a person or a group of people have male or female reproductive organs? Please don't laugh, as this issue is important. Many psychologists—including some social psychologists—have to be careful about their language choices when it comes to denoting who participated in their studies. When writing about sexual orientation (which is an issue distinct from issues of gender and sex), for example, the term *gay men* is preferred over *homosexual men* (APA, 2001). The latter term is not only outdated, it also conjures up negative impressions in the minds of many people. In fact, specificity is always best. Thus, when referring to same-sex sexual orientation, use the terms *lesbians* and *gay men*; *gays* is not precise enough. Some people use it to refer to both groups, whereas others use it as shorthand for gay men.

What about you? Will any labels pose difficulties for your social psychological research? Unless gender identity, reproductive issues, or sexual orientation are a central part of your work, you will probably rely on *men* and *women* to describe research participants ("Thirty men and thirty women were recruited to participate in a study on dating behavior"). Note that use of *men* and *women* is favored over the more academical-sounding *males* and *females*, and both sets of terms always supersede antiquated descriptions such as *ladies* and *gentlemen*. Naturally, descriptors such as *girls* and *boys* should be used only when children are participating in the research.

Let's close our discussion of labels by asking whether the term "subjects" is ever appropriate. It is, but not where humans are concerned. The term subjects is reserved to describe or characterize the behavior of nonhuman organisms, chiefly animals (e.g., rats, mice, pigeons), involved in psychological research. Thus, college sophomores who take part in social psychological research are participants, while the white rats running a maze in a learning experiment are subjects (for more on animal subjects and their ethical treatment in psychological research see APA, 1993, 2001).

Institutional Review Boards

Before any piece of research in social psychology (or any other discipline) can be conducted at a college or a university, an Institutional Review Board (IRB) must approve the work. By "approve," I mean that a panel of professionals must review any proposed research—whether it involves humans or animals, whether it is experimental or observational—to make certain that those who will take part are protected by appropriate ethical guidelines. Most IRBs represent a cross-section of a campus's research community. Thus one or two members of the panel might be psychologists (not necessarily social psychologists), while the other reviewers could be from biology, philosophy, sociology, even the English Department. Medical ethicists and theologians are often drafted to serve on IRBs. In order to ensure a broad perspective, some IRBs also recruit at least one member from off-campus, such as a professional from the local community.

Colleges and universities also typically have an Institutional Animal Care and Use Committee (IACUC). This committee focuses on the welfare and treatment of nonhuman organisms involved in any research efforts. Social psychological research involving animals is relatively rare, but it is not unknown. Some of the classic studies in Zajonc's aforementioned work on social facilitation (see chapter 2) actually used cockroaches (Zajonc, Heingartner, & Herman, 1969). More recently, a new generation of social psychologists is examining selective social connections between humans and animals (e.g., Jones & Josephs, 2006).

Some psychology departments also have an "in-house" or department-based IRB, often called the ethics panel. Such ethics panels often review student research proposals or they do a "first pass" at a researcher's project before it is sent on for a full review by the institution's IRB. Preliminary comments and recommendations from a departmentally based review panel can catch problems or identify important questions early on, allowing the investigator to address them then, which may lead to a more expedited review by the IRB.

Keep the IRB's ethical mission firmly in mind: Unless there are clear problems, no panel ever judges the scientific merit of a project or the novelty or worthiness of the ideas contained within it. Rather, the people on the review panel focus on the likely experience of participants who will take part in the work. Will they be subjected to any stress? Is there anything psychologically or physically harmful in the proposed work? What are the risks involved for people who participate? Can steps be taken to moderate or eliminate any psychologically upsetting aspects of a research procedure?

These concerns point to a legitimate question: Are there "risks" in social psychology experiments? In truth, IRBs adopt the view that there is some degree of risk—however minor—in virtually *any* piece of psychological research, even the most innocuous one imaginable. Why? For the simple reason that no one can predict how every participant will react to a given research setting, the materials used, and so on. This is the concept of minimal risk. Although the possibility may be remote, some aspect of a social psychological investigation could remind a participant of a troubling personal event. Imagine, for example, that a psychologist was studying grief as a social emotion and the research procedure involved having participants watch a video of a funeral service. Unbeknownst to the psychologist, one of the participants had recently been bereaved and seeing the film caused that participant serious emotional distress.

Of course, in practice, few people respond negatively to scholarly investigations, but it is any IRB's responsibility to anticipate what problems might occur and whether they can be prevented or reduced. In the case of a study involving induced grief, for example, posting a clear description of the study ("You will watch a videotape of a funeral service . . .") might be sufficient to dissuade grieving or otherwise sensitive people from signing up. An IRB might request that a detailed description of a procedure be made available, for example, or the panel might suggest a researcher identify a less stressful means to induce a mood or an emotion in a group of participants.

The IRB must also weigh the relative benefit of what is to be learned through some research effort over the discomfort—however temporary it might be—of the people taking part in it. We have already reviewed some benefits and costs associated with social psychological research (recall Tables 3.3 and 3.4). Some researchers have offered ways to balance the costs and benefits of doing research (e.g., Rosenthal, 1994b; Rosenthal & Rosnow, 1984, 1991). Figure 3.3, developed by two social psychologists, Robert Rosenthal and Ralph Rosnow, illustrates a simple decision model for doing a cost–benefit analysis of experiments or other research approaches (see Rosenthal & Rosnow,

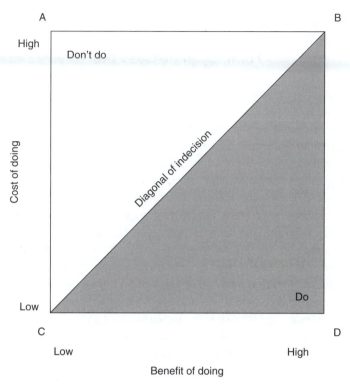

Figure 3.3. Doing a cost versus benefit analysis of whether to do research. Adapted from Rosnow and Rosenthal (1996, Figure 3.1, p. 60)

1984). The important issue here is perceptions of the costs and benefits of research by virtue of how the people involved—experimenters, participants, teachers, students, members of society—define these two terms. Those research efforts that fall at or near region D (i.e., low cost, high benefit) are likely to be performed, whereas those perceived to be at point A (high cost, low benefit) are unlikely to be conducted. Difficulties arise around or along the "diagonal of indecision" lying between regions B and C (see Figure 3.3). Here, researchers, IRBs, and interested observers struggle with whether to pursue research that is either "low–low" or "high–high."

Rosnow and Rosenthal (1996) wisely point out the even this cost–benefit approach is a bit misleading. Although Figure 3.3 implicates the costs and benefits of doing research, it is mute on those associated with *not* doing the research. Some research questions may be very costly to pursue (e.g., the social psychological consequences of war and terrorism, reducing AIDS by changing entrenched cultural beliefs) but the eventual benefits to society could be well worth the trouble. There is also the possibility that the benefits associated with pursuing some research questions may not be recognized by the most thorough cost–benefit analysis. Thus a decision maker might elect not to pursue some question or an IRB might prevent some project from going forward, never realizing the true benefit that might result.

ACTIVE LEARNING EXERCISE   3A

Forming an In-Class IRB

As noted earlier, some psychology departments rely on in-house IRBs to review student research proposals. Some schools even mandate that student research proposals be reviewed by the internal IRB. You can well imagine what a lot of work (albeit important work) that is for a group of reviewers. More commonly, however, students review the work of other students by creating an in-class IRB. I think doing so is a terrific way for you to learn about the ethical issues entailed in doing social psychological research first-hand.

Table 3.5 outlines some steps for creating an in-class IRB. These steps can be modified to the needs of your course, department regulations, and your instructor's plans. Who serves on the IRB, for example, will be determined by the number of students enrolled in the class as well as by how many research projects are conducted during the course. If there is only one research project, then perhaps all members of the class can read and comment on each proposed experiment. If there are several labs during the term, then the IRB membership can shift so that every student in the class gets one opportunity to serve. The most important aspect of this active learning exercise is that the goal is to comment exclusively on ethical issues pertaining to the

Table 3.5   Steps for Creating an In-Class IRB

Step 1	Determine who serves on the in-class IRB (i.e., everyone or a smaller group within the class).
Step 2	IRB members must familiarize themselves with the ethical criteria pertaining to experiments and the professional behavior of psychologists. To do so, they must read and discuss two publications by the American Psychological Association (1982, 2002).
Step 3	IRB forms must be completed for every research project (see Table 3.6) and submitted to the in-class IRB for review.
Step 4	The IRB reviews each form. A proposal is discussed and then approved by unanimous favorable vote. An IRB member is excused from the discussion and vote if he or she is the author of a proposal. When a vote is unanimous and favorable, proceed to Step 6. If not, then proceed to Step 5.
Step 5	When an initial review is unfavorable, the IRB provides written comments and suggestions to the proposal author with a copy to the course instructor. The proposal author is invited to revise and resubmit the IRB form. The IRB is encouraged to ask for additional information or for clarification regarding any procedures. When the revised form is resubmitted, go back to Step 4.
Step 6	The IRB notifies the proposal author and the course instructor in writing when a research proposal passes review.

Source: Adapted from Dunn (1999, p. 151).

experience of the research participants, not to critique the research hypothesis or its execution. Maintaining this focus can be difficult—you may need to keep reminding yourself and your peers about this goal—but the experience will illustrate in microcosm the dilemmas and responsibilities faced by IRB members.

ACTIVE LEARNING EXERCISE   **3B**

Completing an IRB Form

If your institution has any type of IRB, then it must have IRB forms available. Chances are that you can download a copy from somewhere on your institution's web site, fill it out, and then submit it for review (as previously noted, some institutions insist that undergraduate research be approved by the IRB, whereas others allow the course instructor to serve as proxy for the committee). Minimally, most IRBs require relatively detailed information concerning the issues outlined in Table 3.6.

If you do not have an IRB form available, you can create one based on the information shown in Table 3.6. Create a document that provides sufficient detail about each of the 11 items shown in Table 3.6. Some items can be answered briefly; others will require a coherent narrative. Your descriptions should provide

Table 3.6   Information Usually Required by IRBs

1   Researcher's name and contact information (phone number, email address, campus address).
2   Title of the proposed research.
3   Name of the course instructor who is supervising the research.
4   Whether the proposal is a new proposal, a resubmission of a rejected proposal, a renewal, or a request for modification to an on-going project
5   Who will be the participants in the research? How many?
6   Specify any risks to the participants. How will these risks be reduced?
7   Does the research involve deception of the participants? If "yes," the nature of the deception and the planned debriefing procedure must be described.
8   A detailed description of the proposed research, including the research design, what will be behaviorally required of participants, and any procedures designed to reduce risks to the participants.
9   Copies of any surveys, questionnaires, standardized measures, or other stimulus materials that the participants will read or complete during the proposed research.
10   Explanations of how the data collected during the research will be safeguarded and how the participants' anonymity will be maintained.
11   A copy of the informed consent form for the research.

Continued

enough detail so that IRB members—whether they are appointed committee members, or your instructor and fellow classmates—can mentally "walk through" your proposed research from the moment participants arrive until they leave the experimental situation. Again, the IRB needs to know only what participants do behaviorally (however, part of the narrative can probably be later adapted for the Method section of your research paper; see chapter 12).

After the IRB reviews your proposal, you may receive comments, suggestions, or even directives about how to revise your proposed research. Accept these comments in the constructive and ethical spirit they are intended. Any changes requested by the IRB will be meant to safeguard the experience of the participants and to ensure that you are treating them ethically. The IRB may subject your proposal to a cost–benefit analysis (i.e., does the intellectual and empirical gain warrant the methods and proposed procedures?), so do not be defensive about any feedback. Accept it, incorporate it, resubmit the revised proposal to the IRB, and prepare to begin your research project.

Informed Consent is Essential

When people decide to participate in any experiment, their informed consent to do so must be obtained. The term *informed consent* refers to the process whereby participants are told what taking part in the research entails, including any potential risks or benefits associated with doing so. Individuals must be given enough information about a study so that they can make a conscious decision about whether to actually take part in it. As we noted earlier, there is always some degree of risk in any research experience; even a minor risk is still a risk.

Where laboratory-based research is concerned, the key issue linked with informed consent is an individual's right to quit the study at any time and without any penalty. When individuals remove themselves from taking part in a study, they are retracting their consent. Established ethical guidelines clearly state that any participant can withdraw from a study at any point in time and without any need to provide an explanation for doing so. In practice, of course, an individual who elects to end his or her participation is apt to explain why, if only briefly. Still, the ethics of experimentation are clear: The investigator must honor a participant's decision to withdraw *without* question or protest. If any credit or other reward is part of the study (course credit is typical, though some researchers pay volunteers a few dollars for their time), the experimenter must graciously give it to anyone who quits early.

Most importantly, the option to withdraw from the study at any time must be clearly explained at the outset of the study's procedure. Thus participants are informed and reminded of their fundamental right before anything happens. Anyone electing to take part in research has the right to self-determination, as this key passage from the Nuremberg Code attests (Beals et al., 1946–1949, pp. 181–182; see also Katz, 1996):

> The voluntary consent of the human subject is absolutely essential. This means that the person involved should have legal capacity to give consent; should be so situated as to be able to exercise free power of choice, without the intervention of any element of force, fraud, deceit, duress, overreaching, or other ulterior form of constraint or coercion; and should have sufficient knowledge and comprehension of the elements of the subject matter involved so as to enable him to make . . . an enlightened decision. . . . The duty and responsibility for ascertaining the quality of the consent rests upon each individual who initiates, directs, or engages in the experiment. It is a personal duty and responsibility which may not be delegated to another with impunity.

Take careful note of the phrase "each individual who initiates, directs, or engages in the experiment" in the above excerpted passage: This refers to you when you act as an experimenter. You are ultimately responsible for the well-being of the people who take part in your project—whether those people are close friends, acquaintances, peers from your class, or strangers off the street. You must be absolutely focused on making certain that their participation is voluntary, that they may withdraw at any time without penalty, their consent is informed, and that it is obtained properly.

Confidentiality

A major part of informed consent is the expectation of *confidentiality*. Participants must be explicitly told that whatever information they provide in the course of any investigation will be held in the strictest confidence. Neither their names nor any other identifying information will ever be linked to their responses. In practice, the results from most social psychology experiments are reported in aggregate form (see chapter 11); only unique or otherwise noteworthy responses are discussed individually. On the rare occasions when this occurs, researchers always make an effort to remove any details from the solo responses that could reveal a participant's identity. The only exception to this rule is if and when participants consent to have specific information they provided (e.g., detailed experiences) shared publicly, usually in a researcher's professional presentations or publications.

How can confidentiality be maintained during and after a piece of research? In practice, participants' names should never be attached to their questionnaires, any study sign-up sheets (see chapter 10), or other private materials. Most researchers assign each participant a unique identification number, and create a master list containing participants' names and numbers. Most IRBs require that such lists be kept under lock and key, usually in a file cabinet in a secure place. If all of this sounds a bit too cloak and dagger, bear in mind that participants trust experimenters when they say that all private and personal responses will be kept anonymous. It is not an exaggeration to say that the enterprise of conducting research in social psychology is based on trust that researchers will maintain participants' anonymity.

Obtaining informed consent

Informed consent is determined by a person's legal status. The general guideline is age-based: Individuals who are legally adults (i.e., at least 18 years of age) can make decisions for themselves, including whether to take part in social psychology experiments. Thus most college students can provide their own informed consent. Students who are younger than 18 years of age, however, must have the consent of a parent or legal guardian. If you are recruiting traditional college-aged students (i.e., 17 to 24 years of age), before any of them take part in your project, be sure to ascertain that they are 18 or older.

Special permission must also be obtained for some other groups of potential research participants who cannot provide their own informed consent. Young children and minors cannot participate in a research project unless a parent or other legal guardian signs on their behalf. A legal guardian or some other authority must provide informed consent before individuals with mental disabilities or prisoners can take part in any research (APA, 1982). Please note that securing permission from someone else does not mean that the consent of the potential participant should be neglected. Although a designated guardian may make the ultimate decision, the potential participant has a right to have the project explained in detail, and then to agree to or to decline a role in the research. Whenever there is any uncertainty about a person's involvement in a study, an IRB should be directly involved in the discussion so that the individuals' welfare is ensured.

ACTIVE LEARNING EXERCISE   3C

Creating an Informed Consent Form for Your Project

Acquiring the informed consent of the people who will take part in your research is essential; indeed, you are ethically bound to do so. There is a very good chance that your psychology department has a standard informed consent form available for you to use. If so, use it or adapt it as needed. If not, then you will need to create one yourself. Doing so is not difficult. In fact, you will gain the opportunity to ethically think through what people experience during your study.

Informed consent forms abide by the ethical principles for the treatment of human participants espoused by the American Psychological Association (1982, 2002). Table 3.7 lists the information that must be shared with participants so that their informed consent can be obtained. Some experimenters write a script that provides the information outlined in Table 3.7. This script need not be lengthy, rather just a few paragraphs that can be memorized and delivered verbally or read to participants prior to every research session.

Whether you commit it to memory or read it, writing a few descriptive paragraphs covering the information in Table 3.7 is a good idea. When doing so, however, you

Table 3.7 Information to Disclose (Verbally or in Writing) When Obtaining Informed Consent

1   Title of the experiment or study.
2   Describe what the participant will do behaviorally during the research session(s).
3   Describe the expected duration of the session (how many minutes).
4   Research may present minimal or extreme risk to subjects. Describe the extent of risk presented by this research to the participant.
5   Describe the expected benefit for the participant, if any, for taking part in the research.
6   Describe how the participant's records (e.g., questionnaires) will be kept confidential during the research.
7   Describe what will happen to participant records at the conclusion of the research.
8   Inform each participant who to contact if any emotional or physical upset occurs during the session (your course instructor or research supervisor is the appropriate choice).
9   Explain that participation in the research is voluntary. Refusal to participate will involve no penalty or loss of benefit (e.g., course credit) to which the participant is otherwise entitled. Participation can be discontinued at any time.
10 Inform the participant that questions about the research will be answered at the session's conclusion. Inform the participant that your course instructor or research supervisor can answer questions regarding participant rights.
11 Obtain a dated signature for individuals 18 years of age or older, or the dated signature of a legal guardian (if necessary) to authorize the individual's participation.

need only disclose the *behavioral requirements* of the study—what participants will be asked to do—but not the reasons for their actions, the theory underlying the research or, most important of all, the actual hypothesis being tested. Such key details are not revealed until the postexperimental interview or debriefing, which occurs once the research session is over (the importance of debriefing and how to do it is explained in chapter 10). Disclosing the true nature of the research early on would likely bias the participants' responses, change their subsequent behavior, and render the findings of questionable validity and scientific value.

This is an appropriate place for a few words on debriefing, the end of the informed consent process. A social psychologist is ethically obligated to disclose the complete purpose and research methods (including any deception) used in a study to each and every participant. The ethical function of debriefing requires that the researcher explain the need for withholding information and for testing a hypothesis one way and not another, and answers whatever questions participants have. In this case, ethics also serve an educational purpose: explaining to partici-pants why social psychologists examine behavior as they do. The practical side of debriefing is so that the researcher can verify that the experimental procedure and instructions made sense, that experimental manipulations went unrecognized, and

Continued

to assess whether participants were suspicious, and so on. These and others practical matters linked to debriefing are considered in chapter 10.

Table 3.8 contains a sample informed consent form written by a student researcher examining how college students choose elective courses. The student was interested in examining how alliances form between people who are working together in small groups where discussion is a central element. If you read Table 3.8, you will see that its content reflects key points from Table 3.7's guidelines. Take a closer look at items d and e in Table 3.8, which deal with the presence or absence, respectively, of deception. A sentence like that found in item d acknowledges that any "incomplete information" will be provided at the study's conclusion. This honest declaration assures participants that if some deception is present,

Table 3.8 A Sample Informed Consent Form

Informed Consent Form for Choosing College Electives

I give my informed consent to take part in a study of how people decide what courses to take as college electives. I consent to having my responses used in any publication of the study's results with the understanding that my responses will remain anonymous, disguised, and never linked to me individually. I also understand that my name will not be linked to my responses in any of the research records, and that a number only will identify the information collected from me.

a I have been told that my participation in this study will involve a group discussion on choosing elective college courses.

b I was told that the study will take between 45 min and 1 hour to complete.

c I know that possible risks associated with this study are low, that it is unlikely that I will feel physical or psychological discomfort by engaging in a discussion with others. As for benefits, I may learn some new ways to think about selecting my courses in the future.

d [*Use a sentence like this one if deception is present*] I know that if the initial information I have been given is incomplete, I will be given complete information at the study's conclusion.

e [*Use a sentence like this one if no deception is present in the study*] I was told that there are no "disguised" procedures in this study. The procedures are as they appear to be.

f I know that I can withdraw from participating in this study at any time and without any penalty.

g If I have questions or concerns about this study, I can see Dr. Smith, Room 231, in the Psychology Department, Old Main Hall, who is supervising student research this semester.

I attest that I have read and understood this consent form and received a copy.

Subject signature: _____ Date: _____

I attest that I am the subject's legally authorized representative and that I have read and understood this consent form, and received a copy.

Legal representative signature: _____ Date: _____

they will still be treated fairly because the reason for its use will be eventually explained in detail. And, of course, participants will be able to ask questions regarding deception or any other aspect of the project once it is over.

A sentence like the one shown in item e should be used when no medium or high level of deception is part of a study. Informing participants that there are no "disguised procedures" will reduce their suspicion or discomfort about taking part in the project (Sternberg, 2003). Regrettably, many people assume that psychologists are out to trick them, make them look foolish, or otherwise "read their minds" (see the concerns raised by Baumrind, 1964, 1985); thus candor regarding the absence of deception can reduce participants' wariness or anxiety.

One final note about informed consent forms: As experimenter, you are required to keep a signed copy of every form to verify that every participant's permission was properly obtained. As already noted, keep them in a secure place so that the participants' confidentiality is maintained.

Ethical Issues and Field Research

Social psychological research is not restricted to the well-defined control of the laboratory, which means that studies out in the field raise special ethical concerns. "Out in the field" can mean many things, of course, but in the context of this chapter, we need to be especially concerned about ethical issues where obtaining participants' informed consent is not possible or when doing so might create some ethical dilemmas. Consider behavior in public settings: Most of us watch other people all the time. We are curious about people, so we watch them in class, on campus, in the mall, at airports, wherever. Watching people (as long as you are not staring or otherwise intruding into their lives) is a normal human activity. What happens, however, if your "watching" becomes observation, that is, carefully assessing what people do in a public place? Is obtaining their informed consent necessary?

It depends. In the first place, you must give careful thought to how invasive you are being when it comes to the privacy of others. Is what you are doing reasonable? Can people decline to take part in your study or remove themselves from it if they remain unaware they are taking part? No, of course not. This is arguably the key ethical dilemma in field research. Now, public behavior is, after all, public: There is nothing unusual about watching people and thinking about what motivates their actions, but there is something unusual about taking meticulous notes or making detailed observations while doing so.

This leads us to consider what we might call post hoc (after the fact) informed consent. Can you seek someone's permission once your research is done? Perhaps. But you should consider how the people you observed will react. If you are merely observing people and creating no intervention (see chapter 5), then it might be best not to approach them and tell them about your research. Quite a bit of observational research would be regarded as innocuous. On the other hand, if there is some intervention—you leave a wallet with money in it lying on the ground to see if passers-by will take the money or look for the owner—then you should probably explain what you are doing. You cannot assume that everyone will willingly allow you to use the behavioral responses you collect. As Aronson, Wilson, and Brewer (1998, p. 137) note, "Special sensitivity on the part of the researcher is required to avoid embarrassing people and to ensure the mechanisms are available for refusal to be included in the study after the fact." No still means no, and you must follow the (unwilling) participants' wishes to the letter.

When you come up against an ethical problem related to field research (or, indeed, any social psychological research), the best advice is to seek the counsel of experts (e.g., IRB members, your instructor, a philosopher who studies ethics) or experienced researchers. Relying on collective wisdom is wiser and likely to lead to a happier outcome for you and your research participants than is making a solitary decision.

Shared Virtues: Ethical Treatment, Education, and Science

During my college years, I once heard a waggish philosophy professor make the following remark: "All psychologists are liars; social psychologists are even bigger liars." I laughed when I first heard it, but then I realized that the joke was on me and the discipline I was planning to join. Ouch! The subversive beliefs perpetuated by this quote are that social psychologists enjoy telling lies to the unwitting participants who inhabit studies, that social psychology is all about the undisciplined use of deception, even that the pursuit of knowledge is trivial—and trivialized by—the research methods embraced by its practitioners. Of course, my response sounds a bit defensive, as no reasonably educated person believes the philosopher's witty charge. And yet social psychology and the people who teach and research in the field are often criticized for using deceptive practices.

What to do? Or, more to the point, what can you do to help dispel the myth that social psychology is all about lying and deceiving human participants? When conducting your research, you must act as both educator and social psychologist in training. You must adhere to the goals of science and social psychology while endeavoring to teach those taking part in the research why it is worth doing in the first place. You must treat them respectfully and ethically, pledging to maintain their anonymity and to keep their responses confidential. You must share what insights you learn from them with others. If all this sounds lofty to you, then we can focus on some simple ways to treat participants with dignity, courtesy, and the respect they deserve. Suggestions in this vein appear in Table 3.9. Review the contents of Table 3.9 now and again when you begin to recruit actual participants.

Table 3.9 Treat Participants Well: Practical Ethics for Doing Social Psychological Research

Begin and end on time: Do not keep participants waiting to begin a project and do not detain them longer than necessary. Your time and theirs is equally valuable.

Create a rapport: Welcome and treat them in a friendly but professional manner. Thank them when their role in the project is over.

Know your role: Professional social psychologists are smooth. They know the research script—what they will say and when they will say it (see chapter 10). Errors, missteps, and the like will undermine participant confidence in you and your project.

Reduce their anxiety: If there is no deception in your study, tell them that right away—things are just as they seem to be. Inform them that all their responses will be kept anonymous, only reported in summary form, and so on.

Be engaging: The experimental procedure will quickly become familiar to you but it will be novel to each and every participant. Convey interest in the participants and appreciation for their assistance.

Answer all questions: You are representing the discipline of social psychology. Explain the purpose and theory underlying the research. Be sincerely grateful when participants express interest in what you are doing (most will).

Say thank you—one more time: Once the debriefing is over, thank each person again for helping you with your project. Be sincere.

A Last Word on Ethics?

Ethical issues, concerns, and controversies evolve; there is no last word on the matter where social psychological research is concerned. A fine, general discussion of ethical issues in social psychological research, for example, can be found in Kimmel (2004). Social psychologists are duty bound to be vigilant about changes to or expansion of disciplinary materials pertaining to ethics. The APA (2002) provides a set of coherent principles—*Ethical Principles of Psychologists and the Code of Conduct*—for psychologists who work with human research participants (see also Canter, Bennett, Jones, & Nagy, 1994; Nagy, 2005). For further discussion of the ethics regarding the protection of human participants, see Chastain and Landrum (1999) and Sales and Folkman (2000).

In the end, of course, research ethics and ethical practices comes down to you. There is only one way to appropriately treat research participants who take part in your project. Treat them as you would want to be treated in similar circumstances.

Exercises

1 Look through a recent issue of a social psychology journal, such as the *Journal of Personality and Social Psychology* or one listed in Appendix A. Do a content analysis of the journal's articles: How many studies, if any, use an active form of deception?

How do the authors of the studies refer to the research participants (i.e., what labels, if any, are used)?

2   The APA requires that researchers indicate in journal articles (usually at the end of Method sections) that participants were treated in accordance with the discipline's ethical guidelines (APA 1982, 1993) and fully debriefed. Do a content analysis on experimental articles appearing in a social psychology journal to learn what percentage obeyed this rule.

3   Was the deception in Milgram's (1963) study justified? To explore arguments on both sides, read the historic exchange between Milgram (1964) and one of his critics (Baumrind, 1964; see also Baumrind, 1985).

4   Some social psychologists (e.g., Kelman, 1968; Schultz, 1969) argue that role-playing studies—asking participants to act as if they were in a particular situation—are a viable solution to the ethical and practical dilemmas of doing social psychology experiments. Consult these arguments and then identify some advantages and disadvantages of role-playing research.

Chapter 4

Basic Experimental Design

If you're driving into town
With a dark cloud above you
Dial in the number
Who's bound to love you
—*You Turn Me on, I'm a Radio*, 1972,
words and music by Joni Mitchell

If you are like most people, occasionally you probably wonder whether your emotions affect how you think and behave. Are you likely to seek out a friend, for example, when you are feeling low? Some social psychological research demonstrates that anxiety or upset does promote a tendency for people to affiliate with others (Schachter, 1959). Misery very much appreciates company.

More specifically, though, how do moods—those transient emotional states that possess a positive or negative tone—influence our social behavior? Do the dark clouds of a bad mood—say, one triggered by a very low grade on an otherwise easy examination—make it harder for you to pay attention during class? Folk wisdom, common sense, and psychological research (Derryberry & Tucker, 1994; Easterbrook, 1959) suggest that foul moods or negative emotions narrow our focus of attention. We ruminate, we worry, and we search for a solution to our problem (e.g., studying more for the next test, writing a stellar paper, asking about extra credit opportunities). Quite a bit of research examines the impact of negative moods on people's thoughts, feelings, and behaviors; indeed, research identifies three or four discrete negative emotions for every one positive feeling state (Ellsworth & Smith, 1988).

Surprisingly, we know somewhat less about good moods, the fleeting states social psychologists often refer to as "positive affect." In daily life, surrounding circumstance often triggers good feelings. Being served a quick snack (juice and cookies) or given a small gift (a bag of candy), for example, will brighten your mood, but with what consequence? Unlike negative moods, positive moods do not shut us down by narrowing our attentional focus. Instead, when we regard the world as a somewhat rosier place, our focus broadens beyond ourselves (Fredrickson, 1998). Perhaps our momentary delight becomes wrapped up with good thoughts and imaginative actions. Will a small surprise or an unexpected treat influence any subsequent problems that come your way? Can feeling good make you (if only for a short time) more ingenious than usual?

Mentally walk yourself through the following experiment, which tested the hypothesis that positive affect would promote creative problem solving (Isen, Daubman, & Nowicki, 1987, experiment 1). For 5 minutes, groups of men and women watched either a highly humorous film of "bloopers" or an emotionally neutral film on how to measure the area under a curve (although it may sound dull, participants did not rate this math film negatively). Working alone in the same room with the others, each participant was then introduced to the candle task, a classic measure of creative problem solving (Duncker, 1945). After each participant was seated at a table alone, an experimenter read these instructions:

> On the table are a book of matches, a box of tacks, and a candle. Above the table on the wall is a corkboard. Your task is to affix the candle to the corkboard in such a way that it will burn without dripping wax on the table or the floor beneath. You will be given 10 minutes to work on the problem.

Mull over these instructions for a few minutes: How would you solve the problem? Is the solution obvious or is the problem a perplexing one?

The answer requires the problem solver to—I confess that the temptation here is too great—think *inside* the box. If you empty out its contents and then tack it to the corkboard, the box becomes a candle holder. A lit candle can stand upright in the box while being, in effect, attached to the corkboard—and this solution guarantees that no wax will drip on the floor. Once you know the solution, the path to it seems quite obvious, even easy. Still, some problem solvers fail to identify the correct solution before the 10 minutes are over.

What about the mood manipulation, which was represented by the two films? As predicted, those participants who saw the blooper reel were more likely to solve this problem correctly in the allotted time than those who viewed the more neutral film. Other research supports the idea that good moods as well as positive emotions promote us to be more broad-minded in our thinking (see, e.g., Fredrikson, 1998; Isen, 1987; Isen et al., 1987). One way to think about the results is that good moods help us to see things in new, less conventional ways.

But how do we know the research is accurate? How do we know that the good mood group really and truly behaved differently than those in the neutral film group? Why are such differences important to research in social psychology? To answer these questions, we must understand the crucial role that experiments play in social psychology.

The Logic of Experimentation

Psychologists often speak of a "true" experiment, a term that refers to the minimum qualities that must be present in order for an investigation to be trusted to adequately test a hypothesis. A *true experiment* employs random assignment to two (or more) treatment conditions, which allows for subsequent behavior in each one to be compared with the other (e.g., Aronson, Wilson, & Brewer, 1998; Rosenthal, 1995a). By *random assignment*, we mean that each research participant has the same likelihood of being assigned to either treatment condition as all of the other participants. Before sitting down to watch one of the two films, then, each person in the available sample of people had the same chance as the others of ending up viewing the funny or the neutral film. Social psychologists typically use what is known as a random numbers table to assign participants to conditions in an experiment (instructions for doing so appear later in this chapter). As we learned in chapter 1, each treatment condition represents a distinct level of an independent variable that is deemed essential to testing the hypothesis. Isen and her colleagues (1987) predicted that seeing the funny film would lead to more correct solutions in the available time frame than watching the control film.

To be labeled an experiment, a piece of research must have at least two groups, one of which serves as the *control group*. A control group closely resembles the experimental group in every way possible but one: There is no exposure to the main factor of interest, here the positive mood inducer, the funny film. The control group serves as a comparison group for evaluating behavioral responses, a place where nothing should happen and normal, usual, or otherwise typical behavior is expected. In contrast, the *experimental group* represents the introduction of one change into the situation, a place where "different than normal" behavior is anticipated to occur—that is, to be caused by—the independent variable. This familiar and most basic research design is called the *posttest-only control group design* because the dependent variable is introduced only once (i.e., posttest), some time after the independent variable.

I must point out that more complex experiments have more than one experimental group—in fact, Isen and colleagues (1987) actually had two additional groups in the study. For purposes of illustrative clarity here, I elected to focus on only two of them. The rule for manipulating an independent variable is a simple but important one: There must be at least two treatment groups in any experiment and one of them must be designated the control or comparison group.

Let's return to the important role of random assignment in true experiments. The goal of random assignment in experiments is to reduce, even remove, behavioral bias; in fact, this procedure remains the single, best way to do so (Rosenthal, 1995a; see also Bennett, 1998). Random assignment to condition is the great equalizer in experimental research (Aronson, Ellsworth, Carlsmith, & Gonzales, 1990). When properly used, the participants in all conditions in an experiment are assumed, theoretically, to be equivalent to one another at the study's outset. Any between-group difference does not—must not—occur until the experimental manipulation of the independent variable.

For example, random assignment can spread any individual differences possessed by participants equally across the two (or more) conditions in an experiment. *Individual differences* (also known as *subject variables*) refers to unique characteristics we all have—some are stable (e.g., personality, eye color) while others are transient (e.g., fatigue, hunger, flu). And, of course, people share some individual differences—some of us describe ourselves as "morning people" in that we think best early in the day, while others report that they do not hit their intellectual stride until later in the day. In theory, while any of these differences do affect our behavior as individuals (a hungry participant may not listen to an experimenter's directions as well as someone who just ate), their collective effects are spread evenly between the two (or more) groups in an experiment (i.e., hungry as well as sated people are likely to be represented in all conditions). Random assignment reduces the possibility that any differences are more present in one group than the other (or any other).

The experimenter, who introduces one level of the independent variable to each group, then intentionally disrupts this theoretical equality. In practical terms, one group experiences something that is distinct from what the other group experiences. Isen and her colleagues (1987) had already pretested the impact of the two different films on other participants, knowing that the funny film produced good moods and the neutral mood led to middle-of-the-road moods. After watching the different films, each group was temporarily changed in one way only—their respective moods were either elevated in a positive direction or continued to hover around a neutral point. Bear in mind that everything else the two groups experienced was, as psychologists say, "held constant," that is, was exactly the same: same room, same experimenter, same instructions, same everything.

You may be wondering about this issue: Why did Isen and colleagues (1987) bother to show the neutral film? Why did they have the control participants watch any film at all? Why not just have them sit in a room for 5 minutes while the experimental group was laughing away at the funny film in a room down the hallway? These researchers could have done that, but then the people in the control group would have had a somewhat different experience than those in the experimental group. Some might have become bored, others might have begun talking to one another, and so on—who knows? The point is that to really test a hypothesis properly, the experience of both groups should be as similar as possible except for the crucial difference(s) introduced by the experimental treatment. Showing a film, albeit a neutral one, made the group experiences that much more similar to one another.

After experiencing the only introduced difference, the mood induction, each group then received the same directions for the candle task. The dependent variable, the measure of their behavior in response to the independent variable—whether they solved the problem correctly within the allotted time frame—was identical. Each group in any social psychology experiment always receives the same dependent measure. In this case, the dependent measure was an all-or-nothing index of behavior: After watching one of two films and being presented with the task, each participant either solved or did not solve the problem correctly. (There are many different types of dependent variables social psychologists use—we discuss other examples below and in chapter 8.) Isen and her colleagues (1987) used a statistical test (see chapter 11) to compare the number of successes in the positive mood group versus the neutral mood group.

As we already know, and in line with the hypothesis, a greater number of correct solutions was found in the good mood group relative to those in the neutral mood group. This evidence not only supported Isen's hypothesis for this study but also is in keeping with her other work on positive affect (e.g., Isen, 1987). If more correct solutions had been observed in the neutral mood group or if both groups had approximately the same number of right answers, then the "positive mood leads to creativity" hypothesis would be suspect.

No one study—whether it confirms or disconfirms a hypothesis—is sufficient to demonstrate the veracity of a social psychological theory (Aronson et al., 1998). Most social psychologists will test and retest the same hypothesis in several experiments before publishing any results. Their goal is to establish that an experimental effect truly exists and that it can be demonstrated in a variety of situations and with consistent, if different, results (we discuss the relevant issues of experimental validity and reliability in chapter 9). Running experimental variations is a way to exert control over a social psychological phenomenon, to learn how the observed effect "behaves" under different conditions. In fact, if you skim any social psychology journal, it is a rare article these days that presents only one supporting experiment. Most articles contain several experiments that are "packaged" to illustrate a main or original hypothesis, as well as variations on it. (The next time you are in your library's periodical area, take a look at the most recent issue of some social psychology journal to verify this point.)

The qualities of a true experiment are now established. As we will learn later, true experiments are not the only research approaches embraced by social psychologists (see chapter 5). Some social phenomena do not lend themselves to laboratory investigation—they must be studied out in the world, in everyday life, where control is less certain and at times nonexistent. In the meantime, however, we need to consider what specific advantages experiments offer.

The advantages of experiments

One goal of science is to offer an unbiased view of how and why things happen as they do. The goal of social psychology is similar: to offer an unbiased explanation of why people think, feel, and behave as they do in social situations. Critical, informed observation in the form of experimentation is crucial to both pursuits. Why are experiments the *sine qua non*—the truly indispensable part—of social psychology?

Experiments provide certain advantages that other research approaches aimed at explaining the intricacies of social life do not. These advantages include:

- *Careful control.* People are not things; they act and react. Except for participants' behavioral reactions, then, virtually everything that happens in the course of an experiment should be accounted for. Such control allows researchers to rule out alternative explanations for obtained results and to speculate about the social psychological processes that led to the observed behavior.

- *Measurement.* Experimentation is not just about introducing change—it also involves assessing subsequent change. To verify that one variable affects another, experiments rely on well thought out measures to demonstrate that something happened as a result of something else. Measurement in social psychology often links overt behavior with self-reflections or other forms of self-report (e.g., ratings of other people).
- *The identification of cause.* Minimally, an experiment pits one possible explanation for some social behavior against another. This approach allows us to explore why the introduction or removal of some factor necessarily leads to a predictable outcome. The focus on cause and effect is the hallmark of experimentation. No other research method provides such definitive explanations or evidence for them. Experimentation in social psychology involves causes that are seen (e.g., behaviors of self or others) as well as causes that are hypothesized (e.g., thoughts, feelings, emotions, social norms).
- *Developing and testing theory.* An experimental result means little in isolation. One fact or finding generally leads to additional questions, which usually spurs further experimentation. One experiment begets other experiments. A web of coherent ideas drawn from the critical evaluation of the results develops into a theory, which can then be tested further and refined. Some social psychological theories explain the emotion, cognition, and behavior of the individuals, whereas others focus on the same processes in groups.

Why experiments matter in social psychology

The advantages associated with experimentation hold true for research in psychology or any other science. Why do experiments matter so much in social psychology? Social life is complex, too complex to be understood by either passive observation or active participation alone. Planned "interference," the thoughtful introduction of change to assess its effects, however, makes this complexity more manageable. Social psychology experiments represent slices of social life—small, short-term interventions that capture what people do under certain conditions and offer explanations about why they do it. Most social psychology experiments are designed to mimic real life situations and settings (this quality, known as *mundane realism,* will be discussed in chapter 9). Although they cannot capture all the "blooming buzzing confusion" (as William James put it in a different context) of the real social world, well-designed experiments can represent that world in microcosm. Ideally, the circumstances should be highly engaging so that the people taking part focus more on what they are supposed to be doing—say, trying to form accurate impressions of someone they only just met—rather than dwelling on the fact they are taking part in a contrived (socially artificial, staged) situation. In essence, a well-conceived experiment should reflect what happens in everyday life while encouraging the participants to suspend their disbelief in the same way an audience watching a well-performed play or film becomes wrapped up in it.

As we will learn in chapter 5, not all research questions lend themselves to experimentation. Many topics are not feasible to study because variables cannot be manipulated or adequately measured, and some questions would be unethical to pursue experimentally. Still, experimentation remains the single best approach for learning how and why people think, feel, and act in response to other people, ideas, or social processes (e.g., Wilson, 2005).

Turning a Research Question into a Hypothesis

Social psychologists pursue questions about social behavior that can be studied empirically and, as we learned in chapter 2, linked whenever possible to existing research. To study an idea empirically, a research question must be transformed into a hypothesis, a testable question or prediction that is intentionally designed to explain some phenomenon. Isen and her colleagues (1987) tested the hypothesis that positive mood would promote more creative problem solving as compared to neutral mood. In the authors own words: "Our studies are designed to test more directly the proposition that positive affect promotes creativity . . . In these experiments, we investigate whether the creativity promoted by positive affect includes problem solving innovation" (Isen, Daubman, & Nowicki, 1987, p. 1123). This general hypothesis illustrates the qualities of all good hypotheses in social psychology.

As I have argued elsewhere (Dunn, 1999, p. 173), a good hypothesis:

- *is not a question but, rather, a clear statement.* Although we think of hypotheses as "testable questions"—and, indeed, they are—they should succinctly state what issue is being examined: positive affect promotes creativity.
- *is reasonably concise.* A hypothesis should not be too detailed or convoluted—people in good moods should offer relatively more creative solutions to problems than those in neutral moods. Save the explanatory architecture of the hypotheses for the theory supporting it.
- *distinguishes relationships among variables.* Any change in an independent variable (e.g., mood state) should be clearly linked to a predictable and measurable change in a dependent variable (e.g., problem solution).
- *is based on what is already known and aimed at extending this knowledge.* As we learned in chapter 2, very little research is truly original. This observation is not a criticism but a reflection that novel research builds upon established research. Social psychologists and students of social psychology learn and contribute by extending, expanding, and relating new ideas to established research.
- *can be easily understood and appreciated by others.* This quality is especially characteristic of many social psychology experiments. Social behavior is inherently interesting, whether a result confirms a casual observation (e.g., people like people similar to themselves; Byrne, 1971) or counterintuitive (e.g., we think more about an idea when we intentionally try to suppress it; Wegner, 1994).

Thus our own social realities create a bridge between experience and research hypotheses.

- *can be tested*. Although this quality is obvious, it is essential where conducting experiments or other forms of empirical research (see chapters 5 and 6) is concerned. As we learned, mood can be manipulated and problem solving can be measured. A critical test of a prediction is possible: The effects of the presence of an intervention can be compared against what happens when it is absent.

Operational definitions in social psychological research

When social psychologists craft a hypothesis, they are really developing two hypotheses. One hypothesis represents ideas in a broad, descriptive way, while the other operationalizes the ideas in a narrow, testable way. A *descriptive definition* portrays the relationship among variables in an abstract way. Isen and colleagues (1987) focused on the link between positive mood and creative problem solving. Any number of events or experiences can trigger a positive mood—a sunny day, a friendly smile, a delicious aroma, a pleasant memory, an email message from a close friend. Besides the variety of their origins, everyone is familiar with the suddenness and transience of good feelings; they come and they go. Creative problem solving, too, can be framed in many different ways—writing is a form of invention, as is coming up with original solutions to puzzles or avoiding "functional fixation" by using standard materials (a box and some tacks) in novel ways (supporting a candle on a wall). Thus descriptive definitions allow readers and other social psychologists to imagine how a hypothesis might apply to various situations. Descriptive definitions communicate the appeal and applicability of a hypothesis toward explaining social behavior.

In contrast to the conceptual approach of descriptive definitions, an *operational definition* specifies how abstract concepts are transformed into concrete operations that are amenable to manipulation and measurement. Operational definitions force a researcher to think through possibilities and to select one or more that best illustrate the predicted relations among variables. Isen and colleagues (1987) operationalized moods by having some participants watch a short, funny film while others saw a neutral film of equal length. As researchers, they knew that humor induces positive mood, just as they knew that readers (and potential critics) would identify with this form of emotional manipulation—we have all laughed at (been put in a good mood by) funny films (e.g., cartoons, TV sitcoms, movies) in everyday life.

These researchers chose the candle task as the dependent measure because it was already an established, operational measure of creative problem solving (i.e., Duncker, 1945). Although many other such measures are available in the psychological literature, I am sure you will agree that until you know the candle task's solution, the problem is intriguing and highly engaging. Using the box as a stand and not just a box is an inventive insight. There is also an advantage in that there is *one* good solution— participants either "see" it or fail to—allowing for an easy comparison of the number of correct answers in the positive mood versus neutral mood groups.

Please realize that there is no single ideal descriptive or operational definition for any independent or dependent variable forming a hypothesis. A different social psychologist studying the relation between mood and problem solving would have phrased the descriptive definitions in other ways and used a completely different operationalization. Thus researchers must often choose among an array of strong possibilities, any one of which could be used in an experiment. Social psychologists who conduct programmatic research often rely on different *empirical realizations*—how abstract ideas are translated into operational processes (Aronson et al., 1990)—of the same variables in similar hypotheses.

Verifying the same or similar findings in different ways in different experiments allows an investigator to demonstrate whether a given effect is robust. Isen and colleagues (1987), for example, manipulated mood in various ways (e.g., passing out candy bars) and measured creativity using other established measures, such as word association tests (see Mednick, Mednick, & Mednick, 1964). In her research program, Isen varies the descriptive and operational definitions of positive mood and problem solving (e.g., Isen, 1999, 2002, 2004), even going so far as to examine how both are linked to practice satisfaction among physicians (Estrada, Isen, & Young, 1994). Following such a strong and creative lead, a student of social psychology must reflect on and then select the descriptive and operational definitions that will best fit a given research project.

ACTIVE LEARNING EXERCISE 4A

Writing an Operational Definition

You will need to write an operational definition or definitions for your research project. Such practice is an invaluable part of conducting research in social psychology. If you make a quick trip to the library to consult social psychology journals (see Appendix A) or leaf through a textbook on the topic, you will learn about all the different ways social psychologists have operationalized variables appearing in descriptive definitions of hypotheses. Alternatively, take out a piece of paper and spend a few minutes thinking about how many different ways you might operationalize a variable like aggression, romantic attraction, stress, or some variable that interests you. This need not be a formal exercise (we will get to one of those in a moment), just a chance for you to see how many different ways an abstract concept can be rendered into a more concrete form.

Are you ready to begin writing operational definitions for the variables you plan to use in your research project? You may not feel ready—in fact, you may not be entirely certain what your project will examine, let alone what variables you will

Continued

manipulate and measure. Even so, translating descriptive definitions of independent and dependent variables into operational forms is an important skill to develop. Table 4.1 contains an exercise that will help you identify good candidate variables and then refine your thinking about them and definitions for them. If you believe it is premature to operationalize variables, you can return to this exercise when you are ready to do so.

Table 4.1   Writing Operational Definitions

1   Briefly summarize your descriptive theory about some social behavior in three sentences or less.
2   Write a *descriptive definition* for the independent variable(s) and dependent variable(s) from the theory.
3   Write an *operational definition* for the independent variable(s) and dependent variable(s) found in point 2. Focus on using tangible terms and familiar concepts in the *operational definitions*.
4   If you are using research from the published literature (see chapter 2), what *operational definitions* have been used to study these or similar independent variables and dependent variables? Jot down the published *operational definitions* and then compare them to the ones you developed in point 3.
5   Refine the *operational definitions* from point 4. Share them with a peer or your instructor for comment and then finalize the *operational definitions* for the research project.

Note: Adapted from Table 6.1 in Dunn (1999, p. 175).

Independent and Dependent Variables

Variables are an integral part of experimental research. A *variable* is any factor within a piece of research that can take on a different value or can be measured. Social psychologists—indeed, any psychologists who conduct experiments—are concerned with the manipulation of so-called independent variables and the measurement of dependent variables. One means nothing without the other. Both independent and dependent variables are part of a causal chain of events—the introduction of one thing to observe its effect on something else. Part of the sequence is under the complete control of the social psychologist, while the other part is only partially influenced by the experimenter. The rest of that control lies in the hands of the research participants, the people taking part in the study. Their reactions are of keen interest to, but beyond the direct control of, the experimenter.

The "cause" in an experiment is represented by an independent variable. An *independent variable* is the variable whose value is controlled by an experimenter. Within any experiment, an independent variable must have a minimum of two levels, which represent two "values" or "variations," usually the presence of some quality anticipated to lead to some behavioral change, and the absence of that same quality, which should lead to no behavioral change. (More than two levels in an independent variable is absolutely fine, but the logistics of conducting a project increase.) Half of the participants in an experiment are exposed to one quality, while the other half experience the other quality. The independent variable in the experiment conducted by Isen and colleagues (1987) had two levels: the actual treatment condition of interest (e.g., a funny film designed to cause a good mood) and a control condition (e.g., a neutral film of equal length that was not expected to alter viewers' moods).

To reinforce the experimenter's direct involvement, psychologists will often say that they "manipulated" the independent variable to see what effect it had on behavior, that is, how people reacted to it being there. The *effect* refers to whether the treatment or experimental level—the level of actual interest—led to a predicted change in behavior when compared to the control (nontreatment) level of the same variable. The effect, the predicted change, happens to what is called the dependent variable. A *dependent variable* (some authors and researchers call it a *dependent measure* to emphasize its role as a behavioral gauge—the terms are interchangeable) is the outcome variable—that which is effected by the causal influence embodied in the independent variable.

Dependent variables come in a variety of forms—some are self-report, paper-and-pencil-based questionnaires (e.g., rating scales); others are physical measurements that register movement, proximity, or action; still others tap into our physiology (e.g., heart rate) (see chapter 8). A dependent variable is examined to determine if an experimental treatment had any effect, that is, created some measurable change in its value (ideally, of course, one in line with the hypothesis). Put another way, the value of the dependent measure *depends on* the independent variable, the agent of change (unless the variable creates no change or some behavior that is counter to the hypothesis).

How is the dependent variable under only partial control of the experimenter? The experimenter designs the dependent variable and then makes certain that research participants in all conditions (levels of the independent variable) in the experiment receive it. After the independent variable is presented and once the dependent variable is administered, the experimenter's control ends. At that point, the dependent variable then falls under the "control" of the research participants in that it measures or records their behavioral responses, if any, to the independent variable. All of the participants in Isen et al.'s (1987) study were exposed to the same candle task and their solutions within a 10 minute period—whether correct or incorrect—were monitored and recorded. As predicted, more of those in good moods were likely to correctly solve the problem as compared to those in neutral moods.

Independent variables are a behavioral stimulus—they spur people to act one way rather than another. Dependent variables record people's responses, that is, what happens after the stimulus is delivered. The social psychologist's responsibility is to coherently explain the relationship between these two types of variables in any experiment.

ACTIVE LEARNING EXERCISE   4B

Identifying Independent and Dependent Variables in Social Psychology Experiments

At this point in time you are probably convinced that you understand the distinction between independent and dependent variables very well. One creates behavioral change, the other measures it. We reviewed the design and results from the Isen et al. (1987) study several times, for example, and there is a very good chance that you learned about variables and their role in experiments in a previous psychology class. As a teacher, however, I would be remiss if I did not tell you that students routinely confuse these two types of variables until they practice identifying them. Sometimes concepts that seem to be obvious are less so when we are called to demonstrate a skill.

To verify your ability to determine which variable is which, take a few minutes to read the following three partial descriptions of social psychology experiments. Identify the independent and dependent variables in each one. The correct answers are printed at the end of this chapter. If this task proves more challenging that you expected, please review the earlier sections of this chapter once more before proceeding.

1   Obese and nonobese people had an opportunity to eat as much as they wanted from a bowl full of salted peanuts. Half the time the nuts were in small packets in the bowl, the rest of the time the equivalent amount of unpackaged nuts appeared in the bowl.

2   Half of the women taking part in a study supposedly on learning were told they would receive painful electric shocks if they gave wrong answers. The other half were told that the shocks would only tingle and were not at all painful. Before the learning phase took place, the women were asked if they preferred to wait alone or with another person.

3   As part of a marketing study, shoppers were shown five different black pens and told they could choose to keep one if they completed a survey. Half of the people chose a pen and were told to keep it. The other half were told to keep their second choice, as their first selection was the last one of its kind in the researcher's possession. All participants completed a questionnaire wherein they rated how much they liked the pen they were given.

Doing Randomization in Social Psychology Experiments

Issues of error

Randomization is the process social psychologists use to assign an individual or a group to receive a particular treatment based on chance alone. By placing participants at random in one or another condition in an experiment, a researcher tries to eliminate potential sources of measurement error that can undermine detecting cause-and-effect relationships, that is, how the treatment level of an independent variable creates a measurable change in a dependent measure. Beyond the independent variable of interest, anything—any uncontrolled factor or other influence—that contributes to change in a dependent measure is a source of error. Within an experiment, any uneven or erratic difference in how we measure a variable or variables is called *error*. No social psychologist or other researcher can eliminate all sources of error—lots of things influence a participant's behavior besides the independent variable—but an attempt must be made to reduce the effects of such sources as much as possible.

Any experimenter must worry about two sources of error: random error and systematic error. *Random error* refers to the "noise" or the little distractions that occur in any experiment, even the most carefully controlled one. Random error is caused by the various extraneous variables that exist in any experiment (e.g., the room's temperature, ambient noise in an adjacent hallway, the odor of the experimenter's cologne, the clarity of the instructions). The good news for the social psychologist is that random error exists in all conditions with an experiment; as a result, its influence is spread more or less evenly throughout the experiment. The bad news is that this noise—we might call it behavioral static—makes it that much harder for the independent variable to make an impact on the participants' behavior as detected by the dependent measure.

How so? Random error can cause people's behavior to vary a bit even in response to a powerful independent variable. Perhaps the room where an experiment took place was poorly lit, which made it difficult for all participants to read and complete the dependent variable. Note that the real difference between the control and the experimental group is still there; it is simply the case that the difference may not be as strong or clearly observable as it would be if the error were eliminated. Indeed, in the worst case, random error leads a researcher to miss obtaining a real difference between the treatment conditions in an experiment because it looks as if the difference is too small or even nonexistent. In truth, however, the behavioral difference between the groups is real and actually present, but the random noise obscures it.

In contrast, *systematic error* poses a more serious problem for detecting and interpreting cause and effect in social psychology experiments. Systematic error is consistent error, a pronounced source of bias in an experiment, one that masks or disrupts an investigator's ability to determine whether any behavioral differences are actually attributable to an independent variable. Where random error can affect the behavior of all participants in a study, systematic error impacts only what some people do (i.e., those found in only one condition), but it does so in a distorting way.

Isen and colleagues (1987) attributed the heightened creativity in the positive mood group to the effects of the blooper reel. What if the actual source of the enhanced positive mood was not exclusively due to the film but, rather, some unrecognized quality shared by several people in the group? Imagine that several close friends signed up for the study and ended up together in the positive mood group. Their established camaraderie—familiar jokes, comfort with one another, and so on—and not solely the blooper reel led to the good moods which facilitated the creativity needed to solve the candle task. Although localized in the treatment group, the bias was systematic (e.g., perhaps laughter during the film was more contagious because of the friends' established comfort level). The experimenters, however, are none the wiser, continuing to attribute the higher number of creative solutions to the film alone.

The problem posed by systematic error is certainty where the identification and understanding of causal relations is concerned. Despite the fact that the changes in the dependent variable were in the desired direction—more correct solutions in the positive mood conditions—the source of the change is not purely due to the independent variable embodied in the funny film. Another factor, established close relationships among the participants, compromises the clarity of inference. Perhaps the film alone, for instance, would not have elicited enough positive emotion in the group to enhance their individual levels of creativity. The researchers might not recognize a problem until they tried to replicate the experiment and discovered no difference between the control and experimental groups. Aside from reducing inferential clarity, the real damage posed by systematic bias is that its nature or source may not be recognized for quite some time, if ever.

Besides random and systematic error, social psychologists must also be concerned about the impact of *subject variables*. A subject variable is any characteristic possessed by a participant that cannot be controlled by an experimenter but which could influence the participant's behavior. Subject variables are immune to randomization: You cannot randomly assign one participant to be a woman and another to be 35 years old, just as you cannot make one person suddenly have a higher level of self-esteem than someone else. Subject variables are effectively "hard wired" in all of us—they make us who we are and we carry them with us into the experimental situation. Because a social psychologist cannot rule out the effects of subject variables on behavior, these individual differences are usually treated as random error.

A list of some typical subject variables is provided in Table 4.2. You may well discover others in the course of your reading and research. If so, consider recording them in Table 4.2 or in your research notebook.

Could a subject variable ever be a source of systematic error? Although unlikely, it is possible that a researcher could unknowingly recruit a group of people containing a subsample of individuals who all differed from the rest in some methical way. Random assignment might be accidentally violated, such that most of these people sharing a common yet unrecognized feature end up in the treatment condition of the experiment. Their resulting behavior in that group would subsequently be attributed to the impact of the independent variable when, in actuality, the source happens to be

Table 4.2 Some Typical Subject Variables Associated with Social Psychological Research

Age	Club or organization membership
Sex	Health status
Education	Race
IQ or intelligence level	Socioeconomic status (SES)
Marital status	Religion
Sexual orientation	Self-esteem
Introversion/extroversion	Birth order

List other subject variables you identify below:

the subject variable found in the subgroup of participants. Thus the subject variable is somehow related to and affected by the independent variable of interest (and vice versa).

Let's return to the Isen et al. (1987) experiment one more time. We have already considered a case of systematic error in the positive mood group, one posed by a possible situational factor, preexisting friendships. Although it could contribute to systematic error, friendship is not a subject variable because it varies—if one of the hypothetical friends ended up in the neutral mood group, for example, this variable would have had little influence there.

Consider, however, the potentially disruptive effects of a personality factor that is quite relevant to the experience of emotion. What if some of the participants in the experimental group had a higher happiness "set point," the stable average level of positive emotionality linked with genetics (Lykken & Tellegen, 1996)? Conversely, what if some people with chronically lower levels of cheerfulness were assigned to the neutral mood group—would their dispositions artificially maintain the emotional balance there? Although these examples are only thought experiments that seem a bit far-fetched, the reality is that subject variables can disrupt a researcher's ability to delineate cause and effect in an experiment.

Can anything be done to rule out the effects of subject variables? Yes, but only if the researcher becomes aware that one or more such variables are shared by some of the participants. Thus, researchers must always consider what other variables—notably demographic (e.g., age, sex, education, income level) or personality (e.g., self-esteem, extroversion, neuroticism) variables—might interact with the independent variable being tested. The solution some social psychologists use is called a *matching procedure*, a variation on randomization that helps to ensure that a given quality that could create change in competition with the independent variable is spread evenly throughout the experiment. To reduce the random error associated with a subject variable, a matching procedure involves having an experimenter create pairs or groups of people who are comparable to one another on the quality embodied by the subject variable (e.g., pairs of participants who share a similar happiness set-point). Once the pairs are identified, one person from each is randomly assigned to the experimental treatment condition, while the other is placed in the control condition. In the case of more than two levels to an independent variable, more than two participants can be matched on the same dimension and then randomly spread out into the available conditions.

Do subject variables or individual difference variables serve any helpful role in experimental research in social psychology? As long as their influence is recognized and interpreted carefully, subject variables and individual differences can be treated as nonmanipulated independent variables. This term is an admitted oxymoron because I have repeatedly emphasized that independent variables are *always* manipulated— nonetheless, please bear with me for a few moments. As noted before, neither stable individual differences nor any other subject variables can be manipulated—we cannot randomly assign one person to a high level of, say, shyness and another to a lower level. Instead, we can identify people who vary in shyness within the experiment, placing those who are high, medium, or low (for example) into groups and then examining whether measurable differences in the dependent measure occur due to this grouping.

Imagine that a social psychologist is conducting a study on self-presentation skills, one that required the participants to give a speech on some controversial issue to an audience. One of the dependent variables might be the number of verbal errors made during the speech (e.g., pauses, number of dropped or mispronounced words, overuse of "um" and "like"). Shyness would seem to be a relevant variable, as less shy people would be expected to make fewer errors (i.e., they would be relatively more comfortable in front of strangers) than those who expressed higher levels of shyness. To examine the effect of shyness on speech errors, if any, the social psychologist might administer a standard personality measure of shyness (e.g., Jones, Briggs, & Smith, 1986) before the study. Once it was complete, the investigator could examine whether speech errors varied according to whether participants were high, medium, or low on the shyness scale, either in combination with or separately from the independent variable.

Note that there is no control over shyness—we cannot definitively say that very shy participants were more likely to make more speech errors than less shy participants because random assignment did not occur. Instead, we can indicate that the observed comparisons make sense (or not) but that a true account of the causal relationship between shyness and speech errors is unclear. Still, exploring such noncausal comparisons is interesting and suggestive, as we know more than if we did not bother to examine these nonmanipulated variables.

Sampling and randomization

Before we assign participants to one or another condition in a social psychology experiment, we must address a more fundamental issue, one related to both error and randomization—where do they come from? There is a practical as well as theoretical side to this seemingly innocent question. The practical issue of recruiting research participants—getting people to take part in your research—is discussed in chapter 10. We will consider sampling basics here, especially as they inform randomization and experimental design, revisiting more advanced sampling issues in chapter 6 (see, especially, Table 6.1, which lists a variety of sampling techniques, where they are especially relevant to constructing questionnaires and surveys).

Let's turn to the links among populations, samples, and randomization. Unless they are interested in some particular subgroup of people (e.g., adolescents, elderly women, business executives), when social psychologists conduct experiments, they hope their results will describe the typical, usual, or average behavior of *most* people. That is, can the behavior of the individuals who participated in one social psychology experiment at one point in time be generalized—used to explain—the behavior of other people at other times in other places?

In concrete terms, Isen and colleagues (1987) demonstrated that being in a good mood led to more creative problem solving. Can we assume that if a different group of people took part in the same or a similar experiment, for example, that they, too, would do better on the candle task than a novel group of people in the control group? The answer would seem to be a reasonable "yes," indeed, why would anyone expect otherwise? Moreover, the experiment was used to demonstrate a more important point—the candle task was used to operationalize creativity, so what we really want to conclude (following Isen) is that in general, when people are in good moods they behave in more, not less, creative ways.

Thus most social psychologists wish to argue that the behavior of a sample of people who participate in an experiment is representative of the larger population from which they were drawn. A *population* is a group of people—the citizens of the state of Maine, for example, all women, or the students currently hanging out in your institution's student union. Generally, then, social psychologists are trying to characterize most normal functioning adults in everyday settings. If researchers are interested in characterizing the behavior of most people, of course, they are not going to actually conduct experiments involving most people—instead, they recruit a sample of people.

A *sample* is a small group drawn from some larger population. The question, of course, is whether a sample is representative—highly similar to, shares most features with—the parent population. The argument can be made, for example, that one does not get a sense of life in Massachusetts if one only speaks to Boston residents, just as a member of a sorority may have a very different view of student life at a university than a woman who commutes or one who lives in a traditional dormitory. What to do? How can a social psychologist ensure that the opinions and behavior of people in a particular sample are representative of a larger group?

Ideally, researchers would like to have access to a random sample. A *random sample* is a sample drawn from a larger population in such a manner that each member of the population has the same chance as all the others of being chosen. Assuming they are of sufficient size (you would not ask one Massachusetts resident or one student to characterize their respective settings and expect to "know" what life in either place is really like), random samples are theoretically desirable because they are less likely to possess biased qualities.

Where doing psychological research is concerned, random samples have an inherent drawback—they are hard to come by and are relatively rare in behavioral science research (Dunn, 2001). Participants in most social psychology experiments are first or second year undergraduate students, typically students who are enrolled in an introductory psychology course or even a course on social psychology. Social psychologists and their critics often refer to this as the "college sophomore problem," a wry way of questioning whether the science of social psychology can be built on the behavior of a group that is rather distinct from the general population on a variety of dimensions (see, e.g., Dawes, 1991; Sears, 1986). College students are not a random sample in any sense of the word: They elected to be in a psychology course for some reason and they are taking part in research either as volunteers, for modest pay, or to satisfy a course requirement.

Instead of constituting a random sample, the available pool of college research participants is usually called a *convenience sample* by social psychologists. A convenience sample is convenient—a group of people who are accessible and willing to take part in social psychological research. Having people at hand who are willing to help out is a big advantage, one that allows an investigator to do the work of social psychology. Convenience samples are sometimes labeled *haphazard samples* (Dunn, 1999), an apt name because a researcher may well have a collection of people possessing a number of unknown and potentially disruptive qualities (in the sense of a given theory, hypothesis, and variables—recall our discussion of individual differences and subject variables). This is a distinct disadvantage: A nonrandom group may not be representative of a population of interest, which limits a researcher's ability to generalize about the nature of behavior beyond the group.

Social psychologists (indeed, most other psychologists, as well) usually choose to do research and to work with convenience samples as best they can. Indeed, they may have little or no choice if they want to conduct research. If random selection from some larger population is not possible, then they generally opt for the next best thing: random assignment. *Random assignment* involves randomly assigning the members of an available sample of people to the conditions in an experiment. This process ensures that each participant has the same likelihood as the others of being placed in either the experimental or the control condition (or in another group if there are more than two in a study's design). Random assignment establishes the equivalence of groups prior to the introduction of the independent variable, allowing the researcher to engage in causal inference: Any subsequent change in behavior can be attributed to the impact of the independent variable on the dependent variable.

How do social psychologists perform randomization in their experiments?

ACTIVE LEARNING EXERCISE 4C

Performing Random Assignment and Random Selection

"The generation of random numbers is too important to be left to chance" (Robert R. Coveyou, quoted in Gardner, 1975, p. 169).

Chances are that you will be working with a convenience sample when conducting your own social psychological research. Thus you should learn some practical approaches for performing random assignment. I will also provide guidance on how to do random selection on the off-chance that you will have an opportunity to select participants from some larger population of interest (perhaps, for example, you will want to profile student opinion on your campus; see chapter 6).

To perform random assignment, a social psychologist can flip a coin (e.g., "heads" assigns a participant to the experimental group, "tails" places a participant in a control group) or roll some fair dice. However, the best approach is to employ a table of random numbers. A *random numbers table* is a compendium of numbers between 0 and 9 that were generated in an unbiased way. Each of these 10 numbers occurs with the same frequency throughout the table but in a pattern-less way. Table 4.3 shows a sample page taken from a larger table of random numbers (Rand Corporation, 1955). The leftmost column lists the numbers of the rows (in

Table 4.3 Excerpt from a Random Numbers Table

00100	03991 10461	93716 16894	66083 24653	84609 58232	88618 19161
00101	38555 95554	32886 59780	08355 60860	29735 47762	71299 23853
00102	17546 73704	92052 46215	55121 29281	59076 07936	27954 58909
00103	32643 52861	95819 06831	00911 98936	76355 93779	80863 00514
00104	69572 68777	39510 35905	14060 40619	29549 69616	33564 60780
00105	24122 66591	27699 06494	14845 46672	61958 77100	90899 75754
00106	61196 30231	92962 61773	41839 55382	17267 70943	78038 70267
00107	30532 21704	10274 12202	39685 23309	10061 68829	55986 66485
00108	03788 97599	75867 20717	74416 53166	35208 33374	87539 08823
00109	48228 63379	85783 47619	53152 67433	35663 52972	16818 60311
00110	60365 94653	35075 33949	42614 29297	01918 28316	98953 73231
00111	83799 42402	56623 34442	34994 41375	70071 14736	09958 18065
00112	32960 07405	36409 83232	99385 41600	11133 07586	15917 06253
00113	19322 53845	57620 52606	66497 68646	78138 66559	19640 99413
00114	11220 94947	07399 37408	48509 23929	27482 45476	85244 35159
00115	31751 57260	68980 05339	15470 48355	88651 22596	03152 19121
00116	88492 99382	14454 04504	20094 98977	74843 93413	22109 78508
00117	30934 47744	07481 83828	73788 06533	28597 20405	94205 20380
00118	22888 48893	27499 98748	60530 45128	74022 84617	82037 10268
00119	78212 16993	35902 91386	44372 15486	65741 14014	87481 37220

Continued

Table 4.3   *Continued*

00120	41849 84547	46850 52326	34677 58300	74910 64345	19325 81549
00121	46352 33049	69248 93460	45305 07521	61318 31855	14413 70951
00122	11087 96294	14013 31792	59747 67277	76503 34513	39663 77544
00123	52701 08337	56303 87315	16520 69676	11654 99893	02181 68161
00124	57275 36898	81304 48585	68652 27376	92852 55866	88446 03584
00125	20857 73156	70284 24326	79375 95220	01159 63267	10622 48391
00126	15633 84924	90415 93614	33521 26665	55823 47641	86225 31704
00127	92694 48297	39904 02115	59589 49067	66821 41575	49767 04037
00128	77613 19019	88152 00080	20554 91409	96277 48257	50816 97616
00129	38688 32486	45134 63545	59404 72059	43947 51680	43852 59693
00130	25163 01889	70014 15021	41290 67312	71857 15957	68971 11403
00131	65251 07629	37239 33295	05870 01119	92784 26340	18477 65622
00132	36815 43625	18637 37509	82444 99005	04921 73701	14707 93997
00133	64397 11692	05327 82162	20247 81759	45197 25332	83745 22567
00134	04515 25624	95096 67946	48460 85558	15191 18782	16930 33361
00135	83761 60873	43253 84145	60833 25983	01291 41349	20368 07126
00136	14387 06345	80854 09279	43529 06318	38384 74761	41196 37480
00137	51321 92246	80088 77074	88722 56736	66164 49431	66919 31678
00138	72472 00008	80890 18002	94813 31900	54155 83436	35352 54131
00139	05466 55306	93128 18464	74457 90561	72848 11834	79982 68416
00140	39528 72484	82474 25593	48545 35247	18619 13674	18611 19241
00141	81616 18711	53342 44276	75122 11724	74627 73707	58319 15997
00142	07586 16120	82641 22820	92904 13141	32392 19763	61199 67940
00143	90767 04235	13574 17200	69902 63742	78464 22501	18627 90872
00144	40188 28193	29593 88627	94972 11598	32095 36787	00441 58997
00145	34414 82157	86887 55087	19152 00023	12302 80783	32624 68691
00146	63439 75363	44989 16822	36024 00867	76378 41605	65961 73488
00147	67049 09070	93399 45547	94458 74284	05041 49807	20288 34060
00148	79495 04146	52162 90286	54158 34243	46978 35482	59362 95938
00149	91704 30552	04737 21031	75051 93029	47665 64382	99782 93478

Source: Rand Corporation (1955, p. 3).

this excerpt, from 00100 to 00149). The next 10 columns list random sequences of numbers in 5-digit groupings. The random quality of the table allows a user to begin anywhere in the table and to read down a column, across a row, frontward or backwards, and in any single or multiple combinations of numbers.

Doing random selection. To begin, you need to identify some larger population, such as, say, the 30 students enrolled in a psychology class. You want to draw a sample of 5 students from the group of 30—how do you do it? (The following procedure can be contracted for a smaller sample or expanded for a larger one— the logic is the same.)

Shut your eyes and, using the index finger of your dominant hand, place it anyplace on Table 4.3. My finger ended up in column 4 out of the 10 containing random digits, on a string of numbers in row 00115 (see Table 4.3). The string of numbers is 05339. By reading across, I can treat each pair of digits as two-digit numbers for 05 and 33, followed by the single digit 9. Since we are using double, not single, digits, we can join 9 to the first number in the adjacent string to its right (i.e., 15470), which is 1, for 91. This number is followed by 54 and 70. We now have five numbers, but since our sample only has 30 names in it, so far we can only select one name (corresponding to the 5th person). We need to continue moving across the columns in the random numbers table in 4.3 until we select four other numbers between 01 and 30 (excluding 5, of course). If you follow this process, you will obtain the numbers 22, 19, 12, and 18 (this last number was found by linking the last digit (i.e., 1) in row 00115 to the first digit in row 00116 in the first column of random digits (i.e., 8). Assuming the list of 30 students in the psychology class is in alphabetical order, you would select the names corresponding to the 5th, 22nd, 19th, 12th, and 18th place (a nonalphabetized list, such as a seating chart, could also be used). We now have our sample of five people.

What happens when a two-digit number in a string is greater than the highest number in the list (i.e., between 01 and 30)? You simply skip it and read on to the next two-digit pair that is 30 or less. The same process (whether one, two, or more digits) can be used to read upward or downward in a column in a random numbers table. It really does not matter as long as you are consistent. As demonstrated, when you reach the end of a row or the top (or bottom) of a column, simply move down to the next line (or up) or over, whatever the case may be, and then continue the process until the appropriate sized sample is selected.

Practice exercise: List the students in your class and draw a random sample of six names using Table 4.3.

Doing random assignment. The random selection exercise can be readily adapted for performing random assignment. Again, we use random selection when a larger population is known and sampling, for whatever reason, is necessary. Random assignment is typically used when we are working with a convenience sample and we are unaware of the characteristics of the population from which it originates. In practice, we use random assignment to fill the (minimum of two) conditions in an experiment. Here are the steps (adapted from Dunn 1999, pp. 200–202):

1   Obtain a convenience sample of people (let's say there are 20, so 10 people must be assigned to the experimental condition and 10 to the control group).
2   Assign numbers (from 01 to 20) to each name in the sample.

Continued

3   Use a random numbers table, such as Table 4.3, to choose the appropriate number of names (10) to be placed in one condition (the remaining 10 names will comprise the control group).

4   Close your eyes and place an index finger anywhere on Table 4.3. Follow more or less the same procedure described above for random selection. You can begin to search for 10 two-digit numbers between 01 and 20 (skip numbers greater than 20). The first 10 names selected form one group, the remaining names the other group.

Practice exercise. List the students in your class and, using Table 4.3, randomly assign half of them to one group, the remainder to another group.

Additional exercise. How can you use Table 4.3 to assign the members of a convenience sample to one of four conditions in an experiment? Try to be creative but avoid making the assignment process too cumbersome. Be sure that you can explain the logic behind your strategy and do not violate the need for randomness.

Other approaches to performing randomization can be found in Snedecor and Cochran (1980). As ideas, chance and randomization actually have a very interesting place in the history of ideas. For further exploration of their relevant history, consult Hacking (1975) or Gigerenzer et al. (1989).

We now turn to the dynamics of research design, the frames of experimental reference that allow social psychologists to determine causality in social interaction.

Common Experimental Designs in Social Psychology

Social psychologists employ a variety of research designs in their examination of human social behavior. We will review a few of the more common designs in the remainder of this chapter. Please do not assume that the subsequent discussion is the last word on research design. There are more research designs than I can adequately introduce and review in a chapter on basic experimental design. For other experimental designs, please consult the following references (Campbell & Stanley, 1966; Rosenthal & Rosnow, 1991; Shadish, Cook, & Campbell, 2001).

Between-subjects research designs

We begin our review of research designs with what is probably the most common and, therefore, familiar type: the between-subjects design. A *between-subjects* (also known as *between-groups*) *design* is one where the experiment's participants are exposed to one, and only one, level of an independent variable. The practical aspect of this definition is that each condition within an experiment comprises a different group of people (the standard posttest-only control group design fits this mold). Most of the sample experiments we considered thus far have been simple, two-cell or two-condition between-subjects designs: Participants were either assigned to an experimental treatment group or to a control group, and we subsequently compared what happened in each condition. Put another way, different groups of participants have different experiences, and whether the nature of those experiences leads to measurable, behavioral differences is determined by examining the dependent variable.

Simple two-cell designs have both advantages and disadvantages. A clear strength is that such designs, with one independent variable, are relatively straightforward to conduct. A second, related strength is that learning whether the independent variable created a change in the dependent variable is usually easy to determine. These designs are helpful when little is known about a research question. Thus social psychologists often use two-cell designs when they are trying to establish whether a hypothesized effect, as indicated by a between-group difference, is really there.

These strengths, however, can also pose disadvantages in that studies with one independent variable can be limiting where broader information about a topic is concerned. Their "present-versus-absent" quality (e.g., good mood versus neutral mood) does not tell us about the subtleties or complexities of human behavior (e.g., can some positive moods be stronger than others and, if so, with what effect on problem solving?). One way to think about studies with one independent variable is that they create more questions than they answer. The quality of these questions often requires that a researcher manipulate two, three, or even more independent variables within one study in order to address richer behavioral questions. If you think about your daily social experiences, their nature is multifactorial—the result of encountering different levels of different independent variables—and not based on whether one condition is there or not there.

Despite their interest value, the science of social psychology does not advance by doing innumerable studies with one independent variable. Instead, investigators develop theories and expand empirical knowledge by conducting multifactor designs. These designs are commonly referred to as *factorial designs* because they allow a researcher to simultaneously investigate the effects of more than one independent variable on a single dependent variable. Let's begin with the simplest example: an experiment employing two independent variables and a single outcome variable. This popular design (especially with students) is called a 2×2 ("two by two") research design because it employs two independent variables, each of which has two levels. For convenience, Table 4.4 illustrates the two levels of factor A (i.e., A1 and A2) and those for factor B (i.e., B1, B2). This translates into four cells—the experimental conditions represented as A1B1, A2B1, A1B2, and A2B2—in the research design (see Table 4.4).

A common feature of all factorial designs is that by multiplying the number of levels in one independent variable by those found in the other factor (or factors), you will know how many cells appear in the research design (i.e., $2 \times 2 = 4$ cells, $3 \times 2 = 6$ cells,

Table 4.4 A Standard 2 × 2 Research Design

| | | Factor A | |
		Level A1	Level A2
	Level B1	A1B1	A2B1
Factor B			
	Level B2	A1B2	A2B2

2 × 2 × 2 = 8 cells, and so on). As you will see, the introduction of a second independent variable provides more than the knowledge that would be gained by conducting two separate, one-independent-variable (i.e., two-cell design) experiments.

Increasing the complexity of a research design is fine as long as the researcher has a clear and compelling rationale for doing so—adding additional independent variables "because you can" is not a legitimate practice. There must be some compelling reason based in theory or due to an interesting observation from a prior study. As an alternative to creating overly complex research designs, many psychologists adopt a converging operations approach where they conduct multiple experiments designed to explore subtle variations of the same hypothesis (see Aronson et al., 1998 on programmatic research; see also Garner, Hake, & Eriksen, 1956).

In any case, increasing the number of independent variables within between-groups designs necessitates that a researcher recruit more participants to "fill" each cell in the design. How many participants are needed? The answer depends on the nature of the research, the design, and whether an adequate pool of research participants is available. Where student research in social psychology is concerned, I advocate trying to have 10 participants per cell in a research design (if you must, settle for five people per cell, but no fewer; we will discuss participant recruiting issues later in chapter 10). Although it is beyond the scope of this book, there is a formal, statistical procedure called power analysis for determining how many people are needed in order to demonstrate an effect that reaches a particular magnitude (e.g., Cohen, 1988; Kenny, Kashy, & Bolger, 1998).

Let's consider a concrete example of a 2 × 2 factorial design. Spencer, Steele, and Quinn (1999, study 2) conducted a clever study employing a 2 × 2 design, on the consequences of being a member of a stigmatized group. Aside from the interesting result, what makes this study noteworthy for our purposes is that the researchers treated a subject variable as an independent variable—occasionally referred to as an IV × SV (independent variable × subject variable) design (see, e.g., Cozby, 1997). At this moment, you should be thinking "wait a minute—subject variables cannot be manipulated, so how can one serve as an independent variable?"

I applaud you if a thought like that crossed your mind. You are quite correct; however, social psychologists have little choice but to rely on subject variables for comparing behavior in nonrandom groups of people. For example, we cannot randomly assign people to be either male or female, yet sex differences and gender roles are important topics in social psychology. Our inability to randomly assign people to such groupings forces us to be cautious where inferring causality is concerned—however, it does not forbid us from making reasonable speculations.

Spencer and colleagues (1999) explored what is known as *stereotype threat*, a fear that one's membership in a stigmatized group will confirm the stereotype that others hold toward that group (Steele, 1997). The researchers were interested specifically in what would happen to women's scores on a math test when the stereotype that women do not perform as well in math activities compared to men was made prominent. For the first independent variable, the researchers varied how a math test was characterized: Half the participants—men and women—were informed that no gender differences were observed on the test they were all going to take (participants assumed the stereotype that men outperformed women on the test—this message was never explicitly given). The other half learned that a gender difference gave men an advantage on the math test. The second independent variable—participants' sex—was, of course, not manipulated; however, being male or female was used to group participants' responses (see Figure 4.1).

As shown in Figure 4.1, men and women performed about equally well when they believed the test was gender-neutral (see the left pair of bars in Figure 4.1). When the stereotype was activated in the women's minds, however, they performed much worse

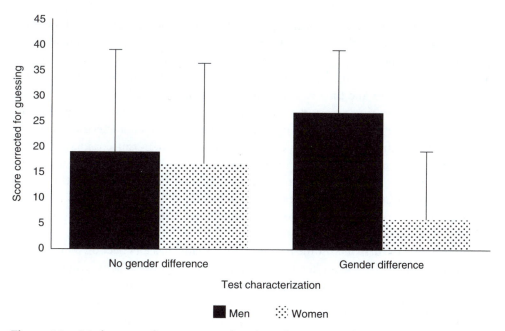

Figure 4.1. Math test performance as a function of stereotype threat and gender. Adapted from Spencer, Steele, & Quinn (1999, Figure 2, p. 13)

Table 4.5   Mean Math Test Scores as Function of Stereotype Threat and Sex

Test characterization condition	Sex		Row means
	Men	Women	
No gender difference	18.9 (20.4)	17.3 (17.9)	18.1
Gender difference	26.7 (13.9)	5.8 (16.3)	16.3
Column means	22.8	11.6	17.2

Note: Standard deviations appear in parentheses. Higher means reflect higher scores on a math test.
Source: Means provided by Steve Spencer (personal communication, March 11, 2006); table based on Study 2 in Spencer, Steele, and Quinn (1999).

on the test than did the men (see the right pair of bars in Figure 4.1). As shown by Figure 4.1, we know that women performed as well as men in the absence of a threatening atmosphere posed by the stereotype, but when the women questioned their skills and grew concerned about how they would be perceived, their performance fell.

What else can we learn from a 2 × 2 design? Take a look at Table 4.5, which presents the same data—average math test scores—from the Spencer et al. (1999) experiment but in numerical form instead of the graphical form shown in Figure 4.1. Like most psychologists, social psychologists examine typical behavior within experiments; that is, they examine the averages or means within each condition (see the four cell means in Table 4.5) as well as those based on each level of the independent variable (see the column means for sex and the row means for the test characteristic conditions in Table 4.5). Thus, by averaging across the two levels of gender, you can examine the row means to see if the math test scores differed based on the test characterization condition (no gender difference versus gender difference). When you compare the row means this way, you are looking to see if they are the same or different from one another. If the means are different in value, this is called a main effect. (At this point, do not worry about whether the means are statistically different from one another—just focus on differences in magnitude—we will discuss the statistical results from the Spencer et al. experiment in chapter 11.)

A *main effect* occurs when some independent variable has an effect on a dependent variable, such that there is an apparent difference in magnitude between two means (or among more than two means) representing the levels of the independent variable. Compare the two row means in Table 4.5: Regardless of their sex, the people in the no gender difference group scored an average of 18.1 on the math test, whereas those in the gender difference group scored a slightly lower average of 16.3. What do we know? The row means tell this story: Those participants who were told that the math test "had shown gender differences in the past" scored slightly lower than those who were told there was no gender difference on the test.

Is there a main effect for test characterization? Possibly, given that the control condition (i.e., no gender difference) scored objectively higher than the experimental (stereotype threat activated gender difference) group. If the means had been identical, say, each condition scored an average of 18, then we would say that there was no main effect for test characterization. Again, we cannot definitively know if a main effect is present until a statistical analysis is performed—vigilant social psychologists examine data tables carefully, however, so that educated guesses can be made. We will see if this main effect is statistically significant in chapter 11.

Was there also a main effect for sex? Yes. Take a look at the column means in Table 4.5. As you can see—collapsing down over the test characterization conditions—overall, the women scored lower (with a mean of only 11.6 on the test) than the men (who scored an average of 22.8) in this study. Again, we are not concerned here with whether this main effect is statistically significant (i.e., whether the men's test average was statistically greater than the women's average); rather, we are simply examining the differences (if any) between two means and interpreting them based on their values. If the two column means in Table 4.5 were equal or very close in value, then we would say that there was no main effect for sex (or if the row means were similar, that there was no main effect for threat group).

As noted earlier, however, factorial designs have a distinct quality that makes them superior to designs with one independent variable. In a real sense, the two main effects we just reviewed represent the results of two separate experiments—that is, by selectively collapsing across one variable or the other, it's *as if* we were examining the results of different experiments. Of course, the data are from the same experiment, which allows us to explore the concept of interaction. An *interaction* occurs when the influence of one independent variable varies at different levels of another independent variable. Similar to verifying the real presence of a main effect, a statistical analysis must be performed. Still, there is a quick way to examine the cell means from a 2×2 to design to see if an interaction is a reasonable possibility. Here's how: If the cell means representing the four conditions are graphed and the slopes of the two lines representing the variables are not parallel (they either do intersect or could if they were long enough), then it is likely there is an interaction. If the lines are parallel and will remain so, then there is no interaction.

The four cell means (representing the four experimental groups) from Table 4.5 (see the center of the table) are conveniently plotted in Figure 4.2. The test characterization groups are noted at the bottom of Figure 4.2 and the plotted lines represent men (solid line) and women (broken line). The slopes of the two lines in Figure 4.2 are clearly different than one another: Indeed, it looks as if men scored higher in the gender differences condition, while women scored lower after the possibility of being stereotyped on the math test was aired. What Spencer and colleagues (1999) actually found through the interaction is that the women in the gender difference (stereotype threat) condition had significantly lower test scores compared to the people in the

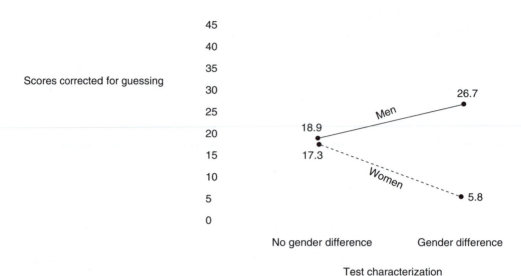

Figure 4.2.   Graph illustrating an interaction between stereotype threat and gender on math test scores. Means provided by Steve Spencer (personal communication, March 11, 2006); data based on Study 2 in Spencer, Steele, and Quinn (1999)

other three conditions (while these other three means differed in magnitude from one another they were not statistically different than one another). We will revisit this issue again in chapter 11.

There is one other interpretive dimension to any interaction: It qualifies the presence, if any, of the main effects. What I mean is that the sex-by-test characterization interaction tells us more than either or both main effects because it simultaneously involves how both independent variables affected the dependent measure. Think about it: One main effect tells us that men score higher than women on a math test, where the other tells us that the stereotype threat group had a lower math score than the no-threat control group. These separate facts do not reveal as much as the interaction, which demonstrated that women performed worse than men on the test only when the threat of the gender stereotype regarding math ability was in the air. Without the factorial design, we could not learn about the interaction, which is more informative—hence we say it "qualifies" or restricts the usefulness of the information from either main effect. In the absence of an interaction, however, we do focus on the interpretive power of either or both main effects (however, main effects and their meaning are always reported in written research summaries).

Figure 4.2 illustrated the plot of one possible interaction—there are many other patterns that suggest that an interaction between two variables might be present. Figure 4.3 illustrates some common interaction plots, as well as the parallel lines indicating that no interaction is present.

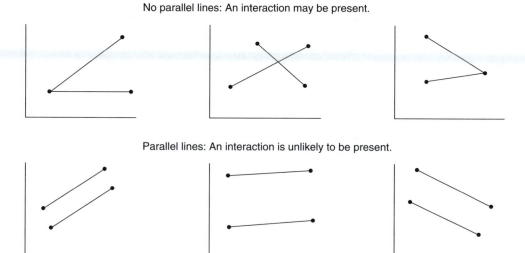

Figure 4.3.   Some sample plotted lines illustrating the presence or absence of an interaction between two variables

ACTIVE LEARNING EXERCISE   4D

Recognizing Main Effects and Interactions

Social psychologists love data. They love to learn whether people behaved differently depending upon what levels of what independent variables they encountered. As a budding researcher, you need to learn to love data. In particular, you need to learn to quickly size up 2 × 2 data tables (Are any main effects present? What about an interaction?) in the course of reading about the results of an experiment (see also Appendix B). Examine each of the tables shown in Table 4.6 (the first one is already done for you). Decide whether there is a main effect for each A variable by examining the column means (if the averages differ, then a main effect is present). Perform the same, simple calculations for each B variable (i.e., examine the row means). Finally, plot the four cell means in the center of each table (parallel lines mean no interaction is present; intersecting or converging lines mean an interaction is there; recall Figures 4.2 and 4.3). The correct answers are shown at the end of this chapter.

Continued

Table 4.6 Practice Makes Perfect: Recognizing the Presence of Main Effects and Interactions in 2 × 2 Data Tables

1.

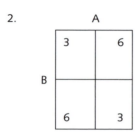

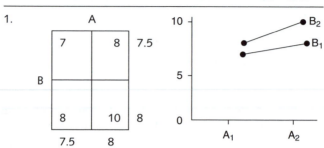

2.

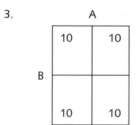

3.

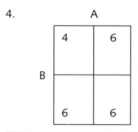

4.

Note: The cell entries are means from hypothetical experiments.

Within-subjects research designs

The scientific logic underlying between-groups designs is clear: They provide a clean way to learn how the presence and absence of key factors affect distinct (if similar in terms of demographic characteristics) groups of people. Yet, if you think about it, our routine social lives are not exactly like between-group research designs: We do not experience one (and only one) level of an independent variable; rather, we tend to encounter all levels of a variable—not all at once necessarily, but at different points in time.

Think for a moment about your experience of mood compared to the mood induction paradigm described at the opening of the chapter (Isen et al., 1987). Your mood probably varies a fair amount during a given day—from good (wake-up coffee at breakfast) to not-so-good (homework to be done) to neutral (driving in the car, sitting in the library)—and the changes from one to another are swift (chatting with a friend you've not seen for weeks, getting an unexpectedly high phone bill in the mail). Our reactions to our shifting moods—how we think and feel, including whether our creativity ebbs or flows—also shift, though we may not realize it unless we focus and think about it. In the language of research methodology, it is possible to expose participants to all levels of an independent variable in order to see how they react and how their reactions, like our moods, change.

To characterize what happens when participants experience all levels of an independent variable and to capture what effects such exposure has on a dependent variable, psychologists rely on within-subjects designs. A *within-subjects* (sometimes called *within-groups* or *repeated-measures*) *design* is one where the same group of participants experiences all levels of an independent variable. In a within-subjects research design, the same dependent variable is administered at several points in time—usually after each condition or level of the independent variable is presented—and not simply once, as is often the case for basic between-subjects designs.

Do within-subjects designs have any advantages over between-subjects designs? The best answer is that it all depends on the nature of the hypothesis being examined; in some cases, a between-groups approach will be better, in others the within-groups strategy will be superior. One distinct advantage of within-groups designs is that they usually require fewer participants than between-groups designs. Why? Think about it: Even a simple 2 × 2 study requires four separate participant groups. If you want 10 people in each group, that's a total of 40 participants. As we will see, conducting a within-subjects design where all participants experience both levels of two independent variables (i.e., four conditions) requires many fewer participants than 40.

Let's consider how this is possible by reviewing an experiment from an area of social psychological research, detecting deception, which routinely employs within-subjects designs. DePaulo, Lanier, and Davis (1983) relied on a within-subjects design in order to examine whether and how well observers could detect lies from truthful statements. Of particular interest was whether people's ability to detect planned lies from "spur of the moment" or spontaneous lies varied. Participants watched filmed actors deliver four remarks: a planned lie, a planned truth, a spontaneous lie, and a spontaneous truth. The participants were asked to evaluate the truthfulness of each remark by guessing whether it was a lie. Although people were able to detect lies at better than chance levels (i.e., they identified lies correctly slightly better than half the time), their ability to detect spontaneous falsehoods was no better than that for the planned ones.

A between-subjects design would have had four separate conditions, two groups who witnessed one of the types of lies and two other groups who saw one of the two types of true remarks. The within-subjects design allowed DePaulo and colleagues (1983) to show all participants all four conditions. As a result, only 24 participants took part in the study, when at least 40 people (and probably as many as 60) would be needed to fill the four cells in a between-subjects design for this research. Naturally, any savings in numbers of people needed also results in a savings of a researcher's time, energy, and effort.

There is another advantage to choosing a within-subjects design, one related to the random error that often emanates from individual differences and subject variables. Since each participant took part in all four experimental conditions, each individual's unique variability could be statistically extracted from the experiment's random error (see, e.g., Dunn, 2001). In practical terms, each participant served as his or her own control group; a person's responses for one experimental condition were readily compared to the same person's responses to each of the other three conditions. Thus any and all individual differences are spread throughout the design, which dilutes their influence and allows a researcher to focus on effects due to differences caused by the levels of the independent variable.

There is one main disadvantage associated with within-subjects designs, however. Any time a group of research participants' reactions are assessed more than once, there is risk of what methodologists call a confounded variable. A *confounded variable* or a "*confound*" is a problem variable that varies systematically with some independent variable of interest. If a confound is not controlled methodologically, an experimenter cannot be sure whether observed changes in a dependent variable are caused by this nuisance variable or, as hoped, by the independent variable. Consider the interpretive problem if all of the participants in the DePaulo et al. (1983) study were exposed to the two lies and two true statements in the same order: Any change in the dependent variable would have been confounded with the order in which the remarks appeared (i.e., if the order of presentation of the independent variables never varied).

To ensure that the independent variables are not confounded with their order of presentation, the researchers relied on counterbalancing. *Counterbalancing* is a procedure whereby each participant is exposed to every level of an independent variable in a random order (e.g., Campbell & Stanley, 1966). Alternating the levels of an independent variable evenly throughout a sample of participants spreads the effects of any stimulus order throughout an experiment—no confound occurs favoring one sequence (e.g., planned lie, spontaneous lie, planned truth, spontaneous truth) over another (e.g., planned truth, spontaneous lie, planned lie, spontaneous truth). Thus the people

Table 4.7 A Within-Subjects Design: A Completely Counterbalanced Presentation of an Independent Variable with Four Levels (A, B, C, D)

Participant	Treatment order	Participant	Treatment order
1	ABCD	13	CABD
2	ABDC	14	CADB
3	ACBD	15	CBAD
4	ACDB	16	CBDA
5	ADCB	17	CDAB
6	ADBC	18	CDBA
7	BACD	19	DABC
8	BADC	20	DACB
9	BCAD	21	DBAC
10	BCDA	22	DBCA
11	BDAC	23	DCAB
12	BDCA	24	DCBA

Note: Counterbalanced ordering (for 24 participants) of a planned lie (A), a spontaneous lie (B), a planned truth (C), and a spontaneous truth (D) in a study on detecting deception (i.e., lie versus true remarks, planned versus spontaneous remarks). Presentation order adapted from DePaulo, Lanier, & Davis (1983).

in the DePaulo et al. study all saw the same two lies and two truths—they just saw them in different orders so that the independent variable was not confounded with the sequence of presentation. Table 4.7 illustrates how the 24 participants in the DePaulo et al. study could have each received a unique order of the four levels of the independent variable.

Instead of conducting a fully counterbalanced study like that shown in Table 4.7, some researchers employ a partial counterbalancing procedure by using a Latin square design. A *Latin square* design is a within-subjects design that allows each condition in an independent variable to appear in every possible ordinal position (i.e., 1st, 2nd, 3rd, and so on). Table 4.8 illustrates a simple Latin square design with four conditions. In lieu of the completely counterbalanced design DePaulo et al. (1983) chose (recall Table 4.7), the researchers could have settled for this design—it is a reasonable, if not perfect, solution to combat the confounding influence of order effects. Latin square designs are often useful when it is logistically too difficult to represent all treatment orders or when too few participants are available. Methodologically, however, it is essential to have the same number of people appear in each group (e.g., if only 4 people were available for each group, the design shown in Table 4.8 could be conducted with only 16 participants). Winer, Brown, and Michels (1991) provide additional information on creating and implementing Latin square designs in psychological research.

Besides confounded variables, within-subject designs also pose interpretive risk in the form of carryover effects (sometimes referred to as contamination effects). A *carryover effect* is likely to occur when one treatment condition at one point during the

Table 4.8   Within-Subjects Design: A Latin Square Design Illustrating an Independent Variable with Four Levels

---

ABCD
BADC
CDAB
DCBA

Note: Each level of the independent variable appears in each of the four ordinal positions.

Table 4.9   Some Carryover Effects Relevant to Conducting Within-Subjects Designs

---

Habituation: Repeated exposure to the same stimulus leads to a decline in response to that stimulus. If participants view the same stimuli throughout an experiment, their attention may wander as the experiment progresses.

Sensitization: An effect that is the opposite of habituation. Being exposed to a given stimulus can provoke stronger responses to subsequent stimuli.

Learning: When participants learn to do a task during the first condition of an experiment, their ability to perform the same (or a similar) task is likely to artificially improve in later conditions.

Fatigue: When the early part of an experiment produces fatigue—participants become tired, distracted, listless, or bored—what they do later is apt to deteriorate despite the presence of an independent variable. Across time, challenging experimental tasks (e.g., puzzles, problems) can seriously reduce their concentration.

Adaptation: When participants must get used to some aspect of an experiment (e.g., learning to answer items in an online personality measure), earlier responses can differ from later responses because of adaptive changes rather than the effects of an independent variable.

Contrast: When an earlier condition is substantially different than a later one(s), later responses can differ from earlier responses because the (actually similar) conditions are perceived differently. Variation in responding is due to some perceived contrast and not the influence of the independent variable.

---

experiment (time 1) affects the behavior following some later treatment condition (time 2; Tourangeau, Rasinski, Bradburn, & D'Andrade, 1989; see also Schuman, 1996; Tourangeau, 2000). The later change in behavior is not due to an independent variable or the order effects associated with confounds. Instead, the mere experience of taking part in an earlier part of an experiment is "carried over" to a later part. For example, by virtue of learning to perform a task at the start of an experiment, people perform it much better by the experiment's end. Similarly, participants may be much more interested when an experiment begins, but their enthusiasm—and attention—flags by the end, which affects their responses to the later independent and dependent variables.

Table 4.9 lists some of the more common carryover effects associated with experimental research. Any one of these effects—and possibly more than one—can plague any within-subjects design. Ideally, the possibility of carryover effects should be considered when an experiment is being designed. A careful researcher will always mention to readers that the potential for carryover effects was recognized and addressed insofar as possible.

Can carryover effects be circumvented? Fortunately, yes. As was true for order effects, counterbalancing is also an effective antidote to the deleterious impact of carryover effects.

Joining between- and within-subject variables: Mixed designs

Researchers have capitalized on the strengths of between-subjects and within-subjects designs by joining them together in so-called mixed designs (sometimes referred to as mixed-model designs or combination designs). A *mixed design* contains at least one between-subjects variable and at least one within-subjects variable. Each of two (or more) participant groups is exposed to one level of the (between-subjects) independent variable and every level of some second (within-subjects) independent variable. Naturally, random assignment to group is essential, as is counterbalancing of the within-subjects factor. Mixed designs are often creative and occasionally unorthodox, which means that a social psychologist must often make modifications or even sacrifices related to the unique demands of the research question (Aronson et al., 1990).

Design Matters

Experiments are the Rosetta stone for the social psychologist: They allow a researcher the opportunity to translate a variety of abstract ideas into concrete, testable hypotheses and empirical realizations that tease apart cause and effect. Experiments provide evidence, support, and meaning to hunches, observations, and full-blown theories about social behavior. Whenever possible, experiments should be the social psychologist's first choice for studying social phenomena. Of course, not all interesting research questions lend themselves to experimental investigation. Fortunately, social psychologists tend to be a creative and adaptive bunch, fitting research methods to the sorts of empirical opportunities they encounter. We will discuss some of these alternatives to experimental research in the next chapter.

Exercises

1 Go to the periodical section of a library and look at some social psychology journals (see the list in Appendix A). Identify the independent and dependent variables in each of several articles. Be sure to make note of their theoretical definitions, operationalization, and, in the case of dependent variables, how they were measured.

2   Using the variables found in question 1, write your own theoretical definitions and operationalizations, and suggest some other ways to measure the same dependent variables.

3   Examine several issues of a social psychology journal. Keep a count of how many experiments rely on between-subjects rather than within-subjects designs. Why do you think this is so?

4   Select a between-subjects design from one of the articles identified above in 3. Can you convert the design into a within-subjects design? Why or why not?

Active Learning Exercise 4B answers: 1 Independent variable: whether nuts were packaged or not; dependent variable: amount of nuts consumed (obesity is subject-variable—it is sometimes treated as an independent variable). 2 Independent variable: whether or not shocks were described as painful; dependent variable: whether the women preferred to wait alone or with someone else. 3 Independent variable: choice or second choice of pen; dependent measure: rating of liking for pen.

Table 4.6 answers: 1 Main effect for A; main effect for B; A × B interaction. 2 No main effect for A; no main effect for B; A × B interaction. 3 No main effect for A; no main effect for B; no A × B interaction. 4. No main effect for A; main effect for B; no A × B interaction.

Chapter 5

Alternatives to Experimental Research in Social Psychology

"Thank You for Not Sharing Your Earthquake Experience" (Sentiment emblazoned on t-shirts that appeared in Palo Alto, California, approximately four weeks after the October 1989 Loma Prieta Earthquake; Pennebaker & Harber, 1993, p. 133).

Disasters happen. People and property are lost. Survivors are left to make sense of the event, plodding through the mental or physical remnants asking questions like "Why me?" or "Why them?" In our time, the bombing of the Federal Building in Oklahoma City, the terrorist attacks of September 11, 2001, the Iraq war, and Hurricane Katrina have all prompted collective soul searching. In the aftermath of these and other calamities, the search for meaning can continue for some time. Seeking answers, people ask each other questions; they offer opinions and share experiences in search of closure (e.g., Horowitz, 1976). Some answers are painful but clear. Other questions about the causes and consequences of such shared traumas will never be answered.

Profound events are worthy of serious empirical scrutiny even if they cannot be examined with the meticulous research designs associated with laboratory-based research in social psychology. Consider a compelling example: Social psychologists James Pennebaker and Kent Harber (1993) undertook a very involved piece of research within one week after the October 1989 Loma Prieta Earthquake which, registering 7.2 on the Richter scale, wreaked havoc in the San Francisco Bay area and caused over 60 deaths. Using random digit dialing (or RDD, a technique for randomly phoning residents related to the sampling ideas reviewed in chapters 4 and 6), these researchers interviewed close to 800 residents of three California cities (San Francisco, Sacramento, Claremont) and Dallas, Texas. The participants were called by phone once within 1, 2, 3, 6, 8, 16, 28, or 50 weeks after the quake and for 10 minutes were asked about their earthquake experiences. Because Pennebaker and Harber were especially interested in social responses (i.e., communicating thoughts and feelings about the quake to others) and psychological responses (i.e., thinking about the quake) to the seismic activity, all participants were asked how many times in the previous 24 hours they had talked about and thought about the earthquake.

Let's look at the responses of the people who experienced the quake first hand, the sample of residents from San Francisco. Figure 5.1 plots the self-reported incidence of thinking and talking about the earthquake among a sample of 275 city residents

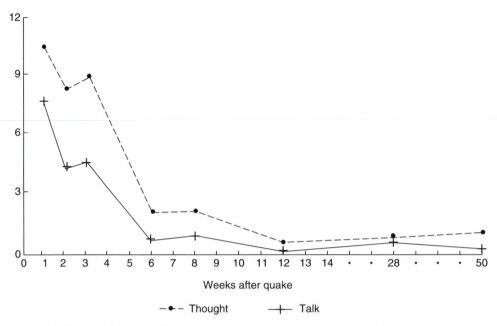

Self-reported number of thoughts and conversations in the previous 24 hours concerning the earthquake among San Francisco residents. Data were based on 275 telephone interviews (approximately 34 respondents at each time point). To control for extreme responses, subjects who reported thinking or talking about the quake more than 25 times in the previous 24 hours were assigned a value of 25 times.

Figure 5.1.   Incidence of thinking and talking about the Loma Prieta earthquake. *Source:* Pennebaker (1993, Figure 9.1, p. 211)

(around 34 people were interviewed at each of the key time points noted earlier). What can we learn from Figure 5.1? San Francisco residents spoke about and thought about the quake a great deal during the first two weeks, so that many people reported that the event "brought the city together" (Pennebaker, 1993, p. 211). After two weeks and up to the eight-week mark, however, chatter about the quake died down precipitously. On the other hand, a fair number of respondents—above 20%—continued to *think* about the disaster (see Figure 5.1). Although they wanted to tell their own stories about what happened, people became much less willing to hear others talk about the disaster (recall the t-shirt slogan that opened this chapter). They became socially constrained, yet they were still mulling the quake's occurrence over in their own minds. As Pennebaker and Harber (1993, p. 133) put it, "A subtle conspiracy of silence was the result" of the collective social constraint.

This intriguing pattern of collective behavior allowed Pennebaker and Harber (1993) to propose a three-stage model of collective coping shown in Figure 5.2 (the curves shown in this figure are idealized but they are based on the pattern of data shown in Figure 5.1). Briefly, they argue that collective coping occurred in three

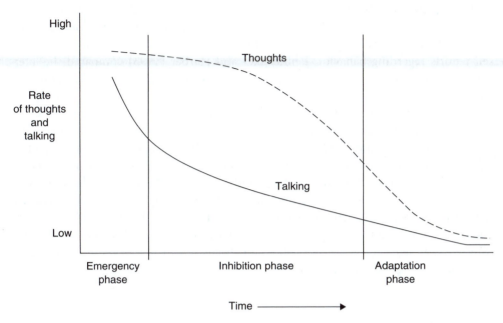

Figure 5.2.   Pennebaker and Harber's (1993) three-stage model of collective coping based on self-reported thinking and talking following the Loma Prieta earthquake. *Source:* Pennebaker and Harber (1993, Figure 2, p. 133)

distinct stages—an emergency phase, an inhibition phase, and an adaptation phase (see Figure 5.2). Thoughts about the event remain relatively high during the first two phases but then finally dissipate in the third phase, where people act as if the event— literal and psychological—is over. In contrast, actual talking about the event declines from the end of the emergency phase through the adaptation phase.

Psychologically speaking, the intriguing story is what happened during the inhibition phase, where people refrained from talking about the event. Lacking opportunity to talk with others about what happened, people continued to reflect on, even ruminate about, the upheaval. Ironically, this community-imposed silence or "holding back" actually heightened people's risk for health problems and psychological difficulties (Pennebaker & Harber, 1993). San Francisco residents reported a greater frequency of foul moods than normal, higher rates of quarreling with their families and coworkers, a jump in minor health problems, and having sleep disturbances in the form of quake-related dreams. In short, not talking but continuing to mentally "stew" about the quake had consequences for the city's residents; opening up to others might have been a preferable course of action (Pennebaker, 1997). Furthermore, the consequences of inhibition were public as well as personal. Compared to the same time period during the previous year, police reports of aggravated assaults grew 10 percent a few weeks after the disaster (Pennebaker & Harber, 1993).

As for good news, about eight weeks later, participants reported returning to normal. The intrusive thoughts about the disaster and the accompanying interpersonal conflict dissipated, eventually disappearing altogether. To demonstrate this return to base-line self-reports regarding behavior, Pennebaker and Harber (1993) compared the later San Francisco residents' interview data with that obtained from the three "control" cities.

The Loma Prieta earthquake is not the only real world calamity affecting large numbers of people that Pennebaker and his colleagues have studied. Pennebaker and Harber (1993) also examined collective responses to the Persian Gulf War through the lens of their proposed model of large-scale coping. Back in the 1980s, Pennebaker examined community reactions to the eruption of the Mount St. Helens volcano (Pennebaker & Newtson, 1983). Pennebaker and his colleagues have also examined the nature of social interactions following September 11, 2001 (Mehl & Pennebaker, 2003) and online chat room conversations concerning the death of Princess Diana (Stone & Pennebaker, 2002). For a broader discussion of inhibition and its role in social life, see Pennebaker (1989, 1997).

Leaving the Comfort of the Lab: Problems and Prospects

As the work by Pennebaker and Harber (1993) illustrates, social psychologists do conduct real life research in real life settings outside the controlled confines of the laboratory. But when researchers leave the lab, difficulties arise. The predictability of the lab is lost; research out in the real world or the field is less predictable—very often it is unpredictable. There are problems associated with conducting nonexperimental studies, that is, research efforts that do not satisfy the requirements of "true" experiments in social psychology (see chapter 4). These problems can include:

- No random assignment to condition,
- No controlled manipulation of an independent variable,
- No conditions representing distinct levels of an independent variable,
- No sensitive dependent variables that allow researchers to directly link cause with effect,
- No control group(s) or use of limited comparison groups,
- No opportunity to debrief research participants.

In short, research in the real world lacks the rigor associated with the lab where between- or within-group differences caused by the manipulation of an independent variable can be cleanly and clearly documented. Research out in the real world is complicated, often hard to do, and sometimes messy. Things go awry and researchers must compensate or go with the flow in an effort to identify interesting, even fundamental, issues in the study of social behavior.

Therein lies the excitement and challenge of doing research where experimental control and exactitude are lessened or even absent as compared to the lab. The loss of rigor need not mean a corresponding loss of vigor. As we learned from Pennebaker and Harber's (1993) work on collective responses to a common disaster, there are ways to capitalize on nature's caprices. If random assignment to condition is not possible, perhaps some form of random selection can be performed. If an ideal control group is not available, perhaps some similar group of people can be identified as a possible substitute. The advantages associated with nonexperimental research include:

- Thinking broadly and creatively about social behavior in actual social contexts,
- Testing out ideas uncovered in the lab out in the field (and vice versa),
- Developing new and creative dependent variables and ways to measure behavior,
- Having opportunity to examine how people respond to or cope with a real social or natural event,
- Using social psychological theory to explain or improve some practical issue in the social world.

Many social psychologists like to leave the relative quiet of the lab for the hurly-burly action outside in the world. Some make it a practice to first identify a social psychological effect in the lab and then examine its influence out in everyday life. In this chapter, we will consider some intriguing research design alternatives to true experiments. These include observational studies, correlational approaches, so-called quasi-experimental designs, survey research, experience sampling approaches and diary studies, Internet-based research, and archival and meta-analytic studies.

Observational Research

The most basic form of nonexperimental social psychological research involves simply looking around and observing what people do. In general, *observational research* involves watching people engage in normal behavior in public settings. In contrast to experimental research, observational research does not interfere in the situation— there is no intervention that might disrupt what is occurring naturally. Most observations are made in an unobtrusive or even "secret" manner so that the individual(s) being observed do not alter their actions. In a real sense, we all engage in a form of observational research any time we are in a public setting—a park, the mall, a sporting event, a sidewalk cafe—that causes us to watch and wonder about what motivates people to perform some acts but not others. Where real observational research differs from casual observation, of course, is that some record is being maintained: An observer or observers takes notes on the behavior being watched.

Here is a simple, off-the-cuff observational study: When walking past large department store windows, do people look at their own reflections or do they avoid doing so? Social psychologically speaking, we might be investigating public displays of self-consciousness (e.g., Fenigstein, 1984; Scheier & Carver, 1985) or naturally occurring situations where self-awareness is triggered (e.g., Duval & Wicklund, 1972). All one would need to do would be to sit on a bench adjacent to a department store and watch what people do.

Of course, an investigator would define what constitutes a "glance"—some concrete behavioral description is necessary so that the observed behavior can be measured. For example, a simple count of (a) how many people walk by and (b) how many subsequently glance at their own reflections could then be recorded. A researcher might also take note of the gender of the passers-by—do women look at their reflections more often than men? What sort of women (or men) look at their reflections? How long (in seconds) do people look at their reflections? How many adjust their hair or clothing after doing so? Does weight, height, age, or other characteristics appear to influence whether people look at their reflections? How can the observations we collect lend support to more "causal" arguments? Even in a simple example like this one, one observation leads to other observations; questions beget other questions. What seemed simple can become more complex—even a casual observation can quickly morph into a theory (albeit one that must be tested in a more rigorous manner).

The virtues of observational research are easy to summarize: It can be done in almost any public place where people gather or pass by. No expensive tools are usually needed; a pad and pencil, a simple checklist, or some other recording device is usually sufficient. Finally, the real and true advantage of observational research is that it can be used to generate ideas—future, potential hypotheses—that can be examined experimentally. Ironically, this strength also highlights the downside of observational research: Its speculative nature does not allow a researcher to determine causality—what internal or external factor(s) led to what witnessed behavior. Still, conducting an observational study can be a great way to begin gathering ideas for subsequent experimental research in social psychology.

ACTIVE LEARNING EXERCISE   5A

Designing and Conducting an Observational Study

An observational study should be simple and straightforward to conduct and, as McKenna (1995) suggests, they can almost always be carried out on a typical college campus or in some community settings. Remember: You are to carefully observe social behavior as it occurs (or does not occur)—you are not supposed to otherwise influence what happens. Table 5.1 lists some possible topics and locales for observational studies.

Table 5.1 Watching Social Behavior: Some Suggested Observational Study Topics and Locales

Topic	Locale
Failing to discard trash or clear table	Cafeteria, fast food restaurant
Wasting of food	Cafeteria, fast food restaurant
Talking or sleeping rather than studying	Library
People's weight and speed of food consumption	Cafeteria, fast food restaurant
Gender and TV show choice (e.g., comedy, romance, crime)	Dorm lounge
Frequency of interaction between people of different races or ethnicities	Various possible locations
Littering and gender	Public park, various other locations
Watching (not watching) reflection in mirror	Campus weight room
Talking during a movie or play or concert	Theater, auditorium
Late arrivals and early departures from class	Lecture hall, seminar, classroom

Here are the steps you need to follow to do an observational piece of research:

1 Develop a hypothesis regarding some naturally occurring behavior.
2 Concretely define the behavior in operational terms (recall chapter 4's discussion of operationalizing variables).
3 Identify what other related variables (e.g., gender) should be considered.
4 Identify a public locale for observing the behavior.
5 Develop a coding system and record sheet for the behavior. How will you tally what you see?
6 Decide whether you need to enlist the help of a fellow observer to help you verify your observations (see the discussion of reliability in chapter 8).
7 Seek IRB approval before you begin any data collection (see chapter 3).
8 How will you display your data? You might want to create simple bar graphs or data tables, for example (see the discussion of tables and figures in chapter 12).
9 Perform the observational research.

Correlational Approaches

Unlike observational research, correlational research allows an investigator to assess the degree of association between pairs of variables. A *correlation* is a measure of association between two variables. As you probably learned in an earlier class, the nature of the association between two variables can be one of three types:

Positive association: As the value of one variable increases (or decreases), the value of the other variable behaves the same way. Here is a favorite example that nicely illustrates positive correlation: The more hours a first year college student studies per week, the higher his or her grades are likely to be at the end of the term. Conversely, fewer hours of study are also positively related to lower grades at a term's end.

Negative association: As the value of one variable increases, the value of the other variable decreases (or vice versa). In other words, each variable follows a direction opposite to that of the other. The more hours spent studying, the fewer hours available for watching television (or vice versa).

Zero or no association: There is no discernable pattern of covariation between the variables being considered. Time spent studying has no relationship with or effect on grades, nor is there any link between study time and discretionary time spent watching television.

The statistical magnitude of the association between two variables is described by a numerical index, the "correlation coefficient." The statistical symbol used to denote the correlation coefficient is r. The value of a correlation coefficient (e.g., Pearson or Spearman, the two most common types of correlations) can range between +1.00 (a perfect positive correlation) and −1.00 (a perfect negative correlation). As the value of a correlation approaches the mid-point between these two poles—that is, 0—there is no association between the variables. The presence of a "+" or a "−" in front of a coefficient (e.g., .25) only indicates the direction of the association between the two variables under consideration—in fact, the plus or minus sign is there to help us readily interpret the relationship—but the sign says nothing about the strength of the association. (APA-style, 2001, drops the "+" for positive correlations, however, the "−" sign is always shown for negative correlations.) Only the coefficient itself indicates that strength (i.e., stronger correlational relationships occur the further a coefficient is from the 0 point in the range between +1.00 and −1.00). Thus a correlation of +.32 is not as strong as the association indicated by a correlation of −.56. It follows, then, that the strength of association of +.76 and −.76 is the same.

Correlational approaches to research are described as passive designs in that a researcher explores how variables "covary"—how their values do or do not change with each other—without any direct intervention or manipulation (Wampold, 2006). Social and personality researchers rely on correlational methods because when an association between variables is established, knowledge of one variable can be predicted from what is known about the other. Thus knowing where one person falls on some measure of personality enables a researcher to predict the likely value of some measure of another related variable, such as another measure of personality or some related construct.

Indeed, one of the more popular, if passive, research approaches is to distribute packets of personality and related psychological measures thought to be associated with each other to a large sample of people. The data from the completed packets are

Table 5.2 Correlations between Social Dominance Orientation (SDO) and Selected Policy Items

Military programs	+.27
Gay and lesbian rights	−.50
Women's rights	−.32
Racial policy	−.46

Source: Sample 3b from Pratto et al. (1994, Table 5, p. 750).

coded, put in a spreadsheet or other data file, and quickly converted into correlational matrices—large tables illustrating all of the associations between each possible two variable pairings. Guided by theory, the researcher then scrutinizes the correlations to learn whether the resulting associations make sense.

Consider the case of *social dominance orientation* (SDO), a personality characteristic indicating the degree to which one prefers inequality among social groups (Pratto, Sidanius, Stallworth, & Malle, 1994). For example, people high in SDO, such as avowed racists, would likely believe that their race is by definition superior to—and by right should dominate—all other races. Those low in SDO, on the other hand, tend not to believe in any such social pecking order, or that the society's "haves" should dictate what happens to the "have nots." Using a correlational research design, Pratto and colleagues demonstrated that knowing how people scored on a measure of SDO was predictive of a wide variety of their social and political attitudes. The researchers developed a 14-item measure of SDO. Participants read each item (e.g., "Some groups are simply not the equals of others," "Some group are just inferior to others") and then rated it on a 1 to 7 scale (from 1 = *very negative* to 7 = *very positive*; for a complete copy of the measure, see Pratto et al., 1994). Different groups of participants completed the SDO measure and many other measures of social, political, and racial attitudes, personality scales, and demographic questions.

Table 5.2 shows correlations between scores on the SDO scale and some selected social policy variables. These data are based on one of several samples included in Pratto et al.'s (1994) study. As you can see, individuals who scored high on SDO had a positive preference for military programs, which emphasize the need for and maintenance of distinctions among different ranks of people. In contrast, high scores on SDO were inversely related to (negatively correlated with) policy issues that tend to reduce or eliminate barriers by promoting the rights of minority or disadvantaged groups (here, gays and lesbians, women, and ethnic minorities).

Look once more at Table 5.2: We have considered these data from the point of view of people who score high on SDO. The same correlations also predict the likely attitudes of low scorers on this personality measure. People low in SDO would be less favorably disposed toward the hierarchical nature of the military (a positive association—lower on one variable, lower on the other variable, as well) and favorable toward promoting the rights of minority groups (negative associations—lower on one variable, higher on the other). Among other findings, Pratto et al. also found that men are more likely to express a social dominance orientation than women, that high-SDO people are drawn to careers that are hierarchical (e.g., business, law enforcement), and that SDO was negatively correlated with tolerance, empathy with others, and altruism (for a broader discussion of SDO, see Sidanius & Pratto, 1999).

There is, of course, one major drawback to all correlational research: Correlation does not indicate causation. This is one of the great dictums of all science and of special relevance to social psychology—social behavior is not always caused by the factors we anticipate. In other words, the presence of a positive or a negative association between two variables does not inform us about the actual origin—the cause—of the relationship. Knowing that there is correlation between one sample's scores on a measure of SDO (variable x) and any one of the policy variables shown in Table 5.2 (a variable y) can be explained in one of three ways: x causes y, y causes x, or some unknown third variable—let's call it z—is causing the association between x and y. We simply do not know which of these directional accounts is the correct one. Thus correlations are interesting, suggestive, and often interpretable—they can even point us in the right direction where answers can be found—but they do not offer causal accounts. As we learned in chapter 4 (and elsewhere in this book), our best course of action for learning how a change in one variable leads to the change in another is by conducting a true experiment.

Please note that we are not ruling out an important role for correlations—they often provide an overlooked insight or highlight an issue that will eventually drive an entire experimental research program. We must, however, remember that correlations only point to possible (and often competing) explanations that must be teased apart using other research methods—again, correlation does not imply causation.

There are some advanced statistical approaches employing correlations that allow researchers to infer causality under particular conditions. These approaches, called structural equation modeling (SEM) or causal modeling, are beyond the scope of this book (see, e.g., Hoyle & Robinson, 2004; Kenny, Kashy, & Bolger, 1998). SEM is a technique for deciding how well data representing a set of variables link to the hypotheses regarding causal connections among the variables. Social psychologists who use SEM build and test models to determine the presence, nature, and extent of causal relationships among variables (e.g., does variable x cause a change in variable y or does some other variable z mediate the relation between x and y; see, for example, Breckler, 1990).

ACTIVE LEARNING EXERCISE   5B

Conducting a Correlational Study on Personality

Correlational studies are ideal for situations where experimental manipulations are either impossible or unethical. Researchers who study alcoholism or drug abuse, for example, cannot require some people to consume liquor or illegal substances (or deny others the right to avail themselves of either) in order to examine subsequent declines in health and psychological well-being. You can imagine any number of interesting issues (e.g., marriage, divorce, sexual orientation, adoption, health problems) that preclude any assignment to a condition or state, let alone random assignment, but can nonetheless be examined through correlational means. And, as we learned from the work by Pratto and colleagues (1994), correlational research is often the choice method for examining how an expressed personality trait can predict responses on related social variables, such as attitudes toward certain groups (e.g., ethnicities) or issues (e.g., affirmative action).

As noted earlier, correlational studies are not difficult to conduct; in fact, they are relatively inexpensive "paper and pencil" procedures. Here are some straightforward steps for executing a correlational study:

Step one. You need to identify some personality trait of interest and then locate an existing instrument or scale designed to measure it. Table 5.3 lists some popular traits for which various measures or scales exist in the social and personality psychology literature (this list is by no means an exhaustive one—list other traits you find or record them in your research notebook). Good sources for personality traits (and occasionally some measures) include introductory text books on the topic. Alternatively, you can look in your library for reference works containing personality measures (e.g., Robinson, Shaver, & Wrightsman, 1991) or search PsycINFO for references that provide personality scales and scoring information. Some psychology departments also maintain files of personality measures students can use in their research (ask your instructor if such files are available at your institution).

Step two. Once you identify a personality trait of interest and locate an appropriate scale or measure (note that shorter personality inventories are generally easier to score), develop a questionnaire containing items that you believe will be positively and negatively correlated with it. For example, if you were studying procrastination, you would want to know how many hours per week a person studied (or not), typical number of hours of sleep per night, how often assignments are

Table 5.3 Some Sample Personality Traits Appropriate for Correlational Research

Altruism	Locus of control
Introversion/extroversion	Self-monitoring
Optimism	Conscientiousness
Self-consciousness	Agreeableness
Masculinity/femininity/androgyny	Procrastination
Shyness	Sensation-seeking

Continued

submitted past the due date (where 1 = *very infrequently* to 7 = *all the time*), and so on. Chapter 6 provides detailed guidelines for writing questions and putting together questionnaires.

The questions you use should have numerical answers, which means that rating scales, behavior counts, or any self-report-based questions that have some range of values can be correlated with one another and with scores on the personality measure you select. Questions requiring answers of "yes" and "no" have a limited range of values, which means that they are not appropriate for conventional correlational analyses. You should also collect descriptive demographic information about your participants, such as age, sex, year in college, major, or whatever information seems relevant (for more on demographic information, see chapter 6). Such information will allow you to characterize your sample for readers (see also the discussion of Method sections in chapter 12).

Step three. After you have collected the measures, created a questionnaire packet, and copied, distributed, and then collected them from a participant sample, all that remains is for you to code the data (per person) and enter it into a file. Correlational analyses can then be quickly and easily performed using a statistical software package or a basic spreadsheet program (most have a correlation option built into them). Obtain a printout of the correlations and look for interesting associations that confirm or refute your theory about how the trait would be linked with the other self-report items. A more detailed discussion of correlational analyses— including reporting correlational results in written form—may be found in chapter 11.

Quasi-Experimental Research Designs

Interesting research questions often precede the availability of ideal methods for studying them. As we learned from Pennebaker and Harber's (1993) efforts on psychosocial reactions to natural disasters, however, social psychologists are flexible, learning what they can whenever and wherever they can. The premise of this chapter is that controlled or true experiments are not always feasible and, in any case, that there is no single, perfect research design. We now turn to the original antidote to the absence of empirical control: quasi-experiments.

A *quasi-experiment* is "close to but not quite" an experiment because it lacks one or more of the following: experimental control, random assignment to condition, lack of a representative control or comparison group, and manipulation of an independent variable. As Wampold (2006) notes, any research design that possesses one or more threats to validity is by definition a quasi-experiment. Threats to validity are design flaws or methodological limitations reducing the confidence researchers place in their ability to make inferences based on research results.

When conducting any quasi-experiment, a social psychologist's chief concern is *internal validity*, whether an observed demonstration of cause and effect is sound. When internal validity is high (i.e., few, if any, design problems exist), then few alternative or competing explanations are likely to account for some set of results. A researcher can be confident about the favored explanation. When internal validity is low, certainty is low; any number of rival accounts could explain a set of findings. We will discuss the two types of validity—internal and external validity (whether obtained results are generalizable to other settings)—in detail in chapter 9.

Quasi-experiments are approximations of true experiments, making the best of what can sometimes be a murky empirical situation. In fact, when researchers conduct quasi-experiments, they often substitute the term "treatment" or "intervention" in lieu of using the term "independent variable." Why? Very often a researcher will study some event over which experimental manipulation is neither possible nor necessarily desirable (e.g., assessing the health and educational benefits of a free breakfast program for disadvantage elementary schoolchildren—would a control group be ethically viable?). Similarly, instead of assessing treatment effects by evaluating dependent variables, quasi-experiments use the term "outcome variables" to reflect the lack of precise control associated with true experiments. Like true experiments, however, quasi-experiments can be multivariate; more than one treatment and more than one outcome can be evaluated in the same study.

Quasi-experimental research is part of the legacy of Donald T. Campbell, a brilliant methodologist and creative social psychologist. I met the late, great Don Campbell on a few pleasant occasions back in the late 1980s when he was teaching at a neighboring university. I once heard him quip that quasi-experiments were sometimes "queasy" experiments. By that he meant their results could be "unsettling," that researchers using quasi-experimental designs in certain settings could never be altogether certain about the true nature of the cause and effect relationships. Some interesting behavior that looked to be caused by one variable might very well be due to the unforeseen influence of another variable, some artifact of the research design, the lack of an adequate control or comparison group, or another uncontrollable quality inherent to the research.

What are hardworking social psychologists to do? Give in to frustration and rethink the virtues of pursuing a topic, or reconcile themselves to the vagaries of research life beyond the serenity and control of the lab? I think that the better part of research valor is to press on and conduct the research. Quasi-experimental designs are not ideal— after all, they are not purely experimental—but they offer a more constructive solution than deciding not to pursue a question. An investigator may not learn the true state of affairs regarding some phenomenon, but some insights will be learned. In some cases, a clever researcher can build a theoretical case by combining results obtained from a mix of experimental and quasi-experimental investigations.

Campbell and his colleagues published a series of very important works on quasi-experimental and experimental research designs (Campbell & Stanley, 1966; Cook & Campbell, 1979; Shadish, Cook, & Campbell, 2001). These are among the most useful books on research design in psychology and the other social sciences. We cannot review all of their insights on methodology, let alone quasi-experiments, due to space constraints. Instead, our review of quasi-experimental designs will be highly selective. We will consider some examples from each of the two main design categories identified by Cook and Campbell (1979): nonequivalent group designs and time-series designs. Other designs can be found in the books by Campbell and his colleagues.

Nonequivalent group designs

Nonequivalent group designs involve two or more groups, at least one of which is exposed to some treatment. In the ideal case, the groups complete the same outcome measure before and after the treatment occurs, so that any change can be documented. Given that random assignment to a group may not be feasible, the groups may differ from one another at the study's outset (hence the label "nonequivalent"). Further, the treatment may be naturally occurring (like the Loma Prieta earthquake) or it may be controlled by someone other than an experimenter (e.g., layoffs instituted as an economic measure by a corporation).

When no randomly assigned control group exists, researchers sometimes create a nonequivalent control or comparison group. Pennebaker and Harber (1993), for example, compared the earthquake responses of Dallas residents (who were completely unaffected) to those of San Franciscans whose lives were disrupted. The design problem is obvious: The members of the control or comparison group may not be from the same population as the treatment group. On the other hand, one can argue that even a nonequivalent control group is better than no control group whatsoever (however, exceptions to this rule exist; see, e.g., Pennebaker, Barger, & Tiebout, 1989). In diagram form, this nonequivalent control design—labeled the untreated control group design with a pretest and a posttest (see Cook & Campbell, 1979)—looks like this:

$$O_1 \quad X \quad O_2$$

$$O_1 \qquad \quad O_2$$

Symbolically, the Os represent a pretest outcome measure (O_1) and a posttreatment outcome measure (O_2). The single X in the upper half of the diagram indicates that the treatment was presented to one group after the first outcome measure. The second group (the bottom half of the diagram) serves as the (nonequivalent) control group, which completes outcome measures at the same points in time. The broken line indicates that the two groups were created without the benefit of randomization. The design is by no means ideal; you can easily imagine many different ways the groups can differ from one another besides the one of interest, the effects on the treatment group's posttreatment outcome. The key here is whether the control group can be shown to share any common experiences with the treatment group. If yes, then several of the threats to the internal validity of this design pose no problem (i.e., history, maturation, testing, instrumentation; these systematic risks to verifying that change is attributable to an independent variable and not some uncontrolled or random factor are discussed in detail in chapter 9; see pp. 237–239). Two other threats—mortality and selection—still pose a problem, however (see p. 239 in chapter 9).

What happens when no reasonable control group exists? Some researchers employ several different comparison groups. Baum, Gatchel, and Schaeffer (1983), for example, used a design called the posttest only design with nonequivalent groups (Cook & Campbell, 1979) which, when diagramed, looks like this:

$$X \quad O_1$$

$$O_2$$

$$O_3$$

$$O_4$$

The researchers examined the stress responses of people residing near Pennsylvania's Three Mile Island (TMI) nuclear reactor, where a relatively serious industrial accident occurred in the late 1970s. As with any accident, there was no forewarning, so Baum et al. could do no pretesting to establish that groups were similar before the event (i.e., the treatment) occurred. Three comparison groups were formed: One group lived near a functioning nuclear power plant, another close to a coal-fired power generator, and a third resided over 20 miles away from any energy facility. Why bother gathering such groups? As with an ideal (randomly assigned) control group, Baum and colleagues wanted to rule out rival explanations for the physical and psychological stress reported by the TMI residents.

What about validity concerns? Interview data from all four groups were gathered simultaneously, thereby eliminating worries about five major validity threats: history, maturation, testing, instrumentation, and mortality (again, see pp. 237–239 in chapter 9). The threat of selection bias—the possibility that members of the treatment group hail from a different population than the control or comparison groups—remained, however, as is often the case in any nonequivalent control group design. The decision to use more than one comparison group was an effort to rule out selection bias as a threat to the study's internal validity.

Time series designs

Time series designs are a form of repeated measures or within-subject designs: The same measure is administered to the same group at several points in time (see chapter 4). One difference between this type of quasi-experiment and a standard experiment

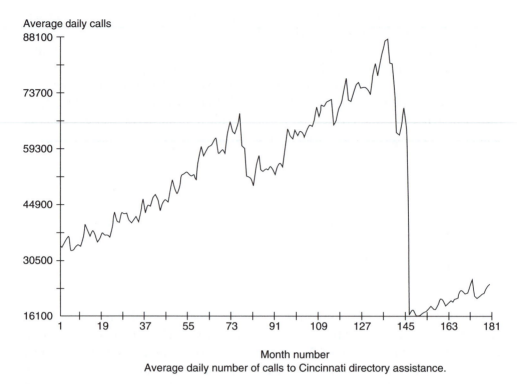

Average daily calls

Month number
Average daily number of calls to Cincinnati directory assistance.

Figure 5.3.   Evidence from an interrupted time series design: The effects of charging for directory assistance in Cincinnati, Ohio. *Source:* Figure 6.1 in Shadish, Cook, & Campbell (2002, p. 175), based on McSweeny (1978)

is that the time frame is usually much broader—days, weeks, or even months between measures, rather than minutes. A second difference is the lack of control over what participants experience between the administrations of the measures. And, just as was true of some nonequivalent group designs, there may be no control or comparison group.

The most basic time series design is the interrupted time series design (Cook & Campbell, 1979), where a single treatment "interrupts" numerous observations collected from one population or group. In diagram form, the design looks like this:

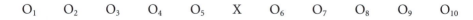

$$O_1 \quad O_2 \quad O_3 \quad O_4 \quad O_5 \quad X \quad O_6 \quad O_7 \quad O_8 \quad O_9 \quad O_{10}$$

The choice of 10 outcome observations is arbitrary; however, more rather than fewer measures are apt to lend credence to any arguments supporting observed changes.

Figure 5.3 illustrates a clever demonstration of the interrupted time series design. McSweeny (1978) examined the effect of Cincinnati Bell's charging a 20 cent fee for local directory assistance calls. As shown in Figure 5.3, imposing the fee (treatment)

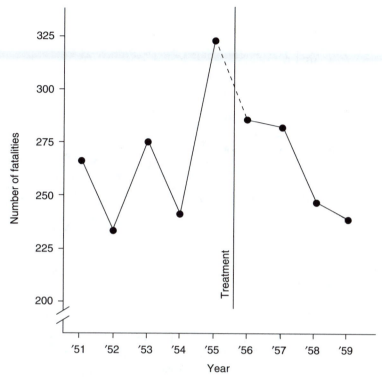

Figure 5.4. Interrupted time series design: highway deaths in Connecticut from 1951 to 1959. *Source:* Campbell (1969, p. 413)

in 1974 led to a sharp and steep decline in the number of directory assisted calls. Even in the absence of a control group, Shadish et al. (2002) suggest that few plausible rival explanations can reasonably account for the drop in calls.

Campbell (1969) himself offered what is one of the most elegant demonstrations of the interrupted time series design. In 1955, Connecticut began a concerted effort to stop speeding on its major highways. A reduction in highways deaths followed: only 284 fatalities in 1956 compared to 324 in 1955. Did better policing of the state's highways lead to close to 13% fewer deaths? Campbell used the interrupted time series design to examine the highway deaths in Connecticut from 1951 to 1959 (see Figure 5.4) and answer this question. A drop did occur once the treatment was introduced, but the decline in mortality rates is not very convincing when you consider how variable the rate was over the 8-year period (see Figure 5.4).

To address the variability problem, Campbell (1969) used a variation on the basic interrupted time series design, one with a control group: the interrupted time series with a nonequivalent no-treatment control group time series (Cook & Campbell, 1979). Admittedly a mouthful to say, the design looks like this:

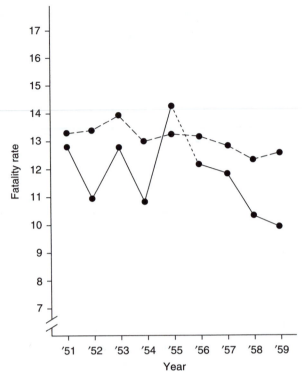

Figure 5.5.　Interrupted time series design with control groups: Highway deaths in Connecticut and four control states from 1951 to 1959. *Source:* Campbell (1969, p. 419)

O_1	O_2	O_3	O_4	O_5	X	O_6	O_7	O_8	O_9	O_{10}
O_1	O_2	O_3	O_4	O_5		O_6	O_7	O_8	O_9	O_{10}

His clever solution was to examine the highway mortality rates from four similar states that did not institute speeding reduction programs during the same time period. Figure 5.5 superimposes the death rates for the four control states over that for Connecticut. As you can see, the number of deaths in the control states is relatively steady across the 8-year period, whereas Connecticut's rate declines fairly steadily once the speeding intervention ensued. In short, the new policy of policing the highways led to a lower mortality rate (bearing in mind, as Campbell did, that other influences were no doubt also at work). Evidence for the decline in highway deaths, however, was less tenable without the support provided by the time series design.

The alternative designs we reviewed so far have largely been behavior based. Instead of only observing what people do and inferring the cause of outcomes, what if we ask them directly why they do what they do?

Survey Research

Survey research is predicated on a basic idea: If you want to know what people think about some issue, just ask them. *Survey research* entails the creation and dissemination of self-report questionnaires designed to gauge people's thoughts and feelings about something—a political (e.g., immigration, foreign policy) or social (e.g., drug use) issue, an experience (e.g., quality of service in a hotel), or an idea (e.g., changing a school's mascot). Our review of survey research will necessarily be brief because chapter 6 is devoted to a detailed discussion of creating questionnaires and conducting survey research.

Survey research takes place out in the field and not in the controlled setting of the laboratory. Surveys can be conducted by handing or mailing out questionnaires, interviewing people in person or by phone, or having them submit responses over the Internet. Most surveys have a similar goal: adequately describing the reactions of a representative sample of people from some larger population (e.g., residents of a town, a city, a state, or a country; students who attend a particular school; registered voters; retirees living in an assisted living facility). Naturally, having access to a random sample of survey participants generally strengthens a researcher's confidence in any conclusions drawn from it (recall the discussion of sampling issues in chapter 4; see also chapter 6).

One of the striking characteristics of a good survey is that a researcher really only needs around 1,200 responses (assuming they were randomly gathered) in order to adequately portray the general opinion of some population. In fact, whether they are national or local in scope, most such surveys can claim a 95% level of confidence in characterizing the opinion held by the population of interest (usually with an error rate of around only 3%). There is one important point to keep in mind about such survey results—the data represent public opinion at one moment in time; thus the knowledge gained reflects current feelings and not necessarily a valid prediction. Opinion changes, often swiftly, which is one of the reasons that public opinion polling during the months leading up to elections is done so frequently.

Approaches to surveying opinion

Surveys are either cross-sectional or longitudinal. A *cross-sectional* survey is designed to collect responses from one or more samples of people at one point in time. The aforementioned election-oriented surveys are usually cross-sectional. In the weeks and days leading up to an election, different samples composed of different voters are surveyed at different times in order to portray the electorate's opinions. *Longitudinal surveys* contact and collect responses from the same sample of people at more than one point in time. The goal is to assess attitude or opinion changes across time (e.g., do people feel differently about health insurance before and after retirement?).

Experience Sampling Methods and Diary Approaches

What if you completed a short survey about yourself—what you were doing, thinking, and feeling, for instance—at several points during the day? What would these mini-assessments reveal about you? An interesting variation of survey-oriented research is called the *Experience Sampling Method* (ESM; e.g., Csikszentmihalyi, 1997; Csikszentmihalyi & Larson, 1987; Moneta & Csikszentmihalyi, 1996). Pioneered by Mihaly Csikszentmihalyi (pronounced "Me-high Chick-sent-me-high-ee"), ESM uses a pager or programmable watch (a "Personal Data Manager" or PDM can work as well) to alert participants as to when they must stop what they are doing to fill out a few pages in a research pamphlet—a mini-diary, really—already in their possession. Csikszentmihalyi and his colleagues usually program the pagers to ring randomly during two-hour blocks of time throughout normal waking hours (say, 7am to 11pm—a week of these diary entries fills over 50 pages). When the pager sounds, participants record where they are, their current actions or activities, and who is with them. Participants also rate their "consciousness" at that moment using close-ended, numerical scales for self-esteem, happiness, concentration, motivation, and other self-report indicators of emotion and well-being. Other open-ended questions (e.g., "What were you thinking about when the beeper sounded?") are often included (Hektner & Csikszentmihalyi, 2002).

What do these brief but repetitive snapshots in time reveal about people, their conscious states, and their social doings? Csikszentmihalyi (1997) notes that large caches of observations from different people allow investigators to portray the nature of daily life. Traditional experiments or surveys capture a moment in time (i.e., a cross-sectional approach)—not many moments across a relatively short period of time (with the exception, of course, of some within-subjects designs; see chapter 4). Yet this form of longitudinal work is decidedly different than most long-term studies—a week of frequent records is different than measuring people's responses only once a month, a few times a year, or across many years. For example, ESM has been used to examine affect (Schimmack, 2003), emotion (Scollon, Diener, Oishi, & Biswas-Diener, 2004), attitudes about work and leisure (Csikszentmihalyi & LeFevre, 1989), gender and affiliation tendencies (Wong & Csikszentmihalyi, 1991), relationships and family life (Larson & Richards, 1994), even driving (Csikszentmihalyi & LeFevre, 1989), among other topics.

Csikszentmihalyi's key interest is often to illustrate those moments in our lives where we become wrapped up in tasks that are challenging and engaging, where we become so focused on what we are doing that we overlook the passage of time. He calls these sorts of peak experiences the "flow effect" or simply "flow" (Csikszentmihalyi, 1997). Such moments are apt to occur when a task requires a high degree of skill and a sufficient level of commitment, and ESM studies reveal we are happiest when we are in the midst of flow experiences (for a list of other qualities associated with the flow experience, see Csikszentmihalyi, 1997). What makes them of interest to social psychologists is that flow moments often occur outside usual venues for social interaction—say, when a person is writing or playing a musical instrument or some interesting, if often solitary, game. Flow never happens when we are watching television for example. Ironically, however, if we enjoy our work a great deal (i.e., our work is play), we often find flow there but not always in pursuit of leisure time activities that are supposed to be linked to our well-being (e.g., sunbathing around the pool).

ACTIVE LEARNING EXERCISE   **5C**

Conducting an ESM Study

Can you conduct an ESM study? Certainly. According to Punzo and Miller (2002), student-conceived and run ESM studies are not difficult to conduct. These researchers had students from two of their classes examine a normal week in the life of a teenager. The teen participants were given electronic beepers and were "paged" at random times. Once a beeper went off, the participants completed some scales and answered some questions.

Punzo and Miller's (2002) student researchers used one of two institutionally owned beepers (i.e., numeric display pagers) that could transmit signals across wide distances. Pairs of student researchers borrowed a pager for a day or two, giving it to a teen participant to carry around along with copies of the experience sampling form (ESF; Csikszentmihalyi & Larson, 1984). A sample ESF is shown in Table 5.4.

Table 5.4   A Sample Experience Sample Form (ESF)

Name: _____
Date: _____ Time beeped: _____ Time filled out: _____
What were you thinking about? _____
_____

Where were you? _____
What was the main thing you were doing? _____
_____

Who were you with?_____
Please choose one of the following responses for each question below and write the numbers in the blanks:
1 = none/not at all
2 = a little
3 = moderately
4 = a lot
Were you making progress on a task?   _____
Were you relating well with someone?   _____
Did you feel positive emotions?   _____
Were you concentrating?   _____
Was it hard to concentrate?   _____

Continued

Using this sample form as a template, you can create an ESF designed to learn about the typical social experiences of a group of people. You might, for example, explore the experiences of fraternity or sorority members, commuter students, student athletes, or representatives from some other on-campus groups. Each ESF should contain the same set of open-ended questions, rating scales, checklists, or other psychological measures—just keep it to two pages or less. Your research participants must be able to complete the ESF quickly.

What if you do not have access to a pager or other beeper device? You will need to be creative. What other small, portable, and hopefully inexpensive devices could be pressed into service as proxy beepers? Some digital watches have built in alarms, as do cell phones. Alternatively, you could call participants' cell phones at random times. When they answer, identify yourself and ask them to complete the ESF (a variation is for the researcher to call participants at random times and interview them via the cell phone, eliminating the need to provide participants with ESF packets). For more ideas on planning and running an ESM study, see Punzo and Miller (2002), Csikszentmihalyi and Larson (1984), Reis and Gable (2000), or Hektner and Csikszentmihalyi (2002).

If you prefer to follow a low-tech route, then you could have participants follow more of a diary approach. They would agree to complete ESF-like measures at certain times during the day or even just once a day, but they have to remind themselves when it is time to complete the measures. If you elect to follow the once-a-day option, then your approach would be consistent with the idea underlying most diaries or private journals, which serve as a repository for individuals' confidential thoughts, feelings, and recollections about the events of some period of time, usually a day. As we will see, social and personality psychologists also make use of existing diaries.

Dear diary: An example

The ESM can be thought of as a sort of diary approach, as research participants are keeping daily (or even more frequent) records of their doings. A traditional diary, however, is a place to record private reflections. Psychologists have shown interest in learning whether what people write in their diaries at one point in time not only characterizes their experience then, but how this early (recorded) experience affects their future lives.

Danner, Snowdon, and Friesen (2001), for example, examined handwritten, one-page autobiographies from 180 Roman Catholic nuns, which were written when the women were around 22 years old. These women were part of the Nun Study of aging and Alzheimer's disease (e.g., Snowdon, 1997). Specifically, in 1930, as each nun took her final vows she was asked to:

write a short sketch of [her] life. This account should not contain more than two to three hundred words and should be written on a single sheet of paper . . . include place of birth, parentage, interesting and edifying events of childhood, schools attended, influences that led to the convent, religious life, and outstanding events. (Danner et al., 2001, p. 806)

Danner and colleagues (2001) decided to explore the possible association between written emotional expression in the one-page diary and longevity (when this study started, the nuns in the sample were an average of 83 years old). The diaries were coded for emotional content (e.g., use of positive, negative, or neutral words). What made the group of nuns interesting was their similarity to one another: They had comparable social, (non)marital, and reproductive lives; had the same socio-economic status and access to medical care; and neither smoked nor drank excessive amounts of alcohol. Of course, these similarities also preclude generalizing any findings to other groups.

Did written emotions predict longevity? Indeed, they did: Positive emotional content was strongly associated with lower mortality risk. In other words, those nuns who expressed their thoughts and feelings using positive words were more likely to be alive and well almost 60 years later than their counterparts who used more negative language. Optimistic outlooks are linked with longer lives (Peterson, Seligman, Yurko, Martin, & Friedman, 1998).

Given the use of old records as keys to psychological states, the Danner et al. (2001) study could also qualify as a form of archival research (see below). However, I elected to place it in this section of the chapter because our focus here is on the role of social information gathered at a key point in time in diary form. For a broader discussion of issues pertaining to the measurement of daily event and experiences, see Stone, Kessler, and Haythornthwaite (1991).

Both ESM and other diary approaches rely on researchers to recruit or track down participants. We now turn to an alternative approach—the Internet—that encourages would-be participants to seek out research opportunities.

Internet-Based Research

The Internet has truly changed everything. Knowledge about anything and everything (and no doubt some things we would be better off not knowing) is literally at our fingertips. The advent of the Internet—the World Wide Web of computers—has also affected social psychological research. Participants need not ever darken the door of a psychology department in order to take part in a piece of research. Instead, they can be virtual participants, electing to take part in online investigations or surveys of human social behavior. In fact, participants can decide when and, thanks to wireless access to the Internet, even where they take part in Internet-based research—they might be right next door or they might be in Nicaragua or the Philippines.

As Fraley (2004) explains, virtually any piece of psychological research that can be done with a traditional paper and pencil approach can be put online (see also Dillman,

2000). The real boon for researchers is that participant responses can be directly entered into an existing and ever-growing data base. There is no need to laboriously read, code, and copy information from a questionnaire for entry into a computer—all that time and toil is gone because participants type in or otherwise select their responses, which are saved by and into software.

Internet-based research also allows social psychologists to think locally (on campus) but to act globally (collecting responses from participants from all over the world). This advantage reduces reliance on the traditional college sophomore samples (recall the discussion of homogeneous participant samples in chapter 4), meaning that the participants in many (any) online social psychology projects are likely to be more diverse, which can enhance claims that the results from a given research effort possess generalizability (this desirable, empirical criterion, also known as external validity, is discussed in chapter 9).

The Internet also allows investigators to:

- Employ web-based questionnaires containing rating scales, checklists, and open or free responses;
- Conduct experiments online from start (instructions) to finish (debriefing);
- Randomize the order in which stimuli, questions, images, or text appears;
- Randomly assign a participant to an experimental condition;
- Measure reaction or response time, that is, how long a participant takes to complete (e.g., reason through, answer) a problem or question;
- Store participants' responses and prepare them for analysis.

Internet ethics

Because people are involved, Internet research is like any other form of research in social psychology: Certain ethical obligations must be met. Anyone who elects to participate in an online project, for example, must complete an informed consent form (see chapter 3). Problems associated with online research, however, include ensuring that participants are old enough to participate and whether time was taken to actually read the informed consent form before "signing" it, that is, proceeding with the experiment or questionnaire. Obviously, any web-based project must pass muster with an IRB (recall chapter 3). Rules vary, however, as noted by Fraley (2004):

> At the University of Illinois at Chicago, getting IRB approval for Internet research is mostly a formality, for two reasons. The first is that Internet participation is fully voluntary; research subjects can withdraw, quite literally, from the research at any time. The second important factor is that we do not collect personal identifying information from our research subjects. In other words, we have no way of knowing from whom the data come. For my university, when our research violates these two conditions, we must submit more complex protocols to the IRB. (Fraley, 2004, p. 274)

Fraley (2004) also suggests that using deception online is not a good idea and should be avoided, thereby reiterating a claim made earlier in this book (see chapter 3). Mild deception that can be dealt with in a face-to-face encounter in a lab is one thing (such mild deception is acceptable to many participants; see Epley & Huff, 1998), but deceiving someone for whom there is no opportunity for direct discussion about the need for intentional "dishonesty" is quite another. The serious concern here is that without an experimenter-to-participant encounter, which is precluded by online research, it is virtually impossible to determine how the use of deception will affect participants. For social psychologists employing the Internet, it is better to be safe than sorry where participant welfare is concerned. However mild it may seem, the best policy is to avoid any level of deception when planning or implementing Internet-based research.

Time, participant loss, and sampling issues

All else being equal, Internet-based research should take a relatively short amount of time. In a lab or even traditional field setting, the proximity and presence of an investigator can probably encourage respondents to complete a whole packet of questionnaires. Online surveys are a different matter, however. If an Internet-based survey takes too long to complete, then participants may simply quit the program. To discourage premature departures, Fraley (2004) suggests that no online study should take more than 10 minutes or so to finish. As an aside, I completed an online survey recently that continually graphed my progress through the materials—as I moved forward to each subsequent page, a bar advanced so that I could gauge how close I was to being finished. I confess that without this indicator of my progress, I might have quit early.

What about participant loss or "dropout" during online surveys or investigations? Should online researchers be concerned? Absolutely. Such participant loss—often labeled "mortality"—poses a threat to a study's validity (see chapter 9). Specifically, participants are much more likely to drop out, that is, quit the online study before it is over, than those who take part in traditional, lab-based research projects. The reason for worry is a standard one: Perhaps the people who drop out are somehow different from those who remain, potentially biasing the intact data that remain. Although the problem can never be entirely avoided, one solution noted by Fraley is to collect information (e.g., sex, age, education, and other useful demographic characteristics) about all respondents early on, in the opening pages of an online experience. Later, you can compare the demographic data collected from subsequent dropouts with that from the individuals who completed the experiment, to assess any between-group differences (e.g., men tended to drop out compared to women). Detailed discussion of the dropout problem is available in work by Frick, Bachtiger, and Reips (2001) and by Knapp and Heidingsfelder (2001).

In a related vein, Vaux and Briggs (2006) note that researchers unknowingly increase their own dropout rate by sending surveys in the body of email messages instead of creating websites where the surveys can be accessed and completed. Surveys in email messages often lose their original formatting, which makes them difficult to read or recreate, thereby discouraging recipients from bothering to fill out and return them. Like a high dropout rate, a lowered response rate reduces a researcher's confidence in the data that are obtained (see Dillman, 2000; Salant & Dillman, 1994).

Who takes part in Internet-based research and how do we know? Do Internet samples differ from the typical samples of people who take part in social psychology studies? We already noted that keeping track of participant demographics early in the online experience is one way to learn about who starts, who finishes, and whether these groups differ in meaningful or consequential ways. Fraley (2004) suggests an obvious possibility: Stick with your same participant population but have them participate online. Although inelegant, this solution ensures that you are recruiting from your local and typical participant sample.

What we do know about broader Internet samples is that they are apt to attract a more restricted audience (at least for now and the foreseeable future) than traditional research. The reason is that people who have access to the Internet are likely to be better educated and somewhat more technically savvy than the average person (Reips, 2000). As the Internet becomes even more common in daily life, this difference in sophistication among samples will likely disappear. Fraley (2004) believes, however, that under the right conditions, Internet samples can be superior to the haphazard samples most social psychologists rely upon. Online respondents can be anticipated to demonstrate a greater range of ages, income levels, careers, and countries of origin. In support of this view, Vaux and Briggs (2006, p. 190) claim that, "As more people gain access to the Internet, samples of Internet users will become increasingly representative of the general population."

Table 5.5 summarizes some of the advantages and disadvantages of Internet-based research and data collection. Before you commit to launching an online social psychology project, be sure the benefits associated with doing so outweigh the costs involved. Unless you already possess some programming skills or are familiar with web site design, using the Internet for a research project in social psychology may be a considerable undertaking. Still, use of the Internet is becoming more common in social science research and some very good "how to" works are available (Birnbaum, 2001; Dillman, 2000; Fraley, 2004). Let's consider an example of how some psychologists used the Internet to characterize and capture people's reactions to a fateful moment in time.

An Internet-based example: Online character pre and post September 11, 2001

Peterson and Seligman (2003) used an online survey to assess whether Americans changed following the terrorist attacks on September 11, 2001. The presence of some change in American attitudes (e.g., "People in the United States have forever changed") was voiced repeatedly in the days following the loss of the World Trade Center towers, the crash of Flight 92 in Pennsylvania, and the damage and loss of life sustained at the Pentagon. As data were collected before and after the attacks, the researchers were able to determine whether—as popular lore would have it—citizens became nicer, more spiritual, and more affectionate people. For their part, Peterson and Seligman also wondered if people developed less pessimistic or more courageous outlooks, and if so, for how long.

Table 5.5   Some Advantages and Disadvantages of Internet-Based Research in Social Psychology

Advantages

Some samples (e.g., computer users, college faculty and students) are highly representative, so generalizing beyond them is unnecessary.

Data collection can be speedy and less error-prone than traditional methods.

Materials are virtual rather than physical (i.e., no paper needed).

Internet surveys can be cheaper to conduct and analyze than traditional surveys.

Internet surveys and experiments can reach or attract more people than traditional methods.

Participants can take part in research in their own time.

Fewer item completion errors or skipped items are associated with online surveys (e.g., Kiesler & Sproull, 1986).

Responses on the Internet are often honest and less susceptible to social desirability bias (e.g., Dillman, 2000; Kiesler & Sproull, 1986).

Disadvantages

Lack of genuine social interaction.

Participants cannot ask an experimenter any questions or for help.

Delivery of participant incentives (e.g., course credit, modest remuneration) is difficult.

Lack of similarity to everyday life or experiences (low in mundane realism; see chapter 9).

Samples are not necessarily random.

Samples may not be representative of population of interest.

Start-up costs can prohibit Internet-based research.

Lack of computer skills in a researcher can inhibit Internet-based research.

Ample pretesting of online experiments and surveys is sometimes needed.

As part of their research program in positive psychology, these two researchers developed a measure of people's positive traits, the *Values in Action* (VIA) *Classifications of Strengths* (see also Peterson & Seligman, 2004). Peterson and Seligman argue that the presence of positive traits (e.g., bravery, gratitude, self-control) within an individual enable him or her to have positive experiences. The authors created an online version of the VIA so that they could collect sufficient self-report data to verify the instrument's validity (see chapter 9).

Between January 2001 and June 2002, 4,817 people completed a version of the VIA online. The VIA measures people's responses to 24 character traits (see the list in Table 5.6). Ten different items assess each strength. Participants read an item and then respond to it on a 5-point rating scale (where 1 = *very much unlike me* to 5 = *very much like me*). Table 5.6 shows the average scores on the VIA before September 11 and then one and two months later (note that the responses shown here are based on a sub-sample of 1,396 people).

Did people represented in the sample change in the aftermath of September 11, 2001? Peterson and Seligman (2003) found that seven strengths showed a positive

Table 5.6   Character Strengths Before and After September 11th: Mean Scores on the Values in Action Inventory of Strengths

Trait	Mean before 9/11 ($n = 906$)	Mean 1 month after 9/11 ($n = 295$)	Mean 2 months after 9/11 ($n = 195$)
Appreciation of beauty	3.75 (0.66)	3.81 (0.66)	3.80 (0.62)
Bravery	3.63 (0.58)	3.70 (0.58)	3.72 (0.62)
Creativity, ingenuity	3.73 (0.71)	3.75 (0.66)	3.87 (0.62)
Curiosity, interest	3.99 (0.55)	4.03 (0.54)	4.08 (0.55)
Equity, fairness	3.91 (0.51)	3.95 (0.48)	3.98 (0.51)
Gratitude	3.83 (0.59)	4.02* (0.58)	4.01* (0.57)
Hope, optimism	3.56 (0.67)	3.68* (0.66)	3.80* (0.67)
Industry, perseverance	3.60 (0.64)	3.67 (0.68)	3.75* (0.65)
Integrity, honesty	3.94 (0.46)	3.97 (0.47)	4.03 (0.49)
Judgment	3.92 (0.49)	3.98 (0.50)	4.03* (0.56)
Kindness	3.87 (0.52)	3.99* (0.47)	4.01* (0.51)
Leadership	3.62 (0.54)	3.73* (0.53)	3.78* (0.58)
Love of learning	3.84 (0.64)	3.87 (0.61)	3.87 (0.66)
Love, intimacy	3.88 (0.58)	4.02* (0.57)	4.05* (0.53)
Perspective, wisdom	3.79 (0.53)	3.81 (0.49)	3.86 (0.54)
Prudence, caution	3.48 (0.57)	3.52 (0.55)	3.54 (0.64)
Self-control	3.28 (0.63)	3.30 (0.63)	3.31 (0.65)
Social intelligence	3.70 (0.55)	3.76 (0.52)	3.85* (0.55)
Spirituality, faith	3.36 (0.88)	3.57* (0.83)	3.57* (0.93)
Teamwork	3.48 (0.54)	3.65* (0.53)	3.73* (0.56)
Modesty[a]	3.26 (0.66)	3.33 (0.64)	3.27 (0.69)
Forgiveness[a]	3.57 (0.66)	3.54 (0.66)	3.69 (0.65)
Playfulness[a]	3.80 (0.60)	3.86 (0.59)	3.86 (0.66)
Zest[a]	3.62 (0.67)	3.58 (0.65)	3.66 (0.66)

Note: Standard deviations are in parentheses.

[a] Modesty, forgiveness, playfulness, and zest were not measured in the early versions of our survey (see the text). Before September 11, $n = 689$ for modesty and 471 for forgiveness, playfulness, and zest. Post-September 11 scores on these scales did not differ from pre-September 11 scores (t texts, $ps > .05$).

* Mean different from pre-September 11 mean by t text ($p < .01$).

Source: Reprinted from Peterson & Seligman (2003, p. 382, Table 1).

increase one and two months following the tragedy: gratitude, hope, kindness, leadership, love, spirituality, and teamwork (see the traits with asterisks listed in Table 5.6). Other traits—chiefly those not conceptually related to caring for others (e.g., integrity, love of learning)—did not vary with respect to this date of destiny. Peterson and Seligman suggest that the seven virtues that did change allowed people to feel a sense of belonging that encouraged them to turn to others in beneficial ways. Their social worlds were changed, and they reported acting and feeling in ways meant to create connections with people in days and weeks following the event. Several months after the events of September 11, subsequent responses to the VIA indicated that self-reported strengths rating receded somewhat.

These Internet-based data are only suggestive, of course. Peterson and Seligman (2003) happened to have this project up and running for a different purpose—like Pennebaker (e.g., Pennebaker & Harber, 1993; Pennebaker & Newtson, 1983), they sought to capture a sense of a psychological moment in time to assess collective reactions to it. Peterson and Seligman readily admit that true change may not have occurred—respondents chose when and whether to take part in the online VIA (i.e., before or after September 11) and their responses were restricted to one point in time: People offered either a pretest or a postevent response, not both. Ideally, change in positive traits would be measured across time, that is, longitudinally, rather than in the necessarily cross-sectional manner the researchers were forced to use—September 11 was an awful, if historical, moment of happenstance.

Yet Peterson and Seligman's (2003) work nicely illustrates that reactions to "calendar-based," real world events can be documented using the Internet. Online approaches like this one are interesting to social psychologists because they happen in "real time." How can social psychologists study events long after the fact, when such ideal records are nonexistent? Are any materials available that can shed light on and insight into past social behavior?

Archival Research and Meta-Analysis

Consider these nonexperimental research results, which share one characteristic in common—the investigators relied on data that were collected independently and for some other purpose:

- The need to belong to some group is so powerful that, particularly among sports fans who "pull together," it may contribute to a reduction in suicides. In the US, for example, between 1984 and 1994, fewer suicides occurred on Super Bowl Sunday than on comparison Sundays (Joiner, Hollar, & Van Orden, 2006).
- Presidential candidates who gave pessimistic nomination speeches went on to lose 9 out of 10 elections between 1948 and 1984 (Zullow & Seligman, 1990).
- Riots, murders, and rapes appear to be related to the weather; hotter days predict higher rates of aggression (Anderson, 1989; Anderson & Anderson, 1984; Carlsmith & Anderson).
- As student newspaper reports became less emotional following the accidental deaths of 12 students during the construction of the traditional bonfire at Texas A&M University, student visits to the university's health center and medical clinic increased dramatically. However, illness rates returned to preaccident levels within two months (recall the social stages of coping model discussed in the opening pages of this chapter; Gortner & Pennebaker, 2003).

What makes these examples interesting is that the researchers used existing records—suicide rates, long published (and possibly forgotten) speeches, weather reports, crime stories, college newspaper articles, medical records—to propose and demonstrate social psychological phenomena. No new data were collected; existing information was gathered and then organized or somehow reorganized. No research participants ran through their paces in any experiment or study. In fact, the data were long a matter of public or private record: filed but accessible, mute but speaking volumes when examined in a new light.

Researchers do not only intentionally collect social psychological data. Many times, researchers take advantage of data that already exist by placing some interpretive framework on information gathered by others. Archival research is a prime example of how social psychologists make sense of preexisting information concerning all sorts of public and private social behaviors. An *archive* is some storehouse of knowledge or source of information. An archive can be as simple as a set of files pertaining to a topic, a computerized database, or an extensive collection of objects. In the minds of many people, the term "archive" connotes old, even ancient, information, but this is not always true. A contemporary research library is an archive of sorts, as is your high school or college transcript or the local phone book. Similarly, we associate archives with documents but groups of objects in general can be archival. A collection of stamps, matchbooks, campaign buttons, or bumper stickers can all be considered an archive of sorts.

Archival data, or archival material that can be converted into "measures" of behavior, are sometimes referred to as nonreactive or unobtrusive measures (Webb, Campbell, Schwartz, Sechrest, & Grove, 1981). A *nonreactive measure* is one employed so that research participants remain unaware their behavior is being measured or evaluated (specific examples of nonreactive dependent measures are presented in chapter 8). In contrast, reactive measures are those psychological instruments, such as surveys or questionnaires (see chapter 6), or even direct interviews, that invite participants' attention, curiosity, and even speculation about researchers' intentions. Bias is always possible in any type of social psychological research, but its potential presence is lessened when—as in the case of archival data—the original participants remain truly unaware that their responses are being tallied or reviewed.

In practical terms, doing archival research in social psychology requires a researcher to systematically delve into records or other documentation that shed light on some research question. What sorts of records or documents? Psychologists have been known to examine court records, want ads, personal ads, newspaper stories, old posters, films, crime reports or statistics—really, any account that describes the behavior of a person or people from which psychologically relevant information can be drawn.

Table 5.7 lists some possible sources for archival data—you will no doubt think of others (jot them down at the bottom of the table or in your research notebook). Naturally, researchers hope that their chosen database will be objective and unbiased. They must take steps to ensure these qualities are present, including identifying inaccurate

Table 5.7 Some Archival Sources for Social Psychological Research

Newspapers	Hospital or medical records
Magazines	Telephone logs
Court reports or records	Resumes
Yearbooks	Letters
Diaries	Clinical case files or records
Census data	Email correspondence
Personal ads	Family photo albums
Accident reports	Graduation or other student records
Videotapes	Public speeches
Obituaries	The Internet
Letters to the editor	"Hits" on an Internet web site
Wants ads, classified ads	Graffiti
Sales figures	Recyclable materials, trash

or missing information, correcting erroneous or false entries, and verifying that the original record keepers avoided making subjective judgments (unless such judgments support a researcher's hypothesis, such as uncovering selective bias; see, e.g., Gould's, 1996, reanalysis of data on race and brain size).

Let's consider a popular source of timely information we can all relate to and access with relative ease: the sports pages of the newspaper. Lau and Russell (1980; see also Lau, 1984) read and coded the attributions—personal, causal judgments—of athletes, coaches, and sports writers in the daily sports pages. Their interest was to see how these individuals explained the win or loss of a team following a baseball or a football game. Specifically, Lau and Russell tested a particular prediction of attribution theory, namely that we are motivated to make internal (self-related, often self-enhancing) explanations for our successes (i.e., wins) and offer external (situationally dependent, often beyond our control) accounts for our failures (i.e., losses; see, e.g., Miller & Ross, 1975). The researchers predicted that quotations from postgame interviews or analysis would reveal self-serving bias, that is, relatively more internal attributions would be offered in the case of wins than for losses.

Lau and Russell (1980) developed a coding system and systematically evaluated sports articles from eight daily newspapers during the autumn of 1977. As anticipated, they found a clear motivationally based trend where success was attributed internally: About 75% of the attributions of a winning team were internal, whereas less than 55% of those from losing teams were internal. The researchers also found that more attributions were offered after unexpected outcomes (e.g., a team was favored to win but lost) than expected ones (e.g., a losing team lost, a home court advantage prevailed).

Lau and Russell (1980) raised an important methodological point about archival data: Interpretation can be in the eye of the beholder, which means that researchers must be careful their desire to confirm a hypothesis does not bias their work. Consider two hypothetical attributions a player from one team might make regarding the other team's performance: "Those guys played a better game that we did" and "Our team played a worse game than they did." These two comments reflect and report the same conclusion, and as such, are typical in player interviews and newspaper stories. But look again—in the study of causal attributions for success or failure, the first one would be labeled as "external" (i.e., the other team played better than we did) while the second would be coded as "internal" (i.e., we played worse than the other team")— speaking methodologically, which is which (see also Monson & Snyder, 1977; Ross, 1977)? And what does that decision harbor for psychological explanations for motivation where the perception of success or failure is concerned? The point is that the archival researcher must take care to think through the different ways that a mute fact—an observation, a recorded comment, a quotation—is interpreted before deciding which account is definitive. Because this example of archival research is not experimental, there will always be some doubt about how to precisely interpret a causal judgment of a win or a loss. Following Lau and Russell, however, a conscientious researcher should always point out potential flaws where interpretations and conclusions are concerned.

What about an archival source that is not dependent on the printed word? Can images, specifically, posed pictures, be used to explore social psychological theory? Harker and Keltner (2001) conducted an interesting study relying on a familiar photographic archive—college yearbook photos taken at age 21—and linked them to the same people to learn how they were faring socially and emotionally 30 years later. These researchers explored the claim that individual differences in emotion do shape our personalities and life outcomes across time. Using the Facial Action Coding System (FACS; Ekman & Friesen, 1978), trained raters coded positive emotional expressions displayed by women in college yearbook photos drawn from the Mills College senior classes of 1958 and 1960. These same women were part of the Mills Longitudinal Study, a long-term research project tracing the lives of graduates from this private women's college in Oakland, CA (Helson, 1967). Previously, at ages 21, 27, 43, and 52, these participants completed various psychological and self-report measures, including some focused on emotionality, affiliation and nurturance, competence, and long-term life outcomes focused on marriage (marital status, satisfaction, tension) and personal well-being.

Very often, we judge people's personalities and presume the presence of particular attributes based on their facial expressions. Thus, to add a degree of realism by treating the women's emotional expressions in a more active social vein, Harker and Keltner (2001) had a group of male and female undergraduate students carefully examine a sample of the yearbook photos. These untrained judges were asked to form impressions of the women based on their photos and to reflect on what meeting the women might be like (e.g., a positive or a negative experience) and to rate the women's personalities.

As predicted, the presence of genuine, positive emotions in the photos were associated with the women's self-reported personality traits including affiliation, competence, and low negative emotionality from the early 20s though adulthood. Moreover, positive emotionality (denoted by sincere rather than false smiles) was an effective forecaster for good marital outcomes (being or remaining married, high levels of marital satisfaction, low tension with spouse) and personal psychological well-being across three decades. What about the student judges' judgments of the photos? The students' personality judgments were related to the women's self-reported personalities (e.g., a warm smile was judged to predict a warm personality, which it did). The students anticipated that actual encounters with those women with positive facial expressions would be positive rather than negative. Pictures are worth a thousand words, at least where the expression and anticipation of favorable, pleasant emotions are concerned.

A decided strength of Harker and Keltner's (2001) study is the judicious mix of established record (data coded from photographs) with self-report measures of personality and social well-being (e.g., marital status, stability, and satisfaction) and even the expectations of observers 30 years after the yearbook photos were taken. What about shortcomings? The researchers acknowledge that no photos of men were used in this project, and existing research demonstrates that women tend to smile more and with more strength in high school and college yearbook photos than do men (e.g., LaFrance & Banaji, 1992). This difference is worth considering and exploring empirically. Finally, Harker and Keltner make the observation that the photos are "silent" when it comes to explaining whether positive emotional expressions or positive experiences are the key to good outcomes across time. Again, the nonreactive nature of archival methods can be a strength when it comes to preventing subjectivity from clouding conclusions. On the other hand, the absence of relevant reactive measures prevented these researchers from addressing this interesting point.

Still, archival methods offer unique opportunities to social psychologists. The strengths of archival research include:

- Data can be quantitative (e.g., counts of something, sales figures) or qualitative (interviews, case studies)
- The data are already collected—they need only be verified for accuracy and analyzed in light of the researcher's hypothesis.
- No manipulation of independent variables is necessary (of course, a researcher must be scrupulous about drawing definitive causal conclusions).
- Unusual, rare, atypical, or long past behaviors or beliefs can be examined in light of current theory or social experience.

However, enthusiasm for the archival approach must be appropriately tempered by reality. There are some drawbacks to this method, such as:

- Data may be false, fabricated, incomplete, or otherwise suspect.
- The original record keepers were not intentionally developing an archive for future researchers.
- Any conclusions cannot be causal, only suggestive.
- Archival methods often identify questions that can only be answered by additional, experimentally focused research.

Perhaps the ideal approach is to mix archival research with other methods including, of course, experimentation. Really, no method or research tool should be used in isolation or relied upon exclusively. And in any case, "No [single] research method is without bias" (Webb et al., 1981, p. 1). Overdependence on any one research approach not only opens the door to bias and error, it is simply not very creative.

Summarizing studies of social behavior: Meta-analysis

Related to but distinct from archival research is a technique for performing a study of separate studies on the same psychological topic (Glass, 1976). In other words, an existing archive aimed at understanding one psychological effect or observation is analyzed. A *meta-analysis* is an advanced statistical technique that assesses the effects of independent studies examining the same psychological effect or phenomenon (e.g., Cooper & Hedges, 1994; Ling, 2004; Lipsey, 2001; Rosenthal, 1991). When performing a meta-analysis, a social psychologist will search the literature for all studies exploring a particular hypothesis or demonstrating a specific effect or finding. In a sense, the published or otherwise obtainable literature serves as an archive of sorts. Meta-analytic techniques allow a researcher to combine together all the results of disparate studies that used different samples of people, different dependent measures, and found significant as well as nonsignificant differences between groups. A meta-analysis provides a way for researchers to verify the existence of some effect by identifying it as a consistent and predictable pattern of behavior.

A successful meta-analysis benefits future researchers who elect to study some social psychological effect further. The results can help researchers gauge how difficult it can be to observe a small, medium, or large effect when planning to conduct a study. An effect size indicates the measured strength of association among some variables in a study or the observed magnitude of some experimental result (e.g., Cohen, 1988). Effects sizes are a good guideline to determining how many participants will need to be recruited for a given study (cf., power analysis in chapter 4).

Social psychologists often perform a meta-analysis to summarize quantitatively what is known about a particular question or topic. During the writing of his doctoral dissertation back in the 1950s, for example, Robert Rosenthal unwittingly discovered what has become known as the *expectancy effect* (also known as the "self-fulfilling prophecy"; we specifically discuss how expectancy effects can be problematic for experimental research in chapter 10). Rosenthal observed that how he interacted with research participants often led them to behave in accordance with the hypothesis being tested in his experiment. His (research) expectancies affected (influenced) the participants' behavior. Any social psychologist wants to confirm the experimental hypothesis, of course, but for the right reason—because the observed effect is both true and real; not because the participants unknowingly recognize and comply with the experimenter's wishes. Expectancy effects have been demonstrated in the context of animal learning (that's right—an animal, in this case a rat—learns and confirms expectations "transmitted" from a student trainer; Rosenthal & Fode, 1963) and in the classroom (students randomly labeled "intellectual bloomers" subsequently outperform their peers—but only the teachers knew who was or was not expected to bloom; see Rosenthal & Jacobson, 1968).

What is truly remarkable about the expectancy effect phenomenon is the number of studies conducted since the 1950s that verify the presence or influence of the effect. Indeed, in 1978, Rosenthal and Rubin published an article summarizing 345 studies using meta-analysis (see also Rosenthal & Rubin, 1980). No doubt many additional studies have appeared since this 1978 meta-analysis—expectancy effects are robust. A more recent publication by Rosenthal (1994a) offers a short but reflective (and quantitative) account of the importance of expectancy effects, which are found in management settings, nursing homes, and courtrooms, probably anyplace where people have the opportunity to influence one another.

Meta-analysis is obviously an advanced topic, one dependent on statistical sophistication and deep knowledge regarding a research question or area of inquiry. Nonetheless, meta-analytic studies are not only becoming more common in the social psychological literature, they are extremely useful when it comes to supporting theoretically based arguments with actual, demonstrated results. As a student of social psychology, it is possible that you will come across a meta-analytic study in the course of doing library research for your research project and accompanying paper—thus you should be familiar with the concept. Table 5.8 lists some review articles related to social

Table 5.8   A Sampling of Topical, Meta-Analytic Review Articles

---

Conformity

Bond, R. U., & Smith, P. B. (1996). Culture and conformity: A meta-analysis of studies using Asch's (1952b, 1956) line judgment task. *Psychological Bulletin, 119,* 111–137.

Deindividuation and Anti-Social Behavior

Postmes, T., & Spears, R. (1998). Deindividuation and antinormative behavior: A meta-analysis. *Psychological Bulletin, 123,* 238–259.

Gender Differences

Eagly, A. H., Crowley, M. (1986). Gender and helping behavior: A meta-analytic review of the social psychological literature. *Psychological Bulletin, 100,* 283–308.

Eagly, A. H., & Steffen, V. J. (1986). Gender and aggressive behavior: A meta-analytic review of the social psychological literature. *Psychological Bulletin, 100,* 309–330.

Feingold, A. (1994). Gender differences in personality: A meta-analysis. *Psychological Bulletin, 116,* 429–456.

Physical Attractiveness

Eagly, A. H., Ashmore, R. D., Makhijani, M. G., & Longo, C. (1991). What is beautiful is good, but . . . : A meta-analytic review of research on the physical attractiveness stereotype. *Psychological Bulletin, 110,* 109–128.

Feingold, A. (1992). Good-looking people are not what we think. *Psychological Bulletin, 111,* 304–341.

---

and personality psychology that relied on or incorporated a meta-analysis. You will also note that all these citations are from the journal *Psychological Bulletin*, which frequently publishes meta-analytic reviews.

Guidance for performing actual meta-analyses is available in the work cited previously (see especially Rosenthal, 1991, 1993; Cooper & Hedges, 1994). Finally, for would-be meta-analysts, guidelines for writing meta-analytic reviews are also available (e.g., Rosenthal, 1995b).

Conclusions

"Social psychologists should not be one-trick ponies" (Mark & Reichardt, 2004, p. 284).

As this chapter has amply demonstrated, there is more to life—research life and the methods it embraces—than the stalwart true experiment. Experiments in general may offer a more certain insight into the nature of what factors directly cause the richness of much social behavior, but by no means *all* social behavior. Unusual, unexpected, or ethically demanding events, as well as situations that do not lend themselves to random assignment, careful control, and direct manipulation and measurement of variables, are still worthy of critical study. Social psychologists have evolved and adopted a diverse array of techniques aimed at filling in gaps in our understanding of why people behave as they do when real or imagined others are present.

Social psychology would be shortsighted if only true experiments were the source of ideas, insights, and theories. Instead, the ideal approach to learning about people is to use an array of methods that complement one another. Some of the most creative researchers examine an effect first in the controlled confines of the lab before venturing out into the field, where niceties of control and causal inference are more difficult to obtain. Still other researchers observe an event in the real world and then later, once they understand it better, only then do they attempt to recreate and "harness" it in the lab. The point is that a variety of different methods are used depending on the unique circumstances researchers face. Social psychologists are creative and resourceful; they are not limited in their vision or the methods they can use. They are certainly not—nor should be they—one-trick ponies in the search for adequate explanations of social behavior.

Exercises

1 Select a sight on or off campus and conduct a brief observational study (see Table 5.1 for potential sites and behaviors). What difficulties, if any, did you encounter when coding behavior? Would a second observer agree with your coding system and observational record? Why or why not?

2 What changes in rules have occurred on your campus lately? Have these changes resulted in any behavior changes? Describe a quasi-experiment that could be designed and conducted to demonstrate whether any changes actually occurred.

3 If you were to conduct an ESM study, what daily experiences would you want to examine? What do you think a record of ESFs would reveal?

4 Identify some archival sources that could be used to characterize the students who attended or are currently attending your institution. What would these sources reveal?

Chapter 6

Developing Questionnaires and Surveys

One of the most famous moments in American political history involves faulty surveys. In the 1936 presidential election, political pundits and polls predicted that Alfred Landon would handily defeat incumbent Franklin Delano Roosevelt. Following the first Tuesday after the first Monday in November, however, the result was actually a landslide victory by Roosevelt the Democrat over Landon the Republican. What happened?

The culprit was an understandable overconfidence caused by polls based on non-random sampling of the electorate. Pollsters relied on surveys of registered voters drawn from phone books, automobile registrations, and lists of magazine subscribers. Although these data sources proved to be accurate in earlier elections, the Great Depression drove low wage voters—those who had no phones, cars, or subscriptions—to cast their votes for Roosevelt. Wealthier folks still voted for Landon, of course, but their numbers paled in comparison to the mass of poorer voters. The rest is political history, history that repeated itself in the 1948 election when underdog incumbent Harry S. Truman defeated the anticipated winner Thomas Dewey (a famous photo from the time shows a triumphant Truman holding up a Chicago newspaper declaring that "Dewey Defeats Truman"; see Figure 6.1). Dewey's presidential aspirations, too, were done in by bad polling coupled with voters who switched their allegiance at the last minute.

In our time, we are used to political polls being relatively accurate, just as we are accustomed to answering lots of surveys and assorted questionnaires. Social and personality psychologists rely heavily on surveys and questionnaires in their research projects. Indeed, it is the rare study that relies exclusively on behavioral measures. Most experiments or other investigations have at least one or more self-report measures. By "self-report," I refer to any survey, questionnaire, rating scale, or other measure that is language-dependent. Behaviorally speaking, self-report measures ask research participants what they did in the past, what they are currently doing, or how they anticipate acting in the future. Participants write down a sentence or a paragraph, circle a number, check a box, or otherwise provide some personal, private reaction to a research prompt.

People generally take it on faith that their own responses to such questions are valid indicators of how they think and feel about any number of topics. Social psychological

Figure 6.1.   "Dewey defeats Truman"

research reveals quite convincingly, however, that individuals are often in error when it comes to reporting on the nature or content of various mental states (e.g., Nisbett & Wilson, 1977; Wilson, 2002). In other words, people believe that they are in a unique position when it comes to reporting on their thoughts and feelings, but they may not be (Bem, 1972). What could seem more true than self-knowledge? Who knows you better—what your favorite color is, for example, or why you never eat strawberry ice cream—than you yourself? To question one's own accuracy regarding self-knowledge seems ridiculous, even absurd. Yet various studies illustrate quite convincingly that self-reports are not always reliable and valid indicators of why people behave as they do (for a review, see Wilson, 2002). Let's consider a well-structured example.

Caveat Emptor: Let the (Jam) Buyer Beware

Have you ever taken part in a taste test where you were asked to rank order some product from best to worst tasting? Not all of us have done so in formal settings, but we have certainly done so informally. In fact, our shopping habits reveal our preferences quite well. We choose some salad dressings over others, for example, and many of us would never dream of putting certain soft drinks into ourselves, let alone our shopping carts.

We are confident of our choices and our preferences. We know what we like and, moreover, what products we should or should not buy. If asked, we can quickly offer reasons for our choices and our feelings about them. But how accurate are such explanations? This confidence, no, this certainty, raises a research question: Can we ever think too much about product choices? Can the consequences of our introspection be disruptive by leading us to make poor choices? If so, what might that mean for our responses to more general surveys that make us think about how we feel?

Wilson and Schooler (1991) had undergraduate students take part in a strawberry jam taste test. Participants tasted five jams that had previously been rated and ranked by expert tasters at *Consumer Reports* magazine. The criteria the experts used to arrive at the jam rankings included smell, sugary taste, sourness, and the like. The students were told they would taste spoonfuls before rating their liking for each jam. Before the tasting began, however, half the participants were randomly assigned to a control condition. The others were placed in a reasons analysis condition. The "reasons" participants were specifically instructed to "analyze why you feel the way you do about each" jam sample "to prepare yourself for your evaluations" (p. 183). As they tasted each jam, the reasons tasters listed reasons they liked or disliked each jam (control participants completed an unrelated questionnaire about their college major). At the end of the tasting, participants in both groups rated each jam on a 9-point scale, which ranged from (1) *disliked* to (9) *liked*.

Sounds simple enough, right? Wilson and Schooler (1991) predicted that prompting participants to think about reasons would actually alter their evaluations of the jams. Further, the researchers believed that the reasons analysis manipulation would result in preferences that were less than optimal; in short, the reasons students' ratings were presumed to be less likely to match the evaluations of the *Consumer Reports* expert raters.

What happened? In general, the reasons analysis group's evaluations did not match the ratings given by the control group. As expected, when Wilson and Schooler correlated the experts' jam rankings with the control group's rankings and the reasons group's rankings, greater agreement was found between the former ($M = .55$) than the latter ($M = .11$). What caused the lower agreement in reasons condition? Wilson and Schooler argue that the reasons group brought to mind ad hoc reasons that disagreed with the experts' jam evaluations, prompting them to adopt the attitude (pro or con) toward the products suggested by these reasons.

The problem here, of course, is that, unlike the control group, the reasons students' taste preferences no longer jibed with those of experts. The students changed their minds about how they felt about the jams as they thought of reasons for their feelings. Presumably, many of the new reasons were treated as more important (e.g., "this jam has an unattractive color," "these seeds are too crunchy") than the more legitimate reactions they had when they first tasted the jam. Thus there may be times and situations where we should not analyze the reasons underlying our preferences too much. Of course, not all questionnaire or surveys will prompt us to perform a reasons analysis, and such self-reflection is not always problematic (Millar & Tesser, 1986; Wilson, Dunn, Kraft, & Lisle, 1989). The lesson here is that we, as researchers, should be careful when it comes to asking questions.

The Obvious Advantage of Asking Questions

If you want to know what people think, why not just ask them? Observations like this one are useful when a social psychologist decides to create a questionnaire or a survey. Questionnaires are a general label given to almost any systematic attempt to learn what people think about an issue, a person, or an experience. Most questionnaires require some form of written response or the checking of a box or item in a list. Some are delivered verbally, as is the case during an interview or the debriefing portion of a study (see chapters 8 and 10, respectively). Questionnaires are often administered to learn how people think, feel, or act regarding something. Social psychologists often use questionnaires as a starting point, a way to find out how many people respond to some social situation or event.

Surveys, which were briefly introduced in chapter 5, are also dependent on written or verbal responses. However, the goal of a survey is slightly different than that of a questionnaire. Surveys are designed to characterize the general response of some sample of people in order to capture the likely sentiment of the larger population from which they were drawn. Questionnaires can sometimes achieve this end, but that is not their usual purpose. Instead, most questionnaires simply portray the thoughts and feelings of the individuals who are participating in an experiment or other social psychological investigation. Questionnaires, then, are often used in tandem with other research methods, such as overt measures of behavior (i.e., researchers often want to learn the degree to which people's verbal reports correspond to their actions).

The goal of this chapter is to demonstrate social psychological matters underlying the construction of questionnaires. The main issue here is not the topic you ask about but, rather, the sample you poll and how you ask questions concerning the topic. Where questionnaires and surveys are concerned, the phrasing of questions is a critical matter, one that can profoundly affect what a social psychologist can learn from research participants. Both of the examples that opened this chapter reflect this goal. Landon did not win over Roosevelt and Dewey did not defeat Truman, but such electoral outcomes were anticipated because of sample bias and poor survey methodology. As the Wilson and Schooler (1991) study illustrates, asking people to report their feelings regarding a decision can sometimes be a problem, especially if they lack sufficient knowledge about a topic or have never thought about it before (i.e., sometimes we really don't know how we feel). Note that a lack of knowledge does not prevent people from answering almost any question. Our linguistic abilities provide us with many advantages, not least of which is the ability to construct thoughtful, if completely ad hoc, explanations for almost anything. Most people want to avoid looking foolish, thus they rarely report that they "don't know" why they did one thing or failed to do another. We all like to appear to be consistent, for example, not to mention that sometimes we may actually be unaware that we are constructing an attitude or an answer off the cuff or in the moment.

One last comment before we begin: There is an art and a science to conducting survey research. In this single chapter, I can only introduce some of the most basic principles of survey research, as well as issues that are common to constructing questionnaires and surveys (chiefly, how to craft clear questions). As Schwartz, Groves, and Schuman (1998) wisely point out, most social psychologists are users, not producers, of survey data. Many large data archives are available to social researchers who select from preexisting sets of questions and responses (usually numbering in thousands) to test out hypotheses. When social psychologists decide to conduct a large-scale survey (e.g., national opinion survey), they are likely to contract the services of professional survey researchers rather than attempt the work on their own. Nonetheless, all students of social psychology need a basic introduction to working with surveys and questionnaires like the one provided in this chapter. For a more detailed introduction, consult the Schwartz et al. reference (see also Schuman & Presser, 1981).

Sampling Issues

One of the harsh realities of the social and behavioral sciences is that you cannot poll every person to learn how they think, feel, and behave. Much of the time, researchers rely on various techniques to estimate or "guess" how the untapped majority would likely respond if they could be interviewed. Why bother worrying about people who cannot or did not take part in a study?

Whenever possible, social psychologists want the results of their research efforts to generalize beyond the experiment or study they conducted. This goal is dependent on the source and quality of the participant sample, as well as whatever randomizing techniques were used (recall chapter 4). When crafting and conducting a survey, a researcher wants to accurately portray the beliefs or opinions shared by some group. Ideally, the responses of this group can be used to describe the beliefs of others who are similar to but were not included in the survey. Researchers rely on a sample of responses in order to learn what the larger population is apt to be like.

We introduced samples and populations in chapter 4 but a brief review is in order. A sample is a small subset of responses drawn from a larger population of complete responses. When a sample is conceived appropriately—ideally, a random sample is drawn, one with no biasing properties—then a researcher can use the sample's characteristics to infer the qualities of the larger population. Public opinion polls, which usually employ phone interviews, are routinely used to portray how some population—registered voters, retirees, freelance workers, environmentalists—think or feel about some relevant issue. Sampling procedures are used to discern everything from a politician's political standing to the preferred flavor of toothpaste.

Samples and the statistical and methodological logic underlying them are essential to social psychological research. Whether we are talking about a class, a college, a county, a state, or an entire nation, most populations are simply too big to be handled on a case-by-case basis. Thus complete or "exhaustive" sampling is rarely done, usually only when a researcher considers the population to be small enough to be completely measured. If you live in a campus dormitory, for example, you could collect responses from everyone on your floor or perhaps even the entire building. If you did so, you could claim to be able to describe the opinions of the "entire" population of your floor or the dorm as long as you made no attempt to generalize beyond it (this particular polling method is actually called a *census*, which is time-consuming, rarely feasible on a large scale, and done for a specific purpose, such as the national census designed to characterize the US population). You could not be certain, for example, if the opinions you gathered were similar to those found on another floor in another dorm elsewhere on campus.

As we will see, there are other approaches to sampling besides the simple random sample, which is rarely used in psychological research, and random assignment to condition. As you already know, random assignment is very often the method of choice when conducting a social psychology experiment. There are, however, other sampling approaches that researchers use, especially when it comes to conducting questionnaire or survey research.

Probability and nonprobability samples

There are two categories of samples: probability and nonprobability samples. A *probability sample* is any sample where the people in it were chosen by chance (e.g., via a random numbers table, drawing straws, flipping a coin). Simple random sampling is the most familiar and frequently used form of probability sampling (for a review, see chapter 4). A less familiar but sometimes useful approach is systematic sampling. A *systematic sample* is one where the researcher selects every *i*th case found in the sample.

Suppose you are interested in the health habits (e.g., exercise, diet) of medical professionals: Do they practice what they preach to patients? You know that 80 professionals are attending a workshop on your campus and you have a list of their names. You decide to systematically sample and survey 10 of them, so you close your eyes and pick a starting point on the list with your pencil—you happen to land on the fifth name. You then choose 10 names by sampling every eighth name (i.e., 80 divided by 10 is 8) after the starting point (i.e., 5 + 8 = 13, followed by 21, 29, 37, 45, 53, 61, 69, 77, and 5). Upon reaching the end of the list, you must return to the beginning (after the 77th individual, the next eighth person is number 5).

Systematic sampling is quick and easy to perform; however, it has a shortcoming. Can we be certain that the resulting sample is at all a random one? Regrettably, no, as each of the medical professionals in our hypothetical sample did not have an equal opportunity of being selected for inclusion in the sample. The problem is that systematically sampling from this or any list imposes a nonrandom order on the process: Every eighth name following the fifth one on the list was chosen. Why is this standardization a problem? Consider the fact that some names (e.g., Smith) occur more frequently than others (e.g., Zimmerman) and that surnames beginning with some letters (e.g., S) will have more last names than others (e.g., Q). Oversampling of some names or names that begin with some letters can result, which means the sample is not (probabilistically speaking) random. Indeed, such convenience trumps randomization so that we cannot presume that this or any systematic sample will allow us to generalize much beyond the sample itself. If generalization to other groups is less critical, however, then systematic sampling is a very viable approach to effectively gauging the opinions of a sample of people.

A somewhat better approach to establishing a probability sample is stratified sampling. *Stratified sampling* is concerned with adequately representing various subpopulations that are present in the larger parent population. Perhaps you wanted to survey the psychology majors who attend your school. Before beginning, you would need to keep a few things in mind. First, at the present time, most psychology majors in the United States are women, so you need to be sure they are overrepresented in whatever sample you create. Imagine your school had 100 women majoring in psychology and 30 men. If you decided on a sample of 10%, then you would poll 10 women and 3 men. Second, you would also want to make certain you were taking into account how many students were at the sophomore, junior, and senior levels when creating your sample (let's assume that first year students are not permitted to declare a major). If there are more seniors than juniors, for example, then you would be certain to poll more of the former according to their percentage representation in the population, and so on for the other groups. Stratified sampling is best accomplished by randomly sampling from a list of names that appropriately categorizes the relevant subpopulations (i.e., senior women, senior men, junior women, junior men).

Stratified sampling is a particularly good choice when the larger population has numerous subgroups whose opinions should be represented in any sample. Certainly you can imagine situations where the representation of racial, ethnic, or religious minorities would matter, or even where proper sampling of age groups, education or income level, or job classification (e.g., white collar, blue collar) would matter. On campus, students' membership in social or political organizations, car ownership (that old devil limited parking again!), athletic teams, and the like can dictate what form stratified sampling will take.

What about sampling procedures that ignore issues of probability for inclusion? *Nonprobability samples* lack randomization altogether, so that the people included in them are not selected by chance or in any way that systematically rules out biasing influences. Social psychologists elect to use nonprobability samples when they seek a quick answer to a question or when they intend to use random assignment once a sample is drawn. Use of a nonprobability sample is also appropriate when randomization is not feasible.

We introduced the most common type of nonprobability sample, the convenience sample, in chapter 4. *Convenience samples* are those comprising whatever people are at hand. On college campuses, where the bulk of social psychological research is conducted, convenience samples are made up of student volunteers who receive modest payment or course credit. A convenience sample drawn in a public place—a park, a mall, a sporting event—simply takes advantage of the (nonrandom) people who are gathered in a given place for whatever reason. Frisbee players in a park or hockey fans screaming in an arena are hardly random collections of people. Still, surveying their opinions is a better source of information than no source of information. Sometimes, of course, these haphazard or accidental samples (another label, meaning that a researcher "accidentally" included whoever happened to be around) are useful: If you want to begin to learn about vicarious aggression, who better to ask than fans at a hockey game? The chief limitation of all convenience samples is that there is really no way to know what biases are present in the responses of those who are surveyed.

Besides convenience samples, researchers sometimes rely on quota samples, which mimic the goals of stratified sampling. A *quota sample* makes an attempt to represent individuals from available subpopulations but without any randomizing element. Perhaps a social psychology student is curious about whether current fraternity and sorority members on the campus miss being allowed to put pledges through some hazing process (virtually all universities now outlaw these humiliating and often dangerous rituals). The student researcher decides to survey three members of each organization (the college has eight fraternities and six sororities), thus a sample of 42 people is needed. Abandoning any attempt to randomly select members from the 14 groups, the researcher simply visits each fraternity and sorority house, administering surveys to the first three people encountered at each place. Besides randomization, adequate representation is also lost, as the student researcher did not bother to worry about the number of members in each "house," their class standing, any leadership role in the organization, and so on. The goal of quota sampling is to create a quasi-representative sample as quickly as possible.

Table 6.1 lists and defines all of the probability and nonprobability samples reviewed in this chapter. Use this table as a quick reference for definitions or when you are considering conducting a questionnaire or survey study.

Table 6.1   A Summary of Probability and Nonprobability Samples

Preferred probability sample and assignment method
Random sample: each individual in a population has the same chance as all others of being selected to be part of a sample.
Random assignment: each individual in a group is assigned randomly to one condition in an experiment or other study.

Other probability samples
Systematic sampling: every *i*th member in a roll or list is included in a sample.
Stratified sampling: random samples of individuals are drawn from subpopulations identified in some larger population.

Nonprobability samples
Convenience sample: also known as haphazard or accidental samples are comprised of people who are available, willing, and interested in taking part in research. There is an attempt to gather people who are somewhat representative of a larger population, but bias, systematic or otherwise, cannot be ruled out.
Quota sample: sampling a number of people representing some special interest group or groups in a sizeable population.
Census: a sample comprising every individual in some population (e.g., residents of a town).

Scales of Measurement

A key assumption of research methodology in psychology is that internal, mental events (e.g., thoughts, feelings) are as measurable as external behaviors (see also chapter 8). This assumption has guided research efforts since the birth of psychophysics in the mid-19th century. The early experimental psychologists gravitated towards the study of the contents of consciousness, as well as memory, vision, audition, touch, and taste. As you already know, the early social psychologists were interested in measuring people's attitudes and how such social thinking affected behavior towards others (e.g., the LaPiere study discussed in chapter 1). Thus the ability to measure thoughts, feelings, and behaviors is a given in psychological research (for background on testing and measurement theory in psychology, see, e.g., Anastasi & Urbina, 1996; Gregory, 2003).

Social psychologists and other behavioral scientists rely on four scales of measurement when conducting research. Two of the scales—nominal and ordinal—are qualitative, while the other two—interval and ratio—are more quantitative. As we will see, most psychologists, especially social psychologists, rely primarily on interval scales. Nonetheless, a working understanding of all four types of scales will be helpful to you.

Although these scales are usually used for self-report purposes (how an individual thinks and feels about him or herself), the measures are often used for "other" reports (e.g., what a participant knows or presumes to be true about a family member, friend, peer, or acquaintance). In social psychology experiments, participants routinely complete scales that assess their reactions to "targets," people they just met or will soon meet. Personality researchers use combinations of self-report and other-report scales in order identify salient traits and behaviors (Funder, 1999, 2004).

Nominal scales

The simplest form of measurement involves naming things. A *nominal scale*, which is occasionally referred to as a *categorical scale*, organizes information by using a name or a label to categorize some observation. Nominal scaling has an "either–or" quality to it: You are either a male or a female, you did or did not graduate from high school, and your eyes are blue, brown, or green. Your social security number is a type of nominal scaling: The government stores information about you based on that number, which is much easier to work with than your actual name. License plate numbers, student identification numbers, apartment numbers, and the like serve a similar purpose. Take careful note of the fact that nominal scales only make qualitative, not quantitative, distinctions.

In the case of nominally scaling a person's sex, for example, a questionnaire asks for respondents to indicate "male" or "female" by "checking one." A researcher can then convert the responses to (arbitrarily) "1" for male and "2" for "female." This coding condenses qualitative information into a form that can later be quickly summarized as percentages or frequencies, or used to group responses to some other variable for comparison. Other individual characteristics are often nominally scaled, including religion, race, ethnicity, year in college, income level, and the like. In fact, when research participants answer demographic sorts of questions in a questionnaire or a survey, most of the items are nominally scaled.

Ordinal scales

Where nominal scales make no quantitative distinctions among categories, ordinal scales consider how observations are ordered or ranked. An *ordinal scale* orders or ranks observations in terms of whether one is greater or lesser than another on some dimension of value. Ordinal scales do not, however, reveal how close or far away observations are from each other. If you graduated fifth in your high school class, for example, then we know that your grade point average (GPA) was higher than the person who graduated sixth but less than that of your peer in fourth place. This simple example illustrates the "greater than and less than" of quality ordinal scales, as well as the scale's lack of sensitivity where absolute differences between observations is concerned. We know the ordering of your class and your rank in it, but not the individual GPAs of the students involved. Ordinal scaling, then, is useful when asking people to list their birth order, their preferences for some things over others (favorite foods, bands), or almost anything that can be ranked or ordered along one meaningful dimension.

Interval scales

Interval scales provide quantitative information about the differences between observations, a marked improvement over nominal and ordinal scales. In theory, the distance between observations on an interval scale is equal, ordinal, and measurable. Yet interval scales lack what is called a "true zero" point, that is, a 0 point below which no observations or ratings can occur. Most familiar standardized tests you know, such as the Scholastic Aptitude Test (SAT), as well as various intelligence or IQ tests, innumerable personality measures, and other psychological tests rely on interval scaling. Practically all of the tests and "pop" quizzes you have completed throughout your life are based on interval scales (including the classic 100 point exam). Finally, the simple, familiar 5 or 7-point rating scales so dear to the hearts and research programs of social psychologists are interval scales (we discuss these in greater detail later in this chapter).

There are two important aspects of interval scales to consider. The issue of underlying magnitude is the first: Suppose two people complete an interval measure of extroversion, one where higher numbers reflect a more sociable and outgoing personality. If one person has a score of 30 on the scale and the other receives a 60, does it follow that the second person is twice as extroverted as the first? No. Interval scales are based on ordered, mathematical relationships, but not ratios. The second point relates to the lack of a true zero point. Unlike ordinal scales, some interval scales, such as the Fahrenheit measure of temperature, can have negative values. If you have ever lived in a cold climate, then you know that temperatures routinely fall below zero, as when the temperature outside is −7 degrees. Interval scaling allows for such meaningful, if negative, numerical indexing of phenomena.

Ratio scales

A *ratio scale* possesses all the properties attributed to the other three types of scales and it has a true zero point. In practical terms, the presence of a true zero point means that although information can be absent, no ratio scale can have a value less than 0. Further, the ratios existing between measurements matter and are presumed to be equal. Ratio scaling is actually common in daily life. Driving speed is gauged on a ratio scale. When a car is standing still, it registers a speed of 0 miles per hour (mph), whereas on a typical highway, the car travels at 55 mph. Weight, too, is based on a ratio scale, which means that a 10 pound weight is twice as heavy as a 5 pound weight. Thus ratio scales possess the most flexible mathematical properties of all the scales of measurement.

Unfortunately, perhaps, few psychologists—including social psychologists—rely on ratio scales. Most use some form of interval scale, which are much easier to create and more convenient to use. However, some early social psychologists attempted to create interval scales that mimicked the idealized properties of ratio scales (i.e., equal intervals between psychological measures). Efforts in this vein include Thurstone's (1929) differential scale and Guttman's (1944) cumulative scale (see also Edwards & Thurstone, 1952). Generally, social psychologists prefer to carefully develop interval scales they hope will approach the idealized qualities of ratio scales.

I want to close this section with some practical information regarding data analyses and scales. Virtually everyone, students as well as researchers, rely on statistical software for analyzing the data collected in their studies. What is probably the most commonly used software package, SPSS (Statistical Package for the Social Sciences),[1] permits users to analyze data based on three scale types: nominal, ordinal, and scale. The last category—scale—refers to data based on both interval and ratio scales. In other words, SPSS does not distinguish between the two, a small but important fact you should know before you begin your analyses. If you are using some other software, you should check to see what, if any, distinctions are made for data from the four types of scales.

Types of Questions: Open-Ended and Close-Ended

As already acknowledged, the essential part of questionnaire and survey research is asking people questions. In order to ask questions so that you learn how people think,

---

[1]   SPSS is a registered trademark of SPSS Inc., 233 S. Wacker Drive, 11th Floor, Chicago, IL 60606.

feel, and behave, a researcher must know how to create questions that respondents can understand and answer appropriately. There are two broad classes of questions used in questionnaire and survey research: open-ended and close-ended questions.

Open-ended questions

Open-ended questions are phrased in ways that allow respondents a great deal of freedom when it comes to offering answers. Open-ended questions do not constrain respondents, who can write (or in the case of an interview, say) whatever they want in response to some prompt. Perhaps a social psychologist who is interested in study-ing jealousy in romantic relationships asks a sample of men and women to answer this open-ended question:

> If you and your romantic partner were attending a party, how would you feel if your partner spent a long time talking to someone of the opposite sex?

Note that this question allows the respondent to interpret a familiar situation in their own way; some respondents will raise the issue of romantic jealousy while others will not. Some responses will be brief ("I'd get mad" or "Who cares?") whereas others will be a long narrative ("I guess if my girl spent too much time with another guy I'd get upset and wonder what he was up to. If I knew him already it wouldn't matter but if he was a strange dude then I'd get pretty mad at him and probably at her too. . . ."). A decided strength of open-ended questions, then, is that they are often very motivat-ing to respondents, who can choose how much or little to say (Hoyle, Harris, & Judd, 2002).

This particular jealousy-related question also presumes a heterosexual relationship. For appropriate balance, a similar question focusing on "talking to someone of the same sex" should be added. Alternatively, a respondent's sexual orientation could be determined earlier in the questionnaire.

Open-ended questions are an excellent way to collect a large number of detailed responses that can help a social psychologist develop or refine hypotheses regarding some social behavior. Again, if you want to know what people think about some topic, then why not simply ask them to explain their thoughts to you? The strength of open-ended questions can also be a weakness: How can a researcher make sense out of so many detailed and often lengthy responses? When reading open-ended answers, a researcher should look for similar, frequent responses, which suggest that people share a common perspective. A researcher's goal is to categorize people's responses to search for themes or patterns. In the case of romantic jealousy, for example, the researcher would code the open-ended responses in search of self-reported anger, upset, distress, unhappiness, and the like. Additionally, the researcher might want to determine whether male and female respondents provided different kinds of answers pointing to jealous responses (e.g., Buss, 2000).

Of course, some open-ended responses are unintelligible. A respondent's hand-writing can be difficult to decipher, for example, or the response can be an incoherent "word salad." Alternatively, people often jot down answers that appear to have little to do with the question being asked. The problem is that a researcher cannot determine if the intent of the question was missed or misunderstood, or whether the respondent just felt like writing about something else. Other respondents will leave the space below the question blank or even draw a picture. The point here is that some responses will defy categorization so that little or nothing can be learned from them. Fortunately, many respondents will provide rich detailed answers that can be mined for ideas or insights into social behavior.

One more caveat regarding open-ended questions: Don't ask too many of them. If you ask too many open-ended questions, participants can become fatigued or even annoyed. In either case, the quality of the answers—and thus their usefulness to you—will suffer. A lot of open-ended questions means a lot of data coding, which will take a great deal of time. You may get more information than you need or can use. Instead, focus on asking a few good questions that should elicit a reasonable number of codable responses. Indeed, a very good idea is to balance the number of open-ended questions with a good sampling of close-ended questions.

Close-ended questions

Close-ended questions allow respondents a limited amount of freedom in terms of how they can respond. In general, most close-ended questions provide a few categorical responses respondents can choose from or they permit the selection or entry of some numerical response. Close-ended questions are a form of "forced choice" question, the kind that requires respondents to choose one response (or occasionally more) from a prescribed list of options. Any standard "yes–no" sort of question is a close-ended question, for example:

Do you have a high school diploma? _____ Yes _____ No (check one)

A related close-ended question with more alternatives could look like this one:

During high school, which of the following math-related courses did you complete (check all that apply)?

_____ algebra I
_____ algebra II
_____ geometry
_____ calculus
_____ computer science
_____ statistics
_____ other math course _____

In an example like this one, a list of alternatives can jog respondents' memories, allowing them to correctly describe their educational background. Being asked to provide an open-ended response to a similar question can result in a wrong or incomplete answer, especially for those respondents (like me) for whom high school is a vague memory. A second virtue is that preexisting categories allow a researcher to subsequently code respondents' answers quickly and efficiently, much more so than is the case for the laborious work associated with keeping track of open-ended responses. Finally, no list of alternatives is likely to be complete so, as shown in the above example, adding a brief, open-ended option ("other math course") is often a good idea.

Many numerical questions qualify as close-ended and are usually phrased in ways that allow respondents to answer using whole numbers. If you were surveying people about their exercise habits, you might ask them:

About how many hours per week do you work out or exercise? _____ hour(s)

Obviously, some people do not work out at all, so they can enter "0", whereas others exercise for less than an hour. They might enter .5 for half an hour or jot down "<1" meaning "less than an hour," and so on. Answers to numerical questions like this one can be reported as frequencies ("50 respondents exercise for 2 hours a week, 20 for an hour, and 5 for less than an hour"), a percentage ("Sixty percent of the respondents exercise for 3 hours or less per week"), or an average ("Most people in the sample exercise for an average of 2.5 hours per week").

The most common and useful numerical scale: The Likert scale

By far the most typical and familiar numerical questions are based on interval rating scales. Social psychologists depend heavily on rating scales for questionnaires used in experiments or other studies, as well as for survey work. The most common form of numerical rating scale is the Likert (pronounced "Lick-ert") scale, which is named for its creator, social scientist Rensis Likert (1903–1981). Likert scales come in a variety of forms, but they all share some common features and psychological assumptions. First, all Likert scales either rely on having respondents make numerical choices in order to reflect some reaction to a stimulus question (e.g., circling a number) or making a response on some continuum (say, marking an "x" on a line) that can later be measured and converted into a number.

Second, psychologically speaking, Likert scaling presumes that people's opinions or attitudes (recall the LaPiere study from chapter 1) fall on a continuum of some sort, that their views are not "polarized" or lumped together at one or the other extreme. Unlike "yes–no" sorts of questions, Likert scales allow respondents to report fine shades of meaning and depth of feelings. The extent of a respondent's support for some statement or idea is gauged on a graduated scale of possible response options.

Table 6.2 illustrates some of the more common forms of Likert scales. As you can see, each statement is accompanied by some rating scale (numerical, verbal, or continuum-based) that is anchored at the extremes by divergent points of view (usually some variation of "strongly disagree" and "strongly agree" or "strongly approve" to

Table 6.2 Some Standard Likert Scale Type Questions to Assess Opinion

a. Circle a number that best reflects your opinion:

Lowering the legal drinking age for alcohol from 21 to 18 is a good idea.

1	2	3	4	5
Strongly disagree				Strongly agree

b. Circle a number that best describes how you feel about the proposed tuition increase.

1	2	3	4	5	6	7
Strongly disapprove						Strongly approve

c. Put an "x" on the line shown below at the point that best illustrates your personal view: Students should not be allowed to process during graduation exercises unless they have completed all requirements for this honor.

Oppose [_____] Support

d. The new apartments being built on campus should be reserved for senior and junior level students exclusively. Place an "x" in the space that best describes your attitude.

Strongly disagree	Disagree	Tend to disagree	Tend to agree	Agree	Strongly agree

e. The Armed Services should be allowed to recruit on campus. Place an "x" in the space that best describes how you feel about this issue.

Strongly disapprove	Somewhat disapprove	Neutral	Somewhat approve	Strongly approve

"strongly disapprove," though, of course, other anchor labels are used). Respondents can select intermediate positions between the extremes in order to elect a more moderate or even a neutral position. Perhaps for this latter reason, most numerical or verbal Likert scales are either 5 or 7-point scales (see examples a and b in Table 6.2). Of course, a respondent is always free to select the mid-point along a continuum (see example c in Table 6.2).

Some researchers prefer rating scales that force respondents to come down on one side of an issue or the other (see d in Table 6.2). These researchers argue that people really do feel one way or another about issues, ideas, or people, that we are never truly neutral or ambivalent about anything. Still, I believe it is prudent to consider that as researchers, we may recruit some people in our studies who truly have never given much thought to some issues (e.g., legalizing marijuana). Thus we need to allow them to express the absence of a solid opinion at that point in time, something a neutral option allows (see example e in Table 6.2).

Many social and personality psychologists assume that almost *any* numerical rating scale qualifies as a Likert scale. In practice, many students and researchers refer to any generic numerical scale as a "Likert" scale. Strictly speaking, this label is inaccurate. In actuality, there is a proscribed procedure for creating a Likert scale. First, a researcher drafts a large number of statements concerning the research issue. Some sample from the population of interest evaluates them using whatever rating scale (e.g., 5 or 7 points) the researcher chooses. The final selection of scale items is made by determining which individual items are positively correlated with the total score (sum) of all the items. The items with strong positive associations are retained. Items with low correlations are dropped because they are less likely to discriminate between people with very positive or very negative attitudes towards the issue.

The final Likert scale should be made up of some number of items (a good range is between 10 and 20) that are phrased in both pro (e.g., "Increased taxes will improve public education") and con (e.g., "Good education does not result from higher taxes") directions about an issue. To determine an individual's score on the Likert scale, all ratings need to be in the same direction. The individual's ratings on the con items, for example, would need to be reversed (i.e., a rating of "1" on a 5-point scale would become a "5," a "2" would be a "4," and so on). The ratings for all the pro and reversed con items would then be summed. An individual with a high score would have a favorable attitude toward increasing taxes for education, while a person with a lower score would be less favorable towards higher taxes.

Admittedly, this sounds like a lot of work, especially for what is likely to be a short-term research project. Here's the good news: I am not suggesting that you adopt this procedure and abandon creating ad hoc numerical rating scales, what we will call "Likert-type" scales. I do, however, want you to know how ideal Likert scales are developed. Social psychologists frequently use Likert-type scales and other types of scales that resemble but do not adhere to the underlying theory, assumptions, or construction procedures advocated by their creators. Social psychologists are very flexible, adapting to constraints imposed by time, a participant sample, or the experiment or field situation where data collection is occurring. The great advantage of Likert-type rating scales is that they permit respondents to quickly and accurately portray their opinion regarding an issue. Subsequently, these responses can be quickly coded and analyzed. Naturally, most questionnaires will contain several Likert-type scaled items coupled with some mix of other close-ended and open-ended questions.

Writing Clear Questions

The actual writing of questions for a questionnaire or a survey is part of a larger process. Table 6.3 outlines a process for conducting a questionnaire or a survey study

Table 6.3   Steps for Executing a Questionnaire or Survey Study

Step 1:	Identify a topic and, if necessary, define a sample (see Table 6.1 for sampling approaches)
Step 2:	Determine the type of instrument (e.g., paper-and-pencil questionnaire, face-to-face or phone interview, Internet-based survey, experience sampling method; see chapter 5)
Step 3:	Draft the initial questionnaire and ask peers and professionals to critique it (see Active Learning Exercise 6A)
Step 4:	Pilot test the questionnaire on a few people, use their feedback to improve question clarity, and revise the questionnaire (see Active Learning Exercise 6B)
Step 5:	Administer the survey to the intended group or sample(s)
Step 6:	Code and analyze the data and then share the results in a report or other publication.

(as we already learned, the latter is more dependent on sampling issues than the former). The steps outlined in Table 6.3 capture the main activities of student researchers who are developing questionnaires and surveys. The steps needed for a large-scale survey are more detailed and involved (e.g., Schwartz et al., 1998); however, the goals of accurately portraying the "sense" of a sample or a population are the same. Keep this process outlined in Table 6.3 in mind as you learn how to write good questions that can inform your research effort.

When writing questions, three criteria should guide you:

1   *Content*: Do the questions adequately evaluate the topic of interest? Do the questions reasonably represent the breadth of the topic? Would other social psychologists agree that the topic is covered by the questions?
2   *Clarity*: Are the questions written in the plainest language possible? Have complex words been replaced by simpler ones? Are familiar terms used in place of unfamiliar, unusual, or rarely heard words?
3   *Shared meaning*: Do respondents interpret the questions the way the experimenter intended? Are respondents understanding the questions and reacting to them as anticipated? Questionnaires and surveys are not one-sided exchanges—both parties should agree on what is being asked and how it can be answered.

Once the questions are drafted, a fourth criterion comes into play:

4   *Length of the questionnaire*: Is the questionnaire an appropriate length? How many questions are too many? A questionnaire that is too long will alienate respondents, whereas one that is too short will not provide sufficient information for the researcher's purposes.

These four criteria shape a questionnaire or a survey's content and length. Keep them in mind as you learn about the additional guidelines that follow.

Phrasing

Social psychologists are likely to write questions or items that focus on one of three issues: what respondents know about something (e.g., factual knowledge); what they feel, think, prefer, or anticipate (e.g., attitudes, beliefs); and how they have acted in the past or expect to act in the future (e.g., behavior). Any questionnaire or survey is likely to contain items that touch on one or more of these issues. How the items are phrased in order to elicit clear, interpretable responses is important.

Be brief. When writing an open-ended or a closed-ended question, strive for brevity. Shorter questions tend to be more focused than longer ones and, in general, are easier for respondents to understand. Perhaps you are interested in people's close relationships, specifically their perceptions of close friendships. Here is the same item for a rating scale (anchored "strongly disagree" to "strongly agree") phrased in two different ways:

> When I think about my relationships with others, I realize that I have the right number of close friends for me.
>
> I have the right number of close friends.

The second item captures the same meaning as the first but in a much briefer form. When developing questions or items, the first step is to write down as many as you can. Once you have a reasonable list, edit each one so that needless words are omitted.

Phrase things positively. Positive statements are understood more quickly and easily than negative statements. Further, the presence of negative key words or phrases ("No indictment yet") can lead people to make unintended, even implicit social judgments (e.g., Wegner, Wenzlaff, Kerker, & Beattie, 1981). When writing a questionnaire or a survey, difficulties arise when people write questions that incorporate double negatives. A *double negative* is a statement or question containing two negative ideas that impede understanding. Consider this example:

> No one should be allowed to not pay taxes.

Clearer, simpler phrasing in a positive vein is:

> Everyone should pay taxes.

Don't use leading questions. A *leading question* is one that presumes what the answer should be in the course of asking the question. Leading questions can bias respondents' answers so that while researchers get the desired response, they do so for the wrong reason. Here is an example drawn from current events:

Most Americans honor the flag as an embodiment of our nation's heritage and values. Are you in favor of an amendment to ban flag desecration?

Leading questions can be a not-so-subtle attempt to persuade people to change their minds or at least to endorse a certain opinion this one time. Thus they have no place in a questionnaire or survey designed to learn how people actually feel about something.

Avoid jargon. What appear to be everyday terms for social psychologists and other social scientists are often easily misunderstood by respondents. Terms like "marital status," "sexual orientation," "party affiliation," and the like should either be explained in context or avoided altogether. When asking about a person's marital status, for example, an open-ended question like this one is probably not a good idea:

What is your marital status?

This short and simple question is actually imprecise. Instead of writing "I am married" or "I was divorced last year," some respondents might be moved to write a long and detailed narrative about their hopes for meeting the right person, how dating is difficult where they live, and so on. Instead, a few shorter, closed-ended questions might focus a respondent's replies:

1 Are you married? _____ yes _____ no
2 If you answered "no" to item 1, have you ever been married? _____ yes _____ no
3 If you answered "yes" to item 2, are you _____ divorced _____ a widow/ widower?

Naturally, a researcher must address the trade-offs imposed by having more than one question dealing with a standard demographic matter. An alternative might be a question like this one:

Are you currently married or living with a partner? I am _____ single (never married) _____ single (divorced) _____ single (widowed) _____ married or living with a partner

If a researcher wanted or needed to know whether a person was married more than once, an additional question or two might be needed.

Various psychological inventories, especially those that measure depression, are excellent models of how to avoid jargon, technical terms, or other "psychobabble." Respondents are not asked to think about depression using the terms bandied about by psychologists. Instead, they are asked to report how often in some time period, say, the last week, they have "felt blue," "cried," "could not get going," and the like. Basic, easily understood words and phrases like these are meaningful to practically everyone. Keep such straightforward language in mind as you craft questions.

Reading level or age appropriateness. Know your target audience—say, middle-aged people or middle school students—before you begin to write any questions. And in doing so, you should imagine someone who represents the theoretical average of that audience. If the words and content of your questionnaire do not fit your audience, they will neither understand what you are asking nor will their answers provide you with much useful information. It follows, too, that topics should be age and audience appropriate: Issues you present to college students are going to be more mature in content than those you would present to elementary school-aged students. A good rule of thumb for writing questions is to emulate local newspapers, most of which are written and edited so that anyone with a rudimentary education can read their contents. Pilot testing the draft survey on members of the target group is also a good idea (see Active Learning Exercise 6B below).

Double-barreled questions. Written language is not like spoken language. When we speak, we routinely run multiple ideas together with few breaks, yet almost everyone understands what we mean. This rule does not hold for written language, especially when questions are being asked. Running ideas together is not only confusing to read, it reduces the likelihood that people's responses will be meaningful or useful. When asking people to rate themselves, for example, the most common error is to ask people to answer two things at once.

> I am hardworking and honest (circle one):   True   False

These compound questions are called double-barreled questions. Some people think of themselves as honest and hardworking, but others do not. If people are really and truly honest to themselves and the researcher, then some will admit that they are not hard workers. Thus separating these concepts into two distinct items makes more sense:

> I am hardworking (circle one):   True   False
> I am honest (circle one):   True   False

I don't know. Previously, we noted that people rarely admit that they don't know about something or lack an opinion. They may decline to say "I don't know" in order to avoid embarrassment. Some of the time, however, respondents are prevented from electing this option because the researcher forgot to add it to the questionnaire or survey. Such forgetfulness is natural as an enthusiastic researcher becomes so interested in crafting focused questions that the fact that some respondents have never thought about the matter at hand is never considered. When people have an opportunity to admit that they "don't know," many will use it appropriately (Schuman & Presser, 1979).

There are two remedies to this problem. First, unless you are certain that all the people comprising your sample know a good deal about the topic of the questionnaire, you should assess "I don't know" or "no opinion" sorts of responses. When writing Likert-type items, for example, the neutral point in the scale can be converted to "Don't know" or "no opinion." The usual string of descriptions might be "strongly disagree," "disagree," "no opinion," "agree," and "strongly agree." In the case of open-ended questions, the general instructions at the start of the questionnaire could indicate that writing down "no opinion," "I don't know," or the equivalent is a legitimate response.

A second remedy is to rely on what are called filter questions. A *filter question* is designed to separate respondents who know about an issue from those who don't. A filter question appears before a single or set of substantive questions pertaining to an issue. For example:

> Are you a college graduate? _____ yes _____ no
> If you answered "yes," then please answer questions 1 to 14. If you answered "no," then please skip down to question 15.

In this example, people who have college degrees are supposed to answer the next 14 questions. Respondents who are still in college or who did not graduate from one are supposed to skip these questions and to continue with question 15.

Avoiding unnecessary conclusions. When writing a questionnaire or a survey, a researcher can easily make some assumptions about respondents that are unwarranted. Conclusions about research participants are drawn before we know anything about them or their opinions. Consider this simple example:

> How old is your car?

Many people, perhaps Americans in particular, cannot imagine life without a car nor can they envision not owning one. Yet many people in the world (and quite a few in the United States, especially residents of New York City) don't drive and don't own a car. In the spirit of filter questions, unnecessary conclusions can be avoided by writing two questions instead of one:

> Do you own a car? _____ yes _____ no
> If "yes," how old is your car? _____ years

Other questions that presume certain conclusions deal with careers and occupations (some people do not work for a living), employment (a person may have lost a job, quit, or be searching for a new one), education (not everyone went to college, not everyone completed high school). Similar care must be taken when asking about an individual's past behavior, "When you voted in the last election, which of the two senatorial candidates did you select?" As political scientists and ample newspaper stories can attest, voter participation tends to be low. You must never assume anything is true about your respondents—allow them to tell you about themselves freely and openly. Avoiding drawing unwarranted conclusions about respondents will not only lead to clearer and cleaner data, you will not risk antagonizing, embarrassing, or otherwise frustrating the people you have enlisted to help you with your research.

Never ask all-or-nothing questions. The careful phrasing of questions should demonstrate differences among people by revealing a range of responses. Questions that limit people's range of reactions—they all affirm the item or they all disagree with it—do not provide much information. Such "all-or-nothing" questions pose a problem for respondents and researchers. What do I mean by an all-or-nothing question? Imagine asking people to rate their level of agreement with this item:

> A responsible government feeds its starving children.

Feeding starving children? It is hard to imagine anyone disagreeing with this statement. What about this item:

> Poverty can never be eliminated.

Will poverty always exist? Most of us hope not, so very few people would be moved to agree with this statement. Certainly, *some* poverty has been eliminated and more can be, so this statement seems a bit extreme.

Statements like these illustrate what social psychologists refer to as ceiling and floor effects in the crafting of questionnaires and surveys. As was illustrated by the first example, a *ceiling effect* occurs when virtually all respondents are moved to agree with the statement (i.e., on a 7-point scale where higher numbers reflect greater levels of agreement, respondents circle a "6" or a "7"). Ceiling effects reflect responding at higher levels to a question. What about almost exclusively lower levels of response? The second item shows a *floor effect* where most people are moved to disagree with what is said (i.e., circling a "1" or a "2" on the same 7-point measure of agreement). Unless you are specifically trying to restrict your sample or the opinions represented within it, no item should prevent participants from sharing a range of responses.

Sequencing questions

Besides the phrasing of questions, the order in which they appear in a questionnaire or survey can matter a great deal. There are two issues to consider: the literal effects of order and what survey researchers refer to as context effects.

Question order. Unless there is a compelling theoretical reason for it, research participants should never be surprised. This rule holds true for respondents who complete questionnaires and surveys. If you are asking questions dealing with a controversial topic (e.g., abortion, sexuality, capital punishment, prayer in schools), you should not show your hand too soon. By that I mean that you want to introduce the topic gradually, with sensitivity, not abruptly. Begin the questionnaire with straightforward questions and move on to the more sensitive topic. As you do, bear in mind that the language you use, the tone of the questions, and the perspective you adopt—I assume one of scholarly neutrality—all matter. If you appear to have an agenda or to present a bias in the minds of your respondents, their cooperation and sincere willingness to share what they think or believe will dissipate. Thus the ordering of questions matters a great deal: Moving from noncontroversial to more controversial topics—all the while acknowledging the existence of divergent opinions—will demonstrate your sincerity. Later, this sincerity will manifest itself in the report you write, wherein you faithfully and accurately portray the reactions of your respondents.

Is there an ideal structure for questionnaires and the sequencing of questions therein? Although "local conditions" regarding a research topic (e.g., institutional rules, composition of and number of participants in the sample, printing costs, time available for respondents to complete the questionnaire) can have some influence, a reasonable structure to follow is this:

- Open with interesting but not overly challenging questions that engage the respondents. These "openers" should emphasize the purpose of the study and have clear relevance (Dillman, 1978). You want to make the respondents confident that they can complete the questionnaire without difficulty and that doing so will be a positive experience.
- After the opening questions, turn to the main focus of the questionnaire. If the topic is a controversial one, remember to gradually introduce the subject matter (a good idea is waiting to the second page before presenting any truly divisive issue). As noted earlier, topically related questions should appear together with appropriate filter questions. Skipping around, moving from one topic to another and back again, irks respondents. Your questionnaire should flow logically forward, never back.
- Novice researchers tend to believe that asking demographic questions first is a good way to begin—not so. These questions are best placed at the end of the questionnaire. When they get there, most respondents will be comfortable with the questions and their answers, so they will be willing to share private or personal information with the researcher. Suspicious or skeptical respondents simply won't answer the demographic questions; however, there is little reason to assume their earlier responses are "tainted" or "biased."

Context effects. Survey researchers have learned that ordering of questions is not the only factor that can affect the nature of participants' responses. Information that appears earlier in a survey can actually influence the responses people give later. These "carry-over effects" are problematic because an earlier question or questions can bias responses that appear much later in the questionnaire (Tourangeau & Rasinski, 1988; Tourangeau, Rasinski, Bradburn, & D'Andrade, 1989; see also Tourangeau, Rips, & Rasinski, 2000; see also chapter 5's discussion of within-subject research designs). People's earlier reactions to some issue, especially one that is sensitive or socially controversial, can alter the responses that follow later in the survey.

Here are two items from a phone survey dealing with abortion:

> Please tell me whether or not you think it should be possible for a pregnant woman to obtain a legal abortion if there is a strong chance of a serious (birth) defect in the baby.

> Please tell me about whether or not you think it should be possible for a pregnant woman to obtain a legal abortion when the woman is married and does not want any more children.

When the question concerning a potential birth defect came first in the survey, the number of pro-choice responses to the question dealing with the married woman fell (Schuman & Presser, 1996). When the married woman question was listed in advance of the birth defect question, however, respondents tended to give it favorable support.

The real concern here is that such carry-over effects alter how respondents are thinking about a questionnaire's topics as they work though it—these alterations do not, however, shed much light on how people really feel about the matter at hand. Carry-over effects create inconsistent responses that may mask not only what people think or feel, but how they typically behave. The real drawback is that unless different question orders are tested, survey researchers will not know that any carry-over effect is present.

Such carry-over effects are unlikely to be a concern for your social psychological research. Nonetheless, you should know about them and their detrimental effects, especially when it comes to reading about and critically evaluating large-scale surveys reported in the media.

Being sensitive

I thought about titling this subsection "Sex, drugs, and alcohol" because invariably several students in my social psychology methods classes very much want to study these topics. In particular, students want to know about their peers' sexual habits and orientations, use of recreational drugs, and how much beer is being consumed in a normal week. We might also add cheating on tests or plagiarizing papers to this list.

Such curiosity is understandable but usually has little relevance to social psychological research.

The golden rule where sensitive topics are concerned is a wise one: Only ask about sensitive issues—private, personal matters—if you must. Let's assume you have a sound, theoretically based reason for doing so. How should you proceed? As noted earlier, make way to the main issue gradually, not abruptly. When asking a sensitive question about a sensitive topic, such as illegal drug use, it is often best to give respondents a range of options. As Pelham (1999) suggests, people might be reluctant to answer a bold question like:

Do you regularly smoke marijuana?

A better approach is to reduce the tension by focusing on legal as well as illegal substances, as well as giving respondents a range of response options, as in:

Check any of the following substances you have ever used:

_____ Caffeine
_____ Marijuana
_____ Aspirin
_____ Alcohol
_____ Cocaine
_____ Methamphetamine

The social consequences of admitting one has smoked (if not inhaled) marijuana seem less dire when it is grouped with cocaine and methamphetamine. If people feel less inhibited then they are likely to be more honest. This is one example. How you approach other sensitive topics will depend on their nature and that of the population being questioned (e.g., although some cheating occurs in both groups, high school students are probably more honest about it than are college students). The best advice is to develop questions on such topics thoughtfully, asking yourself how you can ask probing questions without implying that you are passing any judgment on the respondents.

Last words on wording for questionnaires and surveys

As always, there is much to learn about this area of social psychological research. If you decide to conduct a project using a questionnaire or a survey technique, be sure to consult any of the numerous resources available (e.g., Converse & Presser, 1986; Schuman & Presser, 1996; Schwartz et al., 1998; Sirken et al., 1999; Tourangeau et al., 2000).

ACTIVE LEARNING EXERCISE 6A

Writing and Revising Questions

Reading about how to construct questions is not as useful as actually drafting some questions. Now that you have finished reading about how to write good questions, I suggest you actually try your hand at a few. Here is a step-by-step guide for doing so.

1 *Choose a topic for the questionnaire or survey*. Select a topic and identify key issues and resources. Imagine you were interested in what people think about the repeal of laws requiring that motorcyclists wear helmets. Before writing any items, explore the relevant issues (e.g., individual rights, public safety, insurance costs) and resources (e.g., accident rates, traffic fatalities) related to the topic.

2 *Draft an initial pool of items*. If you have difficulty drafting items, try the brainstorming exercise from chapter 2 (see Active Learning Exercise 2A).

3 *Critique the initial item pool*. Review this first pass at item development using the question writing guidelines presented in this chapter, which are summarized in Table 6.4. Using Table 6.4, revise, add, or drop items as necessary.

4 *Seek the counsel of experts*. Ask your instructor and class members to review your draft items. Revise, add, or drop items based on their feedback.

5 *Add an informed consent form and, if needed, a list of demographic questions to the items*. Ethical principles must be followed when conducting a questionnaire or survey study. Respondents should be informed whether

Table 6.4 Summary of Question Writing Guidelines

Keep the questionnaire or survey short and focused.
Write brief questions.
Phrase questions positively (no double negatives).
Avoid leading questions.
Eliminate jargon from items.
Match the complexity of words and ideas to the reading level of the audience.
Do not write double-barreled questions.
Provide respondents with opportunities to answer "I don't know" or "no opinion."
Use filter questions as needed.
Never draw unnecessary conclusions about respondents.
Do not use "all-or-nothing" types of questions.
Place demographic questions at the end of the questionnaire or survey.
Lead into sensitive or controversial topics gradually.

their responses will be kept anonymous, for example, and how their responses will be used (e.g., published in a report, used to generate items for subsequent questionnaires). An informed consent form (see chapter 3) should appear before the items and demographic questions should follow them.

6   *Pilot test the items*. Follow the directions found in Active Learning Exercise 6B.

ACTIVE LEARNING EXERCISE   6B

Pilot Testing Questions

This activity combines question writing skills with debriefing skills (see chapter 10). You need to recruit a few peers who are unfamiliar with your project or are otherwise representative of the target population you intend to question. Ask them to complete the draft version of your questionnaire or survey as best they can, and then interview them about their reactions to it (effectively, these are stages shown in Table 6.3).

After each pilot participant completes the draft questionnaire, as the experimenter, you should conduct a debriefing (see chapter 10). During each debriefing, you should explicitly ask about the questionnaire's content and question clarity in order to ascertain that the items were understood as you intended. Naturally, too, you should determine whether the questionnaire's length was appropriate. Any questions identified as difficult or confusing should be revised accordingly or dropped from the final version of the questionnaire or survey. Once the pilot testing is complete, you should begin to collect data from actual research participants or survey respondents.

Social Desirability Concerns, Halo Effects, and Yea-Saying

Survey researchers and measurement experts have long worried about the phenomenon of response bias. *Response bias* refers to an inclination to answer a set of questions in a consistent way not related to their content. Instead of providing thoughtful responses to a series of rating scales, for example, a participant might circle the same number (say, 3 on a 5-point scale) on each scale in order to finish quickly. Using this approach, the respondent might never even read the individual items embedded in the questionnaire. We will consider three common forms of response bias that social psychologists often encounter when constructing self-report measures: social desirability, halo effects, and yea-saying. We then briefly consider the advantage of allowing respondents to remain anonymous.

We like to be liked

People like to be liked. They like other people to think well, not ill, of them. Unfortunately, in the context of questionnaire and survey research, the desire to be well-liked or thought well of can create problems. Specifically, some respondents will go out of their way to provide answers that sound good or that read well but that are largely false or too good to be true. In other words, people share things that portray themselves in the best possible light (e.g., Baumeister, 1982). Sometimes respondents embellish the truth by making it seem more plausible, interesting, or likely. Other times they fear revealing the truth because they believe it may be too upsetting or embarrassing for others and for themselves.

Are you never late and always on time? Do you always tell the truth without considering the consequences to others' feelings? In spite of their faults and shortcomings, do you like and respect everyone? Do you routinely eat all your vegetables, even mushy peas or limp spinach (just kidding)? Even the most punctual person is occasionally late and sometimes a well-placed lie can save the feelings of a friend ("Why, yes, now that you mention it, I *do* like your new hairstyle").

Individuals who claim virtually perfect records when it comes to social life, niceties and all, are probably displaying what is known as social desirability response bias or socially desirable responding. *Social desirability response bias* or *social desirability* is a general tendency to highlight one's favorable qualities while underrepresenting one's less desirable characteristics. Social desirability is trait-like, so that individuals high in this quality always claim virtuous behavior and rarely, if ever, report even the most minor of social vices (e.g., nail biting, backbiting, procrastinating, telling little white lies).

If you think about it for a moment, socially desirable responding makes a great deal of sense. Few people want to admit their minor shortcomings to others because they worry how they will be perceived. For this same reason and with amplified concern, you can well imagine why people are loathe to disclose religious prejudices, racist attitudes, sexual activities that are viewed as outside the mainstream, any number of odd or unusual interests, or sometimes how they truly feel about current sociopolitical issues (e.g., abortion, gun control, gay marriage, immigration policies). The lack of candor on the part of participants is understandable but very disruptive to a social psychologist's search for scientific truth or the ability to accurately portray the actual opinions of some group.

Regrettably, there is no methodological way to eliminate social desirability but it can be controlled somewhat (Paulhus, 1991). Some researchers include any one of a number of available measures designed to identify those participants who are likely to give socially desirable answers to researchers. The most frequently used scale is the Marlowe–Crowne Social Desirability Scale (Crowne & Marlowe, 1960), which taps into people's need to avoid the disapproval of others. A higher score on this measure indicates a strong need for approval from other people. A researcher would have participants complete a packet of psychological measures (including the Marlow–Crowne scale) and then later carefully examine the data collected from participants with high scores on this scale. Data from respondents with high social desirability scores would be removed from further consideration and analysis in the research. Details about this and other social desirability measures can be found in Paulhus (1991).

Other researchers focus on the nature of their research topic and whether it is likely to trigger social desirability biases. Any research dealing with private or personal issues that can be embarrassing to people (e.g., sexuality, academic performance or standing, family problems, beliefs about race and gender) should be approached with care. If the research topic is a sensitive one, there are some modest steps that can be taken to encourage participants to be truthful in their responses. Note that I say "encourage" because deceptive responses cannot be prevented. First, make it clear to the participants at the beginning of the experiment that all of their responses will be held in strictest confidence, that their name or any other identifying information will never be linked to their responses. Second, tackle the sensitivity issue head on: Inform the participants that you are aware that the research topic can cause people some discomfort. Explain that, unfortunately, such discomfort is necessary because asking directly about the topic is the only way that any meaningful psychological information can be acquired. Third, reinforce both these points by reminding the participants that as a student researcher, you are bound to act ethically and in accordance with established guidelines where participant welfare and anonymity are concerned (see chapter 3).

When it comes to eliciting truthful responses, there is a more practical, methodological approach you can take with participant questionnaires. In the Wilson and Schooler (1991) jam study discussed earlier, participants in the reasons analysis condition completed a questionnaire wherein they wrote down reasons why they felt the way they did about each of the jams. The experimenter informed the participants that the questionnaire was only there to help them organize their thoughts, that they would not need to share these written responses with anyone. In fact, before administering the dependent measure (the jam evaluation form), the experimenter took the reasons questionnaire from the participant, noted that it would not be needed any more, and made a point of dropping it in a trash can. I am sure you can see where this is going: Wilson and Schooler later retrieved each questionnaire from the can for further analysis. Naturally, participants were told of this ruse and why it was necessary during the debriefing following the study's conclusion.

Please be aware that I am not advocating active lying. However, when a situation is sensitive (reasons for liking or disliking jam may not qualify, but the methodological approach is useful in this context), impress upon people that their honest opinions matter and are essential to the success of the project. If they do offer any candid responses on paper, you may be able to stage a way for the questionnaire to be "discarded" in the course of the study. You can retrieve it later and explain to the participant why you would like the opportunity to use his or her responses while maintaining their anonymity, of course. If a participant balks or appears otherwise uncomfortable at this request, in the spirit of research ethics, you must destroy the questionnaire then and there without ever examining its contents.

Likes or dislikes can matter

Just as we want to be liked, we often extend the courtesy to others. When someone crosses us, we can sometimes be unforgiving. In daily social life, liking others is a good thing; disliking is a less good thing, but it is a common aspect of social interaction. When it comes to liking or disliking others in the context of subjective judgments in questionnaire research, such monolithic responses can pose problems.

Some participants display what is known as a halo effect or bias. A *halo effect* occurs when a respondent has a tendency to give a target—a person, an object, an idea—an overall positive or negative evaluation. This "like" or "dislike" subsequently determines how the target is evaluated on more specific dimensions (e.g., Cooper, 1981; Thorndike, 1920). When it comes to evaluating someone we know, if we like that person, we can readily overlook one or more of the individual's annoying qualities. In the context of research, such judgmental charity clouds the true nature of a participant's judgment. It's as if judgments can only be global, never specific, so that dimensions of evaluation are never viewed independently of one another.

Positive halo effects are probably more common. In daily life, for example, good-looking people are presumed to be happier, wealthier, smarter, more successful professionally, and to possess better personalities than less attractive folks (Bar-Tal & Saxe, 1976; Dion, Berscheid, & Walster, 1972; Eagly, Ashmore, Makhijani, & Longo, 1991; Feingold, 1992; Moore, Graziano, & Millar, 1987). Halo effects can grant college professors a break when it comes to being evaluated by students. Experience and research show that on 5-point rating scales (where higher is better), students tend to rate their instructors with 4s and 5s. To combat such evaluation inflation, some institutions flip the scale so that lower numbers mean better teaching and make "good" the scale's midpoint. The resulting 5-point scale uses labels like: "superior," "very good," "good," "average," and "poor" (Dawes, 1972; Hoyle, Harris, & Judd, 2002). After all, how many instructors truly warrant a rating of "superior"?

Can anything be done about halo effects in questionnaire research? The answer may well depend on the nature of the questionnaire's topic, any accompanying stimuli (e.g., photographs), and the respondents themselves. There is nothing to be done about people's personal histories, especially how their experiences affect their likes and dislikes. What can be done, however, is that a vigilant researcher will always examine questionnaire and surveys with an eye to consistent extreme ratings. Changing the labels used in Likert-type scales and flipping their direction (i.e., high becomes low) are other possibilities. Beyond these steps, encouraging respondents to take their time and be thorough in their answers is the best one can do.

Yes, yes, a thousand times, yes

Besides social desirability bias and halo effects, creators of questionnaires and surveys need to worry a bit about yea-saying. *Yea-saying* is a form of response bias where respondents agree with any or all of the statements they encounter in a questionnaire. Yea-saying is a type of acquiescence, where people are apt to agree instead of disagree with what they read. A yea-sayer will agree with or answer "yes" to various questions. Nay-sayers, who are less common than their "yes"-oriented counterparts, routinely answer "no" and disagree with whatever statements they come across.

Unlike social desirability bias, yea-saying can usually be dealt with rather easily. The solution is a simple one. If you are asking for peoples' opinions about some topic or social issue, make certain that half the items are phrased in a "pro" direction and the other half are "anti" items. If you were asking your fellow students to share their opinions on tuition increases at your institution, you need items representing both sides of the debate, as shown here:

Frequent tuition increases are essential in order to maintain high quality instruction at colleges and universities.

     _____ I strongly agree
     _____ I agree
     _____ I am uncertain
     _____ I disagree
     _____ I strongly disagree

Given today's cost of living, no academic institution can justify routine tuition increases.

     _____ I strongly agree
     _____ I agree
     _____ I am uncertain
     _____ I disagree
     _____ I strongly disagree

A yea-sayer would be likely to select "strongly agree" or "agree" in response to both types of items (a nay-sayer would select the "disagree" options routinely). A careful examination of questionnaires before coding and analysis will quickly reveal any consistent, acquiescent responders, so their data can be removed from the final sample and from further consideration.

Anonymity or identity?

I want to close this section of the chapter by having you consider whether research participants need always identify themselves. Our discussion of response bias underscores that sometimes there may be decided advantages to allowing questionnaire or survey respondents to remain anonymous. Chief of these, of course, is that we may be more likely to learn how people really and truly think, feel, and behave with respect to some social domain if we maintain their privacy. If they are required to put their name or some other identifying mark (a student ID or other identification number) on their information packet, then they may be less likely to be candid with the researcher. Before you ask people to disclose identifying information of any type, be absolutely certain that you have a research-based reason for doing so. If not, then don't ask for it. Your questionnaire or survey will be a bit shorter and your respondents may be a bit more candid in their responses.

Questionnaire and Surveys as Precursors to Experiments

This chapter has focused on how to construct questionnaires for use in experiments or other studies, as well as how to survey some population to learn what people believe is true about some issue. I would be remiss if I did not close our discussion by mentioning another very good use of questionnaires and surveys: identifying experimental opportunities.

When reading about social psychological research in textbooks or journal articles, students often assume that the experiments just happened, that investigators noticed some interesting social phenomenon and then built an experiment around it. Sometimes this does happen, but very often research ideas also come from nonexperimental investigations. One very good source for potential hypotheses, then, can be information gleaned from questionnaires or surveys. If you have the time available and only a general sense of what sort of social behavior you want to investigate, then doing a questionnaire study might be a good choice for you.

If you were interested in how people use subtle cues to convey information about themselves to others, then you might design a questionnaire aimed at people's preferences for certain consumer goods. Many people spend a great deal of money on so-called designer goods (e.g., purses, shirts with logos or insignias, athletic shoes, particular jewelry, expensive watches). Most college students have less disposable income, but they nonetheless seek a certain look and purchase clothing and related items to send signals to their peers. Of course, fashion changes quickly and trends evolve. What you might do is first survey a sample of peers about what goods are currently "hot" or "not," and then design a subsequent impression formation study using peers decked out accordingly. The peers could act as live confederates in a "get to know you" situation where they meet participants or they could be photographed to serve as stimuli in a paper-and-pencil-based study.

My suggestions here are just that—some off the cuff ideas to get you thinking about how a questionnaire or survey can be used as a springboard for an experimental investigation. Questionnaires and surveys can be ends in themselves, but they need not be. They can also be precursors to something bigger and causally determined. Just as polls direct the decisions of policy makers and the fates of politicians, questionnaire data can help you design an experimental intervention.

Exercises

1   Imagine you want to accurately poll the students at your school in order to learn their opinion on some burning campus issue. What sort of sampling procedure would you use? How would you implement it?

2   Select some controversial social issue and draft some pro and con questions designed to assess people's opinions. Is this task difficult? Why? Should neutral questions ever be used? Why or why not?

3   Consider the typical student: What topics do you believe are apt to elicit socially desirable responding? Why?

4   Design a questionnaire from which you can gather ideas for future experimental research.

5   Locate and complete an online or Internet questionnaire. Write a critique reviewing the clarity of the questions being asked and whether the survey was easy or difficult to complete.

Chapter 7

Introducing a Difference:
Independent Variables

Do things happen to you or do you make things happen? What I mean by asking this question is how much control do you feel you have over what happens to you on a daily basis? The desire for control—one's sense of personal effectiveness and influence in the world—is a strong drive in human nature. We like to feel that we are masters of our fate, but how often is this really true?

Gambling is one domain that encourages people to exaggerate their perceptions of control. As I write this chapter, online poker games and televised celebrities playing poker for their favorite charities are enormously popular. (Indeed, a young man attending another college in my city was arrested after robbing a bank in order to pay his online gambling debts.) Now, poker takes both skill and luck—you have to know what you are doing but you also have to hope that you get a good hand of cards. What about games of chances that don't require skill? Do we perceive control there, as well?

Mentally walk yourself through the following scenario. You work in an office setting. One day, a colleague asks if you and some people you work with would be interested in taking part in a lottery. Your colleague shows you a stack of 227 lottery tickets, each of which has a photo of a different famous football player on it. Each ticket costs one dollar. The tickets are being sold in your office and in another office. Half the time your colleague simply hands over a ticket to a buyer. The remainder of the time, however, he allows a buyer to pick a ticket from the stack. Let's imagine you get to pick your own ticket from the stack.

On the day of the lottery, your colleague approaches you and says, "Someone in the other office wanted to get into the lottery, but since I'm not selling tickets any more, he asked me if I'd find out how much you'd sell your ticket for. It makes no difference to me, but how much should I tell him?" What resale price would you attach to your ticket? Has the value of the ticket changed since you bought it?

Before you answer this question, remember that lotteries are random events, games of chance where every player has the same objective chance of winning (i.e., 1 chance in however many tickets were sold—here, 1 in 227 or .004). Now, then, how much would you charge before you resold your ticket?

Langer (1975) argued that chance situations like lotteries sometimes mimic skill situations so that many people assume that some skill-related variables can influence randomly determined outcomes. Choice is a skill-related variable that many of us pride ourselves on; we may feel, for instance, that we are able to select the best option from an array of possibilities.

Making choices, especially what we see as the "right" or "best" choice, is a way of exerting control, one that works well in settings that are not determined by chance. Unfortunately, we often assume that our ability to make things happen also holds true in chance situations. For example, people are more confident of winning the roll of some dice when they can toss the dice themselves than when another person does it for them (Dunn & Wilson, 1990). Langer coined the term "illusion of control" to refer to situations where people ignore objective probabilities and anticipate personally succeeding at something in spite of the odds (see also Wortman, 1975).

The office workers who were given a lottery ticket—those who had no choice and could not exert any illusory control—requested a resale price of $1.96 on average. The workers who chose their own tickets and felt "control" asked for an average of $8.67! That's quite a difference, especially when the *only* difference was whether one was handed a ticket or got to draw one from the deck. Having choice, then, gave some people an illusion of control—they assumed that picking their own tickets would enhance their chances of winning the lottery.

Langer conducted a series of ingenious studies exploring the consequence of people's often-exaggerated beliefs about control (Langer, 1983). Is there anything wrong with maintaining such beliefs? Should we consider people who overstate their control to be somehow deluded? We'd better not draw such conclusions because other research suggests that illusory control and related erroneous perceptions are actually a hallmark of mental health (Taylor & Brown, 1988, 1994). We actually need these and other positive illusions in order to maintain a sense of personal well-being (Taylor, 1989). That raises an obvious question: If well-adjusted people overestimate their control over things like the outcome of lotteries, does anyone realize they actually lack control over such events? Yes, but those who do tend to suffer from depression. In fact, depressed people turn out to be quite accurate when it comes to appreciating how little control they (and we) have over what happens to us (Abramson, Metalsky, & Alloy, 1989). The perception that one has no control over even minor events in daily life can have consequences for health, well-being, and even mortality (Langer & Rodin, 1976; Rodin & Langer, 1977; Schultz, 1976).

What makes many studies exploring control so provocative, especially those conducted by Langer (e.g., 1975; Langer & Roth, 1975), is that the independent variables involved are commonplace, relatively simple, and found in daily life. Table 7.1 lists some of the conceptual, independent variables and their operationalizations that can trigger a sense of illusory or perceived control. I offer this list to illustrate how powerful the "simple" effects found in daily life can be. You no doubt remember that the independent variable, the causal variable, is controlled by the experimenter who "manipulates" it, presenting one variation to one group and at least one other, different version to another group. As we learned in the study of illusory control, introducing modest change into a situation—giving some people choice, others none—is sufficient to alter

Table 7.1   Sample Conceptual Variables and Operationalizations Related to Illusory Control

Conceptual variable	Operationalization	Source
Choice	Choosing a ticket in a lottery	Langer (1975)
	Causing an outcome to obtain a prize	Wortman (1975)
Skill	Rolling dice	Dunn & Wilson (1990)
	Flipping a coin	Langer & Roth (1975)
Responsibility	Caring for a plant	Langer & Rodin (1976)
Stimulus familiarity	Cards printed with familiar or unfamiliar symbols	Langer (1975)
Competition	Drawing a high card from a deck of cards	Langer (1975)
	Competing against an opponent who appears to be skilled or unskilled	Langer (1975)

how people think about their personal influence regarding future events. This chapter is about how to create change in social situations and to subsequently learn how thought, emotion, and behavior are affected. We will discuss how to conceive, create, and test the effects of independent variables in social psychology experiments.

Conceiving Independent Variables

Although social psychologists conduct research in a variety of settings, their efforts are often associated with highly controlled lab studies. There is a good chance that your first efforts will also be lab-based. For these reasons, we will focus on how to conceive of independent variables in lab-like conditions (naturally, much of the following advice can be adapted to less controlled field settings).

In social psychology, independent variables play important roles in two types of lab-based studies: impact studies and judgment studies (Aronson, Wilson, & Brewer, 1998). This dichotomy is useful for thinking about whether the manipulation of an independent variable has a relatively powerful effect on participants' thoughts, feelings, and behavior or a more subtle influence. *Impact studies* are experiments wherein something relatively pronounced happens to participants. The impact of the situation is usually due to an independent variable, one that is usually highly involving for the participants.

Consider an intriguing impact study exploring regional differences in violence in the northern and southern United States (for a review, see Nisbett & Cohen, 1996). Unlike their relatively cooperative northern counterparts, southerners often feel that insults and other social provocations must be addressed with a tough, even aggressive, response unless (or until) the offender apologizes.

In one study, a confederate unexpectedly insulted participants so that experimenters could assess the participants' facial reactions. Each participant was asked to place a completed questionnaire in a box at the end of a long, narrow, and crowded hallway. On the return trip up the hall, a confederate brusquely bumped into the participant while mumbling an obscenity under his breath. The confederate then disappeared through an adjacent door. As expected, observers found that southerners exhibited more angry facial expressions than the northern participants, who tended to look surprised by the encounter (Cohen, Nisbett, Bowdle, & Schwartz, 1996). Classic examples of impact studies include Aronson and Mills's (1959) severity of initiation study, Milgram's (1974) obedience experiments, Darley and Latané's (1968) research on bystander intervention, Asch's (1951) conformity paradigm, and Schachter's work on affiliation (Schachter, 1959) and emotional lability (Schachter & Singer, 1962).

In contrast, participants take a less active behavioral role in *judgment studies*, wherein they are more likely to be observers who reflect on, remember, and react to some set of stimulus materials. Judgment studies are much less interactive than impact studies; indeed, the interaction in judgment studies is largely based on recalling past events or anticipating what future or imagined ones might be like. Participants simply share their thoughts and feelings—their judgments—about what they read, watched, or thought about. Independent variables in judgment studies can be powerful and dramatic, but the events are usually described as happening to someone else, not the participant. Thus, where an impact study on bystander intervention would assess a participant's reaction to some staged accident, a judgment study would likely describe an accident scenario in print or ask the participant to watch and respond to a filmed mishap.

Masuda and Nisbett (2001), for example, conducted a judgment study on cultural differences in perceiving information in social contexts. These researchers asked Japanese and American university students to watch cartoons of undersea scenes containing plants, sand, rocks, fish, and other sea life. Later, all the participants were asked to recall what they had seen. The American students recalled largely "focal objects," stimuli that stood out in the scenery, such as rapidly darting fish and brightly colored matter. In contrast, the Japanese students focused on contextual matter, taking greater note of the "background" objects, such as plants and rocks (indeed, these students reported 60% more information about the watery environs than did the Americans). One intriguing conclusion is that the context where behavior occurs matters more to Easterners whereas the behavior alone matters to Westerners (see also Chalfonte & Johnson, 1996). Other studies conducted in the judgment tradition include early, classic research on the fundamental attribution error (Jones & Harris, 1967), studies on self-serving biases (e.g., Ross & Sicoly, 1979), the just world hypothesis (e.g., Abrams, Viki, Masser, & Bohner, 2003), salience effects (Taylor & Fiske, 1975), as well as much of the social cognition research dealing with judgment under uncertainty (e.g., Gilovich, Griffin, & Kahneman, 2002; Nisbett & Ross, 1980).

Types of independent variables

Just as there are two broad types of social psychology experiments, there are also two types of independent variables used in experimental social psychology. Before we describe these two types of independent variables, we need to establish their logic based on the some ideas from the history of experimental psychology (see, e.g., Leahey, 2004). All experimentation in psychology relies on what is referred to as "S-O-R" psychology: "S" refers to the presentation of a stimulus to an organism—the "O," which can be human or animal—in an effort to discern the "R" or response. Most often, the stimulus in experimental psychology is, of course, some independent variable designed to create change in one group but not another. Ideally, the response is a behavior, but with humans, self-reports, ratings, and the like are used alongside more traditional overt behaviors. Psychologists focus their theorizing on what happens inside the organism, for example, how thoughts, emotions, personal histories, and so on can elicit particular responses.

Social psychologists also do a variant of S-O-R psychology in that they try to explain how a social stimulus, some social independent variable (a person, other people, customs, folkways, the self), elicits social behaviors (actions, feelings, emotions, facial expressions, comments). Social psychologists, too, hypothesize about the internal, mental processes (e.g., emotion, cognition) that connect social stimuli to social responses. Indeed, most experiments are designed to demonstrate behaviors that are believed to result from social beliefs people acquire through experience and socialization. Social psychologists generally use one of two types of independent variables in their experiments: those causing behavior directly and those causing behavior indirectly.

Independent variables can cause behavior directly. An independent variable causes behavior directly when some external stimulus causes a participant to react in a predicted manner. When an independent variable serves as a direct cause of behavior, its role is usually concrete and straightforward. In the study of interpersonal attraction, for example, ample evidence points to the favorable effects of *propinquity* or physical proximity (e.g., Eckland, 1968; Festinger, Schachter, & Back, 1950; Segal, 1974). A person will often form a close friendship or a romantic attachment based simply on whether and how often contact with another person occurs. Consider life in the typical college dormitory: Proximity to others (hall or suite mates) leads to friendship because of the sheer number of chance encounters that occur. What make such an obvious external situation variable so interesting is not merely that bonds form, but that the bonds are so strong and long lasting (e.g., I am still good friends with the men who lived on my hall in my freshmen dorm well over 25 years ago). Interestingly, individuals we like the least can also be identified based on their proximity to us (Ebbesen, Kjos, & Konecni, 1976).

In practical, experimental terms, varying where research participants sit, whom they sit with, work on tasks with, and so on can be a means to establish the beginnings of social bonds. Thus situational constraints can serve as an independent variable, one having a direct impact on behavior, such as an increase in reported liking for another or others, as well as enhanced affiliative behavioral displays (e.g., head nodding, eye contact, smiling). Lower liking and fewer affiliative tendencies would be predicted for participants who had less contact with one another, sat farther away from each other, and so on.

Independent variables can cause behavior indirectly. How can an independent variable cause behavior to occur indirectly? In many cases, the independent variable of interest affects or creates some internal state in the participant. Such internal states are often emotions or other feelings. These internal states, in turn, promote some behavioral response in the participant; hence the connection between the independent variable and the (eventual) behavioral response is indirect.

Consider a clever study conducted by Schwartz and Clore (1983) that examined how we use our current feelings as information for making relatively complex judgments about our lives (see also Clore, 1992). Using phone interviews, these researchers asked Midwesterners to rate how happy they were with their lives on either a sunny or a gloomy, overcast day. The respondents in one condition (the no prompt group) indicated they were less happy and satisfied with life on the overcast days, suggesting that they based their outlook on the weather (those phoned on sunny days reported being relatively happier and satisfied with life). Just before being asked to report on their mood and satisfaction with life, a second group of participants was asked "How's the weather down there?" Schwartz and Clore assumed that this prompt would cause the respondents to initially attribute their current mood and life satisfaction to the weather (sunny or gloomy) but that subsequently, they would not use these corresponding feelings to judge their life satisfaction. Sure enough, the prompt kept people from factoring the weather into their sense of overall happiness and life satisfaction—when the weather was "discounted" from the judgment, they reported similar levels of satisfaction regardless of the weather.

In this study, Schwartz and Clore (1983) assumed that people's feelings were already influenced by the weather but that being prompted (or not) to reflect on the likely source of the moods would affect subsequent—and more complex—judgments (deciding contentment with our lives is hardly a simple matter). In other words, internal states already causing some behavioral response (i.e., self-report regarding happiness and life satisfaction) were further affected by an intervention—a prompt—designed to lead to further reflection on the source and appropriateness of feelings. This further reflection was hypothesized to lead to an adjustment in judgment, one causing, in turn, an emotional correction. Compared to the simpler, direct effects of propinquity, the effect of the independent variables (sunny or foul weather, prompt or no prompt) was more indirect.

Further refinement: Mediator and moderator variables. Besides the two broad categories of independent variables, social psychologists are also concerned with how variables exert mediating influences (i.e., a "go-between" variable linking some X to some Y) and moderating (promote or inhibit) effects (Baron & Kenny, 1986). A *mediator variable* is one that is presumed to create the connection between an independent and a dependent variable such that some external, physical event leads to an internal psychological change and its consequences. A mediator variable explains the nature of the relation or connection between a predictor and an outcome variable. Fiske (2004), for example, notes that in its original formulation, the frustration–aggression hypothesis did not specify any particular emotional state connecting the blocking of a desired goal (frustration) to subsequent reactions (aggression; see Dollard, Doob, Miller, Mowrer, & Sears, 1939). One obvious and logical candidate emotion is anger, which could be a mediating mechanism between frustration and aggression (i.e., a blocked goal is frustrating, anger results, which in turn leads to a violent, physical response). Unfortunately, the causes of aggression appear to be more complex than the frustration–aggression hypothesis would suggest (e.g., Baron & Richardson, 1994; see also Berkowitz, 1993).

However, let's continue to reflect on the possible causes of aggression in considering moderator variables. Moderator variables explain the strength of the relationship between two variables; they can be quantitative (e.g., score on exam, amount of praise) or qualitative (e.g., social class, race, religion, sex). As such, a *moderator* can enhance or reduce the likelihood that particular behaviors will occur. Consider this: Most independent variables are not of the "present or absent" variety; rather, they are a matter of degree. Thus the relative amount of frustration could be the key: Larger (or lesser) frustrations would be anticipated to lead to greater (or lesser) amounts of aggression. Similarly, perhaps a cue can moderate aggressive behavior (recall the Klinesmith, Kasser, & McAndrew, 2006, experiment discussed in chapter 1). We know, for example, that the presence of guns or other weapons (the so-called "weapons effect"; Berkowitz & LePage, 1967) can lead to aggression—do some weapons (e.g., pocket knives, paddles) lead to lesser levels of aggressive response than others (e.g., butcher knives, clubs)? Exploring the impact of different sorts of cues could serve as a test of and for moderating variables.

Can one operationalization of an independent variable represent all possibilities?

Whether the study is a judgment or an impact experiment, when deciding to construct and manipulate an independent variable, a researcher's goal is simple: to manipulate a practical variable that represents a conceptual variable but not to manipulate anything else. By practical variable, I refer to the empirical realization or operationalization of some abstract idea or social phenomenon (recall chapter 4). There is no single perfect way to represent a conceptual variable empirically. The practical approach a researcher chooses—his or her operationalization—should be sufficient to convince interested parties, especially fellow researchers, that it is a good representation of the conceptual variable of concern. More to the point, a given operationalization of an independent variable effectively serves as a stand-in for other, possible operationalizations of the same variable. Remember, the higher order concern is with the conceptual independent variable being manipulated and its effect on the dependent variable; its operationalization is a practical matter.

What is the importance of this point when it comes to doing research? Students often worry that they will not hit upon the ideal independent variable to manipulate in an experiment. Let me dispel a counterproductive myth: There is no ideal or perfect way to operationalize any independent variable—there are many ways to do so. Your goal is to identify an operationalization that will work and seem plausible given your research context (e.g., a lab, a dorm room, a classroom, on the street, in a mall). Inducing a good mood on the street (e.g., leaving $1 bills on the ground for passers-by to pick up) is different than in the lab (e.g., having participants watch an uplifting film), but both methods lead to a similar psychological state.

I am not suggesting that established independent variables and ways to manipulate them should be avoided in favor of new variables or interventions. Quite the contrary: Established wisdom is just that, and looking to the literature is always a good idea (see chapter 2). By all means, use whatever reliable variables, methods, or techniques you know about. I want to reiterate that there is no single best way to do anything or to operationalize any variable. So try your luck and develop a new approach or rely on one that is tried and true. The choice is up to you.

Providing Context for the Independent Variable: Instructions

Research participants will generally do whatever you ask of them (sometimes to their own and a study's detriment; see chapter 10's discussion of demand characteristics). But you must ask, which means that your instructions must be crystal clear. In experimental research, instructions are typically delivered to participants orally by an experimenter and then reiterated in written form. For instructions to work—to help participants fulfill their important role in research—they must possess several qualities.

Instructions must be involving. Whether a cover story is involved or not, tell participants things that will get their attention—what the study is about, what will happen, what their role is, and what they will do. In fact, *give* them something to do. Engage their help, ask for their assistance, give them a small responsibility, anything that will keep their attention focused on what is happening and going to happen shortly. The work should not be overly challenging or taxing, nor should it be mindlessly dull (unless creating boredom is an empirical goal; see Festinger & Carlsmith, 1959).

Instructions must be simple and straightforward. Complexity is the enemy of independent variables that engage participants. Similar to the crafting of questions discussed in chapter 6, what you tell participants to do must be clear. Whether presented in written or spoken form, or a combination of both, be sure to construct them using basic, everyday language to convey what will happen in the study and what the participant's role will be. Define any technical terms or unfamiliar language for the participants. Abundant use of examples can sometimes help as well.

Build in redundancy. Tell participants what they are supposed to do, either orally or in writing, and then tell them again. You need not be condescending about this repetition. Build it logically into the procedure. Minimally, after the instructions are shared with the participant through whatever mode (spoken, written, or via computer), go over them once more. This can be done in a friendly, helpful manner:

> I just want to remind you that in the next phase of the study, you will be reading about someone you will later meet. Be sure to learn as much as you can from the individual's file. As I noted a few minutes ago, you can take notes using the notepad if it helps you to organize your thoughts about him.

Instructions should be task-oriented. Besides being involving and easy to understand, instructions should give participants something to do. Left to their own devices, participants' minds will wander, their motivation to take the experiment seriously will drop, and they may even begin to try to figure out the study's hypothesis (see the related discussion of participant curiosity and demand characteristics in chapter 10). If you keep participants busy, they will not get bored and they will need to show the experimenter that they know what they are supposed to be doing. By the participants "doing something," the experimenter gets behavioral confirmation that the instructions were understood (or not).

Always verify that instructions and procedures are understood. Watching what participants do or fail to do is not the only way to determine if instructions (and the independent variable that may be linked to them) were taken seriously. Instead of waiting for participants to ask for help or sheepishly admit they forgot what they are supposed to do next, ask probing questions. Such questions will need to be tailored to the specific procedure in a given experiment. Your inquiries should be friendly but straightforward so that participants receive the clear impression that their role in the experiment is important. Make certain that the answers you receive indicate that the participant's role in the experiment, and the duties associated with it, are clearly understood. Answer any pertinent questions the participants do have in as much detail as necessary. When their questions are not relevant to their role or the procedure, inform them that you will explain everything when the experiment is over.

Plan for piloting

Before beginning actual data collection, set aside some time for pilot testing the independent variable and the experiment. A pilot test is a run-through of the experiment from start to finish that allows an investigator to determine that things will run smoothly and that, in particular, the independent variable is certain to create the desired (predicted) change in the dependent variable. Piloting the study allows a researcher to get out the kinks, to correct or change aspects of the experiment, improving the likelihood that it will succeed. How much time is needed for pilot testing? That depends on the complexity of the study, but a few days should be sufficient. Where successful research is concerned, pilot testing the independent variable can make all the difference.

Delivering the Independent Variable

Before we turn to considering some of the different ways independent variables can be introduced to participants, we need to highlight one feature they all should share: consistency. All participants should be provided with or exposed to the same information, depending, of course, upon which level or condition of the independent variable they will experience. Note that the term "consistency" does not necessarily mean some form of lockstep standardization. The reality of running an experiment with real live people taking part in it is much like everyday life; you cannot completely predict what will happen, who will say what to whom, or what questions will be asked or information ignored.

Thus experimenters and confederates (if any) must be watchful, making certain that participants more or less experience the same thing. Some flexibility is permitted of course. As Aronson, Ellsworth, Carlsmith, and Gonzales (1990) note, the goal is not pure standardization—everyone getting the same information—rather, the goal is making certain that all participants grasp the instructions and what is going to happen in the course of the experiment. Keep this goal in mind as you learn about ways to deliver independent variables.

Delivery via authority: The experimenter

The most straightforward way to deliver an independent variable is by having an experimenter present it to the research participants. Typically, the key information that places a participant in a given condition is provided orally at some point during the experimental procedure. Oral delivery requires that the experimenter know the script (see chapter 10) and that a mechanism exists to indicate which level of the independent variable the participant is to receive. To reduce the possibility of experimenter bias (see chapter 10), the ideal situation is one where the experimenter does not know a participant's assigned condition until the last possible moment (e.g., use of a preset schedule). Alternatively, some experiments involve more than one experimenter—experimenter 1 greets the participant and describes the study, experimenter 2 runs the participant through the procedure, experimenter 1 briefly returns to administer the independent variable, and experimenter 2, who is unaware of which level of the independent variable is in play, returns to administer the dependent variable. In this scenario, one of the experimenters remains "blind" to the participant's assigned condition and thus is less likely to influence the participant to behave in a way that will confirm the hypothesis.

A classic study on fear and affiliation nicely demonstrates how an experimenter can deliver the independent variable (Schachter, 1959). In this study, Stanley Schachter and his colleagues were essentially interested in demonstrating that "misery loves company." To induce fear (or not), groups of women participants met the experimenter, a Dr. Gregor Zillstein, who wore a white lab coat and explained that the study involved electric shock. In the high fear condition, Dr. Zillstein was quite authoritarian, as well as aloof. He delivered the independent variable by telling the group:

> Now, I feel I must be completely honest with you and tell you exactly what you are in for. These shocks will hurt, they will be painful. As you can guess, if, in research of this sort, we're to learn anything at all that will help humanity, it is necessary that our shocks be intense. . . . I do want to be honest with you and tell you that these shocks will be quite painful but, of course, they will do no permanent damage. (Schachter, 1959, p. 13)

In contrast, the low fear group met a friendly, warm, even engaging Dr. Zillstein. He allayed their fears regarding the shocks by explaining that:

> I have asked you all to come today in order to serve as subjects in an experiment concerned with the effects of electric shock. I hasten to add, do not let the word "shock" trouble you; I am sure you will enjoy the experiment. . . . We would like to give each of you a series of mild electric shocks. I assure you that what you will feel will not in any way be painful. It will resemble more a tickle or a tingle than anything unpleasant. (Schachter, 1959, pp. 13–14)

After delivering the independent variable, Zillstein explained that the participants would need to wait a while before taking part in the experiment. He casually noted that he wanted them to complete a brief questionnaire indicating whether they preferred to wait alone or with another participant. In actuality, the study was effectively over (no shocks were actually administered) and the questionnaire was the dependent measure. Confirming Schachter's (1959) prediction, individuals who received a high fear message preferred to wait with others, while those in the low fear condition were generally content to wait by themselves. This experiment capitalized on the fact that participants look to experimenters for guidance. An articulate experimenter can readily present the independent variable in a manner that commands participants' attention (cf., Milgram, 1974).

Personal delivery: Confederates and peers

A second way to introduce an independent variable is by having either a confederate or a peer present it to participants. We already reviewed the important roles that confederates can play in social psychology experiments (see chapter 3). You may, for example, recall how a group of confederates successfully delivered the independent variable—group pressure—in Asch's (1956) study of conformity. Their unanimity led a substantial minority of research participants to knowingly give the wrong answer in the line judgment task. Similarly, when a confederate "defected" and joined the participant by giving a correct answer, the participant was often willing to stand up against the social pressure. Participants, then, understandably treat confederates as peers who can provide information and sometimes solace within experiments. Of course, as we saw with Cohen et al.'s (1996) experiment on regional reactions to insults, confederates can also deliver an independent variable by confronting or intentionally upsetting a participant.

What if peers deliver the independent variable but not by acting as confederates? On occasion, an experiment can use the mere presence of participants as an independent variable. Consider one of the most convincing displays of what is know as the *diffusion of responsibility*, a reduced urgency to seek help in an emergency due to an assumption that others will help or take note of the problem. In an experiment by Latané and Darley (1968), college-aged males completed a questionnaire in a room, either alone or in a group of three people. These researchers hypothesized that people are more likely to notice an emergency and to take action when they are alone than with a group of strangers. While the participants were completing the questionnaires, smoke began to pour into the room through a vent. Solo participants usually noticed the smoke within 5 seconds. Most got up, smelled it, waited a few moments, and then went to report it. When the men were in groups, however, everyone kept working, even when the smoke filled the room completely, obscured their vision, and caused some to cough. Indeed, out of 24 men who comprised eight three-person groups, only one person got up to report the smoke within the first 4 minutes (the experiment lasted only 6 minutes).

What makes the Latané and Darley (1968) study so elegant is that the peers influenced one another without any instructions from the experimenter (other than those directing them to complete the innocuous questionnaire). The experimenter left the room prior to the staged emergency but watched it unfold through a one-way mirror. The participants' determination to fill out the questionnaire while (perhaps) not appearing foolish in the eyes of their peers ("No one else seems concerned so that can't be smoke coming out of the wall") served as a powerful independent variable. When they were all alone, however, participants had no one to look to for social guidance or feedback—they had to rely on their own intuition about whether the smoke qualified as an emergency.

Written delivery

Written instructions designed to deliver the independent variable are commonplace in both impact and judgment studies. Written instructions often come in the form of a sheet of instructions or even a booklet. More involved written instructions will have boldface directions embedded in them (e.g., **If You Have Any Questions, Ask Them Now**) or appearing at the bottom of the page (e.g., **Do Not Turn the Page Until You Are Instructed To Do So**). Such instructions can make the experiment seem more artificial than real life; indeed, the directions will remind some participants of standardized testing sessions. In point of fact, delivering the independent variable through written means is a way to introduce a high degree of standardization: Participants learn what they need to know, including being exposed to the appropriate level of the independent variable (it's very easy to change the content of key pages while making them look similar to one another), at a pace set by the experimenter. This high degree of control is helpful but it does make the experience seem relatively far removed from daily life, at least the life outside mass test sessions. As an experimenter, you need to consider how best to balance the benefits of standardized written instructions as a way to deliver the independent variable with the drawbacks in doing so.

Other forms of delivery

Instruction sheets and booklets are not the only option. Under the category of other modes of delivery of independent variables, some researchers have tried using taped instructions (e.g., Milgram, 1974), where participants appear at an appointed time and activate a tape recorder, cassette player, or the equivalent. The participants then listen to the experimenter's directives and carry them out as best they can. The advantage of taped instructions is twofold: uniformity and decreased experimenter bias. By uniformity, I mean that every person who listens to a given tape hears the same instructions from the same person in the same order. No errors can be made because the instructions are set. As the experimenter is not physically present, there is no chance that he or she can subtly, unintentionally cue the participant into giving the desired (hypothesis-consistent) behavior (see chapter 10's discussion of ways to reduce experimenter bias). These strengths, however, can also be drawbacks. Consider this: Taped instructions are usually played only once and, without an experimenter present, there is no guarantee that the participants are taking the proceedings seriously. Moreover, if they become confused or forget what to do, there is no one present to answer their questions.

As for other delivery systems, some researchers have tried delivery of the independent variable over the telephone. Once again, Stanley Milgram was a trailblazer. In one variation of the obedience paradigm, for example, after giving the most essential instructions, the authority figure left the room and gave subsequent directions to the participant "teacher" by phone (Milgram, 1974). Can phoning be used in a less emotionally charged experiment? Certainly. Participants might arrive for an impression formation study, read a folder of standard directions, and then dial a number to contact the experimenter, who could then provide the crucial information representing the (random) manipulation of the independent variable. This approach has the benefits of uniformity and the opportunity for contact (albeit by phone) so that participants can ask questions. Given that cell phones are now so commonplace, perhaps you can think of a creative but methodologically sound way to use them to present instructions and to manipulate the independent variable. Of course, any phone method still suffers from being less involving than having a real flesh and blood experimenter present (but see an elegant study on social perception and self-fulfilling stereotypes where the phone played a key role; Snyder, Tanke, & Berscheid, 1977).

Finally, some researchers have tried delivery of the independent variable in an online computer approach. Given the ubiquity of computers in daily life, few participants, especially students, are apt to be put off by this approach. On the other hand, the quality of the online materials, especially their clarity, matters. The same concerns that are associated with web-based research apply here (see chapter 5). Once again, having immediate access to a flesh and blood person, the experimenter, is apt to trigger a higher level of engagement from participants than the artificial immediacy of a website or instructions and independent variables sent via email. Of course, there are bound to be clever exceptions and research opportunities in this vein. I am simply suggesting that in general, there is no substitute for close, personal contact with an experimenter.

One more time: Instruct, repeat, and probe

At the risk of repeating myself, I must remind you that embedding the independent variable within the body of some set of instructions is fine as long as participants will take notice of it. To ensure they do, you must present the instructions in a steady, natural manner. You must also repeat the key points in a friendly, helpful way, and not in a way that is apt to elicit suspicion from the participants. Finally, you should probe the participants by asking them if they have any questions about the procedure, the role they are playing, or anything else pertaining to the experiment "so far." If past participants struggled with some aspect of the independent variable, for example, then you might want to gently probe in that direction. On the other hand, if past participants had little or no difficulty, then do not tempt fate by drawing attention to the issue. Simply ascertain whether they have any general questions. If they ask any questions that pertain to the experiment's purpose and the like, gently tell them you will be happy to discuss those issues once the experiment is over. Tell them that "for now, I need to be sure you understand your role so that we can go on to the next phase of the experiment."

ACTIVE LEARNING EXERCISE   7A

Developing Independent Variables

As I noted previously in this chapter and in chapter 4, there is no single best choice for an independent variable nor is there a "right way" to transform a conceptual variable into a good operationalization. Yet, as a researcher, you must develop an independent variable or variables for your project. This exercise is meant to help you develop some independent variables.

1   *Define your conceptual variable(s).* What social behavior do you want to examine? Do you have a theory in mind or are you relying on an existing theory from social psychology?

2 *Look to the literature for ideas on operationalizing the independent variable.* How was the conceptual variable operationalized in the published literature? How many levels did the operationalized independent variable tend to have in the studies you found?

3 *Brainstorm your own operationalization.* Instead of relying on published work, come up with your own operationalization of the independent variable and how to manipulate it. Begin by thinking of how the independent variable appears in everyday life. Where and how does it occur most frequently? You may want to use Active Learning Exercise 4A to help you with this task.

4 *Will your experiment be an impact study, a judgment study, or some other research approach?* As you identify possible independent variables and ways to manipulate them, be sure to consider what type of experiment you envision doing.

5 *Will your independent variable cause behavior in a direct or an indirect way?* An important part of designing an experiment is thinking through the social psychological processes involved. Be sure to determine whether you are seeking to change participants' behavior using direct or indirect means.

6 *How do you intend to deliver the independent variable?* Will you use an experimenter, a peer, a confederate, written instructions, or some combination to present a distinct level of the intended independent variable to an individual or to participant groups?

7 *Seek feedback on your ideas for independent variables.* Share your first pass at an independent variable with your instructor and peers from your class. Be certain to explain both the conceptual and operational definitions for the variable. Be open to suggestions that can improve the delivery of the independent variable or the experiment.

How Many Independent Variables? A Reprise

Independent variables shed light on causality and it can be tempting to add "just one more" to learn more information about the extent of or limits to some social phenomena. As noted in chapter 4, however, the more independent variables you add, the more you must manipulate. In that chapter, we noted that each independent variable increases the complexity of any factorial design. Each variable must have at least two levels—some will have more than that—and simple multiplication indicates how many results cells or conditions must be filled with participants (i.e., a 2×2 design has 4 cells, a $3 \times 2 \times 2$ design has 12 cells, and so on). More is not necessarily merrier. The addition of any independent variable must be justified. Reasonable justification involves adding an independent variable that has not yet been examined in relation to the social behavior being studied. Unreasonable justification is adding an independent variable because you can, or you think it would be "interesting" or even "fun"—some theoretical support is necessary. Without such support, you risk muddying the results and having difficulty making any sense out of them.

If you do identify one or two additional independent variables that you think would be interesting to examine, then consider a practical solution. Conduct two studies. In the first study, demonstrate that the basic effect exists (here I imagine you would manipulate one or two independent variables, but not three). Once the basic effects are established and the results are known, then run a variation of the experiment incorporating the additional independent variable (I would not try to manipulate more than three variables in one study until you are a more experienced investigator). With two experiments, you have a nice package of studies and are well on your way to learning the virtues of conducting programmatic research.

Individual Differences as Independent Variables: Prospects and Problems

Can individual difference variables, such as subject variables or personality traits, serve as independent variables? This issue was discussed in some detail in chapter 4 (see p. 88). In a theoretical sense, the answer is no: No nonmanipulated variable can serve as an independent variable. Doing so changes an experimental investigation into a correlational study. Suggestive observations may be found, but definitive cause and effect relations remain elusive.

Practically speaking, of course, nonmanipulated independent variables are used throughout social psychological research (some are shown in Table 4.2). Consider sex: Researchers interested in sex roles routinely describe how men's behavior differs from women's in domains ranging from domestic life to achievement settings. There is no random assignment allowing a researcher to make one person a man and another a woman, but we nonetheless talk about sex differences, albeit often in cautious, non-causal terms.

Should you consider examining individual difference variables in the course of your research? Yes, absolutely. Minimally, you should check to see whether the men and women in your study behaved similarly or differently from one another. You might also consider examining how an individual difference variable, such as a personality trait, can serve as an independent variable. Think about a trait like self-consciousness, or an acute sense of self-awareness of being an individual, especially in those situations that promote a sense of being socially ill at ease (e.g., formal dinners, job interviews). Some people are naturally more self-conscious than others, and you hypothesize that this trait affects the accuracy of first impressions. Due to their own self-focus, individuals who are high in self-consciousness attend to fewer details about new acquaintances than do those low in the trait. It follows that people who are low in self-consciousness would like to recall more details about strangers met in casual encounters.

You cannot create a trait experimentally—traits, after all, are hypothesized to be permanent qualities—but you can certainly create a temporary state by heightening self-consciousness in some participants relative to others. To accomplish this feat, for example, some randomly assigned participants might have to deliver a spontaneous speech while being filmed (high self-consciousness) while others would have to write down a brief speech with no performance element (low self-consciousness). After the induction, you could stage a brief meeting between each participant and a confederate, followed by a memory test. The induction method would allow you to control and treat this trait-like state as an independent variable. You would then be able to observe how self-consciousness affects behavior and to discuss it in a causal way.

Verifying Cause and Effect: Manipulation Checks

How does a social psychologist know if an independent variable had the hypothesized effect? Is checking the dependent measure—how participants reacted to the independent variable—sufficient? Sometimes yes, sometimes no. Most social psychologists want to be sure that the independent variable had the anticipated impact on research participants' thoughts, feelings, or actions. Of course, their subsequent behavior is an important vindication of a researcher's theory, but as we have noted throughout this book, people are often unaware of what factors do or do not influence their behavior. As Nisbett and Wilson (1977) noted in their classic review of verbal reports on mental processes, research participants often remain unaware that a stimulus led to a response, that a response occurred, or that the stimulus even affected a response.

The message here is that wise researchers also seek to verify that their independent variables were perceived as anticipated. To do so, many researchers rely on what are commonly called manipulation checks. A *manipulation check* is a measure that follows the independent variable and is designed to discern whether participants actually experienced the variable's different levels. In other words, a manipulation check is a safeguard designed to demonstrate that the manipulation worked. For example, a manipulation check can be used to verify that critical instructions were heard and understood by participants. A manipulation check can also be used to demonstrate that participants experienced a psychological state integral to the successful completion of the experiment.

There are two types of manipulation checks, internal and external ones (Rosenthal & Rosnow, 1991). An *internal manipulation check* is given during the course of the experiment, sometimes shortly after the independent variable is presented and other times during the debriefing portion of the experiment. Perhaps you were interested in learning whether embarrassment promotes an increase in prosocial behavior. Half of your participants experience a staged accident—they "accidentally" bump into a table, which then collapses, spewing several stacks of papers all over the floor. These participants experience the high embarrassment condition. Participants in the low embarrassment condition are also led to accidentally bump into a table, but it does not collapse—instead, a pencil falls to the floor. Following this mishap, you administer a brief questionnaire supposedly designed to prepare the participant for the next phase of the study. Embedded in the questionnaire are some items designed to assess embarrassment. If the manipulation of the independent variable was successful, compared to the low embarrassment group, individuals in the high embarrassment condition should report higher levels of social discomfort and awkwardness.

Compared to internal manipulation checks, external manipulation checks have one distinct advantage: They do not disrupt the flow of an experiment's procedure. An *external manipulation check* is given outside the confines of the actual experiment and involves a different group of participants. Essentially, the experimenter runs a simulation study where he or she asks this other group of people to reflect on how they would react if they were faced with the events as laid out in the proposed experiment (e.g., "Would you feel embarrassed if you knocked over a table full of papers? How embarrassed would you feel?"). External manipulation checks are often done during pilot testing and do represent a reasonable way to determine how the actual, future research participants are going to feel about and react to the independent variable.

Keep in mind that good manipulation checks are hard to develop. Administering extra questionnaires, especially before assessing the dependent variable, can unknowingly highlight the hypothesis as well as the independent variable for participants. Whenever possible, making use of naturally occurring manipulation checks is the ideal solution. By "naturally occurring," I refer to some indirect way the participants disclose what they are thinking, how they are feeling, and the like. Behaviors do speak louder than words, of course, especially given Nisbett and Wilson's (1977) warning that people may not be able to adequately or accurately report on what they are experiencing during the course of an experiment. Naturally occurring manipulation checks, such as having judges code participants' facial expressions for the display of particular emotions (e.g., shame, embarrassment), represent a good solution.

In the case of the hypothetical manipulation of high versus low embarrassment, however, I believe there might be a naturally occurring manipulation check wired into the situation. Besides the embedded embarrassment questions, the experimenter might also keep track of the number of times each participant issued an apology following the staged accident. Think about the last time you damaged something belonging to someone else or did something embarrassing in the presence of others—how many times did you apologize for what happened? We might legitimately expect that high embarrassment participants would say "I am so sorry" and make similar comments more times for scattering an experimenter's papers about the room than a low embarrassment participant would for dropping the experimenter's pencil. Thus the relative number of apologies issued per person, a naturally occurring manipulation check, would be some nice additional evidence to support the check done through examining the embarrassment questions.

What happens if a participant's response to an internal manipulation check reveals that he or she either did not understand the independent variable as intended or misinterpreted key instructions during the study? Besides determining whether an independent variable registers with participants, manipulation checks can be used to maintain the integrity of an experiment's data. When one or two participants clearly offered responses due to an error in understanding, an experimenter can legitimately remove their data from further consideration. Dropping any data, of course, is a rather big decision: Not only is the collection of the information hard work, when you remove someone from an experiment, you not only lose that person's responses, you reduce the statistical power available during the analysis stage (i.e., you reduce the chance you will find a detectable effect). The best course is to determine prior to the actual data collection what sort of responses to the manipulation check warrant the discarding of data (bearing in mind that if several participants "fail" the manipulation check, then you should question the effectiveness of the manipulation and not the veracity of the participants—you may need to revisit the experimental procedure).

When deciding on a manipulation check, the best advice is this: Be creative. With this advice in mind, let's turn to an exercise designed to help you be creative.

ACTIVE LEARNING EXERCISE   7B

Developing a Manipulation Check

When it comes to developing a manipulation check, be as subtle as possible. Do not disrupt the flow of the experimental procedure or cause participants to think too much about what they did, are doing, or will soon do in the study. Here are some questions designed to help you to design a manipulation check to verify the effectiveness of your chosen independent variable (recall Active Learning Exercise 6A).

1   *Will you design an internal or an external manipulation check?* If the latter, do you have sufficient time available for a pilot study?
2   *If you do an internal check, will it occur during the experiment or during the participant debriefing?*
3   *If you conduct an internal check, will you use a self-report measure, a behavioral measure, or some other method (e.g., observation of participants' facial expressions)?*
4   *If you conduct an external check, be certain that the pilot participants are from the same population as the eventual participants you intend to use in the experiment.* If you rely on some self-report measure, can it be readily presented during the experimental procedure without affecting (biasing) participant responses to the dependent variable? Perhaps the manipulation check can be given after the dependent measure is collected, either during or just before the debriefing. If you decide to use a behavioral manipulation check, select some naturally occurring behavior that is conceptually related to the independent variable (e.g., apologies and embarrassment).
5   *Seek feedback.* Share your draft of the manipulation check with your instructor and classmates. Use any suggestions that improve the manipulation check.

The Best Laid Plans (and Independent Variables)

Novice students of social psychology are apt to believe that the meticulously described studies found in social psychology journals or introductory books just sprang forth whole and complete from the minds of some clever researchers. I am here to tell you that, in the words of the old song, it "ain't necessarily so." Things don't always go as planned. Few memorable social psychology experiments just happen or are the result of sudden, blinding insight or intuition. Instead, memorable studies are actually the result of much toil, many tears, and quite a bit of sweat, not to mention careful think-ing and the thorough researching of past relevant efforts. In many respects, conducting a quality social psychological experiment—one that "works" so that the intended independent variables creates the expected change in the indicated dependent vari-ables—is similar to staging a good play. Not only are there bits of theater involved (e.g., a cover story, roles for experimenter and participant, a setting), the "show"—the actual running of the study—cannot go on until everything works, from sign-up to debriefing (see chapter 10).

The independent variable plays a crucial part here. If it fails to create a change in behavior, preferably the behavior predicted by the hypothesis, then there is no reason to proceed with data collection. Thus pilot testing the experiment is critical. But what happens if you pilot the experiment and the independent variable does not appear to be causing the expected change or *any* change in the dependent variable? When this happens, a researcher needs to explore possible reasons and remedies for the situation.

Perform an internal analysis

The manipulation of the independent variable may have been quite effective—it just may have been more effective on the behavior of some participants than others. In other words, some participants may be more susceptible to the influence of a given independent variable than other participants. The key, of course, is identifying the factor or factors that allow the independent variable to create greater behavioral change in some people. Doing so involves conducting what is commonly referred to as an internal analysis.

An *internal analysis* is a careful examination of obtained data with an eye to exam-ining a possibly influential variable that was not manipulated in the experiment. Variables identified through an internal analysis are very often subject variables, those individual qualities people carry with them into the experiment and which are largely immune to experimental intervention. Schachter's (1959) previously noted research on fear and affiliation involved a particularly fruitful internal analysis. Recall that participants in the high fear condition (they were threatened with painful electric shocks) expressed a greater desire to affiliate with others than did those in the low fear (no pain) condition. In a series of variations on the original study, Schachter found that the positive relationship between anxiety and affiliation was much more modest and often had to be teased out of the data. Why?

Schachter (1959) concluded that some participants must be more prone to seek out company when anxious than were the others. He guessed correctly that first-born and only children would be more likely to affiliate when anxious than later-born children. His rationale is simple: First-born and only children experience a more anxious parenting style than later-born children; mom and dad's faith in and skill at childrearing grow with their experience. As parents, they probably responded more quickly to quell anxiety in first and only children than those born later. As a result, first-born and only children grow to prefer—are more comfortable—being with other people when upset relative to later-born children. The data bore out Schachter's speculation: Ordinal position matters in the presence of anxiety. First-born and only children expressed a greater desire to wait with others prior to the supposed shock portion of the experiment than did later-borns. Mystery solved.

Of course, performing an internal analysis can provide insight but it also introduces a familiar problem: the violation of randomness. The internal analysis changes a causally focused experiment into a correlational study. Ordinal position in the family—birth order—cannot be manipulated the way a high or low fear communication can be presented. Yes, birth order and affiliative tendencies are correlated, but in a causal sense, Schachter could not prove why definitively. Internal analyses often reveal compelling evidence and arguments as to why an experiment did not turn out as anticipated, but they do not always prove how one variable affects another as is done in a true experiment.

Ask participants but be wary

The most obvious recourse for a researcher is to ask a few participants what they were thinking about during the experiment, especially when they were exposed to the independent variable. This sort of debriefing is different than that usually associated with experiments (see chapter 10). Instead of assessing suspicion, a researcher is intent on learning how participants were interpreting the dynamics of the experiment, particularly whether the independent variable was noted and with what effect, if any. It is quite possible that a manipulation that seems apparent to the researcher who created it is barely noticed by research participants. Similarly, there may be some situational distractions—noise, other people, unclear instructions, interesting or odd objects present in the lab setting—that weaken the impact of the independent variable. If so, discussing the experimental procedure with a few participants may uncover the problem and suggest ways to correct it.

The caveat to this approach is that, as noted previously, people often do not know what aspects of a situation influence them and which do not. In one of Nisbett and Wilson's (1977) studies, for example, some participants watched a film while a confederate created a highly distracting noise (he ran an electric saw) in an adjacent hallway. Other participants watched the same film but it was out of focus. A control group watched the film in relative peace. Later, the members of all three groups were asked to rate the film's interest value, their sympathy for the protagonist, and how much other viewers would be touched by it. The experimenter apologized to the noise and out of focus groups, asking them to note next to each rating whether the distractions influenced their conclusions. In reality, neither the noise nor the bad focus had any effect on participants' ratings, which were analogous to those made by the control group. Interestingly, most participants in the poor focus group did not think the projector affected their ratings. The participants exposed to the power saw's noise, however, incorrectly claimed that the noise did impact on their ratings. The methodological moral is clear: Participants are often unaware of what factors influence their behavior (for more discussion on people's foibles at recognizing causal influences, see Nisbett & Wilson, 1977; Wilson & Stone, 1985; see also Wilson & Dunn, 2004).

Thus you are free to seek out participants' opinions and observations, but you must be wary of them. Although they may sincerely want to help you determine why the independent variable is not eliciting behavior as hypothesized, their intuitions might not accurately reflect their thoughts during the task. Participants are often unaware of what factors actually affect their behavior.

Impact: Increase obviousness

Is an impact study actually impacting on behavior? Is a judgment study too subtle and clever to capture participants' attention? A second possibility is that the presentation or manipulation of the independent variable is not obvious enough. In other words, the independent variable registered in the minds of the participants, but it was neither sufficient nor powerful enough to change their behavior. As perceivers, people are not ideally equipped to adequately, let alone accurately, detect covariation, or how one variable changes behavior in the presence of another (e.g., Jennings, Amabile, & Ross, 1982). They do best when the connections are clear and ideal, that is, obvious.

What can be done to combat the problem of nonobviousness? First, any verbal directions involving the independent variable should be revised with an eye to emphasizing its presence. Perhaps the independent variable needs to be mentioned more than once or even twice. Second, participants should be encouraged to ask questions so the experimenter is certain that all parts of the procedure are understood. Third, when the independent variable is presented as a pictorial stimulus (e.g., a photo, a graph or other graphic image), perhaps it needs to stand out from the rest of the experimental context (Borgida & Nisbett, 1977; Nisbett & Ross, 1980). Perhaps the image can be presented or framed in some way that is colorful and attention getting, but not garish. Fourth, consider the research context: Is the setting spare or cluttered? If there are too many interesting or unusual distractions present, then perhaps the failure of the independent variable to capture participants' interest is obvious. By making the setting plain and even somewhat barren, then by default the independent variable may be more attention getting.

Reconsider the hypothesis

A final possibility is one that researchers do not like to consider: Perhaps the hypothesis is simply wrong. That is, people may respond to the independent variable in a way not captured by the hypothesis. If the hypothesis is incorrect, then there should be no surprise regarding the participants' failure to demonstrate the anticipated reaction to the independent variable.

How can a researcher determine if a favored hypothesis is in error? Sometimes a period of trial and error—running several participants through their empirical paces, asking them about their experiences, and then evaluating the (non)impact of the independent variable—is necessary. Once these steps are followed, a researcher should carefully evaluate the behaviors assessed by the dependent measure. How are the participants reacting to the independent variable? Are participants' behaviors similar within each level or condition of the independent variable? If so, do the participants' reactions reveal any interesting or unexpected behavior patterns? When patterns emerge, the researcher may want to "listen to the data" and reconsider the nature and accuracy of the hypothesis.

There is no shame associated with hypothesis revision in the course of research. In fact, remaining open-minded to other possibilities is a hallmark of high quality research in psychology. Pavlov's (1957) discovery of classical or instrumental conditioning, for example, occurred when he noticed that dogs in his digestive studies anticipated the arrival of food rewards (they began to salivate) when they heard their tenders coming down the hall. Instead of ignoring this unexpected behavior, which was not at all relevant to the work going on in his lab, Pavlov studied it. The Russian physiologist's study of such basic learning revolutionized subsequent theories about human learning.

In a similar way, the social psychologist Shelly E. Taylor noticed and then further explored an initially puzzling finding. Taylor (1983, 1989) was interested in the onset of depression among women who are diagnosed with breast cancer. When recruiting women to take part in the study, she struggled to find enough depressed cancer patients. Most of the women she encountered were coping with their conditions by engaging in a rather strategic form of social comparison: They looked to real or imagined women with cancer who were *worse off* than themselves. Taylor found that these "downward" social comparisons had uplifting psychological qualities (e.g., "I may have had a mastectomy, but I'm not having as much difficulty adjusting as my friend who had a double mastectomy"). Further, she concluded that instead of being in psychological denial, the women in her sample were effectively combating their disease in a very positive, reality-based way.

The take-home message here is this one: Be open to unforeseen possibilities in the course of doing social psychological research. Social psychology is a "hands on" science. The craft of experimentation is best learned by doing it. Reading about research, even in a book like this one, is no substitute. Much memorable and interesting research occurs when the researcher is attune to serendipity—accidental, unforeseen discoveries—in the data.

Keep a Causal Focus

Without a cause, there is no effect. Social life is rife with interplays of cause and effect; thoughts, feelings, and actions have consequences for ourselves and the people around us. Many of these consequences can be observed and even controlled so as to be understood. Independent variables are the one factor that is under complete control of the social psychologist. Independent variables are arguably the one experimental feature that has defined social psychology in the minds of generations of students and in the hearts of researchers. Some of the most memorable research in psychology is from social psychology, and what makes the work memorable is the impact of independent variables on behavior. Keep a causal focus in mind as we turn to the topic of the next chapter, the measurement of behavior.

Exercises

1   Examine a recent issue of a social psychology journal. How many studies were impact studies? How many were judgment studies?

2   Look through a recent issue of a social psychology journal to create a tally of how independent variables were presented to research participants (e.g., verbally, written instructions, behaviorally). What is the most common mode of presentation? Why do you think this is so?

3   Design a manipulation check for one of the studies cited in an article you found for exercise 2.

4   Review the contents of Table 7.1: What other conceptual variables trigger a sense of illusory control? How would you operationalize these variables?

5   Use your answer(s) to exercise 4 to design an impact study and a judgment study.

Chapter 8

Measuring What Happens: Dependent Variables

Consider the common pen. Can the pen you write with tell us anything about you or your social behavior? On the face of it, this is an absurd question. The pen itself doesn't tell us anything, rather, it is the wielder of the pen, the writer, from whom we learn something (consider, for instance, the adage that "the pen is mightier than the sword"). And what we learn is likely to be based on what the writer writes—right? We focus on what people say in writing to learn something about them, their thoughts, feelings, and opinions. How could a pen alone tell us anything about people? Some readers are probably thinking, "Well, people who use fountain pens are kind of old fashioned, which might reveal their stodginess" or "I use whatever pen happens to be lying around—who cares" or "Pens? Who uses pens anymore? I use my laptop." What if writing instruments can be more than just tools for recording our thoughts? What if—sometimes, anyway—they serve as objects revealing things about us. Let me show you what I mean.

Individuality and a sense of choice in daily life are important parts of life in Western culture. If you are American or European, then you know what I mean: You assume that you have a great deal of personal freedom and you express it by what you wear, eat, say, and, naturally, how you behave. This pronounced sense of "agency," or how we express our sense of power or influence in the social world, is not always found in other cultures or cultural contexts (Markus & Kitayama, 2004). Yet even minor choices can speak volumes about who we are. Social and cultural psychologist Hazel Markus and her colleagues at Stanford University asked American students and Indian students to select one pen from a collection of five pens—one pen was blue and the other four were red. Stop: Which color of pen would you choose, a red one or a blue one? American students routinely chose the singular blue pen, while the Indian students always chose the common red pen (Nicholson, 2006; see also Connor Snibbe & Markus, 2005; Kim & Markus, 1999; Stephens, Markus, & Townsend, 2007). Conclusion: We express ourselves through the choices we make even when those choices are modest ones.

We are not done with the pens yet: In a variation of this first study, Markus and her colleagues took away the pen at the moment some of the students made their choice, saying "No, actually you can't have that pen. Here, take this one instead." All students were then told to try out their new pen, either one "chosen" or one "given" to them, and to rate it. What happened? The Americans liked the pens they originally chose; those who were "given" a different pen devalued it. Again, our culture promotes freedom and choice, and we do not like to have either one threatened. What about the Indian students? They showed no preference for either the pen they freely chose or the one that was given to them. Sometimes a pen is just a pen. Does this result surprise you? Consider the fact that the culture of India, as well as Eastern cultures generally, is more about community than individuality.

Wait—we are still not done with the pens. Let's focus on American culture exclusively now for a moment. Markus repeated the pen experiments in two subcultures of Americans, some from the middle class and others from working-class backgrounds (Stephens et al., 2007). Working-class participants routinely selected the majority pen and demonstrated no pen preference when either they or the experimenter made the choice. Any guesses about the middle-class folks? They liked the unique pen, especially when they chose the pen themselves. How do we explain these differences in choice?

Markus and colleagues argue that different groups conceive of personal agency in different ways. Middle-class people view themselves as individuals with the freedom to choose and master their own destinies. In contrast, working-class people, similar to the Indian students from the earlier studies, focus on community and family issues. Standing out is a less desirable choice for working-class people, while their middle-class counterparts may bristle at fitting in. Of course, reality is more complex than what can be revealed by one's choice of pens. But pen choice is not the issue—it is a convenient vehicle, a measure of something else, here the values associated with culture and class, perceived freedom and choice (see also Connor Snibbe & Markus, 2005; Kim & Drolet, 2003).

What can we conclude about common pens? As we learned here and in the last chapter (and really throughout this book), social psychologists are often very creative when it comes to exploring—I almost wrote exploiting—the stuff of everyday life. Measurement is key. Sometimes the choices we make do speak louder than words because they reflect our perceptions when we are not consciously monitoring our actions. This chapter is about dependent variables, the value of which is dependent on the impact of the independent variable. Much of what we do—our behaviors and our self-reports—can be measured; these acts depend upon what is happening to us, including how we are feeling and thinking at a point in time. Dependent variables show us "what happens" in an experiment or field study by illustrating how one group (or more) differs from a control condition. As we will see, like those red and blue pens, dependent variables themselves are mostly silent—the social psychologist must make a case for why a given measure is sufficient for representing some meaningful psychological state.

Behavioral Dependent Measures

A dependent variable or measure is the variable that is *not* under the control of a researcher. Rather, the value of the dependent variable depends upon the reactions—

thoughts, feelings, actions—of the research participant to the independent variable. Where independent variables must have at least two levels or conditions, dependent variables are the same, that is, constant, across the number of conditions in a study. The value of the dependent variable as a measure of some outcome only changes based upon the influence of the independent variable.

Behavioral dependent measures are used because they represent visible, external indicators of people's psychological states. When two people spend the time together gazing into each others' eyes, smiling genuine (or Duchenne) smiles (e.g., Frank, Ekman, & Friesen, 1993), and remaining physically close (e.g., Arkin & Burger, 1980), for example, a social psychologist can reasonably assume that these observable behaviors indicate friendship or interpersonal attraction. When individuals remain physically distant, exchange few smiles, and make little or no eye contact, then their actions suggest they are strangers and not attracted (at least not yet) to one another.

Where social behavior is concerned, then, behavioral dependent measures involve tracking what people do when interacting with or planning to interact with other people. Of course, behavioral dependent measures are also revealing of people's thoughts and feelings when they act *as if* others—whether real or imagined—were present as witnesses (Allport, 1985). Ideally, too, behavioral measures are concrete and codeable.

Why do the latter two criteria matter? A social psychologist will want to be able to employ measures that are easy to use and about which there can be little disagreement regarding what behavior is revealed or what it means. For example, it's possible that good friends who are shy or socially withdrawn might not sit near one another, smile, or look into each others' eyes for significant periods of time, yet most people who have a relationship with one another would display such behaviors. No behavioral measure is ideal because we must infer and explain a link between it and some internal, hypothetical, psychological state. The hope is that most observers—whether fellow social psychologists, students of the discipline, or interested readers—will agree that some concrete behavior or set of actions is representative of purported feelings, thoughts, emotions, and so on (just as pen choice can sometimes indicate the presence or absence of social agency; see also chapter 9).

Codeability matters in that a researcher wants to be able to keep an accurate record of what each participant did in the course of an experiment. Participants' responses are measured and then coded (usually, but not always, as numbers) in preparation for data analysis (see chapter 11). There should be no doubt about what a participant did or did not do behaviorally. Whenever behavioral measures are used, a participant's reactions to them should be both concrete and codeable.

There is one additional, compelling reason to choose behavioral measures: They are often less reactive than verbal measures. When conducting research, the mere act of observing or asking about people's behavior can change that behavior independently of any planned treatment. In experimental social psychological research, *reactivity* refers to the way in which a particular dependent variable can interact with an independent variable, thereby creating a false effect that would not have occurred if some different dependent variable were used. The problem is that if a researcher relies on only one dependent measure, there is no way to know whether it is a reactive one.

A classic example of reactivity is the still controversial *Hawthorne effect* (e.g., Adair, 1984; Jones, 1992; Parsons, 1974; Sommer, 1968). The word "controversial" applies here because some scholars believe the purported effect is real whereas others claim its scientific status is dubious at best. In any case, in the later 1920s and early 1930s, employees at the Hawthorne plant of the Western Electric Company were studied while they worked (Roethlisberger & Dickson, 1939). Basically, researchers concluded that the workers' behavior changed—for example, productivity increased—simply because they were aware they were participating in an experiment. In other words, "being watched," and not any innovative worker training programs, caused their changed performance. Labeling a finding a "Hawthorne effect" highlights the possibility that observed change occurred due to participant reactivity and not the impact of an independent variable. Although reactivity is often a concern in field research where experimental control is limited, it can also pose problems for traditional experimental research (Campbell & Stanley, 1966).

Here is a hypothetical example of reactivity in a social psychology experiment: Imagine you were studying factors that *prime* or activate certain representations or associations in memory dealing with the development of friendship between strangers. You ask pairs of participants to get acquainted with one another for several minutes by talking about where they are from, their college majors, hobbies, and favorite televisions shows. You assume that this exchange will trigger thoughts related to how camaraderie and closeness develop once we meet new people. After the interaction, each member of a pair is given a questionnaire that asks various things about the nature of close but nonromantic relationships. A control group consists of participant pairs who neither meet nor interact with one another; they complete a filler task (writing about their last vacation) before answering the questionnaire.

Analysis of the questionnaire reveals that individuals who interacted in pairs correctly identified and positively endorsed interpersonal factors that predict friendship. By comparison, members of the control group chose fewer of the correct, predictive factors. Does this mean that actual social interaction primes people to look for and act on friendship cues? Not necessarily. No behavioral data, such as observations, were collected during the peer pair interactions. Perhaps no priming actually occurred there; rather, once the experimental group members began to complete the questionnaire they guessed that the "getting acquainted" manipulation was about friendship formation. Relative to the control group, the experimental group responded by calling upon shared cultural stereotypes regarding friendship (e.g., "smiling promotes friendship"). They scored higher on the measure than the control group not because of any priming effect per se but because most of them correctly guessed the experiment's purpose (i.e., "They want to see if I know how people learn to like one another—this should be easy"). In short, the questionnaire led to reactive responses that, while consistent with the hypothesis, were not due to any priming effect.

What, if anything, can be done about the problems posed by reactivity? Reactivity becomes less of a concern when a researcher relies on overt measures of behavior separate from or combined with verbal measures of behavior. The reason that overt measures are less reactive is that research participants are often unaware that their behavior is being measured (the Hawthorne effect studies being an exception; recall, instead, the pen choice studies by Markus and colleagues). In the case of friendship development, for instance, a researcher could decide to look for priming effects during the actual paired interactions rather than relying exclusively on an after-the-fact self-report measure.

Measuring what people do

Human behavior is diverse. People do so many things that the issue is often not so much what to measure but how to go about measuring it. To begin, social psychologists usually decide whether the behavior is part of the person—a facial expression, a movement of the body, something spoken, and the like—or something outside of but nonetheless caused by the person. By outside the person, I mean something that happens because of what the individual does, such as an action the person performs.

When I was an undergraduate student, for example, I once took part in a social psychology experiment where I got to choose a gift, a paperback novel from a group of books. My choice of one book rather than another is an example of such outside behavior (of course, a researcher might want to know the reasons, my thoughts and feelings, underlying my preference). Note that whether the behavior is part of the person or something outside the person, the behavior is overt—that is, obvious, explicit, and completely out in the open.

The chief advantage of measuring overt behavior is that witnesses—readers, fellow researchers, students of the discipline—are apt to agree that the measure is an appropriate one. To use a familiar example, does it make more sense to ask people whether they would help someone who has had an accident or to see what they do behaviorally when presented with an actual, if staged, accident? I think you will agree that what we anticipate doing does not always match what we actually do when faced with a challenging circumstance (cf. Darley & Latané, 1968). Our (overt) actions truly speak louder than our words.

In general, behavioral measures should be as specific as possible. Thus a measurement of "how quickly a bystander walks over to help the fallen confederate" is a better measure of helping than is the vague "helping behavior." This specific measure illustrates an important second quality: Measures of behavior need not be all-or-nothing indicators—they can be more sensitive than that. Instead of tracking whether a bystander offers to help (or not), this sample-specific measure tracks behavior on a time continuum—how much time passes before aid is rendered. *Reaction time* is the amount of time that passes between the presentation of some stimulus and a person's measurable response to it. Shorter reaction times associated with offers of assistance (which could be measured in seconds on a stopwatch) could indicate a stronger disposition to help. Longer reaction times might suggest confusion or a lack of awareness of the need to help, as would no offer of aid at all (in advance, a researcher would decide on an "end time" for the helping opportunity, say, 5 minutes). The advantage of measuring reaction time—also called *response latency*—is its quantitative nature. Quantitative dependent measures can be analyzed using statistical techniques in order to demonstrate between-group differences (see chapter 11). Easily interpreted tables and figures showing, for example, means (averages) for each level of the independent variable can also be created (see chapter 12).

Besides reaction time, what other quantifiable dimensions of behavioral dependent measures are there? Here are several to consider:

Frequency. How often does something—a behavior, thought, or feeling—occur? In the first of a series of clever studies on self-reported thought suppression, Wegner and colleagues seated individual students at a table with a microphone and the sort of bell you associate with a hotel's front desk (Wegner, Schneider, Carter, & White, 1987; see also Wegner, 1994). For five minutes, the student said whatever came to mind into the microphone. For the subsequent five minutes, the student was told to continue thinking aloud while *not* thinking of a white bear. Every time he did think of such a bear, he was supposed to ring the bell (most participants rang the bell six times and talked about the bear out loud, as well). Using simple frequency measures, Wegner discovered a rather ironic effect associated with thought suppression: Not only is it difficult to suppress a thought, when you do so, the thought actually becomes more frequent (Wegner, 1994).

Duration. Behavior is rarely all or nothing. How long does some behavior occur? When participants are emotionally aroused and delivering (false) electric shocks to a confederate as part of an experiment (e.g., Milgram, 1963, 1974; Prentice-Dunn & Rogers, 1980; Zimbardo, 1969), for how long do they press the button that supposedly delivers the shock? The duration of this behavior is another way to operationalize the relative strength of an aggressive response.

Proximity or distance. How close physically does one person get to another (e.g., Hall, 1966)? How close do we allow others to get to us? To measure interpersonal comfort, an experimenter could count the number of floor tiles lying between a participant and a confederate. Fewer tiles would serve as a proxy measure for greater levels of comfort or social ease.

Amount. How much of something will people spend or wager? Simple games of chance are popular ways of assessing people's willingness to take risks, and tokens such as poker chips, play money, and occasionally real money or other materials (e.g., gift certificates, coupons) are used in experiments. In an experiment involving illusory control (recall chapter 7), Dunn and Wilson (1990) observed people's willingness to risk more poker chips with the roll of a fair die when the stakes were low than when they where high. The number of chips retained by the end of the experiment could be "cashed in" for a modest reward, while a chip deficit meant a participant had to perform some onerous tasks.

Speed. How quickly will participants try to escape from a perceived threat? In a series of field experiments, Ellsworth, Carlsmith, and Henson (1972) found that staring at drivers motivated them to stop for briefer periods at a stop sign than drivers who made no eye contact with an experimenter.

No doubt you can think of other dimensions where behavioral dependent measures can be quantified so that statistical analysis and group differences (attributable to the effects of an independent variable) can be demonstrated.

Of course, using a quantifiable dependent measure is not always necessary. On occasion, observing participants' choices can be quite revealing. Consider this elegant study dealing with past guilt and a desire to currently feel clean. Zhong and Liljenquist (2006; see also Carey, 2006) wondered whether people will get an urge to clean themselves when prompted to remember a questionable deed committed in the past. In one experiment, undergraduate students were asked to recall doing something unethical (e.g., betraying a friend) or something ethically worthy (e.g., returning a lost wallet to a stranger). After doing some reflection, the students were told to choose one of two free gifts, either an antiseptic hand-wipe or a pencil. Those students who focused on past dishonorable deeds were two times more likely to choose the wipe than the pencil compared to those who had recalled an ethical action. Note that some modest quantification is still involved here (i.e., counting the number of people per condition who chose which type of gift) but that the dependent variable does not vary on a continuum.

All of the examples cited so far place the behavioral dependent variable close in time to the presentation of the independent variable. Generally speaking, this sort of temporal contiguity between the two types of variables is necessary in order to demonstrate predicted effects. Nonetheless, some social psychologists have executed studies where the presentation of the independent variable occurs quite a long time before any dependent variable is actually measured.

A study by Cohen, Garcia, Apfel, and Master (2006) illustrates this time lag using an intriguing example. Following stereotype threat theory (recall the study by Spencer, Steele, & Quinn, 1999, discussed in chapters 4 and 11), these researchers tested whether a 15-minute in-class writing assignment on "self-integrity" could improve the grades of a group of African American seventh graders. Students in the experimental group read a list of values, selected one, and wrote about why they chose it. Those in the control group saw the same list, chose the least important value, and then wrote about why this value might be important to someone else. This manipulation occurred at the beginning of the fall semester and the dependent variable—the students' grade point averages (GPAs)—was not measured until the end of the year. African American students who wrote about their own important values ended up with GPAs approximately one-third of a point higher than African Americans in the control group (the GPAs of white students in the treatment group did not differ from white students in the control condition). Cohen and colleagues were so surprised by this close in the achievement gap between races that they waited to publish the findings until they successfully replicated the experiment a year later.

Aside from the need for resources to conduct such studies, permission to work in a school setting, and the need for an expansive time frame, are there any drawbacks to such behavioral dependent variables? Actually, yes. Although the results obtained by Cohen et al. (2006) are both provocative and promising, more research needs to be conducted before the link between the treatment variable and the dependent variable are presumed to be solid and causal. Multiple factors, and the need to account or even control for them, come into play when the time lag between these variables is such a long one (see the discussion of threats to internal validity in chapter 9). On the plus side, other social psychological interventions involving people's self-perceptions and subsequent effects on academic performance exist (see Wilson, 2006). As a budding social researcher, however, you should be encouraged by such work to sometimes take the long view where measuring dependent variables is concerned.

Measuring intentions and future commitments

Whether in the lab or the field, not all social behaviors of interest can be examined as they occur. Much of social life involves anticipating the future, our hopes and fears, our role there, and what we expect to do. Given people's abilities to look ahead, there are no doubt many behaviors worth study that have not yet occurred or will not happen for some time. Until they actually occur (and if they occur), we cannot study future behaviors directly; however, we can measure people's intentions. For example, political pollsters continually interview eligible voters in the weeks and months leading up to an election in order to get a sense of which candidate is favored by the electorate. People's actual votes may change by Election Day, of course, but documenting such intentions across time reveals much about how opinion can be influenced by campaign ads, current events, and scandals, to identify a few causal factors. In our own daily lives, most of us routinely make public commitments to perform certain demanding tasks (e.g., "Well, I plan to finally clean out the garage this weekend," "I am absolutely going to begin writing my paper long before it's due"). Sometimes we follow through and carry out the intention, other times we fail to do so. The point is that, psychologically speaking, at one point in time we were sincere in our belief regarding the intended behavior. Such declarations are worthy of study.

Measures of intention or future commitment are commonly labeled *behavioroid measures* (e.g., Aronson, Ellsworth, Carlsmith, & Gonzales, 1990; Aronson, Wilson, & Brewer, 1998). A classic study of compliance conducted by Cialdini and colleagues (1975, study 1) illustrates how straightforward and useful behavioroid measures can be. These researchers were exploring the *door-in-the-face technique*, a method for inducing compliance whereby a refusal to perform a large request increases the chance that a later, smaller request will be granted.

Experimenters approached college students between classes and asked whether they would be willing to escort a group of juvenile delinquents on a two-hour tour of a zoo. When this was the only request made of them, very few students (about 16%) agreed to serve as escorts. Before being asked to go on the zoo trip, other students were asked whether they would be willing to act as counselors to some juvenile delinquents for a two-year period. Not surprisingly, no one agreed to this large request; however, 50% of this second group subsequently agreed to take some juveniles on the two-hour zoo trip. Refusing to agree to perform a large request ensures that many people will feel obligated to comply with a smaller request (for a discussion of other related social influence techniques, see Cialdini, 2000).

The behavioroid measure was simple, powerful, and easily understood by the students: Will you or won't you be willing to performing a demanding task in the future? Note that agreeing to go on a two-hour zoo trip is still quite a commitment, especially when the request is sudden, unexpected, and unplanned. This commitment pales in comparison to the two-year volunteer stint, however. As a behavioroid measure, people's willingness to volunteer was sincere (or, if they declined to help, we can assume that they still took the requests—large or small—quite seriously).

On occasion, similar compelling or convincing behavioroid measures eliminate the need for actual behavioral measures. Think back to the guilt and cleanliness study presented earlier (Carey, 2006; Zhong & Liljenquist, 2006). In a related study, the same researchers found that people who were encouraged to think about their own past transgressions against others were more likely than a control group to volunteer to help others with a school project. There was one interesting qualifying factor, however: If the participants were given the opportunity to wash their hands after their period of reflection, the likelihood that they would subsequently commit to helping out with the project fell by almost half. Sometimes, then, having participants commit to performing some behavior is as powerful as actually having them do the behavior. When conducting an experiment, behavioroid measures possess a practical side that should not be overlooked.

Behavioral measures in disguise: Unobtrusive measures

Unobtrusive measures are an alternative to behavioral or behavioroid measures that avoid triggering any reactivity; indeed, participants are completely unaware that their behavior is being observed, let alone measured. Such measures can be concealed, hidden, or nonobvious in a research situation. Social psychology laboratories, which usually comprise suites of rooms, typically have one-way mirrors. These mirrors allow researchers or research assistants to observe participants' behavior during the course of an experiment. Often, for example, one-way mirrors enable trained coders to look for and maintain records of behaviors in keeping with the favored hypothesis. Wilson, Dunn, Bybee, Hyman, & Rotondo (1984, study 1), for example, relied on one-way mirrors to observe and record for how long participants played with some puzzles in an attitude–behavior consistency experiment. In a companion study (study 2), watching from behind a one-way mirror, these researchers coded the emotional content of participants' facial expressions as they watched a series of scenic slides.

Besides one-way mirrors, hidden cameras and tape recorders are sometimes used to record behaviors occurring when neither an experimenter nor a confederate is present during an experiment. These sorts of concealed methods do pose ethical concerns, as the researchers are, in effect, "spying" on the participants, albeit for a good reason (see chapter 3). Minimally, the use of such methods must be justified to and approved by the local IRB, and researchers must prove there is no reasonable alternative approach that does not rely on any masked tools. At the end of every experiment session, the participants must be told about any nonobvious measures or methods during a careful, systematic debriefing (see chapter 10).

Besides measuring what people do, another possibility is to examine what they leave behind or the changes they introduce into situations. Very often, physical remnants can be a revealing source of knowledge about social behavior (Webb, Campbell, Schwartz, & Sechrest, 1999). Researchers have been chiefly interested in examining two categories of physical remnants, accretion measures and erosion measures.

The things people leave behind constitute *accretion measures* (Webb et al., 1999). Think about it: What could someone learn about you by examining your material goods, such as the contents of your backpack or the objects in the room where you sleep? What would your weekly trash reveal about your eating or recycling habits? Consider your own personal security: Do you routinely lock the door to your room, apartment, or home? Does your "locking" behavior reveal anything about your sense of security and personal safety? Sechrest (1971), for example, speculated that women were probably more conscious of personal security than men. To verify this hunch, the researcher determined the relative number of locked cars parked next to men's and women's dormitories. Some examples of accretion measures are noted in the top part of Table 8.1. No doubt you can think of some others.

Table 8.1   Some Unobtrusive Dependent Variables: Physical Trace Measures

Accretion variables	Sample physical traces
Spending habits	Contents of trash or recycling
Affluence or frugality	Contents of trash or recycling, Length of cigarette butts
Places where smokers gather	Cigarette butts on the ground
Diet	Contents of trash or recycling
Listening habits	Station settings on car radio
Sexual or social attitudes	Graffiti in restrooms
Boredom in the classroom	Graffiti on desks
Political philosophy	Bumper stickers on car, signs posted on home or in yard, graffiti in public places
Popularity of an exhibit or display	Finger and nose-prints on display cases
Use of public parks	Trash and refuse left on ground
Erosion variables	**Sample physical traces**
Safety habits	Wear and tear of seat and shoulder belts in cars
Popularity of books or magazine	Wear and tear of covers and pages
Boredom in the classroom	Damage to student desks and chairs
Popularity of exhibits	Wear and tear of carpet, tile floor
Use of public parks	Wear of benches, picnic tables, fences, gates
Preferred pathways	Brown spaces or paths cut in lawns

Erosion measures constitute the second category of unobtrusive methods for assessing behavior. By erosion, Webb and colleagues (1999) mean how people's contact with things and places causes actual, visible, physical wear and tear. On my campus, for example, a set of paved pathways was laid out in one of the quadrangles behind a main academic building. The goal was to encourage students to use the paths so as to preserve the green space and some plantings on it. What happened? Despite the presence of the new paths (which were largely ignored), students continued to take the shortest route across the quad, thereby cutting a clear dirt trail in the lawn. Eventually, the groundskeepers bowed to the inevitable and installed a permanent, paved path in place of the worn shortcut. In this case, wear and tear was quite revealing: The students made their walking preferences known behaviorally.

Erosion measures are often apparent in public settings, especially museums. The next time you visit a gallery, look to see how many exhibit cases have finger and nose prints on them. Note also that when such grime appears at or below your waist level, it may indicate that the contents of a case are especially popular among younger children. Similarly, popular exhibits in art museums often lead curators to repaint walls (too many handprints) and replace floor tiles (too much foot traffic). The need for such repairs suggests that large numbers of people are passing through to look at the art. Imagine, then, what a continually sparkling clean gallery suggests about the popularity of its contents. The bottom part of Table 8.1 contains some examples of other, unobtrusive erosion measures.

ACTIVE LEARNING EXERCISE **8A**

Creating Creative Dependent Measures

As already noted, overt behavior is all around you. As a student of social psychology, your goal is to develop creative ways to measure people's actions. The goal of this exercise is to help you develop behavioral dependent measures based on your own everyday experiences.

Overt behavioral measures. Athletic events are popular on most college or university campuses. Both athletes and spectators exhibit a variety of behaviors—actions on the sidelines, cheering or jeering, wearing team insignias—that reveal their involvement in the event or loyalty to the team. Go to a game, watch the team and the fans, and create a list of behaviors that are specific and codeable. Are the behavioral measures you identify quantifiable? Are your chosen measures good operationalizations of the prevailing school or team spirit? Why or why not?

Continued

Behavioroid measures. Under what conditions are the people you know likely to express their intentions for the future? Be on the lookout for potential behavioroid measures in your daily life. Here is one common example I am sure you have witnessed: Once the calendar turns to the new year, many of us embark on new diets or exercise regimens (or plan to do so). Such commitments are often touted during the busy and food-filled holiday season leading up to the new year. What sort of behavioroid measure(s) can you create to capture people's new year's resolutions? If this context seems to be too narrow, then identify some behavioroid measures linked with people's desires to reduce bad habits while instilling new, presumably better (e.g., healthier) ones.

Unobtrusive measures. Go and explore some familiar place on your campus or in an office setting, for example, where many people come and go each day (e.g., the library, the student union, the gym). What physical trace measures—erosion or accretion—can you identify there? What traces reveal whether people use a space or simply pass through it? What physical indicators suggest people's preferences (e.g., waste, foodstuffs, seating)? Do people seek to connect with others in the space or do they want privacy? How do you know?

Your own research project. If you are making sufficient progress on your social psychological research project, then you will need to develop an appropriate dependent variable for it. Will you rely on a measure of overt behavior, a behavioroid measure, or an unobtrusive measure? How will this dependent variable be linked to your independent variable?

Verbal Measures

Despite the fact that we have already discussed the use of verbal measures in great detail in chapter 6 when we learned about surveys and questionnaires, we need to note again their importance to social psychological research (but see Baumeister, Vohs, & Funder, 2007). Why are verbal dependent measures so important? If we are interested in studying the origins and purpose of social behavior, then shouldn't our focus be on what people do, their actions rather than their opinions or comments in passing?

Social psychologists rely on verbal dependent measures for two main reasons: convenience and precision. As already acknowledged, verbal measures are easy. Such measures are easy to construct, easy to administer, and easy for research participants to understand and to respond to. There is another side to such convenience: Some social behaviors are difficult to study because people are overly conscious of their actions. That is, under certain conditions or in certain situations, people carefully monitor or control their behavior so that it does not accurately reflect either their thoughts or feelings, especially those directed at other people. I am thinking, for example, of situations involving prejudice or discrimination towards African Americans.

Many White Americans now hold rather egalitarian values when it comes to matters of race, resoundingly rejecting prejudice, racism, and discriminatory actions. Yet while many Whites disavow racist beliefs (e.g., there are genetic differences among the races where intelligence is concerned), they nonetheless harbor more subtle prejudicial thoughts (e.g., Blacks are less self-reliant than Whites, Blacks benefit too much from affirmative action; Gaertner & Dovidio, 1986; McConahay & Hough, 1976; see also Sidanius & Pratto, 1999). Overt behaviors will not reveal lingering prejudice, especially among individuals who work with and live among and socialize with members of minority groups. Only private, sometimes anonymous, verbal measures can document such prejudicial thoughts (as can some nonverbal, physiological, and implicit measures, which are discussed later in this chapter).

What about precision, the second reason for using verbal dependent measures? In many situations, a given social behavior is obvious, yet its very obviousness prevents a researcher from discerning fine shades of meaning or getting at how people actually feel and sometimes act despite the image they project. Consider how we act in our public lives versus our truly private lives, especially when our lifestyle affects our social standing with some groups. Use of a verbal dependent measure in addition to a behavioral measure can be quite enlightening about the social psychology of real life.

Here's an intriguing case. People who live in "special interest houses" on a college campus presumably take the interest quite seriously. Kitts (2003) studied students who elected to live in vegetarian houses where there were strict prohibitions against eating meat and fish (perhaps your school has one). Yet Kitts found that some residents were more observant of the rules than others, and that most of them admitted to breaching their vegetarian regime (typically by eating fish) in private on occasion. They did so in secret because they wanted to protect their fellow vegetarians' sensibilities ("I never want to gross them out that I eat meat") and their own welfare ("I don't want my housemates to guilt me out"). In this example, private verbal reports revealed a great deal more than public behavior, thereby allowing Kitts to provide a more perceptive account of students' choices, lifestyle, and actual eating habits.

Varieties of verbal measures revisited

As we learned in chapter 6, there are a host of different types of ways to ask and receive answers to either close-ended or open-ended questions. I am not going to revisit all of the suggestions presented in chapter 6, but I do recommend that you review that chapter's contents before making any final decisions about what sort of verbal dependent measures you will use in your research project. What I am going to do here is to remind you of the variety of different sorts of verbal measures you can use in social psychological research. I am also going to offer some suggestions about constructing verbal dependent measures that were not offered earlier in the book.

Table 8.2 Some Open-Ended and Close-Ended Verbal Dependent Variables

Open-ended
  Paper and pencil measures (e.g., questionnaires)
  Surveys
  Free recall measures
  Serial recall measures
  Cued recall measures
  Interviews
  Narrative methods

  _____
  _____

Close-ended
  Paper and pencil measures (e.g., questionnaires)
  Personality inventories
  Rating scales
  Surveys
  Recognition measures

  _____
  _____
  _____

Table 8.2 lists a variety of verbal dependent variables you should consider. Naturally, this list is not an exhaustive one. As always, your goal should be to select a verbal measure that theoretically and practically supports whatever behavioral dependent measure you decide to use. Few studies in social psychology rely exclusively on verbal measures or behavioral measures. Some combination of the two is typical. Note that space is provided in Table 8.2 for you to jot down other verbal dependent measures that you learn about in the social psychological literature or that you discover on your own.

Let's turn to some final suggestions for constructing verbal dependent measures.

When asking for numerical responses, be specific and concrete. Research participants are often asked to estimate how often they do or think about something ("About how often do you tell 'white lies' in order not to hurt someone's feelings?"). Although this phrasing invites an open-ended response, a researcher would be better served to offer a distinct and limited set of responses, such as:

Never
Once a week
A few times a week
Several times a week
Once a day
More than once a day

Presenting participants with specific responses ensures that all the responses are based on the same shared metric rather than people's idiosyncratic sense of measurement (and the six responses shown above can easily be coded by a researcher as ratings of "1" to "6" for analysis). For example, when you use descriptions such as "a couple" or "a few," do you mean "two" and "three," respectively? Many but by no means all people ascribe these particular numbers to those particular words. Thus, whenever possible, either provide explicit numbers for people to respond to or define your terms clearly for them.

Keep the content of your questions relevant to your participants. The content of your questions should be both group and age appropriate. Thus, if you are interested in the experience and pressures involved in joining an on-campus group, such as pledging a fraternity or a sorority, you must be sure your research participants either went through "rush" (a period where unaffiliated students explore life in a fraternity or sorority) or joined one of these organizations. Having "independent" students take part in the research is not going to inform you about the process of becoming a member of one of these social organizations.

Similarly, be sure to screen your participant sample with an eye to the relevance of your questions for them. Questions about gender, religion, race, culture, social class, for example, can be interesting and quite important when it comes to portraying social life. You must, however, ensure that such questions are relevant to all the members of your sample.

To ensure acquiring the sample you want and need for your research, be sure to list any participant qualifications on whatever sign-up method you are using to recruit participants (see chapter 10). There is nothing wrong with positing such qualifications ("This study is about women's views of feminism, thus we are only interested in having women students sign up to participate") as long as you do so in an open and honest manner. Always ask yourself this question: Is there anything about the listed qualifications that could offend anyone? If so, then briefly and honestly explain why you are limiting your research project to certain people or groups.

Be aware of the distinction between recognition and recall measures. On occasion, a social psychologist will want to assess people's memories for some event or for something about the self or some other person. A thorough review of social psychological issues pertaining to memory and related mental representations are beyond the scope of this chapter and book (but see, e.g., Moskowitz, 2005; Smith, 1998). Measures of recognition or recall are sometimes used in studies of impression formation. A *recall* task asks a participant to produce some item from memory, such as a fact, a word, a description, or an impression. There are three basic sorts of recall tasks. A *free-recall* task requires participants to repeat learned items in any order they can recall. In contrast, *serial-recall* tasks anticipate that participants will repeat items in the exact order in which they were originally heard or read to them. Finally, *cued-recall* tasks call for participants to memorize a list of paired items (e.g., "friendly – Latino"). When given one item from the pair later, participants are expected to recall the item's mate correctly.

Using a recall task, for example, a researcher could present people with a written description of some target person. Later, after completing some unrelated task, participants are asked to write down all the information they can remember—that is, recall—about the target. The researcher can examine recalled information to learn what is remembered accurately (perhaps salient characteristics, such as race, gender, and so on), the number of facts recalled, and the order in which the information is remembered. Often items learned last are recalled first, the so-called recency effect. Similarly, primacy effects are also often observed, where items learned early on are recalled better (perhaps due to rehearsal) than information appearing later. Of particular interest to some social psychologists would be facts that participants "recall" that were not part of the written description; social perceivers often fill in the blanks, judging what additional qualities about a person should or could be present.

When participants perform a *recognition* task, they are asked to select or identify previously learned material from some array of other related information. Multiple choice and true–false tests are basic examples of recognition memory tasks. A social psychologist might want to measure how well participants learned whatever detailed information was presented during the instruction phase of an experiment. A recognition measure could be used as a manipulation check at that point before proceeding to the next phase of the experiment. For more detailed information on memory processes in psychological research generally, see Tulving and Craik (2000).

Some additional verbal dependent measures

Interviews. Another way to learn how people think, feel, and act is to interview them. Interviews can be conducted in a face-to-face manner or over the telephone, and they are often used in place of surveys or questionnaires because a researcher wants an opportunity to delve deeper into people's opinions about, or reaction to, some topic. An interviewer, usually the experimenter, asks a participant a series of questions in a relatively set order. The individual focus inherent in an interview allows the interviewer to depart from the list of set questions as warranted by the interviewee's comments. Structured interviews tend to rely on close-ended questions, whereas more freewheeling interviews use open-ended questions.

Conducting an interview sounds easy enough, but doing so well entails a couple of challenges. The primary challenge to an interviewer is to remain open and unbiased when listening to and keeping track of participant responses. No matter how unusual the response, a good interviewer should remain unflappable. A second challenge involves how to adequately and thoroughly keep a record of participant responses. Some interviewers rely on a check list composed of close-ended questions while others give the interviewee free rein to disclose whatever comes to mind. Either the interviewer must be able to write verbatim statements quickly and accurately or some recording device (e.g., a tape recorder) must be used. Asking a participant to pause in mid-thought while the interviewer finishes jotting down some comment can be disruptive to the interview and to the research process. Once a transcription of the interview is complete, some interviewers invite interviewees to review the documents for accuracy; such verification is fine for journalism but can introduce a bias into social psychological research.

There are decided strengths to interviewing as a research technique. The exchange between interviewer and interviewee can be a great source of ideas for future experimental work. Outside of a debriefing (see chapter 10), researchers rarely have the opportunity to learn from participants in a back-and-forth manner. The physical presence, too, of an interested, motivated interviewer can encourage participants to take the exercise quite seriously, thereby resulting in higher quality data.

As for drawbacks, interviewing is very time-consuming and clearly not as efficient an enterprise as administering surveys or questionnaires. A good interview is part art and part science, and it is dependent on the interviewer's demeanor. If the interviewer is not comfortable in the role, interactions will be awkward and little valuable verbal information will be gathered. More problematic still, however, is the bias that can be introduced during the interaction if the interviewer is aware of whether a participant is in the experimental or control condition. To reduce the possibility of bias here, it is always a good idea to keep the interviewer unaware of a participant's group assignment. For more detailed guidance on planning and conducting interviews, see, for example, Gubrium and Holstein (2002), Houtkoop (2000), Mishler (1986), Schuman (1981), Schwarz, Grove, and Schuman (1998), and Seidman (1998).

Verbal protocols. Protocol analysis is a familiar tool in experimental and cognitive psychology (e.g., Ericsson & Simon, 1980, 1993; Newell & Simon, 1972). A *protocol analysis* involves giving a research participant some problem to solve and then having the individual "think out loud" while solving it. In theory, a participant's "online" verbalizations, as it were, should reveal the steps being used in the course of thinking through some situation. Similar to some interviews, a detailed transcript (the protocol) is prepared for subsequent analysis (e.g., identifying key moments in the participant's thinking that indicate how he or she sought a solution). The study and integration of data from several protocols is often used to describe the presumed process of reasoning people use in a given domain.

The use of verbal protocols is relatively uncommon in social psychology, possibly due to the critical evaluation of research relying on verbal reports of mental processes (Nisbett & Wilson, 1977). Under some circumstances, of course, asking people taking part in a social psychology experiment to describe their on-going thoughts (as opposed to reflecting back on what led them to some conclusion or trying to explain why they performed some behavior) approximates protocol analysis. Ericsson and Simon (1993) argue that bias is introduced in a protocol when participants are asked to explain their cognitive processes but not when they say what they are thinking out loud.

A related, if somewhat retrospective, technique used in social psychology to study people's responses to persuasive messages is called *thought listing* (Cacioppo, Harkins,

& Petty, 1981; Cacioppo & Petty, 1981; Petty & Cacioppo, 1981). Research participants are given some period of time (e.g., 3 minutes) during which they list all the thoughts they had while they read or heard some persuasive argument ("record only those ideas that you were thinking during the last few minutes"; Cacioppo & Petty, 1981, p. 315). Later, a group of trained judges evaluate the listed thoughts to determine favorable or unfavorable responses in light of the persuasive communication.

Other Types of Dependent Measures

Standard behavioral or verbal-dependent measures do not exhaust research possibilities for social psychologists. Other distinct approaches that complement or supplement behavioral and verbal dependent variables exist, including nonverbal measures, implicit measures, physiological measures, bogus pipeline methods, and narrative approaches.

Nonverbal measures

Nonverbal measures would seem to be behavioral measures because they involve acts that lack or do not rely on words. Perhaps because nonverbal measures of behavior are so subtle and yet they are all around us all the time, social psychology ascribes special status to them. *Nonverbal measures* are designed to assess actions or cues that people use to convey meaning independent of verbal comments. Consider, for example, how often you use nonverbal clues to infer how a person is feeling. Happiness or dejection in others, for example, is often apparent to us, even when no words have been uttered. Do they look relaxed? Are they smiling and looking you in the eye? Or are they looking away and nervously wringing their hands? Categories of nonverbal behavior include voice tone and pitch, facial expressions, hand gestures, body lean and orientation (e.g., towards or away from others), eye contact and gaze (DePaulo & Friedman, 1998).

Of course, nonverbal cues routinely accompany what people say and, in fact, such cues often reveal people's underlying intentions. Thus how you say something is often as important as what you say. For example, have you ever heard one person say to another, "Nice dress" or a similar remark and recognized immediately that the intent was sarcasm (i.e., what an *ugly* dress?)? Social psychologists are interested in measuring nonverbal behavior linked with people's speech because it often reveals how they are feeling. Moreover, nonverbal reactions often reveal people's "true" feelings because such reactions are not always under voluntary control. All too often, people "leak" their true emotions despite protests to the contrary ("I'm not mad at you—really, I'm not"; Ekman & Friesen, 1969). How close a person sits to another, as well as the relative number of smiles directed at that person, readily reveals whether attitudes are positive or negative (Hazlewood & Olson, 1986).

Implicit measures

Nonverbal measures are ideal because they are less subject to conscious control or distortion than verbal reports. Many social psychologists are increasingly interested in a particular nonverbal measure, so-called *implicit measures*, which are used to assess people's automatic positive or negative reactions to objects or other people. Considerable research has been conducted on implicit prejudice (e.g., Greenwald & Banaji, 1995), where people associate positive or negative characteristics toward different social groups. The chief advantage of implicit measures is their subtlety; people cannot censor their habitual reactions—thoughts or feelings (e.g., unfriendliness, fear)—toward a social category (e.g., Black people). Thus a research participant can claim to possess a positive attitude toward a group but his or her response to an implicit measure might reveal the opposite attitude, one lying below conscious awareness (for reviews of recent social psychological research on unconscious processes, see Hassin, Uleman, & Bargh, 2005; Uleman & Bargh, 1989; Wilson, 2002).

To measure implicit, prejudiced attitudes, most researchers use the *Implicit Association Test* (IAT; Greenwald, McGhee, & Schwartz, 1998). Participants are asked to complete two sorting activities as fast as possible. The assumption is that participants' reaction times reveal how they feel about some *target* (e.g., race, ethnic group, sport). One activity requires them to place the target in the same category as a list of words with positive meanings (e.g., nice, fair, beautiful). In the second activity, the target is placed with some negative terms (e.g., unkind, ugly, dishonest). To determine how participants actually feel about a given target, a researcher compares the speed with which the two sorting activities occur. If the target is associated with the positive terms more quickly than the negative terms, the participant is presumed to have a positive implicit attitude toward the target. However, if the target is linked more quickly with the negative terms than the positive ones, then the implicit attitude is identified as negative. You can take an online version of the IAT at https://implicit.harvard.edu/implicit/.

The main drawback of the IAT is that it takes some time to complete, and some researchers question the measure's validity (e.g., Brendl, Markman, & Messner, 2001; but see Nosek, Greenwald, & Banaji, 2007). On the other hand, people's responses on the IAT have been linked with a variety of nonverbal, prejudiced reactions, including making or failing to make eye contact, tentative spoken exchanges, and the presence or absence of smiles (e.g., Dovidio, Kwakami, Johnson, Johnson, & Howard, 1997). Regarding preferences for some groups over others, both younger and older individuals display a bias toward the young over the old, and many people who complete the IAT carry a moderate to high level of prejudice favoring White targets over Blacks (Nosek, Banaji, & Greenwald, 2002).

Physiological measures

Measures of physiological states—bodily processes—in the study of social behavior are not new. Social psychologists sometimes measure blood pressure, heart rate, pupil dilation, as well as galvanic skin response (GSR), a change in the electrical properties of skin (i.e., sweat) in response to a stimulus that triggers excitement or anxiety. Such measures are outside people's conscious control, thus researchers can employ them as unbiased dependent variables.

Unfortunately, physiological measures often require sensitive and rather expensive equipment to employ. Such equipment requires training for users, as well as routine maintenance, which means it is not likely to be available for use in student research projects. Many physiological measures also have a conceptual drawback: They measure the presence or absence of general bodily arousal but they fail to differentiate among various types of arousal. Consider a measure of GSR: Despite the fact that being frightened and being thrilled are distinct types of emotional experiences, most of us are likely to begin to sweat in the same way whether we are watching a scary movie or an exhilarating sporting event. Naturally, objective physiological dependent measures should be supported by self-report and observational measures. For more detailed discussion of physiological measures and their use in social psychological research, see Cacioppo and Tassinary (1990), Cacioppo, Tassinary, and Berntson (2000), Petty (1983), and Wagner and Manstead (1989).

Noninvasive measures from social neuroscience. One new area of physiological inquiry in social psychology is worth mentioning. The subdiscipline of *social neuroscience,* which examines how brain processes influence social cognition, emotion, and interpersonal relationships, among other topics in social and personality psychology, uses noninvasive tools including functional magnetic resonance imaging (fMRI) and positron emission tomography (PET).

These "high tech" tools are obviously beyond the scope of anyone's first foray into social psychological research, but I do think it is important to understand the potential of social neuroscience. Let's briefly consider how fMRI can be used to shed light on our social experience. fMRI is an imaging technology that allows researchers to observe brain structures and to measure changes (e.g., blood flow) happening therein while a person is performing some cognitive task. Eisenberger, Lieberman, and Williams (2003), for example, conducted a study to determine whether the brain bases of social pain are similar to those associated with physical pain (see also Panksepp, 2003). To test the effect of social pain, the researchers chose to examine how people feel when they are socially excluded—ignored, passed over, ostracized—by others. While playing a computerized (virtual) ball tossing game with others, participants were eventually excluded from play by their opponents. As anticipated, brain activity following this mild ostracism paralleled that found in studies of physical pain and was associated with self-reports of anguish. The promise of fMRI data are that they can be linked up with more traditional, social psychological research on the effects of being socially excluded or even dropped by others (see Williams, 2002, for a review of traditional social psychological research on ostracism). For an introduction to social neuroscience, see Cacioppo and Berntson (2004) and Cacioppo, Visser, and Pickett (2005).

False physiological feedback: The bogus pipeline

I would be remiss if I did not mention a classic dependent measure designed to ensure truthful responses from research participants—the bogus pipeline (Jones & Sigall, 1971). This paradigm was created to convince research participants that an experimenter could actually "read their minds" by discerning when they were being truthful. Well in advance of being connected to a fake lie detecting device in a lab setting, Jones and Sigall assessed participants' attitudes in a pretest session. Participants' pretest responses were then used in concert with the pipeline device to demonstrate that honest opinions and feelings could be measured. From that point on, the majority of participants were willing to disclose how they truly felt about various stigmatized groups (e.g., people with disabilities, Blacks). The bogus pipeline proved to be an excellent measure of attitudes as dependent variables, a methodological innovation social psychologists used to obtain true responses towards ideas, groups, and social issues (for a review of the bogus pipeline's effectiveness as a research tool, see Roese & Jamieson, 1993).

Narrative approaches

Narrative approaches represent a new, qualitative approach to dependent variables that is gaining popularity in social and personality psychology. By *narrative*, I mean the personal stories people tell in order to make sense of their own lives, both for themselves and for other people (e.g., McAdams, 1993). Research on narratives suggests that people connect their experiences with different aspects of their self-concept in order to develop a coherent identity, albeit one that can change across time and circumstance. People are especially likely to search for meaning and purpose in their lives following critical moments or major transitions (McAdams, Josselson, & Lieblich, 2001).

Use of narrative approaches by having participants write about their own lives is one way to collect a great deal of rich, interesting information about social life and personal development. On the other hand, a researcher must have some organizing theme or coding scheme to impose order on so much information (similar concerns were raised about open-ended measures in chapter 6). Smaller scale narrative studies using selected self-reports as dependent variables are no doubt possible. For ideas, consult Josselson, Lieblich, and McAdams (2002), McAdams (1993), and McAdams et al. (2001).

Some Practical Issues for Administering Dependent Variables

Will the presentation of a dependent variable change a participant's behavior for the wrong reason (i.e., reactivity)? What can be done to reduce participants' suspicion, curiosity, or wariness regarding the delivery of dependent variables in studies? How

can a researcher be sure that administering a dependent variable won't alert participants about the hypothesis being studied? We already noted that many behavioral
measures have an advantage over verbal measures—people are often less likely to
notice them and, in any case, behavior is often harder to monitor or control than are
thoughts. There are a variety of simple steps a researcher can consider so that a study's
purpose and the main dependent variable are not linked together.

Attend to issues of privacy and sensitivity.   Keep participant reactivity in mind. If your
project is designed to ask questions about sensitive or private matters, remember that
people are often too embarrassed or inhibited to reveal how they actually feel about a
topic or to describe their relevant past behavior. Topics such as sexuality, controversial
social issues (e.g., abortion), race relations, and the like will often induce participants
to give less than candid answers.

What can be done? In the first place, make certain that you really and truly want
and need to conduct research on sensitive or private issues. There are many other
social psychological topics that do not arouse participant concern or suspicion. Second,
if you pursue one of these topics, then take great methodological pains to assure participants that honest responses are needed and that you will keep those responses
anonymous. To do so, behaviorally illustrate how you will maintain anonymity by
having participants place completed questionnaires, for example, in a container with
other surveys. Explain that informed consent forms (recall chapter 3) will be kept
separate from any data collected from them (an ethical practice which should be
observed in any case). Third, admit that the topic of your project is one that often
raises concern. Without revealing your hypothesis, explain why the topic is important
and try to enlist the participants' help as research collaborators and not simply as good
sources of social information. The main point is that sincerity and candor can often
encourage research participants to approach your project with interest, engagement,
and truthful responses.

Disguise a dependent measure.   A dependent measure need not announce itself. Why
not disguise it so that participants are not aware their actions have been measured?
Subtle, nonreactive or unobtrusive behavioral measures were already suggested as
good indicators of people's mental states or dispositions. Another approach can be to
closely observe what participants do at the critical moment in an experiment, thereby
collecting behavioral observations that are consistent with the hypothesis. In the case
of verbal measures, disguising the dependent variable can be as straightforward
as embedding a key question or questions with some filler items within a
questionnaire.

Remove the dependent variable from the situation.   To reduce participant suspicion,
some researchers complete the main part of the study (i.e., delivery of the independent
variable), claim that the study is over, and then begin a debriefing. In the course of
the debriefing, for instance, the experimenter asks the participant to complete an

additional, short set of questions. The actual dependent variable is embedded therein and the participant is none the wiser until the actual debriefing subsequently occurs. Alternatively, a researcher might inform participants that they will take part in two separate but unrelated studies. After the first study is supposedly over, the dependent variable is presented as an unrelated part of the second study. Again, due to the cover story regarding the two studies, the participants are unlikely to link the actual dependent variable with what came before.

Consider nonverbal dependent measures. Instead of asking participants directly how they feel about another person through an interview or a questionnaire—both of which are apt to trigger social desirability concerns (recall chapter 6)—look to subtle nonverbal measures of affect. There is a large literature on nonverbal behavior, much of it concerned with social psychological processes (for a review, see DePaulo & Friedman, 1998). Proximity or interpersonal distance was already suggested as one way to assess one person's liking of another (e.g., Hall, 1966). Making eye contact is another (Exline, 1971). Before employing a nonverbal dependent variable, a conscientious researcher will search the relevant literature to make certain that the behavior has been validated as a reliable indicator of the desired psychological state.

ACTIVE LEARNING EXERCISE   **8B**

Developing Dependent Variables by Looking to the Literature

Coming up with just the right dependent variable for a study can be a challenge. Keep in mind that you need not reinvent the wheel in order to find one that will work for your purposes. Several times in the course of this book I have suggested that you look to the literature for ideas. Borrowing and adapting existing dependent measures is entirely appropriate as long as you credit the creator by citing his or her work in your research report or summary (see chapter 12). Here are two suggestions:

Develop dependent measures based on an article you think is interesting. Look through a recent issue of a social psychology journal or look up a study you admire. Review the description of the dependent variables in the Method section of the article. What makes the measure a good one? Is it compelling and involving? Clever and unobtrusive? Well-written? How could you adapt it for your own research? Can you think of ways to improve it? Write a paragraph describing the original measure, why you think it is a strong one, and how you might use it.

Continued

Develop dependent measures linked to an article relevant to your project. Look through the articles you gathered for your own project. Are there dependent measures that would fit your project well? Should they be adapted or altered? How might the measures be improved for your purposes? Write a paragraph describing each original measure, why you think each is of potential use, or is a strong one, and how you might use it for your own project. Be sure to indicate how the different levels of your independent variable will affect each measure.

Reliability and Dependent Variables

One final, important concern for dependent variables is their reliability. When psychologists talk about reliability, they are not referring to whether a measure can be trusted or whether it is dependable—those characteristics refer more to the validity of a construct or a measure (see chapter 9). *Reliability* refers to a measure's degree of consistency or stability; however, there are a few ways a measure can be consistent. The first is the measure's consistency across time. Many measures, such as intelligence (IQ) tests and some personality inventories, assume that a person's score at one point in time should be approximately the same at another point in time, even if the interval is quite large, say, several months or even longer. Social psychologists use these sorts of reliability measures less often than other psychologists, as most of their experiments are designed to create some change in response due to the impact of an independent variable on a dependent variable. However, if a social psychologist wanted to recruit participants with a particular trait—say, shyness or optimism, for example—then the use of a consistent personality measure would be very important.

A second type of reliability is often related to dependent variables that contain a variety of items all designed to measure the same construct. *Internal consistency* refers to how well a collection of similar items are associated with one another. Technically speaking, this form of reliability is determined by the degree of intercorrelations among a group of related test items or a collection of subtests. Imagine, for example, that you were developing a new personality scale designed to measure modesty to identify individuals who rarely call attention to themselves or their actions. A common approach is to write a large pool of items and to then pilot test them on a group of people. The initial run of analyses involves correlating all the responses to the items with one another. To create a reliable measure, those items that are highly associated with one another (i.e., tapping into the same construct) are retained, whereas those with low correlations are dropped. The decision to retain some items while dropping others usually involves examining what is called an *alpha coefficient*, a numerical index of internal consistency reliability. According to Rosenthal and Rosnow (1991), a reasonable alpha coefficient for tests used for clinical purposes should be .85 or higher, levels which indicate the measure is dependable. Alpha levels for experimental work—including experimental social psychology—can be lower and still be used, but I would suggest using care with anything under .70. Sometimes a researcher will revise some items or write new ones and then conduct a second pilot test (and recalculate internal consistency) in order to prepare the measure for use. For a more technical discussion of internal consistency, see Cronbach (1951). Before deciding to use any published scale in a research project, you should examine its internal consistency reliability to be sure it reaches an acceptable level (such information is available in the publication introducing the scale or, in the case of purchased products, in the test booklet accompanying the copies of the measure).

A type of reliability often found in social psychology experiments is called *interobserver reliability*, that is, the degree to which observers agree about what behavior they are observing, coding, or otherwise describing. Earlier, when discussing unobtrusive measures, I cited research by Wilson et al. (1984, studies 1 and 2) where coders observed and recorded participants' puzzle play and facial expressions from behind a one-way mirror. Interobserver reliability was obtained in both studies by correlating the observations of one observer with those of the other (i.e., a high positive correlation indicated that both observers effectively saw the same behaviors). The utility of this form of reliability is an error check, a way to ensure that the measurement of dependent variables (how long each puzzle was played with by each participant; the number, strength, and duration of each participant's smiles) is accurate. Ideally, the observed correlation between two observers' ratings should be above .80, preferably closer to .90.

Let's close with one important observation about any dependent variable or other measure, one that nicely sets up the topic of the next chapter. Just because a dependent variable is reliable does not mean that it is valid, that it is truly measuring what it is suppose to capture in terms of behavior, verbal report, or psychological construct. An unfair or poorly constructed test will remain so, and people taking it more than once will still score badly on it. Reliability, then, while important, is only one important aspect of a measure. Researchers must be sure that their dependent variables are tapping into the intended social phenomena.

Exercises

1   Review the "pen" study conducted by Hazel Markus that opens this chapter. Can you think of other everyday choices or objects that reveal how different cultural groups display understandings of agency? How would you measure these dependent variables?

2   List some possible behavioral dependent variables that could represent the quantifiable dimensions noted in this chapter (e.g., frequency, duration, speed, proximity).

3   You are planning a study on people's willingness to donate blood to a local blood bank. Identify some overt behavioral, behavioroid, and unobtrusive measures for the study.

4   Review the section discussing unobtrusive measures and then walk around your campus to identify physical evidence pointing to possible erosion and accretion measures.

Chapter 9

Validity and Realism in Research

Are you behaviorally consistent? Do you always do what you say you will? Can your future actions be more or less predicted from what your friends and family know to be true about you? Put another way, do you ever think of yourself as an inconsistent person? Perish the thought! Most of us would not like such a label. We like to think of ourselves as consistent, reliable, dependable people. But are we? When do our self-conceptions change due to our actions? More to the point of this chapter, how can social psychologists convincingly demonstrate that our desire to appear consistent depends on links between thought and behavior when we cannot "see" thoughts or truly measure them? What information do social psychologists use to verify that the causes of our social behavior are just what the theories predict them to be?

These are good questions, the sorts of questions that should push us to do a bit of soul searching. Before we do so—after all, we have this whole chapter to mull over these issues—mentally place yourself in the following situation. You are recruited to take part in an experiment. For an entire hour, you carry out a series of rather boring activities, including turning some wooden knobs embedded in a board round and round. When, at last, you finish, the experimenter tells you that the research deals with how people's expectations influence their performance.

The experimenter, who seems a bit upset, then tells you there is a problem. There is another participant, someone just like you, waiting outside. This person must be told that the experiment—that dull collection of activities you just finished—is really quite interesting. Normally, there is a helper around whose job it is to convince participants that this is true. Alas, for unforeseeable reasons, the helper couldn't be here right now. The experimenter pleads: Would *you* be willing to fill in for the helper? He also tells you that you will be paid for your trouble.

You agree to help—after all, you will be aiding an important research effort and you will also be compensated. You meet the next participant and tell him what a terrific time you had performing the experiment. He looks incredulous. "Are you sure? I heard from a friend who took part in this a week ago that it was dull, dull, dull." "Not at all," you counter, "it's great fun. And you'll get some exercise turning things. I am confident you'll enjoy this experiment. Really." Once you finish telling your "white lie," you are asked to complete a survey dealing with how people react to experiments. One of the questions in this survey asks you to rate how much you enjoyed the knob-turning exercise, the very same exercise you swore up and down was "very interesting" but which, in fact, was extremely boring. How enjoyable would you say the experiment turned out to be?

Before you answer this question, there is one more bit of information to consider: How much were you paid to lie to the waiting participant? Some participants were paid $1 for telling the lie; others were paid $20. (This study, conducted by social psychologists Leon Festinger and J. Merrill Carlsmith, was conducted in 1959, a time when $20 was a tidy sum of money.) What do you predict to be true of your subsequent rating of the knob-turning exercise—would you rate it more favorably if you were paid $1 or $20, and why?

People who are not familiar with this classic piece of social psychological research are usually quick to say that the $20 would motivate them to rate the activity as quite interesting. Indeed, $20 is a reasonable motivator, but as is always the case in any experiment, we must ask the fundamental question, "Compared to what?" Although $20 is sufficient justification for filling their role, $1 is not. According to Festinger and Carlsmith (1959), $1 was "insufficient justification" for performing the two actions— turning the knobs in the first place and then telling a lie about the activity to an innocent stranger. Thus, compared to those people in the $20 condition, those paid $1 rated the experiment as relatively more interesting. How? Why?

Festinger's (1957) theory of cognitive dissonance suggests that people are motivated to maintain a strong sense of consistency in their thoughts. When two thoughts are "dissonant" or in conflict with one another (e.g., "I spent an hour doing a boring and repetitive task and only got paid $1 for it!"), we need to mentally smooth them over to reduce the arousal and psychological tension we feel (e.g., "Have I been duped?"). Being paid so little for doing so much, especially when the work was tedious and meaningless, coupled with being asked to lie to someone about the experience, leads to a great deal of psychological dissonance. In such a circumstance, the afflicted individual feels compelled to do something to relieve, reduce, or release this tension. The usual way to achieve this end is by changing our minds in order to justify our actions (e.g., "Say, although I only got $1 for my trouble, I like the idea of advancing science and, anyway, turning those knobs was sort of fun"). Being paid a dollar for all your trouble is not enough, so participants in the $1 condition were more likely to reduce their feelings of dissonance by rating the experiment as relatively more enjoyable as compared to those in the $20 group (see Figure 9.1). Earning that large amount of cash served as sufficient justification for performing the dull task and telling a lie ("Sure, the work was dull and I had to lie about it, but hey, it's worth $20!"), so these folks experienced a relatively low level of dissonance. In turn, their relative rating of the experiment was less enthusiastic and more candid than the $1 group.

Cognitive dissonance proved to be a robust theory and one of the more popular areas of empirical inquiry in social psychology (Cooper, 2007). A couple of thousand studies on the topic can now be found in the psychological literature. Despite its obvious popularity as a construct (e.g., Harmon-Jones & Mills, 1999), how do we

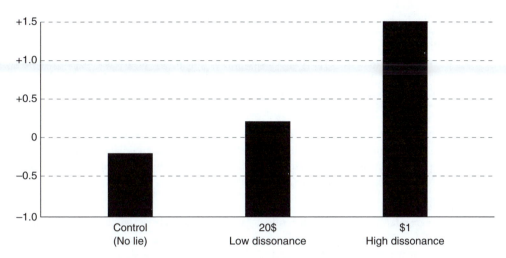

Figure 9.1. Demonstrating insufficient justification: Ratings of enjoyment from Festinger and Carlsmith (1959)

know that this social psychological phenomenon is real? What evidence do we have that dissonant cognitions lead to tension, which leads people to seek ways to reduce their sense of arousal by, for example, rationalizing their behavior to themselves? After all, Festinger and Carlsmith (1959) only measured self-reported enjoyment of a bogus experiment after it was over—they did not measure any "cognitions" nor did they prove that such thoughts changed prior to completing the survey. How can we be sure that what we believe we know about social behavior is actually true?

These are all good questions, the sorts of questions that conscientious researchers routinely ask themselves. These questions lead to the topics of this chapter: the roles of validity and realism in social psychological research. As we will see, these two terms refer to distinct qualities that are desirable in any psychological research, especially that aimed at explaining social behavior. The general focus in this chapter will be to demonstrate that social psychological descriptions of thoughts, feelings, and behaviors are both accurate and correct when examined using rigorous research methods and scientific inference. We begin with the issue of validity, which comes in three main forms where research is concerned: internal validity, external validity, and construct validity (Campbell, 1957; Campbell & Stanley, 1966; Cook & Campbell, 1979; Shadish, Cook, & Campbell, 2001). Some of the key questions addressed by each form of validity are shown in Table 9.1. We begin by considering internal validity.

Trusting Research Evidence: Demonstrating Internal Validity

When should we trust the results of an experiment or field study? One answer to this question involves demonstrating the presence of internal validity. *Internal validity* is

Table 9.1   Questions Addressed by the Three Forms of Validity

Internal validity

  Does the research reveal the hypothesized causal relationship between the independent and dependent variable? Are the causal findings trustworthy? Is the observed change in the measured variable due exclusively to the effect of the manipulated variable?

External validity

  Can we use this sample of behavior to make predictions and draw conclusions about behavior in other populations? Do the results of the present research have implications for other people at other times in similar or related settings? Can findings from an experiment or other study be used to draw generalizations about behavior?

Construct validity

  Do the independent variable and dependent variable adequately represent the theoretical constructs? Are the operationalizations of these variables appropriate representations of the actual constructs? How do the operationalizations of the constructs examined in the present research relate to other, established operationalizations of the same constructs?

a necessary quality of any and all experimental research: There is clear evidence that any change in a dependent variable is attributable only to the influence of the intended independent variable. The "clear evidence" referred to here, of course, is that any confounded variables, uncontrolled variables, or other extraneous factors are ruled out as having any effects on the observed results (recall the discussion in chapter 4). Internal validity, then, is about the nature and direction of causality. No experiment can be labeled a true experiment unless it has internal validity. Indeed, without internal validity, the results of any experiment cannot be trusted.

What about field studies or really any social psychological research that is conducted out of the controlled confines of the laboratory? In ideal circumstances, *any* piece of social psychological research should demonstrate internal validity. As already acknowledged, however, control and the ability to accurately assess cause and effect linkages between variables recede when we leave the lab (see chapter 5). Social psychologists must content themselves with trying to rule out competing explanations for results obtained outside controlled settings. Sometimes this is possible in nonexperimental or quasi-experimental research; other times, not.

Researchers often speak of experiments that are "high" in internal validity, which generally means that the research design and the methods used effectively ruled out rival explanations for the obtained results. We know something happened so that the independent variable affected the dependent variable in the predicted manner and probably for the reasons anticipated by the theory and hypothesis. Research with high levels of internal validity gives social psychologists confidence in drawing conclusions about causality, which in turn allows them to expand theory, develop new hypotheses, and design and execute new experiments or other studies. When an investigation is said to have "low" internal validity, the reverse state of affairs is present. The researcher and those who learn about the research are unsure about the veracity of the findings. Confidence where causality is concerned is low. In this case, we also know that something happened, but we are not altogether sure why or whether the results can be trusted or used in subsequent investigations.

How can a social psychologist rule out rival hypotheses and demonstrate internal validity? The short answer is this one: Conduct a true experiment (see chapter 4). The slightly longer answer is this one: Randomly select participants (if possible) and randomly assign them to conditions in the experiment (essential). Doing so controls for any individual differences participants carry into the situation. By its very nature, a true experiment isolates the participants from outside influences (ideally, both random and systematic variation) so that the independent variable of choice can be directed toward the dependent variable of interest.

Naturally, as was discussed earlier in chapters 4 and 5, the ideal, true experiment is not always possible. Research into many real life social behaviors can be messy in that cause and effect is hard to discern. Instead of giving up or restricting all research to the lab (which would result in limited portrayals of social behavior), researchers must be on the lookout for ways that a study's internal validity could be compromised. Cook and Campbell (1979; see also Judd & Kenny, 1981; Shadish et al., 2001) draw attention to what they call various "threats" to internal validity.

General threats to internal validity

Randomization usually allows researchers to assume that alternative explanations for obtained results are either eliminated or pose minimal problems. When randomization is violated or cannot be performed, however, drawing casual conclusions becomes problematic. Cook and Campbell (1979; see also Shadish et al., 2001) systematized the "threats" to internal validity: competing accounts, rival hypotheses, troublesome or otherwise confusing influences. Careful researchers, even when they conduct a rigorous experiment with random assignment and a high level of control, still evaluate whether any threats to the project's internal validity exist. Researchers who do field research, applied studies, or any research where randomization and control are either compromised, limited, or nonexistent, must pay special attention to these threats. If a threat to internal validity cannot be reasonably ruled out, then the findings will be of limited use. We will discuss seven of the threats identified by Cook and Campbell. Discussion of other threats to internal validity can be found in Cook and Campbell (1979), Judd and Kenny (1981), and Shadish et al. (2001).

History. What happens when some event outside a researcher's control occurs at the same time as the presentation of the independent variable? Perhaps the event and not the manipulated variable is the cause of any observed change in the dependent variable—but how would a researcher know? The threat known as *history* can literally be some major national or international event—a moment in history—that changes people's outlooks and their actions in the course of a study (it could also be a local event, albeit one affecting the population being sampled for inclusion in a study). History or "historical influences" are probably a greater threat in the context of longitudinal studies, but you can well imagine how certain shared events (e.g., September 11, 2001, the crash of the space shuttle *Columbia*) could change people's actions even in a brief experiment of less than an hour. People could be preoccupied by some crisis so that their attention wanders from the experimental task, thereby weakening the effects of independent variable and the dependent variable designed to assess its impact. Ruling out the effects of history is easier in a controlled laboratory setting than in field or other applied settings containing myriad sources of interest and distraction.

Maturation. Research participants change across time—they mature in various ways. In long-term research projects, people's social and political attitudes can be expected to change, and they are also aging, which can mean some physical and mental transformations occur. When projects are short in duration, like most social psychology experiments, is *maturation* a concern? It can be a threat in the sense that people "mature" over the course of an hour or so; some may become hungry, others may be tired, and so on. Regardless of the time frame, these changes represent a threat to a study's internal validity because they represent an influence that is independent of randomization and the manipulation and measurement of key variables. What can be done? When research projects are long-term efforts, researchers must be vigilant for maturational influences in the same way they must look out for historical events as threats. For short-term projects, a savvy researcher schedules data collection at times when people are apt to be at their best—neither too early nor too late in the day, for example, or just after meal times rather than before. Such simple precautions reduce maturation as a systematic, if not random, source of error and threat to valid inference. By the way, as a threat to internal validity, *maturation* is sometimes confused with *history*. To remember the difference between the two, think of maturation as something internal or biologically based, whereas history is an external influence, something outside of the person.

Testing. *Testing* is a broad term referring to ways that behavior can change independently of an intervention, particularly when participants are asked to complete the same measures. When people complete the same measure—a quiz, a questionnaire, a set of rating scales—more than one time, they can become test savvy, responding more quickly and less thoughtfully than on prior administrations of the measure. Any change in self-report or performance is not necessarily attributable to an experimental variable; rather, it is possibly due to familiarity with the measure. Some respondents, too, can become bored or annoyed when completing the same measure repeatedly (especially in a short-term experiment) so that their responses become reactive and extreme. To combat the effects of testing, some researchers administer the same or similar measures at different times or go to pains to convince participants that they are taking part in two separate, unrelated studies, not one (see chapters 8 and 10).

Instrumentation. Errors and biases linked with *instrumentation* issues occur when measurement devices, whether paper-and-pencil or mechanized, are altered. Occasionally, an experimenter will decide to add a new measure to a study after half of the participants have already completed it. How can the investigator be sure that the new measure did not change how the other half of the respondents reacted? Sometimes equipment—a computer or its program, a puzzle, a reaction time device, a tape recorder—must be repaired, recalibrated, or even replaced in the course of data collection. A researcher must make certain that instrumentation effects did not occur before or after the necessary change. Such effects can range from measurement errors linked to the device (e.g., poor quality recordings) or undue attention from participants (e.g., a jazzy MP3 player might draw more interest than a standard tape recorder).

Selection. The simplest source of *selection bias* is when no random assignment to the conditions in an experiment occurs, so that an investigator is never sure whether the people in one condition differ along some influential dimension from those in other conditions. Since random assignment is the sine qua non of a true experiment, selection is unlikely to be a problem in most lab studies (still, a vigilant researcher would make certain that no a priori differences exist among participants, so that, say, mostly first-year students ended up in one group while senior-level students were predominant in another group). Selection issues can plague research done in field settings, especially those where participants are transient (e.g., malls, sporting events, public streets).

Mortality. People quit studies all the time. Although it might be rare for a participant in an hour-long experiment to suddenly express a desire to leave, it happens (recall chapter 3). Dropout rates—participant attrition—can be fairly high in studies that follow people across some period of time, say, a few weeks, months, or less commonly, several years. *Mortality* is a problem if an investigator has no idea why participants withdrew or never came back. The risk is that the dropouts differ in substantive, psychological ways from those who stayed in the study. The hope is that few people will cease participating and that those who do leave do so for unsystematic reasons. A motivated researcher will take pains to learn why some people quit a study in order to rule out the possibility that some systematic bias is causing some people to leave while others remain (for an extended discussion of mortality as a threat in applied research, see Hoyle, Harris, & Judd, 2002). It is also worth noting that in many longitudinal studies, especially those involving thousands of people, mortality in the true sense of the word occurs: People die due to natural causes, accidents, disease, and so forth. A researcher must take every effort to be sure that the individuals remaining in a study do not differ from those who withdraw from it for whatever reason.

Statistical regression. On occasion, a researcher will intentionally recruit participants who display extreme qualities on some dimension—say, very high or very low levels of self-esteem—in order to assess their reactions to some independent variable. *Statistical regression* effects pose a problem when such extreme scores are anomalies, that is, participants' true scores tend more toward the average. For whatever reason, probably random error, people sometimes overperform or underperform on measures. (If you have ever been well prepared for a test and then "bombed" it or done well when you barely studied, then you are acquainted with statistical regression.) Extreme performance for most people is atypical, but without evidence of people's usual performance on the dimension being assessed, how will a researcher know? The real danger associated with regression effects is that change (e.g., enhanced self-esteem) can be falsely attributed to an intervention when, in fact, people's self-reported traits are simply approaching their usual (actual) average levels.

Reprise: Ways to enhance a study's internal validity

Besides mulling over Cook and Campbell's (1979) list of threats, there are other steps a researcher can take to increase the likelihood that a project will have a high degree of internal validity:

- *Conduct a true experiment.* Always use random assignment to conditions. If possible, use random sampling of a population prior to random assignment.
- *Pilot test your project.* Before actual data collection begins, verify that participants are reacting to the independent and dependent variables as hypothesized.
- *Ensure that the experimental procedure is involving for participants.* All else being equal, participants should find your experiment to be interesting and engaging. Keep them busy and focused on some activity. Fewer distractions will reduce sources of error. Tips on keeping participants focused can also be found in chapters 7, 8, and 10.
- *Attend to potential sources of bias often found in social psychological research.* Social psychologists take great care to reduce the sources of error and bias in experiments, including so-called demand characteristics and experimenter bias. These topics are reviewed in the context of staging experiments in chapter 10.
- *Carefully debrief your participants.* There is more to learning about social psychological research than theorizing and data collection. Talk to the people who take part in your study to learn what they thought about as they took part in it (see the debriefing discussion in chapter 10). Participants know best: A thorough and honest debriefing can often reveal sources of error or procedural problems that a researcher would never recognize.

Generalizing to Other Settings: External Validity

Internal validity is essential to social psychological research. If we cannot trust the veracity of the results, then we cannot use them to explain or explore the causes of social behavior. If we are assured that our research effort has sufficient internal validity, what then? Most social psychologists want to conclude more from their efforts than to outline cause and effect in one setting. They also want to extrapolate from this one setting to other settings. They want to explain the behavior of other research participants or, really, other people, in other settings and other places and other times, including, of course, everyday (real) life. In short, most social psychologists want their research effort to possess external validity.

External validity refers to whether research findings can be generalized from one setting to another. As Aronson et al. (1998) note, external validity involves the "robustness" of some psychological phenomenon. When you read about a social psychological experiment in a journal or the newspaper, do you focus exclusively on the reactions of the people who took part in the study? Or are you like most readers, who muse about the findings in light of their own everyday experience? Most of us are automatically drawn to think about, if not question, an experiment's external validity because applying the observations to our own lives is one way to make sense of them.

A quick anecdote: Years ago I was shopping at a clothing sale with my wife. She was in a dressing room trying on an outfit when a young man ran up to the cashier and said "This is a stick up." I froze with fear and immediately thought back to what I knew about people's reactions to emergencies as outlined by Latané and Darley (1969). (Yes, I know, you are now wondering just what kind of person I really am—who thinks about empirical findings during a stick up?) I was scared. I was also frozen. And I remember thinking—is this a real stick up or a joke? Should I try to warn my wife? Moments later, the clerk and the "hold up guy" burst out laughing. They were friends; in fact, both were clerks at the store. I was relieved and (internally) embarrassed. Thank goodness, I thought, that I didn't make a fool of myself, and yet isn't that one of the worries of people who hesitate to act in the face of emergencies? My point is that the Darley and Latané's observation that emergencies can often seem ambiguous to people who are caught up in them or just watching really hit home to me at that moment. Up to that point in time, I never doubted the conclusions of the bystander studies, but I suddenly felt them as real and powerful, and oh so externally valid.

Of course, my experience (or your experience, for that matter) is not necessarily grounds for claiming that external validity regarding any social psychological phenomena exists. To demonstrate that findings are indeed externally valid at other times and to other people and in other places, what must be done? In a validity sense, a researcher needs to demonstrate that the findings observed in one setting (a controlled lab) can be replicated in another setting (say, another lab) or, ideally, settings (several other labs or, even better, out in some field settings). How, then, can external validity be achieved? Through replication.

External validity via replication

Repeating an experiment to replicate—reproduce, duplicate—an effect is a powerful way to demonstrate external validity. By definition, a researcher will be finding the same effect with other participants at another time and (possibly) another place separate from the first demonstration of an effect. *Replication* does not mean just repeating the basic outline of an experiment from beginning to end. Replication or more appropriately still, a *conceptual or systematic replication*, involves verifying that a cause and effect relationship exists and can be demonstrated using different independent variables, different dependent variables, and different research designs that nonetheless all suggest that the same phenomenon is at work.

Virtually all of the major findings in social psychology are based on extensively replicating findings in order to verify them. If you glance through any introductory social psychology book, you will find numerous studies cited to support basic findings concerning helping behavior, interpersonal attraction, social influence, aggression, and so on. (As an exercise, look through a social psychology text, pick a topic, and see how many references are cited in support of some representative effect.) In the ideal case, then, different social psychologists replicate a reported effect in their own laboratories, sometimes integrating it into their own research programs. Reproducing results in novel circumstances with different participant groups is another way to establish the external validity of a social psychological effect.

College sophomores as threats to external validity

There is one issue linked with social psychological research that often causes critics to raise questions regarding external validity: the nature of the participants who take part in most experiments. Think about it: If most social psychology experiments involve undergraduate students who are participating to complete a course requirement for Introductory Psychology 101, are their reactions a sufficient foundation for describing the behavior of all people, most of whom are not college students? More than one wag has called social psychology the "psychology of the college sophomore" (ouch!). The fear, of course, is that any empirical insights obtained from college-aged "volunteer" participants limit generalization to that population alone (e.g., Sears, 1986).

Why is generalizing from a college population to other groups sometimes unwise? The average college student is apt to be quite different from the average person. For one thing, college students tend to be of above average intelligence. They may also be younger in age and, therefore, experience, than the typical person. Issues of social class and socioeconomic status are also relevant; college students are liable to come from homes that have higher than average incomes. The main concern is that any of these differences or some combination of them can render the reactions of students as distinct from the hypothetically average person.

Our concern about the importance of external validity is more than any of these obvious between-group differences. In point of fact, different groups can react to the same independent variable quite differently, thereby yielding distinctly different behaviors. To properly establish external validity, knowledge of group differences needs to inform theory and prediction. Recall the work by Markus and her colleagues (Connor Snibbe & Markus, 2005; Stephens, Markus, & Townsend, 2007; see also Nicholson, 2006) on pen choice, which opened chapter 8: Middle-class participants chose a unique color pen (e.g., the solo blue pen instead of one of four red pens), one that made them stand out from the group. In contrast, working-class participants (like the Indian students) preferred to blend in by selecting a color that did not make them stand out (i.e., one of the red pens rather than the single blue one). Without correctly taking into account social class or cultural norms (Eastern versus Western ways) as a mediating variable, the results would not make sense nor could external validity be properly explained.

Context matters

Research contexts and the nature of the research being conducted can also affect external validity. We have considered lab-based research rather extensively in this book, and we have had a few occasions to discuss field-based research. What we have not reviewed much is the distinction between basic and applied research in social psychology. The term *basic research* usually refers to scientific efforts aimed at creating new knowledge concerning social psychology based on established theory. Whenever possible, basic research employs true experiments or methods that emphasize internal validity. In contrast, *applied research* often tackles social problems or concerns (e.g., drug addiction, HIV transmission) that are difficult to study using traditional experimental methods. Some applied research is conducted in private industry with an eye to using social psychological insights in marketing or consumer contexts.

Table 9.2 outlines the main distinctions regarding basic and applied research in social psychology by comparing the research location, topics pursued, focus, setting, and time considerations. Take a few moments and review the table's entries. There are few surprises in the left side of Table 9.2: Basic research remains true to the paradigm of the true experiment insofar as it is possible to do so. Internal validity is the chief focus. Based on the entries in the right side of Table 9.2, much field-based research appears to value external validity.

Table 9.2   Research Contexts: Comparing Basic and Applied Approaches to Social Psychology

	Basic	Applied
Place	College or university	Government Business/industry Health settings Schools
Topics	Researcher-initiated	Client or issue-initiated
Focus	Internal validity	External validity
Setting	Laboratory	Field
Time frame	Low pressure, few deadlines	High pressure, multiple deadlines

Source: Adapted from Hedrick, Bickman, & Rog (1993).

Can we assume that a basic research finding will be replicable in an applied context? Before answering this question, think about the bias most social psychologists are apt to display when asking such a question: Why is the focus always on the basic research side of things? Consider the question in reverse: Can we assume that an applied finding— one obtained in a field setting of some sort—will be obtainable in an impoverished, if highly controlled, basic research effort? Generally, the best answer to either question is that replication is necessary and needed before any conclusion can be drawn.

Some contexts, especially impressive laboratory facilities, can elicit high degrees of participant involvement and cooperation, as well as a clear demonstration of a hypothesized result (recall Table 9.2). Should a researcher assume that the same result can be obtained in a less inspiring context? This is the precise question Milgram (1974) asked when he sought to replicate the original obedience effects. Milgram noted that the prestige of Yale University could have promoted participant compliance to a high degree. To verify that the obedience to authority effects transcended setting, Milgram fabricated a research company in a shabby storefront in the industrial city of Bridgeport, CT. Although the compliance rates did drop—slightly fewer people went to the highest levels when it came to shocking the mild-mannered confederate (recall chapter 3)—the overall rate of obedience to the authoritarian experimenter remained very high. Thus Milgram was able to show that the context had little effect, that the paradigm used in his research as well as the results themselves, were externally valid.

Enhancing external validity

Is there any sort of research approach that guarantees a high degree of external validity? Actually, yes, there is one. Passive observational research is very high in external validity (Pelham, 1999; see also chapter 5). As you might guess, of course, simply observing behavior and being forced to infer what factors are causing it poses some limits of its own. By watching and meticulously recording how medical professionals interact with each other, for example, we might learn a great deal about the social hierarchies present in hospitals and clinics. We would be unlikely, however, to learn about the origins of the hierarchies or the factors that maintain or occasionally undermine them. To learn about those issues, some form of active intervention would be needed. Although observational research can be high in external validity, the internal validity associated with pinpointing cause and effect tends to be quite low.

How can you enhance external validity in your own research? Here are three suggestions:

Choose a sample whose characteristics are similar to the larger population of interest. Sampling and the composition of a sample are key to establishing external validity. If your goal is to examine how rituals in collegiate organizations (e.g., fraternities, sororities, athletic teams, service clubs) increase group cohesiveness, then your sample of research participants should be college-aged students enrolled in college rather than high school students, college graduates, or mid-career real estate executives. Besides sharing characteristics in common with the larger population from which they were drawn, in the ideal situation, the sample should, of course, be a random one.

Design the experimental setting so that it mimics everyday life. A second way to enhance a study's external validity is by ensuring that the research setting is the same as or highly similar to locations experienced in everyday life. Research findings drawn from having participants form a first impression of a flesh and blood confederate is likely to prove to be more generalizable than having participants read a collection of piecemeal facts about a hypothetical individual. In real life, we meet and form impressions of strangers all the time. Relatively few of us—except, perhaps, people screening resumes for particular job openings—pass judgments on others by reading organized lists of facts. Although experiments based on the latter sort of approach can certainly have external validity, greater faith in the generalizability of results is apt to be associated with the former scenario. We will return to the importance of this realism criterion shortly when we discuss the distinction between mundane and experimental realism.

Replicate observed results in different contexts. Instead of simply hypothesizing or arguing that results are generalizable, adopt an empirical stance and prove your case. Follow Milgram's (1974) lead and verify that the same basic results (or subtle variations thereof) associated with an influential independent variable can be found in distinct contexts.

In praise of external invalidity

Must all psychological research, especially social psychological research, be externally valid? In other words, is there any compelling reason to abide research that is not really generalizable beyond some highly controlled laboratory settings? Mook (1983) made the provocative argument that it may be more important to know what *could* happen in controlled circumstances, however narrow and unlikely they may be, than to know what really *does* happen. In other words, some results will not generalize outside of artificial, experimental situations that bear little or no resemblance at all to the real world. Mook claims that in some circumstances a researcher need not be concerned with external validity at all. On some occasions, a researcher's goal is exclusively to test some narrow hypothesis derived from a well-articulated theory. Whether the results apply to other people in other places at other times (they probably will not) is immaterial. To bolster his argument, Mook cited Milgram's (1974) obedience studies, noting that our daily lives do not compel us to give fake shocks to innocent victims at the command of authoritarian scientists. It is not the scenario per se that matters; rather, it is the implications of the work—the fact that otherwise normal people can be thrust into abnormal situations that compel them to behave in monstrous ways.

That the experimental situation in the Milgram (1974) studies of obedience was artificial and hardly illustrative of real life is not the point To quote Mook (1983, p. 379), "A misplaced preoccupation with external validity can lead us to dismiss good research for which generalization to real life is not intended or meaningful." No doubt some social psychologists will question such wisdom by noting that the careful, critical study of social behavior implies a certain level of external validity. Perhaps, but Mook's thoughtful observations are one way to reconsider the critical reception often given to data drawn from artificial or otherwise socially "barren" studies that lack real people or any sort of real interaction. Thus interesting, if off-beat or unlikely, ideas are still worthy of being tested—they just may not generalize beyond the narrow limits of their testing grounds. Mook's real insight is to consider whether external validity, unlike internal validity, is really more of a question about a piece of research rather than a required criterion that must be met (Ferguson & Bibby, 2004).

The Social Psychologist's Challenge: Trade-Offs Between Internal and External Validity

Both internal validity and external validity are important to research in social psychology. Of the two, internal validity is the essential quality for any piece of research. Without it, little or nothing can be done with a set of results. While not essential, as already established, external validity is a good quality for any research effort to possess. What we have not yet discussed is how to consider the inherent trade-offs that exist between these two types of validity.

By trade-offs, I mean the relative advantages and disadvantages that exist between research that is conducted in highly controlled settings (those high in internal validity) versus those investigations that are conducted in less controlled, real life settings (those high in external validity, such as applied or field settings; Dunn, 1999). We noted this trade-off back in chapter 1 when the distinction between lab and field research was first introduced. Figure 9.2 should look familiar, as it is very similar to Figure 1.1. Figure 9.2 illustrates two continua, one for control and another for generalizability and, unlike Figure 1.1, identifies internal and external validity as important concerns. As suggested by the top part of Figure 9.2, the rigors of lab settings allow a researcher to exert a great deal of control so that outside influences, such as uncontrolled or other nuisance variables, have little or no effect. The downside to such control, of course, is portrayed in

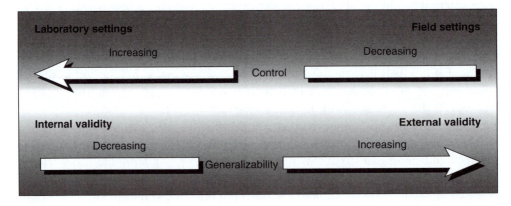

Figure 9.2.   The trade-off continua for lab versus field settings and internal versus external validity. Adapted from Dunn (1999, Figure 7.1, p. 219)

the bottom part of Figure 9.2: Higher levels of control usually mean lower levels of generalizability. A highly controlled setting looks little or nothing like a real life situation or event, which means that the social psychologist is not able to draw strong inferences about very much in the way of social behavior. In contrast, most real life settings have little or no control present in them, but they have vigor; the give and take of cause and effect is apparent, but accurately describing its nature is more difficult.

The major trade offs are these: The more control a researcher exerts, the less the findings will represent any real world situation; generalizability is sacrificed for internal validity. We know more about less where internal validity is concerned. As a researcher moves into the real world, the more relevant, the more generalizable, the research becomes. At the same time, drawing precise, causal conclusions is problematic. Regarding external validity, we know less about more.

So what are clever, hard-working social psychologists to do? Should they sacrifice the hurly-burly of the actual, often messy, social world for the isolated, limited, if highly predictive, lab, or vice versa? The best answer is one that you probably anticipated by now: They should embrace both. That is, some research should emphasize the rigor and clarity of the controlled lab, while other studies should emphasize the multivariable, multicausal nature of applied settings. As you well know by now, no one experiment is ever ideal. Only when several investigations are performed can a researcher begin to offer a full and more complete account of some social psychological phenomenon.

I can almost hear several readers reacting at this point by saying, "That's all very well for professional social psychologists, but what about students like me? What should we do? We don't have the time or maybe the inclination to run a bunch of different studies." Fair enough and true enough. What a student researcher should do is to design the best single experiment that can answer one focused question. Naturally, internal validity is an important consideration, which means that a lab study is a good bet for a first or only try (i.e., get the social phenomenon to behave). On the other hand, there is no reason why a student researcher cannot conduct a less controlled investigation in a field setting as long as the potential threats to internal validity and the benefits of external validity are both acknowledged.

ACTIVE LEARNING EXERCISE   9A

Evaluating Your Project's Internal and External Validity

This active learning exercise is designed to help you evaluate the relative degree of internal and external validity associated with your research project. Ideally, you should review the questions listed in Table 9.3 before you begin to collect any data so that procedural adjustments to enhance validity can be made. If such a review is not possible before the project is conducted, then you should certainly answer

Continued

the questions shown in Table 9.3 before beginning to write up a project summary in APA style or presenting your work in some forum (see chapter 12). Any threats to internal validity or limitations to external validity should be identified and discussed in your research summary. Use the questions in Table 9.3 to guide your thinking about your research design or to reflect on the applicability of your findings.

Table 9.3   Evaluating Your Project's Internal and External Validity

Some questions regarding internal validity
- Is your project a true experiment (random assignment, manipulation of an independent variable, measurement of a dependent variable)? If no, then your project's internal validity is either low or nonexistent. Explain why a true experiment could not be conducted and/or explain the validity concerns present in the alternative research design you used.
- Have you made sure that the participant sample possesses no characteristics that could compromise the effect of any independent variable(s) or the measurement of any dependent variable(s)? If no, then explain whether the project's internal validity is affected.
- Have you ascertained that the common threats to internal validity did not compromise the findings from your research design? If no, then explain in what way(s) the project's internal validity is affected.
- Does the research design seem to be free from participant demand characteristics and experimenter biases (see chapter 10)? If no, then explain whether the project's internal validity is affected.
- Did your debriefing of participants reveal any concerns regarding participant suspicion, clarity of the experiment's procedure, or similar? If yes, then explain whether the project's internal validity is affected.

Some questions regarding external validity
- Are the participants in your study representative of some larger population to which you plan to generalize the findings? If no, why not?
- Are the participants college students or a different population? If the latter, will their participation promote the study's external validity?
- Are you replicating an established effect in a novel setting (e.g., moving from the lab to the field, or vice versa)?
- Does the research setting mimic some everyday event or situation?

Making It Real: Mundane, Experimental, and Psychological Realism

Let's now turn to the issue of realism, which may help you decide how to refine some aspects of your project's procedure. Realism is often discussed as a topic within external validity. Although I do not disagree with that approach, certain aspects of realism are such important considerations in social psychology research—more so than other subareas of psychology—that I believe it warrants a separate section of this chapter.

I recently read about a psychologist who studies consumer behavior, notably how packaging and portion size affect our consumption (the sad reality is that despite what we all believe, packaging really does influence our buying and eating behavior; see Severson, 2006; Wansink, 2006). What struck me as especially interesting is that this researcher, Brian Wansink, has his student participants make their eating decisions in a kitchen setting, which is actually a lab. Wansink or his research assistant can sit comfortably behind a one-way mirror and observe what people do, especially how and how much they eat. Although it sounds a little odd to eat in a kitchen-lab setting, this kitchen is cozy and it seats eight people. And my guess is that, as borne out by Wansink's consistent findings, participants find that they are quite at home in this setting. Put another way, the results appear to have a high degree of external validity due to the nature of the research setting.

What should research settings be like? How similar is a given research setting to a place or situation encountered in daily life? If we study eating behavior, must the setting be like a kitchen or dining room, for example? Will studying the same phenomenon in a mostly empty room have any effects on participants' choices or consumption patterns? Questions like these highlight a quality of social psychology experiments known as *mundane realism* (Aronson & Carlsmith, 1968). Specifically, mundane realism refers to how much the characteristics of an experiment—its procedure, setting, tasks, people, background—are similar to daily life. Or, if you will, is the experiment itself, not only its findings or implications, high in external validity?

Most social psychologists and readers of social psychological research, students as well as critics, assume that the more "lifelike" an experimental setting appears to be, the more seriously participants will behave within it. When an experiment's stage, if you will, is really and truly compelling, then it may lead participants to suspend disbelief (e.g., they are eating in a real kitchen, they are on a real date, they are interviewing for a real job), if only for a short time. The setting may seem so real, so mundane or commonplace, that they forget for the moment that they are taking part in an experiment.

When I was a graduate student, for example, one of the experimental psychologists in the department studied the effects of ethanol (the alcohol found in beer, wine, and liquor) on various psychological processes, including learning and memory. Believe it or not, this researcher created a lounge-like setting, referred to as the "bar-lab," where his participants who were aged 21 and over could consume a variety of alcoholic and nonalcoholic drinks before completing various experimental tasks. The bar-lab had overstuffed couches, comfy chairs, indirect lighting, ashtrays, and some artwork on the walls. In short, the researcher created some convivial, if artificial, surroundings that were high in mundane realism where the consumption of alcohol was concerned. This lounge helped participants relax while concealing a variety of tools related to the study of ethanol consumption and psychological processes.

A second quality, *experimental realism*, is a complement to mundane realism. Experimental realism is the degree to which a study becomes involving and meaningful to participants. Do the tasks or activities used in an experiment prove to be interesting, engaging, or otherwise gripping to participants? Do participants take the study's procedure seriously while acting in a spontaneous, rather than a stilted or self-conscious, manner? The paradigms used by Milgram (1974) to examine obedience and Asch (1955, 1956, 1961) in his study of conformity were high in experimental realism—participants took the respective experiments very seriously (recall chapter 3's discussion of each)—if not mundane realism.

One popular research paradigm that is high in experimental realism is the so-called Prisoner's Dilemma, a game using payoffs for the two players involved. The game's name comes from the predicament two criminals face when they are questioned separately by police after they committed a crime together. When players trust one another and cooperate, each can receive a high payoff or reward. Lower payoffs occur when players mistrust each other and one or both "defect" from a cooperative strategy. Like hypothetical criminals, players must decide whether to help one another by working together (sticking to the same story about what did or did not happen) or defecting (acting against one another by confessing to receive a lighter sentence). The Prisoner's Dilemma paradigm has been used to simulate everything from business decisions between competing corporations to war strategy between hostile nations (for a recent application of the game in social psychology, one illustrating how situational pressures override purported personality qualities, see Liberman, Samuels, & Ross, 2002). This game is obviously low in mundane realism but quite high in experimental realism—participants become very involved in it, often risking modest tokens, rewards, or even small amounts of money. Researchers, too, argue that the game illustrates the dynamics of real-world settings (e.g., Dawes, 1980; Schelling, 1978).

Mundane realism and experimental realism are independent, not opposite, concepts. A study can be relatively high on one property and low on the other, or high or low on both properties. Although social psychologists often seek a high degree of external validity in their research designs, some studies have low levels of mundane realism. Your familiarity with Mook's (1983) defense of external invalidity will indicate why this is so. If any experimental caution is in order, I should probably counsel you to be wary of conducting studies that are low in experimental realism. If participants do not take the procedure seriously or are too distracted by a setting's mundane qualities, they may miss the impact of any independent variables or not be aware of reacting at all to the dependent variables (see the relevant discussions on enhancing the effect of these variables in chapters 7 and 8, respectively).

A third experimental quality related to experimental realism should also be considered. Coined by Aronson, Wilson, and Akert (1994), *psychological realism* refers to how much the psychological processes elicited in an experiment are similar to those found in daily life. Psychological realism is an important consideration when a given experiment might be low in both mundane and experimental realism. Recall Wegner's thought suppression studies involving white bears and other stimuli, which were introduced in chapter 8 (see, e.g., Wegner, 1994; Wegner, Schneider, Carter, & White, 1987). The research setting was hardly typical of everyday life: Participants were isolated in a room, talking into a microphone, and clanging a little bell every time a white bear came to mind.

Were these studies high in experimental realism? Not really—although reporting your ongoing thoughts is initially a challenging activity, people grow accustomed to doing so fairly quickly. I think you will agree, however, that the experimental realism is much lower than that found in Prisoner's Dilemma games or in the Asch (1956) or Milgram (1974) studies. Yet in daily life, we all try not to think about or remember certain things—if not white bears, then perhaps embarrassing things we did or said recently or in the past. Wegner's research is very high in psychological realism because it captured a typical, essential psychological process that happens to everyone on occasion. We all try to suppress something, sometime. So we should not necessarily criticize certain types of social psychological research if the phenomenon under examination is high in psychological realism (for other examples of studies high in psychological realism, consider research on the automatic processing of social information; see, e.g., Devine, 1989; Gilbert & Hixon, 1991; Greenwald, McGhee, & Schwartz, 1998; Langer, 1989).

ACTIVE LEARNING EXERCISE 9B

Enhancing Mundane and Experimental Realism

There is no single way to enhance the mundane or experimental realism found in any study. Whether you focus on one or both forms of realism, how you enhance it will depend on the nature of the research topic, the facilities and equipment available, and, ultimately, where the research is conducted—in the lab or out in the field. Although I cannot anticipate what specific research topic you will pursue, I will hazard a guess that that you will probably conduct your research in a classroom, an office, a dorm or apartment, or some relatively empty room your institution makes available for student research. As an undergraduate student, I collected data in my apartment, campus classrooms, psychology department research spaces (i.e., small office like cubicles), and once in a lounge area in the university's Student Union.

Given the typicality of such spaces, there are a few steps you can take to enhance participants' experience of realism. Table 9.4 lists some suggestions aimed at heightening mundane and experimental realism. These suggestions tend to be global in nature. Specificity, again, is difficult because I do not know what topic you are pursuing. Please do not try to use all of the suggestions in Table 9.4 in your project. Select one or two from each category, for example, if you feel the suggestions can tighten up some aspects of your project by making the setting seem more familiar or by encouraging participants to take the situation seriously.

Continued

Table 9.4   Suggestions for Enhancing Mundane and Experimental Realism

---

Enhancing mundane realism

   Make the research space comfortable, even homey.

   Be sure the space is neither too cluttered with objects or too barren or neat.

   Hang some attractive (but not distracting or provocative) photos, pictures, or posters.

   Use indirect lighting (lamps) instead of ceiling, especially fluorescent, lights.

   Locate comfortable chairs; make a table or desk less sterile by covering it with a simple tablecloth.

   Ambient noise (e.g., people walking and talking in the hallway, low music, the hum of traffic) can make an experimental context seem more like everyday life.

Enhancing experimental realism

   Make the research space look serious and scientific by removing extraneous objects.

   Seat participants in front of the experimenter, who should be seated behind a desk or table.

   Use overhead or fluorescent lighting.

   Hang charts and graphs on the wall; write research designs or equations on any blackboards.

   If a desk is visible, make certain that whatever is on it looks neat and orderly.

   Have experimenters wear white lab coats and carry clip-boards.

   Use tasks (e.g., problems, puzzles, games) that are challenging but not insoluble (unless this quality is related to the independent variable or the theory being tested).

   Use white noise to reduce distractions.

(Re)Considering Construct Validity

In experiments and quasi-experiments, *construct validity* addresses how well the practical manipulation and measurement of variables characterize the true nature of and relationships between variables as theoretical concepts. Do our concrete operationalizations adequately represent the abstract concepts they are designed to represent? In a study of physical attractiveness and liking, for example, does the independent variable (e.g., an attractive confederate vs. an unattractive confederate) influence perceivers' perceptions by calling upon shared sociocultural values of beauty? Does the dependent variable (e.g., frequency of participants' positive verbal and nonverbal behaviors toward a confederate) measure behavioral reactions based on participants' beliefs about beauty?

Adding a discussion devoted to construct validity at this point in the book may strike some readers as odd because the topic has been touched upon in virtually every chapter so far. We first learned about construct validity when operational definitions were introduced in chapter 4. We refined our knowledge of construct validity when we considered how to craft questions, questionnaires, and surveys designed to accurately assess verbal reports and responses (chapters 6 and 8), how to effectively construct and manipulate independent variables (chapter 7), and how to successfully measure behavioral outcomes by creating appropriate dependent variables (chapter 8). The content of these and other chapters is designed to promote construct validity in social psychological research (especially your research) by reducing measurement errors, eliminating inadequate operationalizations of variables, and appropriately streamlining experimental procedures, tasks, and instructions so that participants understand their roles and responsibilities.

When conducting an ideal experiment, construct validity is bound up with internal and external validity so that:

- The experiment and what occurs within it should be under the experimenter's control (i.e., high in internal validity)
- The experiment should contain well-conceived independent and dependent variables that connect to intended conceptual variables (i.e., high in construct validity)
- The experiment should reveal results that can be generalized to other situations with other people (i.e., high in external validity).

Beyond construct validity

Besides construct validity, social psychologists sometimes attend to other forms of validity, especially when they are developing methods for examining novel constructs or those that have received little or no research attention (e.g., Campbell & Fiske, 1959). Three such forms of validity are defined in Table 9.5. As you can see, each one

Table 9.5   Three Other Forms of Validity

Face validity

How well does an instrument or measure seem to assess what it is designed to assess? Does a measure superficially appear to fit a given construct? For example, do the questions on a self-esteem measure appear to tap into people's feelings of confidence and self-worth (e.g., "People like me," "I make friends easily").

Convergent validity

To what degree does the measurement of one theoretical variable relate to other measures and variables? For example, does a measure of self-esteem correlate positively with conceptually linked measures, such as extroversion, social intelligence, and assertiveness.

Discriminant validity

Different measures should tap into distinct and different constructs; researchers should be able to discriminate one measure from another. How do we know that one variable is conceptually distinct from other variables? To what degree does the measurement of some theoretical variable remain unrelated to other measures? Is a given measure distinguishable from other measures? For example, there is no reason to anticipate that a measure of self-esteem should be correlated with (unrelated) measures of math ability, sensation seeking, or procrastination.

is a variation on the theme of how well a given operationalization connects to some theoretical variable.

Validity and Realism via Replication

I opened this chapter by discussing one of the true citation classics of social psychology, Festinger and Carlsmith's (1959) experiment concerning insufficient justification and cognitive dissonance. I noted that Festinger's (1957) theory posited that cognitive dissonance creates arousal and psychological tension among dissonant thoughts (e.g., "I smoke and smoking causes cancer"), so much so that we are motivated to rationalize our thoughts and actions (e.g., "Oh well, everybody dies of something—do you have any matches?"). For decades, researchers assumed that the arousal implicit in the theory represented a valid psychological construct despite the absence of direct evidence. There was, of course, ample indirect evidence: As already noted, study after study demonstrates the efficacy of the dissonance construct. Technical advances and interest in using physiological measures enabled researchers to demonstrate quite clearly and convincingly that dissonance leads to an aroused state of uncomfortable tension. Dissonance researchers found that research participants who felt an uncomfortable degree of dissonance were indeed aroused—they showed increased perspiration and a heightened heart rate (e.g., Cacioppo & Petty, 1986; Croyle & Cooper, 1983; Losch & Cacioppo, 1990). The lesson? Sometimes it takes a while to definitively verify a psychological construct, but it can be done, especially when many social psychologists pursue related questions using a variety of techniques within a research area.

The other lesson is that validity and realism are enhanced by such replication efforts. Thus you may prefer to conduct a replication study instead of conceiving of an original experiment on a novel topic. I believe that is a fine and worthy approach to take. I suggest you consider conducting a conceptual or systematic replication rather than a direct replication. By repeating a basic experiment on an established effect (but methodically varying some aspect of the original approach), you increase the likelihood that your experiment will obtain a meaningful result, as well as refining or extending existing findings. By doing so, you will have to wrestle with issues of internal, external, and construct validity, as well as make some decisions regarding the degree of mundane and experimental realism in the execution of the study. Thinking through such issues and then tackling them empirically is a great way to promote the validity and realism of social psychological results.

Exercises

1   Choose a social psychology journal article describing some research you believe is well done. Review the findings using the validity questions shown in Table 9.3. Did the authors do a good job of establishing internal and external validity? Why or why not?

2   If you are conducting a lab-based social psychology project, review your research design in light of the applied issues shown on the right-hand side of Table 9.2. If you were to move your project to an applied setting, would your hypothesis and research design change (hint: Imagine running your study in a nonlab setting)? How could your project be applied to understanding everyday life?

3   Based on your answer to exercise 2 above, would moving your study to an applied setting affect the internal or external validity of any findings? How so?

4   Search through a recent issue of a social psychology journal and locate a study you believe is high in psychological realism. Why do you believe this is so? What about the study's relative levels of mundane and experimental realism?

Chapter 10

Conducting Social Psychology Experiments: Practical Matters

By now, you are something of an expert in social psychology. You have read about many social psychology studies in this book. Perhaps you took an introductory social psychology course earlier in your education. If you are conducting your own research project, then you have probably been reading relevant research in journals and library books. So I have a question for you: Is there anything research participants won't do in an experiment?

When you learned about Festinger and Carlsmith's (1959) seminal demonstration of cognitive dissonance at the opening of chapter 9, you saw that people will do a dull, repetitive task and then lie about how interesting it is to others. Milgram's (1974) obedience studies demonstrate all too well that otherwise harmless people can be compelled to believe they are delivering high levels of electric shock to an innocent victim. You also know that we are sometimes willing to deny even a modest truth—say, how long one line is compared to another—in the face of the pressure to conform (Asch, 1956). Is there a point beyond which most participants will say, "No thanks— I'm done now"? Maybe, but maybe not.

Imagine you sign up to participate in an experiment being conducted in your institution's psychology department. You show up on time and are ushered into a room and then seated at a desk. A friendly experimenter explains the task you will complete: You will add together thousands of rows of numbers. You begin your task. Time passes. One hour. Then two. You are still adding row upon row upon row of numbers. Hours three and four pass. After five and a half hours the experimenter tells you to stop. Would you stay that long? Would you perform that relentless task for that long? When do you think you would refuse to continue? How much time would pass before you would quit?

Before you answer these questions, let's rewind and start over. What if you took part in the same experiment but with this addition: After you have added all the rows on a sheet of paper, the experimenter tells you to tear the worksheet into a minimum of 32 pieces before adding the numbers on the next one. In other words, after doing the laborious calculations, you would destroy all evidence of your effort before beginning again. Would you recognize this task as not only futile but also quite ridiculous?

From the comfort of wherever you are right now, the answer seems obvious: Of course you would stop work—you would refuse to continue! You might not even agree to do the task for a few minutes! And as for the first study's description, you would not do that tiresome adding for even one hour, let alone almost six hours! Well, don't be so sure. These two studies were actually conducted by psychologist Martin Orne (1962). Orne, who studied hypnosis, was trying to find a dull and completely meaningless task that nonhypnotized people would either refuse to perform or would work on only for a short time. Guess what—he gave up. He was unable to find an experimental task that people would refuse to perform. Given what you know about social psychology and the power of situations, do you truly believe you would behave differently than the participants in Orne's (1962) studies?

Orne (1962) suggested that people have the capacity to make the meaningless seem meaningful. Thus doing a dull and mindless task can seem consequential, for example, when it is done in the context of a scientific investigation. After all, it is routine not to know a study's purpose until it's over; college students who are required to take part in psychology experiments as an introductory course requirement are so informed before they sign up for any study. Further, people assume that scientists have good intentions, that science is important, so it follows that helping out by doing what looks to be a silly activity is (nonetheless) a good thing. In fact, Orne labeled this sort of cooperative acquiescence the desire to be a *good subject* (we would now say *good participant*, but the older term is an established one in the methodological literature). Virtually all people who take part in experiments aspire to fill this role because the reality is that people will do almost anything they are asked to do—or compelled to do—in the context of social psychological research.

Adopt the perspective of a critic for a moment: Is such compliance a good thing? Can such cooperative behavior pose any problems for social psychologists and their research? Are some participants too helpful? Can the good subject effect be a bad thing for drawing conclusions about social behavior? Good subjects or, rather, good participants, want to give experimenters what they seek, some desired behavior that fits a cherished hypothesis. The problem, of course, is that a desired behavior may be happening for the wrong reason. Instead of being caused by an independent variable, for instance, confirmation comes from the misplaced good will of participants who discerned what was expected of them (see also chapters 4 and 7).

This chapter is about the nuts and bolts of conducting a social psychology study. As such, it may be the most "hands on" chapter in the book because it contains five Active Learning Exercises. You are now well positioned, having already acquired the tools you need to design an experiment or other study. Now you need to pull it together by recruiting and running participants through their research paces. Before you do so, however, you need to learn about the pitfalls associated with bias, which can come from participants (as in the good subject effect) or from experimenters who unknowingly cause results to fit their expectations. To detect sources of such bias, we will review classic problems and their remedies. We will also discuss the all-important matter of conducting a thorough debriefing of participants. Before we do so, however, we need to set the experimental stage.

Setting the Stage

Where will your research project take place? In the lab, that is, some controlled setting, or out in the field? Social psychological research occurs in either setting. As you think about setting the stage for your study—deciding where to collect your data—keep in mind that the choice of setting is probably determined by two factors: convenience and the nature of your research question.

Convenience is an easy issue to address. Is there any research space available to students at your institution? Does the psychology department, for example, allow students to use research rooms (if there are any) or classrooms for data collection? If the answer is no, perhaps you can use other campus facilities that will provide some degree of privacy and control. Such spaces might include but are not limited to (as noted in chapter 9) rooms in the Student Union or a dormitory. If you have some convenient space available for research, then by all means use it.

What about the nature of your research question? You probably already have a good idea about whether your research question is likely to be categorized as basic or applied social psychology. Basic research questions tend to lend themselves to more controlled lab settings, while applied issues are often best studied in field settings. If you decide to do your work in a field setting, be certain that you have permission to do so (e.g., if you work in some business, say, an office or a fast food restaurant, be certain to ask your supervisor for permission to do your research). Second, be certain that your research design is not too complicated for the setting. Given that this is probably your first (and potentially only) research experience in social psychology, keep the design simple so that the procedure goes smoothly. This criterion is especially important in field settings. If you collect data in an office setting, for example, you do not want to disrupt the normal business being done there. Neither your coworkers nor any customers should be disrupted by whatever your study entails. Be certain, too, that your work meets all the ethical guidelines we discussed in chapter 3, especially informed consent.

Once you decide on a setting, you need to develop a *cover story*, a plausible description for participants about the reason you are conducting a research project and their role in it. A good cover story provides participants with a rationale for what they will be doing, one that should allay their fears and keep them from being overly suspicious about the research (including what you, the researchers, are *really* trying to find out). Cover stories do not need to be overly detailed and, in any case, they should be truthful unless candor will affect participant behavior in ways that are disruptive to the hypothesis being tested. If at all possible, avoid using deception in your cover story and in the experiment itself. Sometimes deception is necessary in social psychology research, but not in most student research (recall chapter 3).

Of course, there is a difference between active deception and offering an incomplete account of your study. Please note that you do not need to reveal all the specifics of your research in the cover story. For example, if you were examining what demographic characteristics trigger prejudicial reactions to people of different races and social classes, you would not reveal the study's actual purpose until its conclusion.

Prior to that time, however, you could inform participants that they would "be forming impressions, making social judgments, and rating different groups of people." This cover story is true, if not very specific. By waiting until the debriefing to "fill in the blanks" for the participants, a researcher can maintain the integrity of their responses. Disclosing at the outset that the research deals with "prejudice, race, and social class" would likely cause participants to be on their social-cognitive guard so that their responses might be cautious and subject to social desirability biases. In contrast, the nonspecific cover story might not trigger such reactions.

Whenever possible, research settings should be:

- *Involving*: Active participants are less likely to be suspicious or distracted participants, which means the impact of independent variables is enhanced and internal validity is maintained.
- *Familiar*: No setting should generate participant curiosity. Although drab, classrooms or (empty) research rooms are still rooms, familiar spaces that need not arouse suspicion.
- *Logical*: Ultimately, what happens in the course of the study, what participants are asked to do, should make a great deal of sense to them. Creating a logical sequence of events is not difficult if experimenters follow a script that makes sense. Everything should happen for a reason.
- *Simple*: Less is always more. The place, the materials, and the cover story—really everything—should be as simple as possible. You are assessing people's typical reactions to (presumably) typical social psychological events, not filming an epic love story or putting on a Broadway musical.

Where field settings are concerned, consider these issues:

- *Use an available, established setting.* You are conducting a student project, not your life's work. Capitalize on available field settings—a public place or private office (again, with permission)—but do not try to create your own field locale from scratch (see Table 9.2 for sample settings).
- *Consider data collection at a collective event.* Why not study people's reactions to some shared event, such as an outdoor concert, a civil demonstration (e.g., parade, march, protest), or a sporting event (e.g., football game, hockey playoff)? Such events are clearly involving and possess a "simple" quality—everyone is there for more or less the same reason, which reduces some of the uncontrollable sources of variability.

Deception revisited: Think carefully before you decide to deceive participants

Should you rely on some form of deception in your social psychology project or is it best to avoid deceiving the participants in your study? The pros and cons of deception were discussed in detail in chapter 3, so I will not repeat them here (however, I suggest you review chapter 3's discussion before proceeding). My own feeling is that deception can be justified when there is no other way to obtain the information that you need, or on those rare occasions when the topical area requires it. In general, I believe that most student projects should not rely on deceptive practices except for the simplest kind, such as withholding key information regarding the nature of the hypothesis or the topic itself. Sometimes, too, a well-conceived, if false, cover story can represent a mild form of deception (but recall Table 3.2).

If you decide that deception is essential to your project, then be sure that your research design is carefully reviewed by your course instructor and by your departmental or institutional IRB. As noted in chapter 3, any of these reviewers may require you to significantly alter or even to drop the deceptive elements from your final design. If deception is retained, be certain that it is clearly, carefully, and gently explained to participants during the debriefing portion of the study. The golden rule clearly applies here: Treat others as you would want to be treated.

Recruiting Participants

You cannot conduct research without people to take part in it. Who is your participant population? Who will be your sample? These are important considerations (see chapter 4), as is the method you will use to recruit participants. Recruitment is only part of your responsibility—some form of credit may need to be doled out to participants so that they may fulfill their own course requirements. This chapter's first active learning exercise deals with these two important tasks.

ACTIVE LEARNING EXERCISE   **10A**

Participant Pools, Sign-up Sheets, and Giving Credit

Participant sign-ups. How will you recruit participants? Many psychology departments maintain *participant pools* for faculty and student research. Study participants are usually students from introductory-level psychology courses who must take part in research to complete course requirements. If a source for recruiting participants is already established, use it. Many pools now allow volunteers to sign up online. If your department has a participant pool, speak to your instructor or the pool's supervisor about whether you can use it and how to post a notice about your study.

Continued

Other departments simply post research opportunities on a bulletin board. This method may be old-fashioned but it is still effective. A standard sign-up sheet, one used for the course elective study introduced in Table 3.8, is shown in Table 10.1. Participants need to know a study's title; a brief description of what they will do; the available dates, times, and place for participation; and how to contact the experimenter (see Table 10.1). In turn, the experimenter should provide a slip of paper for participants to jot down the date and time of their appointments (these slips should provide the research location, the experimenter's name, and his or her phone number or email address). Wise experimenters always remind participants about scheduled appointments a day before (so it is important to acquire participants' phone numbers or email addresses).

Giving credit when it's due. Few people, especially students, volunteer for research unless there is some incentive for participating. If your institution gives extra credit for research participation, then there is probably a student credit form available for your use. If not, creating a credit slip is easy. A sample credit slip is shown in Table 10.2. Be sure to make the slip look professional and to have your

Table 10.1   A Sample Sign-up Sheet for Recruiting Participants

---

College Course Elective Study

As a participant, you will take part in a discussion with other students about what factors influence you to choose courses outside your major or general education requirements. The study will take between 45 min and 1 hr to complete.

Samuel Andrews is conducting the study. He can be reached by phone at extension 2727 or by email: sandrews@college.edu.

If you sign up to participate, please come to Old Main Hall Room 110-A at one of the dates and times noted below. Please print your name, and phone number or email, in one of the open slots below.

Date: Thursday, December 1 at 3:30pm	Friday, December 2 at 3:30pm
Your Name Phone/Email	*Your Name Phone/Email*
1.	1.
2.	2.
3.	3.
4.	4.
5.	5.
6.	6.

To remind yourself about your agreement to participate in this study, please tear off one of the slips provided below and write down the date and time on it.

[Printed slips of paper labeled "College Course Elective Study, Old Main Hall Room 110-A" would be attached at the bottom of the sign-up sheet.]

Source: Adapted from Table 5.5 in Dunn (1999, p. 156).

Table 10.2   A Sample Participant Experimental Credit Slip

Psychology Department Research Participation Credit Form

To be completed by the participant:

Name_____

Course title_____ Course number_____

Your instructor's name_____

To be completed by the experimenter:

Study's title_____Date_____

Credit awarded (circle):   15 min $^1/_2$ hr $^3/_4$ hr   1 hr   other: _____ hrs

Instructor's name_____

Experimenter's name_____

Experimenter's signature_____

To receive credit, submit this form to the Psychology Participant Pool Coordinator, Room 225, Old Main Hall

instructor authorize its use. Finally, always inform participants about where they must submit their slips in order to receive credit for research participation.

What if there is no participant pool or established bulletin board for posting a sign-up sheet announcing research opportunities? You must get creative and devise ways to recruit participants. Here are a few suggestions (consult your instructor or check out the relevant rules on your campus before you try any of them):

- Create an attractive poster that contains the information noted in Table 10.1. Place the posters (with appropriate permission) around campus. Since you will be counting on "true" volunteers, course credit is probably not possible. Instead, offer participants some refreshments for taking part.
- Announce a lottery where people who agree to participate in your study have a chance to win a gift certificate to a campus store or popular event (e.g., a concert).
- Approach people in a public place (e.g., the Student Union, the library) with a sign-up sheet and ask them to consider participating. Be sincere and explain that their participation will be helping you to complete a course requirement. Respect their privacy: No means no.
- Create a simple, one-page sign-up sheet containing most of the information from Table 10.1 (again, presuming that credit is not a possibility) and ask psychology instructors if they would be willing to pass one around in their classes.

As a last resort, ask your friends, room or dorm mates, the members of your fraternity, sorority, or team, and anyone else you can legitimately invite, to take part.

Continued

Have another student in your class do the same and then swap the lists so that neither of you knows who is taking part in the respective studies. In the end, you may have to ask friends or acquaintances to participate in your research project. Although far from an ideal solution, enlisting the aid of people you know will still enable you to get experience conducting research in social psychology.

Demand Characteristics

All people are curious; participants in social psychology experiments even more so. As the research by Orne (1962) amply demonstrated, participants are usually biased towards wanting to help researchers. How else can they be biased? Orne coined the term *demand characteristics* to refer to the cues available in almost any experiment that guide participants toward identifying the hypothesis being tested or otherwise suggest how they should behave. Whether participants are correct is beside the point—their behavior changes because of other factors besides the all-important independent variable being manipulated. Demand characteristics are somewhat different from reactivity (see chapter 8), which occurs primarily when dependent measures alter the very behavior they were designed to assess and separately from the influence of an independent variable. Any demand characteristic poses a problem when the attention of a participant is directed away from a study's procedure, instructions, presentation of manipulated or measured variables, and so on. Demand characteristics reduce a study's internal validity by prompting second guessing or a misguided desire to help or otherwise cooperate with the experimenter.

On rare occasions, instead of acting in a compliant or cooperative manner, some demand characteristics lead participants to be highly reactive. Such participants become intentionally inattentive. They do not listen to the experimenter or follow directions well, often asking argumentative questions or intentionally completing questionnaires or other measures in a contrary manner (e.g., giving ratings that are the opposite to how they actually feel, writing silly or flippant answers, leaving both open and close-ended questions blank). Fortunately, perhaps, reactive participants are less common than the aforementioned "good subjects," but the behavior of both groups undermines the coherence and causal focus of the study.

Fortunately, there are various ways to reduce demand characteristics. Table 10.3 (drawn from Aronson, Ellsworth, Carlsmith, & Gonzales, 1990) lists some of the common approaches social psychologists use to combat demand characteristics; you may think of others in the process of conducting your research. You need not employ all the tactics shown in Table 10.3 in your study: Which ones you choose to use will depend on your research design, the topic, the procedure you use, and the variables involved. One of the best ways to determine the presence of demand characteristics is by pilot testing the study on some naïve participants and then carefully debriefing them afterwards.

Table 10.3 Tactics for Reducing Participant Demand Characteristics in Social Psychological Research

Adopt a compelling cover story: Satisfy participant curiosity or suspicion with a convincing rationale for the research.

Avoid self-report measures: Instead of focusing on what people say, examine how they behave. Keep in mind that verbal measures can trigger social desirability biases.

Study an obscure hypothesis: When a research question is not obvious, participants are less likely to identify it (e.g., Weber & Cook, 1972).

Deploy dependent variables outside the research situation: Inform participants they will take part in two experiments so that the independent variable in one will not be linked with the dependent variable in the other. Alternatively, administer the main measures during the debriefing, when participants believe the experiment is winding down or even over.

Invite the participant to be the "experimenter": When participants believe they are not the focus of a study, their suspicion and vigilance both drop (e.g., Aronson & Linder, 1965).

Ask participants for help: Sincerely inform participants that they can help you the most if they are willing to behave in an honest and trusting manner (e.g., Fillenbaum, 1966).

Employ involving things to do: Keep the participants occupied doing activities as part of the study's procedure so that there is no time for them to be distracted by potential demand characteristics.

Try bias-reducing research designs: Assign participants to a condition in advance and make certain the experimenter does not know which treatment is being examined at any given time (see Campbell & Stanley, 1966, for specific design examples).

Source: Adapted from Table 6.8 in Dunn (1999, p. 195).

Reducing Experimenter Biases

Where Martin Orne's (1962) research revealed pitfalls of participant demand characteristics for social psychological research, the work of Robert Rosenthal shed light on an equally vexing problem: experimenter bias (e.g., Rosenthal, 1966, 1967, 1969, 1976; see also Rosenthal & Rosnow, 1991). While participants are on the lookout for cues regarding how to act or what question is being studied, experimenters can unknowingly be providing them with hints or clues about hoped-for behavior. By far the biggest source of experimenter bias turns out to be such experimenter *expectancy effects*, which were introduced earlier in chapter 5. To recap, an experimental expectancy effect (or self-fulfilling prophecy) is a research artifact that occurs when an investigator unintentionally, nonverbally, and behaviorally discloses the hypothesis to participants. The participants respond to the researcher's expectations so that their actions increase the chances that the hypothesis will be established as true. The problem, of course, is that their confirmatory behavior is not due to the research design or the impact of the independent variable but instead to the revealed hopes of the researcher.

Expectancy effects in social psychological research disrupt the link between determining true cause and effect; an observed effect is falsely attributed to an empirical intervention rather than the unintended help of an investigator. Once any false finding is unknowingly published in the social psychological literature, it can be very difficult to undo its influence on subsequent theory and research. Thus social psychologists should always be on the lookout for potential experimenter bias, and should replicate all findings.

What is the chief source of experimenter bias in social psychological research? Experimenter knowledge. What I mean is that an experimenter can know too much about a study, including:

- the theory behind an experiment or other study
- the hypothesis being tested
- the level of the independent variable a given participant is being exposed to
- how a participant responds to a dependent variable.

On the surface, these four points seem to be both obvious and unavoidable. After all, how can an experimenter, the person who presumably conceived of a study, not know what is happening within it? In the first place, many social psychologists reduce or even eliminate considerable experimenter bias by employing naïve experimenters. That is, the individuals who run studies from start to finish remain unaware of the hypothesis being tested and the theory behind it (some investigators have actually deceived their experimenters by giving them a false hypothesis; see Cialdini & Ascani, 1976). However, employing naïve experimenters is costly, time-consuming, impractical and, in any case, not terribly appropriate for a student project. After all, you are supposed to learn about the ins and outs of doing social psychological research. Getting someone to do your work for you would defeat that purpose.

How, then, can some experimenter biases be reduced? If you cannot employ a naïve experimenter, perhaps you can enlist the aid of a second person—a collaborator or coinvestigator—to help you with your work. You both may know the theory and the hypothesis being tested, but perhaps one of you can deliver the instructions and the independent variable while the other—who remains unaware of the experimental condition being tested (i.e., experimental or control group)—administers and collects the dependent variable. One or both of you can then debrief the participant. This method—keeping the researchers "blind" to the condition being tested—is one simple way to reduce experimenter bias.

Involving a second experimenter, too, can sometimes be a daunting task. As a result, many investigators rely on what is known as a *double-blind procedure*, where neither the experimenter nor the participant knows whether the participant is in a treatment or control condition. The logic is simple and adopted from medical research, where experimental treatments are pitted against placebos in a research design where neither the researcher or the volunteer knows if a drug treatment is active. Of course, maintaining a true double-blind procedure in a psychology experiment is not easy. At some point, the experimenter may have to know or may simply deduce a participant's condition. Minimally and constructively, an experimenter might not need to learn a participant's condition until the last possible moment, say, when some randomizing device (e.g., a random numbers table, a die toss, a coin flip) is used.

Some researchers use another approach, a mechanized solution based on one suggested by Rosenthal (1966). Following an experimental overview by an experimenter, a participant can be placed in a room in front of a computer. Once the software is loaded, the participant can be randomly assigned to one of several conditions, including a control group. All of the subsequent instructions can be presented on the computer, which will also conveniently collect and store the participants' responses (e.g., ratings, scores, open-ended comments) for later analysis. The experimenter can monitor the proceedings by networked computer from another room, thereby reducing the possibility of bias. The experimenter can then lead the debriefing once the participant finishes with the study and the software. If an appropriate software program is unavailable, a PowerPoint slide show could be used to deliver instructions on individual computers.

In an earlier time—that is, before computers were everywhere—recorded instructions or typed directions were used to reduce bias. The computer does introduce a high level of standardization for combating bias but, as with taped or written instructions, the same overarching problem remains: The setting is less engaging, less like real life. Despite the fact that most of us do interface with computers quite often, we learn more from flesh and blood encounters with other humans. As acknowledged earlier, participants are likely to take an experimental procedure more seriously if they interact with another person. Where automated instructions are concerned, then, the impact of the independent variable and the setting's realism (experimental as well as mundane) may be sacrificed for reduced bias. The social psychologist conducing the research must determine whether this trade-off is worth the trouble.

Rehearsing your script until you can perform it consistently and relatively flawlessly is another way to prevent experimenter bias. As experimenter, you do not begin to collect any data from actual participants until you have memorized the script so that everyone has the same, standardized experience. When the memorization is accomplished, you should recruit three to five participants and have them take part in the experiment to help you practice (their data is discarded as potentially biased). Once you are confident you know the script well, begin the actual data collection.

There is one other technique to prevent experimenter bias that poses no difficulty or great effort for any social psychologist, whether student or professional: Do not look at the data. Rosenthal (1966, 1969) observed that the reactions of the first participants in an experiment affect the experimenter's actions towards all of the participants who take part later. In other words, later participants act like earlier ones, which can mean some experimenter expectancy is passed on to the later participants based on what the first few do. Happily, all you have to do is avoid looking at the dependent measures and other materials gathered from the participants. File them away carefully until the last participant is run—then and only then can you see how the participants

Table 10.4   Some Other Ways to Cope with Experimenter Expectancy Effects

Keep contact between experimenter(s) and participant(s) to a minimum: Use written, recorded, or computerized instructions. Collect data via the Internet or the mail.

Present the most important instructions without interaction: Instead of having an experimenter present the independent and dependent variables, present them in writing (e.g., paper in a file folder) or online (e.g., via a program or email).

Rely on different experimenters across different experimental sessions: Instead of one or two experimenters, try using several at different times.

Emphasize the importance of standardization and sticking to an experimental script (see Active Learning Exercise 10B).

Surreptitiously observe the experimenter's exchanges with participants: Be sure that the experimenter—either through what is said or done—is not revealing the hypothesis to participants. If you are the experimenter, ask your instructor or a peer to watch how you interact with a few participants to make certain you are not creating any expectancies for them.

reacted to your research design. This approach is not only empirically sound, it is ethically appropriate: You can rest assured that you did not bias participants based on their responses.

Other ways to cope with the problem of experimental expectancy effects are noted in Table 10.4. Keep in mind that reducing the interaction between experimenters and participants is the easiest and best way to reduce expectancy effects. As already acknowledged, this reduction also makes social psychology experiments less social. Besides the suggestions offered in this section of the chapter and in Table 10.4, are there any other possibilities? Yes, one important one: Write and then learn a detailed script for your experiment. If you behave similarly with each participant, any bias is apt to be spread equally across the participants, thereby nullifying its impact.

ACTIVE LEARNING EXERCISE   10B

Writing a Script for Your Study

As should be abundantly clear, an experimenter must exert as much control as possible in order to reduce opportunities for error or bias to enter an experiment. Besides taking the precautions we just reviewed, one of the easy ways to do so is by making certain that all participants receive the same information in the same order except, of course, for the critical difference introduced by the independent variable. Table 10.5 illustrates the sequence of events for a typical social psychology experiment with one or two independent variables presented at the same time. As you can see, the experimental and control groups are treated identically every step of the way except when the independent variable is delivered to them. The sequence of events in your social psychology project might differ from Table 10.5, of course, but you will still need to think about when participant groups receive identical or different types of information. How can you ensure that everyone receives the same information? By writing, following, and eventually memorizing an experimental script.

A script, of course, is the text of a play or a film production that tells the actors what to do and, most importantly, what to say. An experimental script serves a similar purpose for an experimenter and any confederates. Each of them needs to know what to say and when to say it (e.g., "Before we proceed to the next activity, I would like you to complete this rating scale . . ."). Naturally, any departure from the script or improvisation should be minimal so that the experiment's internal validity can be maintained (recall chapter 9). Staging directions in the script help in this way as long as they, too, become routine (e.g., collect the rating scales *before* passing out the folder with the target's photograph). Different experiments will have different parts, but most have a typical set of stages where certain key events occur. Once you use the script a few times during data collection, you will not only know exactly what to do, you will also quickly memorize your lines.

Table 10.6, a supplement to Table 10.5, lists the usual types of dialog found in social psychology experiments. Use the contents of Table 10.6 to draft a script for your project. To begin, imagine what will happen at each step in the experiment. As you think about what you should do and say at each step, jot down some notes. Once you have a complete set of notes, sit down at a computer and draft what you believe you will say and do at key points in the procedure. Print out a

Table 10.5 Sequence of Events and Information Provided to Participants in the Typical Social Psychology Experiment

Sequence of events	Experimental	Control
Random selection or recruitment	—	—
Greeting	Same	Same
Rationale for study	Same	Same
Random assignment	—	—
Pretest measure (if used)	Same	Same
Independent variable(s)	Different	Different
Manipulation check(s)	Same	Same
Dependent variables	Same	Same
Debriefing	Same	Same

Source: Adapted from Table 6.16 in Dunn (1999, p. 215).

Continued

Table 10.6   Stages and Sample Dialogue for Typical Experimental Scripts

---

Stage 1: Greeting. The experimenter arrives on time and makes the participant comfortable. Opening comments should remain relatively constant; however, some ad-libbing is fine.

Stage 2: Rationale for experiment and explanation of procedure. As experimenter, deliver the cover story and explain what specifically the participant will do during the study. Consistent dialog is essential here—memorize it.

Stage 3: Questions? The experimenter stops to make certain that the participant understands everything said so far, including the purpose of the research, any directions, and the role he or she is to play. The experimenter should ask a fixed set of questions each time; however, ad-libbed responses are fine, as different participants will ask different questions.

Stage 4: Presentation of the independent variable(s). The experimenter guides the participant through the procedure described in stage 2, presenting the independent variable(s) at the proper time. Consistent dialog is critical here—it should be memorized.

Stage 5: Administration of the dependent variable(s) and any manipulation checks(s). Following stage 4, a participant must complete some measure (e.g., survey, questionnaire, rating scales) and/or perform some behavior that represents the outcome variables of the study. Some way to verify the influence of the independent variable is desirable. Dialog is usually, but not necessarily, limited in this stage.

Stage 6: Debriefing. The participant is fully debriefed by the experimenter. If deception was used, the participant's suspicion (e.g., awareness of the actual hypothesis) is assessed. A debriefing protocol (see Active Learning Exercise 10D) should be followed. Dialog can be scripted but ad-libbing is necessary. A verbal summary of the study's purpose is also provided.

Stage 7: Departure. The participant exits the study with a credit slip and, if desired, a debriefing sheet (see Active Learning Exercises 10B and 10E, respectively). Dialog is gracious and grateful.

Source: Adapted from Dunn (1999, Table 6.2, p. 181).

hard copy of the script, and revise and edit it with an emphasis on clarity and simplicity, as you want to be certain every participant understands what is going on, as well as why, at each stage. Once you have a complete draft, pilot test the script and staging on a practice participant. Don't worry: The first draft of your script is apt to be choppy and incomplete. You will forget a few of your "lines" and have to ad-lib some others on the spot. As you practice it more and become comfortable after running the first few participants, you can refine what you say and do so that things flow seamlessly (again, discard the data from the first few participants as it may be biased due to your initial inexperience with the script).

Record Keeping

Throughout this book, we have focused on ways to generate data in social psychological research. What will you do with the data collected from participants, all the verbal self-reports, ratings of others, observed behaviors, personality scores, and the like? Most data tend to be quantitative rather than qualitative, so you probably will have some collection of numbers based on the responses or reactions of each participant.

Even some qualitative data can be converted into numerical form (recall how fixed verbal responses in surveys or questionnaires were changed into numbers in chapters 6 and 8). Rating scales with fixed category responses such as "not at all," "not very often," "sometimes," "very often," and "all the time" could be given the values 1 through 5, for example. Most of these numbers would be converted to averages and analyzed using statistical formulas (see chapter 11) or otherwise summarized in a table or a figure (see chapter 12). Before any data analysis is performed, what will you do with the raw data? How will you sort it, code it, and save it? (Suggestions regarding how to clean up and prepare data for analysis can be found in DiLalla and Dollinger, 2006.)

Simply put, you will need to develop a system for keeping records of your data. I suggest you do this in two ways. First, create a data record sheet for each participant (see Active Learning Exercise 10C). Keep these record sheets filed in a safe place so that you can consult them as needed.

Second, code the data and enter all the numbers into a computer spreadsheet. Although data analysis will be discussed conceptually in chapter 11, I will not be reviewing elementary statistics in great detail. I assume your instructor will do so or that you have already taken a class or two on this topic. Further, I will hazard a guess that you will rely on commercial software to analyze your data rather than doing calculations by hand. Thus saving your data in a computer file makes the most sense as a second step. As an added precaution—you do not want to lose what represents a lot of hard work—save a back-up copy of the spreadsheet on a different computer, a flash drive, or on your institution's network.

One more thing: Be sure to hold on to the original questionnaires and any other forms that the participants in your study completed. If you misplaced or lost your data record sheets or the spreadsheet files, you could recreate them from the participants' raw materials. Keeping such materials may seem odd to you, but the American Psychological Association (APA, 2001, p. 137) advocates a publishing tradition found in the sciences. Researchers should hold onto their original, raw data for at least 5 years following the publication of a research article. Although you may not be planning to publish your work, you might be able to use it again in the future, especially if you plan to pursue graduate education in social psychology or a related field.

Let's turn to the practical matter of creating data record sheets.

ACTIVE LEARNING EXERCISE   10C

Creating a Data Record Sheet

Keeping accurate records regarding data, including which condition(s) a participant was assigned to, each person's sex, any additional demographic information, as well as the raw data, is important. Loss of any data reduces statistical power, which means detecting cause and effect is made more difficult. Uncertainty about whether a participant was assigned to a treatment or a control group can cause the person's data to be dropped from the analyses completely. Thus, for the welfare of your project, keep accurate data records.

Table 10.7 shows a basic data record. As you can see, the top half of the record contains information about the participant, such as the date the study was conducted, the experimental condition, and so on (note that some numbers are already

Table 10.7 A Sample Data Record Sheet

Data Record

Date: _____

Participant's identification number: _____

Experimenter's name: _____

Time study began: _____ am pm (circle one)

Time study ended _____ am pm (circle one)

Independent Variables

Experimental condition: 1 = control group   2 = treatment group   (circle one)

Participant's sex: 1 = make   2 = female   (circle one)

Any comments:

Dependent Variables

Ratings of stimuli   Reaction time (in milliseconds)

_____   _____

_____   _____

_____   _____

_____   _____

_____   _____

Debriefing

Was a full debriefing performed?   Yes   No   (circle one)

If no, explain:

Did the participant guess the true purpose of the experiment?   Yes   No   (circle one)

If yes, explain:

Is there any reason these data should *not* be included in the analyses?   Yes   No   (circle one)

If yes, explain:

provided, which will make entering the data into a spreadsheet go quicker). The bottom half of Table 10.7 shows a sample record for dependent measures that were collected in this hypothetical study. Obviously, you will need to create a data record that fits your social psychology research project. Your sheet does not need to be elaborate in design but it should have sufficient space for the data for one participant. I suggest you include some descriptive text or labels as a reminder about the study's design, which measures were dependent variables rather than manipulation checks, and so forth. You will be surprised at how easy it can be to forget all the details associated with an experiment once the data are all collected.

Conducting a Postexperimental Interview

No study or experiment ends when the last dependent variable is collected from the participants. One critical matter remains: conducting the postexperimental interview commonly referred to as the *debriefing*. Social psychologists conduct debriefings to learn what participants thought and felt about the research, especially any concerns or fears related to the procedure. Some people, for example, truly believe that psychology experiments can "read their minds" or otherwise uncover their secrets or identify hidden qualities. Nothing could be further from the truth, but it is a researcher's obligation to assuage such fears and to inform the participants about the actual purpose of any project. This educational function is very important.

There is one other reason that social psychologists conduct careful and thorough debriefings: to assess participant suspicion. As already noted, a researcher needs to be on the lookout for participant bias, which occurs when a hypothesis is correctly deduced. Some participants, too, spend extraordinary efforts trying to figure out a project's purpose. They may not discern it correctly, but their efforts detract from their performance so that the impact of the independent and dependent variables is weakened. Researchers must assess suspicion in order to determine if a participant's data are bias-free—if not, a decision to eliminate that person's responses from the analyses must be made.

Here are some guidelines for conducting a debriefing:

- *Take your time.* Neither you nor the participant will learn anything if you rush the debriefing. You are an educator as much as a researcher and, in any case, you need to be sure the hypothesis or other key aspects of the project were not discovered.
- *Encourage the participant to ask questions.* Some participants will have concerns about their experience. Others are simply curious, even excited, about having a role in a scientific investigation. All participants need a bit of time to reflect on the experience and their part in it.

- *Create comfort.* A debriefing is an opportunity to bring participants back to their psychological baselines, how they were thinking and feeling before taking part in the study. Just as most plays and films reach some (often happy) closure, you must ensure the people who took part in your project leave the situation in a mindset close to the one they arrived with.
- *Ensure confidentiality and anonymity.* What happens in the lab stays in the lab. Remind the participants that you will only be using their responses in summary form, joined with the responses of others—no identifying material will be used in any written or oral presentations. Confidentiality and anonymity will be maintained.
- *Enlist their help.* Before you complete the debriefing, ask the participants not to tell their friends or classmates about the nature of project, or what they did or said. Be candid: Disclosure will bias, even ruin, your results and make the experience less interesting for future participants.

On the rare occasion when deception is necessary

No one likes to be tricked or fooled. When deception is used, even for noble purposes, there is always a risk that a participant will be offended or upset. The best approach is to carefully, thoroughly, and gradually explain that social psychological research sometimes explores controversial issues. In the course of doing so, explain that disclosing a project's purpose at the start can taint the results. As you continue, ask the participant if any aspect of the procedure seemed odd or unusual, or if there seemed to be some other purpose to the study than how it was initially described. Allow the participant to explain his or her reaction, if any, and then tailor your explanation accordingly. If the participant thinks everything was normal, then explain the nature of the deception and why it was necessary. Be sure to apologize for having to mislead the participant about the experiment's true purpose, highlighting that the goal was not to lie or deceive but to get at the true causes of social behavior.

I have two other important suggestions regarding the use of deception:

Avoid giving participants false feedback. On rare occasions, a social psychologist will give a participant false feedback, that is, contrived information designed to elicit a response. A common example is to inform someone that he or she earned a very low (or high) test score in order to influence the participant's self-esteem at that moment in time. Research by Ross, Lepper, and Hubbard (1975) found that debriefing after the delivery of false feedback was often not sufficient to dispel the myths that can be created in the minds of participants. Such belief perseverance can be potentially damaging if participants are told falsehoods that are more distressing than information related to performance on a test. My advice is simple: Don't ever give participants false feedback unless the information is truly inconsequential to their sense of self or well-being.

Never, ever make a person feel foolish. No matter what, be sure that every participant understands why the deception was necessary and that it was designed to be effective (i.e., to mislead everyone). Revealing the deception should be done in a friendly, straightforward, and gradual manner. Avoid dramatic "aha!" moments; your role is to be compassionate, not clever.

ACTIVE LEARNING EXERCISE   **10D**

Crafting a Debriefing Protocol

As an experimenter, you have an ethical obligation (recall chapter 3) to inform participants about the true purpose of your research, what you hope to find, and why you became interested in the topic. Aside from ethics, you are also filling an important educational role by teaching people about research in social psychology. You want them to help you confirm your hypotheses about social behavior, but you also want them to leave having had a positive experience.

Practically speaking, too, you want to be sure that your participants did not discern your hypothesis, that they were not suspicious or overly curious about the purpose of your study, and that the procedure, as well as the independent and dependent variables, had the intended effects on behavior. The best way to determine if all these criteria are met is by conducting a thorough debriefing where you can ask questions that will help your research and where participants can satisfy their own curiosity about what you were up to.

Table 10.8 shows the stages and lists the sorts of questions found in a typical debriefing delivered at the end of a social psychology experiment. Most debriefing protocols assess a participant's general reaction to the study, recall of the cover story, presumed purpose of the research (including whether the hypothesis was correctly identified), and the level to which the participant displayed suspicion. Keep in mind that the results of a debriefing can actually help you improve an experiment's design or procedure. People who take part in research often see things that an experimenter will miss, as the experience is both fresh and unfamiliar to them.

You can use this sample protocol to create your own set of questions. Question 1 in Table 10.8, for example, will need to be tailored to fit your project. Different experiments will have different sets of instructions. However, virtually all debriefings in social psychology assess participants' level of suspicion, even when no deception is present. Chances are good that you will need a question like the fourth one shown in Table 10.8. The reason to assess suspicion is that people are wary of being duped, of having their "minds read," or simply feeling tricked. You need to determine, too, whether a highly suspicious participant might have been so

Continued

Table 10.8   A Sample Debriefing Protocol

1   General reaction to the study: "What did you think about this study? Did everything seem to run smoothly? Were the directions clear so that you knew what to do? Did you encounter any problems?"

2   Memory of cover story: "Do you remember the purpose of the study? May I ask you to explain it to me?"

3   Assessing study's purpose: "Do you have any idea what research question this study was trying to answer? (Did the participant identify the correct hypothesis? Check one: _____ Yes _____ No)

4   Assessing suspicion: "Many people are suspicious about what goes on in psychology experiments. Did anything make you suspicious? If so, what was it?" Note to experimenter: If deception was used, gradually and carefully explain its nature and necessity in this instance, including why no alternative was available.

5   Improving the study's procedure: "Can you recommend anything we can do to improve this study? Are there any changes you would make? If so, what are they?"

6   Conclusion and exit: Thank the participant, handing out a credit sheet (see Active Learning Exercise 10A) and debriefing sheet (see Active Learning Exercise 10D) as needed. Remind the participant to contact you if there are further questions (provide your phone number or email address). Ask them not to discuss the study with others, to avoid biasing future data and making the experiment less interesting for future participants.

Adapted from Dunn (1999, Table 5.8, p. 164).

distracted that his or her responses should be dropped from the data set. The same will be true when or if a participant accurately identifies the study's hypothesis.

One final suggestion: Be sure to sincerely thank all participants for taking part in your study at the end of the debriefing. You literally could not do your work without them. There is also a practical reason for doing so. To ensure that details of your study or its purpose do not become widely known by potential participants, close the debriefing by asking each person to refrain from discussing the experience with others.

There is one more debriefing service you might offer to participants—a short, written summary describing the rationale behind your work.

ACTIVE LEARNING EXERCISE   10E

Writing a Debriefing Sheet

Some social psychologists take the idea of "giving psychology away" quite seriously (Miller, 1969a, 1969b). They see experiments as being akin to the classroom, a place where participants can learn about the nature of social behavior while taking part in simulations designed to better understand it. To further participants'

Table 10.9 A Sample Debriefing Sheet

Judging Attractiveness

Are juries truly fair and impartial? Research in social psychology suggests that certain physical characteristics of defendants can bias the judgments made by juries. For example, people often rely on the stereotype that what is beautiful must also be good, leading them to judge less attractive people as somehow guiltier of a crime than those whose physical appearance is more pleasing. In this study, I hypothesized that attractive defendants would receive less severe recommended sentences compared to less attractive defendants. Some participants in this study saw a photograph of a good-looking individual who was on trial for committing a crime. Others received the same information about the defendant but viewed a photograph of a very unattractive person. I believe that my results will shed light on how some jurors decide how severely to sentence criminals.

I want everyone who takes part in my study to enjoy it and to learn something about social psychology. With this goal in mind, may I ask you to please not discuss the study's purpose or any of the procedure with your friends. If future participants know what the project is about, their responses will bias my results. Thank you for agreeing not to discuss this experiment with others.

Thank you, too, for taking part in my research. I will not know the results of my experiment for several weeks. If you are interested in learning about the results or have additional questions, please email me at laura@moravian.edu.

Suggested Reading

Abwender, D. A., & Hough, K. (2001). Interactive effects of characteristics of defendant and mock juror on U.S. participants' judgment and sentencing recommendations. *The Journal of Social Psychology, 141*, 603–615.

education in social psychology, some researchers pass out debriefing sheets at the end of the debriefing. A *debriefing sheet* is a short summary that describes the rationale for a study, placing it contextually in the larger research literature. Some debriefing sheets suggest readings so that truly interested participants can learn more. All such sheets should include contact information, such as a phone number or an email address, so that participants can ask any follow-up questions that occur to them once they leave the research setting. Few do, but it is a research courtesy to extend the offer to all participants (a similar verbal offer should be made at the end of every debriefing protocol; see point 6 in Table 10.8).

Table 10.9 illustrates a sample debriefing sheet. As you can see, the summary shown in Table 10.9 is more or less an extended Abstract (see chapter 12). This debriefing sheet is based on the sample student research paper provided in Appendix C. If you pass out a debriefing sheet, you are teaching participants to appreciate social psychology as a scientific discipline by furthering their knowledge. You are also emphasizing to them that their participation mattered, that their responses were contributions to the expansion of what we know about the causes and consequences of social behavior.

Closing Thought: The Important Role of Pilot Testing

We opened this chapter with Orne's (1962) revelations regarding the "good subject" problem. I want to close this practical chapter with one suggestion about how to be a good experimenter. To ensure that your experiment runs smoothly and to enhance every opportunity for empirical success, pilot test the project. Take the time to run a few practice participants so that you can learn where any gaps in the procedure, script, manipulations, or measurements, might be. Engage these folks in a sincere discussion about what works and what doesn't where your project is concerned. Take their suggestions seriously. Be flexible: Make any and all necessary changes. Their insights about the technical side of doing the research can help you prove your insights about social behavior.

Exercises

1   Write a critique of a published study you find in a social psychology journal. Identify possible demand characteristics or potential sources of experimenter bias. Offer concrete suggestions you believe will improve the procedure, eliminate the problems noted, and enhance the study's internal validity.
2   Draft an experimental script based on a study already published in the social psychological literature.
3   Create a data sheet for a study already published in a social psychology journal.
4   Write a debriefing sheet for a study from the published literature.

Chapter 11

Data Analysis

How do we know some social psychological phenomenon is real? Should we simply trust our senses? Is the best advice to allow our intuition to guide us? What do most social psychologists do in order to convince other researchers that their observations are valid, reliable, and truly descriptive accounts of some social behavior?

Perhaps a simple demonstration is sufficient. In 2000, the late C. R. Snyder, a clinical psychologist who contributed greatly to the study of how social psychological phenomena can inform the study of therapeutic processes and interventions, was interviewed on the popular television show *Good Morning America* (Lopez, 2006a, b). One of Snyder's (1994) scientific contributions was the study of hope or how some individuals anticipate favorable outcomes in the future. Before that day's show began, Snyder had the three cast members—the host, the weatherman, and the medical reporter—complete the Hope Scale, a short, 12-item measure of the degree to which people feel that good things lie ahead (Snyder et al., 1991). Here are two sample items from the scale:

I can think of many ways to get out of a jam.
I energetically pursue my goals.

Respondents rate each item using an 8-point Likert-type scale (see chapter 6) ranging from 1 ("definitely false") to 8 ("definitely true"). Scores on the Hope scale are positively correlated with related constructs, including optimism, self-esteem, and control, and inversely linked to measures of depression and hopelessness (see also Babyak, Snyder, & Yoshinobu, 1993).

On the show, live and unscripted, Snyder had the three cast members take turns performing the cold pressor test, a classical tool from experimental psychology. The cold pressor test is simple but bracing: Individuals plunge a fist into an ice bath of near freezing water, holding it there for as long as they can. As the three participants held their right fists in the icy water, Snyder described hope theory and its link to tolerance for pain to the audience (in case you are wondering, holding your hand—or any body part—in ice water for any period of time *is* very painful—just try it). Simply put, individuals possessing higher levels of hope should be able to withstand serious

Figure 11.1.   C. R. Snyder (1944–2006), a social-clinical psychologist, who helped birth the new subdiscipline of positive psychology

discomfort for longer periods of time than those expressing lower levels of the construct. You might be interested to learn that Snyder was also one of the founders of one of psychology's newest subdisciplines, positive psychology, the scientific study of human strengths and factors that promote well-being (Snyder & Lopez, 2007).

What do you think happened? As Snyder predicted, the scores the cast members received on the scale administered prior to the telecast accurately predicted how long each individual could endure keeping a numb hand in the icy cold water. Snyder was a risk taker in his research, in the classroom, and before a live audience of millions. How did he know that the person with the highest hope score would hold out the longest and the individual with the lowest score would quit first? Was Snyder a good judge of character? Rick Snyder was a colleague and friend of mine, so yes, I would say he was a good judge of people's strengths and weaknesses, but that's not the reason he was so confident (hopeful?) that the demonstration would be a powerful one. (Imagine, for a moment, how the audience and the cast would have reacted if the hope scores were unrelated to the cold pressor test survival times.)

Snyder's confidence was not placed in his showmanship but, rather, in his scholarship. Snyder, his colleagues and students, conducted a great many studies on hope theory. As with any social psychologist, his understanding of the construct (in this case, social phenomena related to hope for the future) grew as it was tested in a variety of settings. Snyder's confidence in the efficacy of the scale and the live demonstration rested on extensive research findings. And his extensive research findings, in turn, rested on planned data analyses which revealed significant results.

By *data analysis*, I refer to systematically collecting and examining observations to answer a question, search for a pattern, or otherwise interpret some research findings. As we already learned in chapter 4, most of the "data"—information—collected in social psychology experiments tends to be quantitative, that is, numbers based on ratings, responses, or behavioral measures. Some social psychological data are qualitative (recall chapter 5), but such nonnumerical analyses will not be reviewed in this chapter (but see Flick, 1998; Lincoln & Guba, 1985; Miles & Huberman, 1984; Taylor & Bogdan, 1998).

Most social psychological research relies on statistical analyses. This chapter offers advice on planning, executing, and writing about the statistical analyses of social psychological data collected in the course of student research. Space constraints prevent me from teaching you the "nuts and bolts" of statistical analysis. I will assume that you already learned about statistics in another class or that your social psychology instructor will advise you on how to do any necessary analysis. Keep in mind, too, that there are many books available on introductory statistical analysis, as well as a variety of software packages that will do the bulk of the work for you. My intent here is simply to persuade you that data analysis is another important skill that social psychologists acquire in the course of their research.

Basic Statistics

How do we know what is or isn't so when it comes to the analysis of data? We rely on statistics. Some piece of data that is represented in numerical form is called a *statistic*. Statistical analysis is the process of testing hypotheses about, and drawing inferences from, data using mathematically based rules. Recall that we discussed some statistical issues earlier in this book when we considered samples, populations, and randomization (see, e.g., chapter 4).

Social psychologists rely on two types of statistics: descriptive statistics and inferential statistics. *Descriptive statistics* are procedures researchers use so they can describe, characterize, organize, and summarize the main qualities of data drawn from a sample. The main descriptive statistic used by social psychologists (and virtually all other types of psychologists) is the mean or statistical average (e.g., the usual or typical level of reported attractiveness of a confederate). Other descriptive statistics address questions involving number (e.g., How many participants were women?), range (e.g., What was the lowest rating? The highest?), and frequency (e.g., How many times did the participant ring the bell?). We will define key descriptive statistics and note some simple calculations shortly.

In contrast, *inferential statistics* enable researchers to generalize about the nature of a population based on the sample drawn from it. Specifically, inferential statistics allow us to assume that what we observe to be true about the behavior in one group of participants in one social psychology experiment at one time is likely to hold true for other people in similar situations at other points in time. Thus Milgram (1963, 1974) argued that the obedient behavior of most of the people who took part in his mock shock experiment was not unique, that virtually any group of adults would have reacted in a similar way. To support this argument, of course, Milgram did not simply point to the average behavior of his research participants (although their uniformity was rather dramatic); he relied on inferential statistics to make the case that the results were caused by the impact of (one or more) independent variables and not due to chance alone.

In fact, inferential statistical tests allow social psychologists to compare people's average responses to a dependent variable following the presentation of an independent variable. Such statistical comparisons allow researchers to determine whether any observed differences in the average behavior in an experimental group (or groups) differs reliably from the average behaviors measured in the control group. This kind of statistical comparison—the difference between mean or average levels of behavior in different participant groups—is at the heart of most social psychological research. Statistics allow social psychologists to make the case that any observed differences (presuming they conform to the hypothesis being tested) are due to the impact of an independent variable and not chance or other random factors. With this focus on average behaviors, let's turn to measures of central tendency.

Mean, mode, and median

Measures of central tendency—behavior at or around some average point—are important to social psychologists, whose efforts are aimed at trying to characterize how *people in general* react to some social stimulus. When considering a set of data, a given measure of central tendency is the single best indicator for describing representative behavior within a sample. Measures of central tendency portray the typical, usual, or common responses. Before we begin, note that some descriptive statistics can be determined by scanning an array of observations. Others require some simple mathematical operations. Still others require more involved calculations or the use of a basic calculator (some of which are programmed to determine the statistics with a push of a button).

There are three common measures of central tendency: the mean, the mode, and the median. The *mean* is the arithmetic average of some collection of observations based on either an interval or a ratio scale of measurement (recall chapter 6). Calculating a mean is rather easy: Sum the available observations and then divide that total by

Table 11.1   Sample Data and Basic Sample Statistics

$N = 10$ scores: 6   7   8   9   10   10   12   12   12   15
The sum of the 10 scores $= \Sigma x = 101$
$M = \bar{x} = 10.1$ mode $= 12$ median $= mdn = 10$
Range $= 15 - 6 = 9$
Variance $= s^2 = 6.69$

Standard deviation $= SD = s = \sqrt{s^2} = 2.59$

the number of observations. When writing about average behavior, the mean is symbolized as *M*. Table 11.1 shows a data set comprised of 10 observations. As you can see, the sum of the observations is equal to 101. Once this sum is divided by 10, the average or mean response is known to be 10.1.

The *mode* is defined as the most frequently occurring observation within some distribution of data. Unlike the statistical average, there is no formula or procedure for calculating the mode. All you need to do is to "eyeball" a frequency distribution of scores and note the score that occurs most often. Take a look at the distribution shown in Table 11.1. The score of 12 is the mode. Why? It occurs three times (review the distribution of 10 scores in Table 11.1). The mode is a descriptive measure—it doesn't reflect the number of times an observation occurs, only that the observation is the most frequent one within a given sample. Can a data set have more than one mode? Certainly. If there were two scores that occurred three times each, for example, then there would be two modes.

The third measure of central tendency, the *median*, is a value that divides a given distribution in half. Fifty percent of the observations fall above the median and the other 50% fall below it. A median (abbreviated as *mdn*) can be determined from ordinal, interval, or ratio-scaled data. When a data set is small, like that shown in Table 11.1, calculating the median is relatively easy. When there is an even number of scores, such as the 10 shown in Table 11.1, the median can be calculated by averaging the middle two scores (i.e., $10 + 10 \div 2$, or 10). In the case of an odd number of scores, simply choose the middle score as the median (i.e., if there were 11 scores, pick the sixth score so that five fall below it and five above it). Larger sets of data require the use of a more involved formula which is beyond our present purposes (any basic statistics text will illustrate and explain how to use this formula).

Which measure of central tendency is the best choice for the social psychologist? That all depends on the data and how they will be used. Averages, for instance, are influenced by extremely high or low scores. Thus all researchers are advised to carefully comb through data sets to be certain that a mean is not being artificially inflated or deflated. Researchers who study income, for example, routinely report the median family income rather than the mean family income, as the latter is unduly affected by the few people in the nation who have incredibly high salaries (in the multimillions of dollars). The mean salary would simply be too high and not at all representative of the typical American income (which, based on 2005 data, was $73,304; U.S. Census, 2007). In contrast, the median income is reported because as a statistic, the median is less sensitive to very high or very low scores (based on 2005 data, the median family income was $56,194; U.S. Census, 2007). Using the simple data set shown in Table 11.1, you can reflect on why this is likely to be so.

Most social psychologists focus on depicting average or typical behavior, so the mean is the index of choice. As you probably already know from reading and working with the social psychological literature, most journal articles report on the mean differences identified as occurring between different conditions—levels of independent variables—in experiments or other studies. Like many behaviors, most social behaviors are believed to be normally distributed, so that they adhere to a "bell-shaped curve." The bulk of the bell occurs in the middle of the distribution, as it denotes the most common and frequent responses, as well as where they fall. Departures from this norm occur towards the two "tails" of the distribution, that is, the locations at the bottom (well below the average) and the top (well above it) where observations are fewer and increasingly rare.

As already noted, too, the mean or average behavior is apt to be a good index of how the *typical person* reacted to whatever dependent variable was administered following the intervention of a given independent variable. Thus most social psychology experiments focus on testing for mean differences between experimental and control groups.

Variance and standard deviation

Beyond focusing on the typical responses found in a data set, social psychologists must also consider how the available observations spread themselves around the average. In other words, are the observations spread far from the mean—responses to the independent variable varied from one another—or are the observations clustered relatively close to the mean? Close clustering suggests that most people responded in the same way to the independent variable. The spread or dispersion of observations within a set of data is referred to as *variability*. Similar to measures of central tendency, there are three indexes of variability: the range, variance, and standard deviation.

The *range* of any collection of observations is easy to determine: Simply subtract the lowest score from the highest one. The range of the data set shown in Table 11.1 is equal to 9 (i.e., 15 − 6). The range, which can be calculated from ordinal, interval, or ratio-scaled observations, does not provide much information about dispersion—only a rough sense of how far the low score is from the high one. As a measure of variability, the range is not sensitive to the number of observations between these extremes.

The second measure of variability is labeled variance. *Variance*, which is symbolized as s^2, is a numerical index of the similarity or dissimilarity of the observations in a data set. When the number representing variance is relatively large, there is a greater degree of dissimilarity among the observations. A smaller variance, in contrast, indicates greater similarity among the observations. The variance of the data set shown in Table 11.1 is 6.69, which means there is not much spread among the observations in the data set—most of the numbers are relatively close to one another in value. Note that the calculation for variance is not shown in Table 11.1, as it is somewhat more involved than the steps used to determine the prior descriptive statistics we have discussed (but the calculation of variance is not difficult—consult a basic statistics text or use a hand calculator, which may do the computations for you with a push of a button).

The third index, the standard deviation, turns out to be the most useful indicator of variability. The *standard deviation* is a numerical index of variability around the mean value in a set of observations. Like variance, the standard deviation describes clustering around the average, but it does so in the unit of measurement upon which the observations are based. The standard deviation is easily calculated by taking the square root of the variance (see Table 11.1). Thus the standard deviation of the data set shown in Table 11.1 is 2.59. When a standard deviation's value is relatively small, then a researcher can assume that most people in the sample responded more or less the same way (they gave the mean response or one close to it). A larger standard deviation points to less uniformity in response, which places people further from the average response. In the sample data set show in Table 11.1, we know that most of the responses fell 2.59 units above and below the mean of 10.1, or between observations of 7.51 and 12.69.

If you read the Results sections of social psychological journals carefully, you will find that means and their standard deviations are very important. The reason is that when coupled with a mean, the standard deviation is a fine index of response error for that mean. Think about it: If everyone in a sample gave the same response (say, a rating of 6 on a 7-point scale), then the mean response would be 6 and the standard deviation would be 0 (i.e., there would be no discrepancy from—or no dispersion around—the mean). As a standard deviation increases in magnitude, then we know that people's responses were associated with more error—more deviation from, less clustering around—the mean.

Standard deviation is symbolized as *s* when it serves as a descriptive statistic or when it is used in inferential statistical tests. When referred to in psychological writing, say, a journal article, it is denoted as *SD*. Like variance, the standard deviation is calculated from observations based on either interval or ratio scales.

Correlation: A reprise

Just a quick reminder: Another basic statistic used in social psychology and personality research is the correlation coefficient. A correlation is a measure of association between two variables. The association can be positive (i.e., as one variable increases or decreases in value, the other variable behaves the same way), negative (i.e., as one variable increases in value, the other variable decreases, or vice versa), or zero (i.e., no discernable pattern). Correlations are symbolized by r, and can range in value between -1.00 and $+1.00$. As the value of a correlation gets closer to either extreme, the relationship between the two variables becomes much stronger and more predictable. Correlations and correlational research were discussed in detail in chapter 5. Calculating correlations is best done using a hand calculator or a software package; however, most basic statistics texts will provide directions for doing so by hand.

Some brief comments on statistical power and effect size

Statistical power—or simply *power*—refers to the likelihood of accomplishing research goals, that is, correctly rejecting the null hypothesis and observing a statistically reliable effect (e.g., a difference between two means indicating that an experimental group somehow differed from a control group). There are advanced, statistically sophisticated methods for determining the level of power needed to observe a hypothesized result; however, this form of power analysis is beyond the scope of this book (but see, e.g., Cohen, 1988; Cohen & Cohen, 1983). There are also practical steps any researcher can take to enhance the level of power in an experiment so as to obtain a desired result (Dunn, 2001). These include:

- *Increasing sample size*. All else being equal, larger samples increase the probability of rejecting a null hypothesis. Practically speaking, instead of having 10 participants per group, for example, try for 15 or 20 or even more.
- *Make the independent variable salient*. As discussed in chapter 7, an independent variable will only lead to a measurable, behavioral difference if participants notice it.
- *Rely on sensitive dependent variables*. More precise or sensitive dependent variables are likely to reveal differences between or among participant groups. Quite often, such dependent variables are well tested, frequently used, and often cited in research publications (e.g., Harris, 1998).
- *Control random factors as much as possible*. Any extra "noise" (e.g., distractions, confusing instructions, demand characteristics) in a research setting adds extra error variance or, in practical terms, reduces the impact of the independent and dependent variables. With the obvious exception of the different levels of the independent variable, in most social psychological investigations, all participants should have approximately the same experience (see, e.g., Table 10.5).

Finally, power is also related to *effect size*, an indicator of the strength of association among variables in a study or the magnitude of an experimental effect. In fact, effect size influences power—the greater the effect size in a study, the greater the power in the study. The effect size of any observed result in an experiment can be described as small, medium, or large. Again, the statistical specifics are not in the purview of our discussion, but you should be aware that many social psychologists routinely report the effect sizes associated with their results. Such information allows readers to not only learn the magnitude of a result but also how difficult it was to observe in the first place (i.e., larger effects are usually more easily detected than smaller effects, which is useful information when planning a study based on prior research). For further discussion of effect size issues, see Cohen (1988) and Rosenthal and Rosnow (1991).

The Role of Data Analysis in Social Psychological Research

Data analysis is a tool for social psychologists to learn whether their theories and hypotheses adequately describe how people behave within or react to particular social situations, other people, or influential variables. I will assume that you are familiar with the sort of basic hypothesis testing taught in introductory statistics courses or described within basic statistics books (i.e., pitting a null hypothesis against a favored, experimental hypothesis, and then either accepting or rejecting the null hypothesis). I will further assume that your research design has at least one independent variable which has at least two levels to it (representing an experimental and control group, respectively) and that some process of random assignment determined each participant's group assignment. Finally, the dependent variable is presumably based on an interval or a ratio scale (recall the discussion of the scales of measurement in chapter 6).

Exceptions to these by now familiar parameters are possible, of course. Traditional experiments or studies with randomization and some control are analyzed using parametric statistics. *Parametric statistics* are inferential tests that make certain assumptions about the population from which some data were drawn. Generally, the assumptions deal with the shape of a population's distribution, namely that it is a "normal" or bell-shaped curve. Most—but not necessarily all—data from an experiment, for example, is likely to be analyzed using parametric tests. Why? Such data are usually based on interval or ratio scales.

When assumptions cannot be met for whatever reason—say, a distribution is abnormally shaped or "skewed"—then social psychologists may fall back on what are called nonparametric statistics. In contrast to parametric tests, *nonparametric approaches* are more or less assumption-free, especially where the shape of population distributions is concerned. Nonparametric tests are often used when there are very few observations available for analysis (for discussion of nonparametric tests, see Siegel & Castellan, 1988). Such tests, which are admittedly uncommon in social psychological research, allow researchers to explore how responses can be categorized (i.e., nominally scaled data) or ranked (i.e., ordinally scaled data). Despite the "distribution-free" nature of these tests, there are some caveats about using them, including:

- *Less statistical power than parametric tests.* Use of nonparametric tests often makes it harder to achieve research goals. Practically speaking, for example, using a test with lower power means that it is more difficult to correctly reject a null hypothesis.
- *Sensitivity.* The scales of measurement associated with nonparametric tests are less sensitive than those used for parametric analyses.

Having a working understanding of the difference between parametric and nonparametric statistical tests raises a very important point for anyone conducting a social psychological research project: Are the data analyses planned in advanced?

Plan analyses in advance

I want to warn you that one of the biggest mistakes beginning social psychologists make is failing to plan their data analyses in advance. By that I mean that their energies are tied up with concerns about theoretical issues (e.g., Is my theory sound?) and empirical ones (e.g., Is the manipulation of the independent variable powerful enough?), but often not with the very real and practical matter of matching the right sort of data to the right sort of analysis. Many otherwise bright people create and execute terrific experiments but never stop for a moment to think about how to analyze the data they collect. An all too common fate of student researchers is that their great research idea yields data that cannot be analyzed using conventional statistical tests. (During graduate school, a friend of mine served as a statistical consultant— I can distinctly remember him shaking his head in disbelief about how many people came to him with data from experiments that could not be interpreted, let alone salvaged for another use.) Instead of using a dependent variable that is based on an interval scale, for example, they have people respond to an ordinal scale, which cannot be evaluated using statistical tests that compare means, for example.

My message here is a simple and important one: Don't let this happen to you! Before you collect any data—no, before you conduct even a pilot test of your procedure—make certain that you are collecting data that can be analyzed using conventional, accepted techniques. A very good idea is to go over your research design with your instructor or some trusted peers who are statistically savvy. Describe the nature of your dependent variable and how you anticipate analyzing participant responses to it. Make absolutely sure you understand how to perform the data analysis and that you are using the right statistical test. Ask your instructor or trusted peer to verify your plan. To help you with this important task, I've designed an appropriate Active Learning Exercise (for a more detailed discussion of planning analyses, see Scherbaum, 2006).

ACTIVE LEARNING EXERCISE **11A**

Planning Data Analyses and Selecting the Proper Statistical Test(s)

Data analysis is an integral part of any research project, not an afterthought. Thus before you collect any data, develop a plan for your analysis. The top part of Table 11.2 identifies a few steps that should be taken before data collection. Step 1 involves determining the nature of the dependent variable, whether it is discontinuous (based on a nominal or ordinal scale) or continuous (based on an interval or ratio scale). The second step discerns whether a dependent variable was administered in an independent manner (i.e., once) or in a dependent approach (i.e., twice, as a repeated measure). Step 3 involves a review of Table 11.3, which presents a series of questions that can help you select the right statistical test for your data. Finally, step 4 involves getting your project underway and actually collecting participant responses.

Table 11.2 Planning and Performing Data Analyses

Predata collection

Step 1 What is the dependent variable's scale of measurement?
- If nominal or ordinal, then the data are discontinuous (i.e., gaps exist between numbers where no intermediate values can occur).
- If interval or ratio, then the data are continuous (i.e., meaningful, intermediate values can occur between numbers along some continuum).

Step 2 Is the dependent variable administered once or more than once?
- If only once, then an independent test is appropriate.
- If more than once, then a dependent test is appropriate.

Step 3 Select an appropriate test for analyzing the data (refer to Table 11.3).

Step 4 Pilot test the project and then begin actual data collection.

Postdata collection

Step 5 Summarize the data and calculate descriptive statistics
- a. Enter data into data record sheets (see chapter 10) and into a spreadsheet
- b. If data are continuous, calculate means and standard deviations.
- c. If data are discontinuous, calculate frequencies or percentages.

Step 6 Perform data analyses identified in Step 2

Step 7 Interpret and write up the result(s)
- a. Use Active Learning Exercise 11B.
- b. Create a table or graph as needed (see chapter 12).

Step 8 Place the results in context: Write a paper, create a poster, or give a presentation (see chapter 12)

Source: Adapted from McKenna (1995).

Continued

Selecting a statistical test

Table 11.3 is designed to help you select the most appropriate test statistic for analyzing your data. Take your time and work your way step by step through the table. To help you make sense of the tests noted in Table 11.3, I will briefly review each one in order of its appearance.

Chi-square (χ^2). A nonparametric test, the chi-square analyzes nominal data based on one variable (e.g., "Are women more likely to believe that altruism actu-

Table 11.3   Choosing an Appropriate Statistical Test

Step 1   Are participants randomly assigned to groups?
         If yes, go to step 3.
         If no, go to step 2.

Step 2   Are participants randomly selected from some population?
         If yes, go to step 3.
         If no, go to step 10.

Step 3   Is at least one independent variable manipulated in the study?
         If yes, go to step 4.
         If no, go to step 9.

Step 4   Are the data from the dependent variable continuous (i.e., interval or ratio scaled)?
         If yes, go to step 5.
         If no, then consider performing a nonparametric test (e.g., chi-square).

Step 5   How many independent variables are being manipulated?
         If one, go to step 6.
         If two or more, perform a factorial (e.g., two-way, three-way) analysis of variance.

Step 6   How many levels does the single independent variable have?
         If two, go to step 7.
         If three or more, go to step 8.

Step 7   What are the two levels of the independent variable like?
         If there are different participants in each group, perform an independent groups t-test.
         If the same participants completed the dependent variable twice, perform a correlated (dependent groups) t-test.

Step 8   Are participants exposed to all levels of the independent variable?
         If yes, perform a one-way repeated measures analysis of variance.
         If no, perform a one-way analysis of variance.

Step 9   Are two (or more) measures per participant collected in a nonexperimental design?
         If yes, consider correlating the measures together (see Active Learning Exercise 5B).
         If no, go to step 10.

Step 10 Inferential statistics are not appropriate for the data you will collect. Redesign the study or consider presenting the results in a graph, a table, or some other diagram.

Source: Adapted from McKenna (1995).

ally exists than are men?") or whether two variables are bound together in some relationship with each other (e.g., "Does a juror's sex affect whether a defendant is given a more lenient or severe sentence for a crime?"). As a test statistic, the chi-square compares observed frequencies collected in a study with those expected by chance. In a one-variable, two-group example, this test examines departures from a 50:50 split. An independent variable is identified as having some effect as the obtained frequencies differ from chance (e.g., 80:20).

Analysis of variance. The analysis of variance (ANOVA) is probably the most common parametric test used in social psychological research. The ANOVA is used to analyze either interval or ratio-scaled data in studies that have two or more groups. The test relies on the *F*-ratio, a number corresponding to the ratio of between-group variance (largely caused by an independent variable) divided by within-group variance (variability of response within each treatment group). To demonstrate that an independent variable caused predicted change in a dependent variable, the amount of between-group variability should be great while the within-group variability should be relatively small. There are basic types of ANOVAs that student researchers are likely to use: a one-way ANOVA, which determines whether any differences exist among three or more groups representing the number of levels in an independent variable; a one-way repeated measures (or within-subject) ANOVA, which considers how the same group of participants react at three or more points in time to different levels of an independent variable; and a two-way ANOVA, which indicates how two independent variables affect a single dependent variable simultaneously (recall the experiment conducted by Spencer, Steele, & Quinn, 1999, discussed in chapter 4).

t-test. The *t*-test, another parametric test, is used to determine whether the mean of one group is different than that observed in another group. This test statistic is perfect for analyzing the data from experiments with one independent variable with two levels (e.g., an experimental vs. a control condition). Like the ANOVA, the *t*-test assesses the relative amount of between-group variability (mostly attributable to the independent variable) compared to the variability found within the two groups. There are two types of *t*-tests typically used in social psychological research. The independent groups *t*-test compares whether the mean in one group of participants is different than that found in a different group of participants. Similar to the repeated measures ANOVA, the dependent groups *t*-test compares the reactions of the same group of participants to the same dependent variable at two different points in time.

Correlation. The Pearson product-moment correlation is used to analyze observations based on interval or ratio scales. When data are based on an ordinal scale, however, the Spearman rank order correlation coefficient can be used (see Siegel & Castellan, 1988).

   This brief review is no substitute for a statistics course. Keep in mind, too, that while I have highlighted the most common tests, my review is selective. There are

Continued

many different types of parametric and nonparametric statistical tests available for social psychological research. I suggest that you speak with your instructor if you are uncertain about what method of analysis will be most appropriate for your research project's data.

After the data are collected

Once the data are collected, what then? Turn back to the bottom part of Table 11.2, which lists the next four steps you should follow. These involve coding and summarizing the data (step 5; see chapter 10), performing the actual data analysis (step 6), interpreting and writing up the results (step 7), and sharing the findings (step 8; see chapter 12). Performing the actual data analyses (step 6) is beyond the scope of this book. However, interpreting and writing up the results of the study is a matter we need to discuss.

Interpreting and Reporting Results

Imagine that your data analyses are completed. Now you get to the real meat of the matter: Did your experiment "work," that is, did the independent variable create some measurable change in the dependent variable? Do your results support your theory or some already established theory in social psychology? What do they mean? How can you put them into words?

One of the key things any social psychologist must do with results is to determine whether any observed differences are significant ones. Where research methodology and data analysis are concerned, the word *significance* means something distinct from its everyday use. When researchers claim that a result is "significant," they do not mean that the finding is important, major, or otherwise noteworthy (although it might be in its own right). Rather, the statistical definition of significance refers to whether the finding is reliable, whether it is trustworthy, whether it allows a researcher to confidently reject the null hypothesis. A good synonym for significance in this context is *detected* (Wright, 1997). In other words, did the statistical test being used detect a reliable difference between an experimental and a control group? "Detect" is a fine word choice, too, because it does not specify whether the difference is large or small, merely that it exists (or not), the original intent of the term "significant." A significant—reliable and detected—difference also allows us to assume that what happened in one sample of people is likely to hold true in other samples of people (of course, this assumption remains to be tested by replicating the experiment).

For most social psychological research, statistical significance is related to significance levels, which are based on probability or *p*-values (also referred to as alpha levels). The *p*-values used in social psychology are most often .05, .01, and .001 (although other levels are possible and occasionally reported). In a journal article, when some test statistic is described as significant at the .05 level, the researcher is really saying that the odds that the detected difference is due to chance (random error) is less than 1 in 20. Put in more concrete terms, if the same study were repeated 100 times, the researcher would anticipate finding the same results by chance or luck (i.e., independently of the effects of the independent variable) five or fewer times. That level of chance "risk"—drawing an incorrect inference 5 out of 100 trials—is deemed acceptable by the scientific community.

The discipline of psychology uses .05 as the minimally acceptable level of significance for rejecting a null hypothesis and claiming a detected difference. When researchers want to use a more stringent criterion for reporting a significant difference, then they rely on *p*-values of .01 (a chance finding happens 1 in 100 trials) and .001 (a chance result occurs 1 in 1,000 trials). Results that fall between .10 and .06 are sometimes reported; researchers tend to describe such findings as reaching a "marginal" level of significance. In other words, the result cannot be trusted as a reliable one but it appears to be suggestive—perhaps a replication using an independent variable with greater impact or a more sensitive dependent variable would lead to a significant difference. Those results that are greater than .10 are described as "nonsignificant": No difference was detected.

So a given result from a given social psychology experiment is either detected or not—it is either declared significant or not significant. When you describe a result, be sure that you do not add unnecessary adjectives that confuse the interpretation of the result. A finding is "significant," but it is not "very significant," "highly significant," or even "incredibly significant."

Stereotype threat revisited

In chapter 4, you will recall that we learned about a study conducted by Spencer et al. (1999) concerning stereotype threat and women's math performance. A brief recap: These researchers posited that the apprehension created by stereotype threat ("compared to men, women do not do as well on math tests") undermines women's math performance. You will recall that stereotype threat was manipulated when half the participants (men as well as women) were told that men tended to perform better on a particular math test. A second group comprising both sexes were told that no gender differences were observed on the test. The participants' sex served as a second (albeit nonmanipulated) independent variable (recall the discussion of subject variables in chapters 4 and 7). Figure 4.1 on p. 99 illustrates the main results: When no stereotype threat was present, men and women performed about the same on the test (see the left side of Figure 4.1). When women were prompted to think about the stereotype, they performed much worse on the test than did the men (see the right side of Figure 4.1). Table 4.5 on p. 100 shows the mean test performance for the four groups (note that standard deviations are shown in parentheses below the means).

As I promised back in chapter 4, we will revisit the results found by Spencer and colleagues (1999) in order to consider how to report the results using words as well as statistical notation. Let's read what the researchers wrote regarding these particular results:

A two-way ANOVA (Sex x Test Characterization) of participants' scores on the test confirmed our predictions. When the participants were explicitly told that the test yielded gender differences, women greatly underperformed in relation to men. But when the test was purported not to yield gender differences, women performed at the same level as equally qualified men. This happened, of course, even though the test in these two conditions was the same. . . . There was a significant main effect for sex, F $(1, 50) = 5.66$, $p < .05$, but it was qualified by a significant sex-by-test characterization interaction, F $(1, 50) = 4.18$, $p < .05$. (Spencer et al., 1999, p. 12)

You will recall that the conceptual interpretation of main effects and interactions was discussed in chapter 4. If you do not remember much about these concepts, then I urge you to turn back to chapter 4 now before reading further.

What did the authors mean by a "main effect for sex"? Turn to Table 4.5 on p. 100. Look at the two means at the bottom of the columns labeled "Men" and "Women," 22.8 and 11.6, respectively. The significant main effect indicates that men, on average, had a significantly higher score on the test ($M = 22.8$) than did women ($M = 11.6$). The F-ratio of 5.66 for this main effect reached significance at the .05 level; that is, an average score of 22.8 is reliably different than an average score of 11.6. To link the descriptive finding with the statistical results, the authors added the statistical notation (i.e., the F-ratio, its degrees of freedom and calculated value, and the p-value) after the verbal interpretation.

What about the other main effect, the one for the test characterization? The authors chose not to report the F-ratio and p-value here, which means that no significant difference between the means for the stereotype threat manipulation occurred. Look at the row means shown on the far right side of Table 4.5. As you can see, the group (men and women together) that was told the test did not predict gender differences scored similarly ($M = 18.1$) to the group that was told the test show a gender difference ($M = 16.3$). The absence of a main effect shows that, in effect, the means are similar in value to one another—one is not reliably larger than (different from) the other.

The authors could have added a sentence like this one to the results:

There was no main effect for test characterization, however; the no gender difference group's test score was similar to the score observed in the gender difference group, F $(1, 50) = F < 1.0$, $p = ns$.

Note that I guessed that the obtained F-ratio for this main effect was less than 1.0 in value, as the actual statistic was not included in the article. When a test statistic does not reach an acceptable level of significance, then the convention is to report the p-value as equal to *ns*, an abbreviation for "not significant."

What about the interaction? Spencer et al. (1999, p. 12) described the interaction both clearly and concisely:

When the participants were explicitly told that the test yielded gender differences, women greatly underperformed in relation to men. But when the test was purported not to yield gender differences, women performed at the same level as equally qualified men.

Back in chapter 4, I told you that one way to determine if an interaction is present is by plotting the four cell means. Such a plot is shown in Figure 4.2 on p. 102. When the plotted lines are parallel to one another, no interaction exists. Lines that intersect, connect, or are otherwise not parallel to one another point to a possible interaction. The only accurate way to determine the presence of an interaction is by performing the appropriate statistical analysis, which Spencer and colleagues (1999) did. As shown by Figure 4.2, women had the lowest test scores when they reacted to the stereotype threat, that is, when they expected that men would score better on this particular test. This possibility is confirmed by Figure 4.2 and by the significant F-ratio linked with the significant (at the .05 level) sex-by-test interaction.

To confirm that the mean of 5.8 (see the mean for women who anticipated a gender difference in Table 4.5) was reliably lower than the other three means, Spencer et al. (1999) performed what is called a posthoc comparison of all means with one another. Posthoc tests are statistical tests applied to data to further clarify results after the main analysis is done. Here is what the authors wrote to shed further light on the interaction (p. 12):

> Student–Neuman–Keuls posthoc comparisons of all possible pairs of means revealed that the mean for women in the gender-differences condition was significantly lower than each of the other means and that no other means differed from each other ($p < .05$).

This additional analysis conclusively shows that stereotype threat affected only one group of women such that their average scores on the math test were reliably lower than those found in the other three groups. In concrete terms, the means of 18.9, 17.3, and 26.7 were no different than one another statistically, but all three of them were reliably higher in value than the mean of 5.8 (see Table 4.5).

There is no single "right" way to report the results of an experiment or other social psychological study. There is a guiding principle, however: Report the findings as briefly and simply as possible. This principle means you need to link a verbal, theoretical explanation of a given result with the statistical notation that allows you to draw the inferential conclusion. When doing so, you are writing for two audiences: those who are familiar with methodological and statistical issues and those who are not. Readers who know little or nothing about data analysis, for example, should be able to understand what you found *without* necessarily knowing anything about statistical notation. Reporting findings in words coupled with statistical notation allows statistically savvy readers to verify that your empirical approach, analysis, and conclusions are both accurate and appropriate.

ACTIVE LEARNING EXERCISE   11B

Putting Results into Words

How can you learn to report results using words and statistical notation? Let me offer a one word answer: practice. How can you get practice? A good approach to learning this skill is by reading and emulating (but not plagiarizing) the work of published social psychologists. Working your way through the data analysis of your own project will also help a great deal.

   The steps outlined in Table 11.4 are designed to help you put statistical results into words for inclusion in an APA-style Results section (see chapter 12). Step 1 requires you to select the statistical test you identified in Table 11.3 and subsequently performed on a dependent variable. (You should have the analysis and its results at hand before you proceed—a printout of a statistical analysis completed by a software package is ideal). The second step entails entering information regarding the statistical test's symbol, the test's degrees of freedom, the critical value for rejecting the null hypothesis, the calculated value of the test statistic, the status of the null hypothesis, and the obtained *p*-value (see Table 11.4). Unless you performed the analysis by hand, most or all of this information should be available on whatever statistical printout you have (otherwise, consult a basic statistics text).

Table 11.4   Interpreting and Writing About Statistical Results

Step 1   Select the statistical test that best matches your analysis plan (check one):

Test	What the test does	Statistical symbol
____ chi-square	assesses categorical difference(s)	χ^2
____ factorial ANOVA	assesses mean differences(s)	F
____ independent groups *t*-test	assesses mean difference	*t*
____ correlated (dependent) groups *t*-test	assesses mean difference	*t*
____ repeated measures ANOVA	assesses mean difference(s)	*F*
____ correlation coefficient	assesses association between variables	*r*

Step 2   Organize statistical notation (record information):
a.   Test symbol (from Step 1 above)   _____
b.   Degree(s) of freedom   _____
c.   Critical value of test statistic (from statistical table or software)   _____
d.   Calculated value of test statistic (from hand or software calculation)   _____
e.   Status of null hypothesis (circle one)   Accept or reject
f.   Obtained significance level (e.g., *p* < .05 or .01) (from statistical table or software)   _____

Step 3   Describe the result in words, incorporating statistical information and notation as needed.

Source: Adapted from Dunn (1999, Table 8.5, p. 280).

The third and final step requires you to revisit your hypothesis in light of the findings from your analysis. A good way to begin is to rephrase the hypothesis as a declarative statement rather than a question. Another approach is to think about what the participants actually did behaviorally during your study, how they responded to the dependent variable. If your results did not match the hypothesis—the participants acted differently than expected—be candid about it (e.g., the means in the experimental and control groups were the same). On occasion, a researcher will discover a significant difference that runs counter to the hypothesis (e.g., people in the control group behave the way those in the experimental group were supposed to, and vice versa), which is one very important reason you need to check your analyses with care. Nonetheless, whatever result you obtain, you must describe it in sufficient detail—not simply that the "hypothesis was not supported." Possible reasons for any results, including unexpected ones, are included in the Discussion section (see chapter 12).

Consider connecting your description of the findings with supporting tables or figures. As discussed in chapter 12, graphic or tabular displays can highlight important relations within data in more direct ways than written text. Just be sure that your writing not only directs the reader to the table or graph, but that it also explains why the data display is important and what it illustrates. Note that the text and table should not provide exactly the same information as each other, just as you should not lead the reader through each and every detail shown in the table or figure. Focus on the highlights or the main results, reserving any detailed review of the findings for the Discussion.

I do have one last suggestion for writing and thinking about results: use the MAGIC criteria. The late Robert Abelson (1995), a noted social psychologist, used the acronym MAGIC—which stands for magnitude, articulation, generality, interestingness, and credibility—as a guide for writing about whether and how well some results support the hypothesis being tested. Table 11.5 defines the scope of each of the criteria. I suggest you consult Table 11.5 when you put your results into words for a paper, a poster, or for an oral presentation.

Table 11.5 The MAGIC Criteria for Evaluating and Writing about Results

---

Magnitude: Are the results strong or weak? To what degree do the results support the hypothesis?

Articulation: How can the findings be summarized using the most basic terms possible? Parsimony is desirable: As long as no essential details are lost, simpler explanations are favored over abstract or complex accounts.

Generality: Can the results be used to explain similar behavior displayed by different people in different places at other times? Are the findings generalizable? Why or why not?

Interestingness: Who will want to know about, learn from, or rely on the results? Can they be used to build theory? Can they be applied to understand behavior in other contexts? Abelson (1995) argued that when findings are really and truly interesting they change the way individuals construe a topic.

Credibility: Do the findings seem to be valid? Are the results believable? Will readers be persuaded by the findings? What will other researchers, including critics, say about the results?

Source: Adapted from Abelson (1995).

Learning from Success, Learning from Failure

Conducting experiments that provide insight into social behavior is part science but it is also part art. Even the best designed experiments do not "work"—provide anticipated results—the first time around. Sometimes not the second time, either. You need to gain experience and a sense of what will and won't work. The only way to do so is to try your hand at research a few times. If at first you do not succeed, then by all means try, try again by redesigning the same study or by switching gears a bit to explore some other topic.

When an experiment fails to confirm a hypothesis on the first try, budding researchers often conclude that their question must be wrong. As you certainly appreciate by now, doing social psychological research well is a demanding enterprise. There are many details that must be attended to at every stage of a project. Little wonder, then, that an experiment might not come out as anticipated on the first trial. Be patient. No experiment or research design is ever perfect, and experience is indeed a great teacher. There will always be some aspect of any project that could be improved.

How can you increase your chances of confirming your hypothesis? Pilot test the experimental procedure to be sure that the independent variable is creating the expected response in terms of the dependent variable. Use manipulation checks whenever possible. Carefully debrief the participants to learn from their impressions and experience of the study. Be flexible. As you conduct an experiment, you may discover that changes to the procedure or possibly to your theory or hypothesis are necessary. As long as you acknowledge such changes in any description of your research, you are fulfilling your obligation to be a conscientious, committed social psychologist.

Exercises

1   Write a paragraph explaining why a dependent variable(s) from your research project needs to be analyzed by a particular statistical test.

2   Draft a sentence or two describing the main finding from your research project, including the supporting statistical notation. Try again by describing the same result using different words. Write a third, different summary of the same finding. Choose the best summary for your project paper.

3   Apply Abelson's (1995) MAGIC criteria to the findings of an empirical journal article from the social psychological literature. How do the results fare when the five criteria are applied? How could the criteria be used to improve the article's Results section?

4   Apply the MAGIC criteria to the result summary drafted in response to question 2 above.

Chapter 12

Presenting Social Psychological Research

Congratulations: You made it. If you are reading this chapter, then you probably finished (or will shortly finish) conducting your first research foray into social psychology. Only one thing remains—sharing what you discovered about human social behavior with other people. Social psychologists tend to share their research in two ways: either in print by writing a journal article, chapter, or occasionally a book, or by giving a professional presentation. Students like you are likely to write a paper or lab report summarizing their research efforts, to give a brief talk to peers during class or at a student conference, or to create a poster that concisely and graphically conveys research findings. I will give you guidance on doing all three of these activities. Before doing so, however, let's consider a social psychological study illustrating the persuasive power of some written communications.

Once upon a time nuclear submarines were imaginary, like Captain Nemo's *Nautilus* in Jules Verne's classic tale, *20,000 Leagues Under the Sea*. Yet the mid-twentieth century's atomic era made the fanciful seem possible, even probable. In the early 1950s, some research participants were invited to speculate on the likelihood that nuclear-powered submarines would come into being. At that time, such subs were only dreams on the drawing board and not the familiar behemoths now roaming our oceans. A few days later, the same people read a paper expressing the opinion that nuclear subs were soon to be fact and no longer fiction. Half of the participants believed the paper was written by the physicist Robert Oppenheimer, a highly credible source (you may know him as the "father of the atomic bomb"), while the remainder learned that the work was by a less credible author, a writer for *Pravda*, the propaganda newspaper of the now defunct Soviet Union. Although the content of the papers was identical, you will not be surprised to learn that participants saw Oppenheimer as more credible than the Soviet journalist; moreover, readers of the work attributed to the physicist showed greater attitude change (i.e., the advent of nuclear subs was now viewed with greater certainty) than those in the other group. Perceived credibility can drive a change in beliefs (Benoit & Strathman, 2004; Petty, Cacioppo, & Goldman, 1981).

This classic persuasion study by Hovland and Weiss (1951) is interesting but not especially striking until one additional variable is considered: time. Four weeks later, both groups of participants expressed their opinions a second time. Unexpectedly, the readers of the paper attributed to the *Pravda* writer shifted their opinions in a favorable direction—they now believed nuclear subs were more likely to be developed in the near future. What happened? Did the author's trustworthiness actually improve? Probably not. Under such circumstances, any positive opinion shift after a lag in time is known as a *sleeper effect*. Sleeper effects occur whenever initially discounted messages are later seen as credible. We change our minds because we forget the nature of our original reservations. Meticulous attitude change research reveals that as time passes, readers or listeners sometimes detach the source of a message from the actual message. Although the *Pravda* group initially discounted what they read based on the source's credibility, a few weeks later, they recalled only the paper's content but not its author.

The sleeper effect's insidious quality is that we may end up agreeing with something because we no longer link an original, questionable source to a message. If your memory is like mine, you may see the sleeper effect as especially troubling—if I'm not careful, I may end up espousing views of people I don't respect or trust. There is some good news here, however. Happenstance can inoculate us against the sleeper effect. Here's how: When prompts or reminders that a source is not credible come *before* the persuasive communication, the sleeper effect is eliminated (Pratkanis, Greenwald, Leippe, & Baumgardner, 1988; see also Pratkanis, 1992). Once people know not to trust a source, they begin creating counterarguments in advance of the message, thereby diminishing its effects. In everyday life, for example, the parents of teenagers may experience this process first hand, as their children often actively question the most reasonable of requests with counterarguments to spare.

As a social researcher, you will want to share your work with others, so it is important to learn what qualities make a presentation appealing as well as persuasive. How can you adapt insights from social psychology to create a persuasive presentation of your research?

Persuasive Communication

Social psychologists have learned a great deal about persuasion since the 1940s and 1950s, when Carl Hovland and his colleagues studied attitude change at Yale University. Known as the "Yale School approach," persuasion research began with the examination of mass communication efforts for the United States Army during World War II. Hovland and colleagues (Hovland, Janis, & Kelley, 1953) argued that persuasive messages have three facets: the *who*, or the source, of a message; the *what*, or the message's context; and the *whom*, or the intended recipient of the message. You should keep these facets in mind as you write about or orally present your research to others. Let's consider each facet in turn.

Who. Why are some speakers more convincing than others? The study of so-called *source characteristics*—the perceived qualities of the individual who delivers a persua-

sive communication—includes the individual's attractiveness and credibility or expertise. Attractive individuals, those who are good-looking or who possess winning
personalities (e.g., actors and models) are more persuasive than less attractive folks
(Eagly & Chaiken, 1975). Similarly, possessing obvious expertise (e.g., a medical
degree) about a topic (e.g., health issues) lends a speaker greater credibility than a
nonexpert speaking on the same issue (Hovland & Weiss, 1951).

Your knowledge of your social psychological research topic lends you a certain
expertise and credibility. You may not have the charisma of an actor or model, but
you can certainly control your appearance. Generally speaking, neatness counts. When
speaking before a group, you are likely to be taken more seriously if you dress appropriately for the occasion than if you sport a t-shirt, shorts, and sandals.

What. Some messages are more persuasive than others, and social psychologists have
spent considerable effort delineating what *message characteristics* influence audience
opinions. If you have ever witnessed a debate, perhaps you wondered whether the
order in which speeches are presented matters—is it better to go first or last? In fact,
order is influential: If speakers appear one right after the other, being the first to
present can lead to a *primacy effect*, where listeners are more likely to believe what they
hear first. If there is a delay between speakers and listeners are supposed to make up
their minds after hearing the second speech, then there is an advantage in going last.
Final speakers hope for a *recency effect*, which occurs when a second message is perceived as more persuasive after a breather following a first talk (Haugtvedt & Wegener,
1994).

When presenting an argument, should speakers outline only those arguments
favoring their position (a "one-sided" communication) or should they explore both
the pro and the con arguments (a "two-sided" communication)? Listeners appreciate
the opportunity to hear both positions, so two-sided talks are often persuasive as long
as the speaker is careful to refute the opposing arguments (Allen, 1991). One more
thing: People are especially likely to be convinced by a message when it does not seem
to have been crafted to persuade them (Petty & Cacioppo, 1986). Perhaps simply
sharing some ideas about the nature of social behavior, its flourishes or foibles, can
attract more attention from an audience than strong appeals regarding the "pioneering" quality of the work. Thus presenting your work with enthusiasm tempered by
appropriate modesty may attract the attention and subsequent allegiance of your audience, whether it's composed of your peers or your professor.

Whom. In the end, the audience, the recipients of a message, matters. Two characteristics that make audiences open to persuasion are quick to summarize: age and intelligence. Younger people—those who are between 18 and 25 or so years of age—are
especially likely to change their minds following a persuasive message. People even a
little older than this age range, however, tend to hold stable beliefs that are resistant
to such entreaties (Krosnick & Alwin, 1989). Smarter people are less likely to be influenced by persuasive messages than those who score lower on intelligence measures

(Rhodes & Wood, 1992). No doubt the former can muster counterarguments with greater ease than the latter. Of course, one other obvious audience characteristic is motivation: Is there some reason they should care about the research topic? Chances are good that a group of your classmates will be more interested in your work than will a group of strangers. Nonetheless, you should work hard to create presentations that speak to both types of audiences.

Now that you know the importance of "who says what to whom," we can turn to matters of form regarding persuasive communications. Let's begin by learning how to write up social psychological research using the writing style promoted by the American Psychological Association.

Writing Like a Social Psychologist: A Matter of (APA) Style

Learning a writing style

American Psychological Association Style, otherwise known as "APA style," is the preferred form of communication in academic psychology. Professional psychologists are used to reading research framed, organized, and compartmentalized by this particular presentation format. Books—including this one—are designed according to the rules of APA style because the assumption is that most readers (i.e., professionals) already know it; others, especially students, need to become familiar with it. The goal of APA-style writing is to convey scientific findings in psychology in a standardized way, one that benefits both expert and novice readers.

Elsewhere (see Dunn, 2008, p. 81–82), I have argued that the benefits of this standardization include:

- *Brevity*: Research findings are explained in succinct and focused ways.
- *Clarity*: A writing style shared by the psychological community fosters the clear presentation of hypotheses, research methods, and results and their implications.
- *Consistency*: An expected and unvarying writing style allows readers, professionals as well as students, to know where particular information can be found in any publication. As a result, writers know how to write up research in ways that benefit readers.

Most psychological journals, as well as many publications in related disciplines (e.g., sociology), rely on APA style. Most students who enroll in psychology courses, especially courses in research methods, learn to write lab reports and other papers using APA style.

What is the best way to learn to write using APA style? The best way to do so is via trial and error modeling: Locate a good model article (an annotated example can be found in Appendix C), draft a paper based upon it, share your draft with someone who knows APA style, use the feedback to revise the paper accordingly, compare the revision to the model, and then seek more feedback. I will advocate that you follow this learning-by-doing approach in the remainder of this chapter.

There is a caveat, of course; I cannot present everything there is to know about the whys and wherefores of writing in APA style in a single chapter. Fortunately, there are other sources offering guidance on successful writing in psychology. Chief among them is the *Publication Manual of the American Psychological Association* (APA, 2001). This book is the official guide to writing about research using APA style. Consider investing in a copy. If you obtain one, it will serve you well as an unabridged reference work to reading and writing in psychology. In the remainder of this section, I will give you an abridged account of APA style, one that will enable you to write up the results from your research efforts in social psychology.

Sections found in APA-Style Papers

Whether you are reading an empirical journal article or a student's lab report, all APA-style writings contain a predictable set of sections that create an outline for the paper. Table 12.1 lists the main sections and, where appropriate, the pages where they are found in a typical manuscript describing the results of an experiment. Take a few moments to look at the contents of Table 12.1. Do the section names seem familiar to you? Can you recall reading articles that were "framed" using these sections (recall your literature search in chapter 2 or Appendix B's advice on how to read a journal article)?

Table 12.1   An Outline of the Sections (with Selected Locations) Found in APA-Style Empirical Papers

Title page: Contains a title, author name(s) and affiliation(s) (page 1).

Abstract page: A brief summary of the paper's contents (page 2).

Introduction: Reviews the relevant literature and describes the hypothesis(es) being investigated (page 3).

Method: Identifies the research participants and provides a step-by-step account of what took place and when during the research procedure.

Results: Describes the analyses used and findings obtained.

Discussion: Reviews and interprets the main findings, highlighting their relevance for future research.

References: An alphabetical list of all sources found in the manuscript.

Appendix: Supporting materials (e.g., stimulus materials) not found elsewhere in the paper; this section is often found in student papers but less frequently in professional publications.

Author note: A brief paragraph sharing contact information regarding the author(s) and acknowledging individuals who aided in the research.

Tables and Figures—Numerical summaries and graphical representations of data

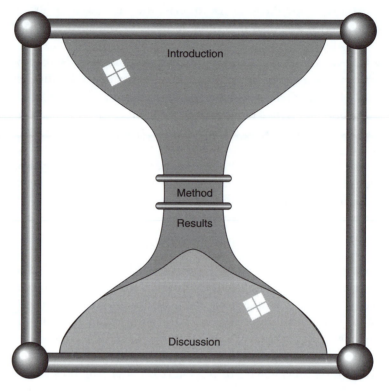

Figure 12.1.   Bem's hourglass model of the APA-style empirical paper. Source: Dunn (1999, Figure 3.1, page 80)

The social-personality psychologist, Daryl J. Bem of Cornell University, claims that the four main sections of any APA-style paper—the introduction, Methods, Results, and Discussion—rhetorically model the shape of an hourglass (see Figure 12.1; Bem, 1987, 1995, 2000). After reading research articles in social psychology, you will probably agree with this characterization: Invariably, an article's narrative opens broadly (the introduction), only to narrow in the Method section where the specific details of the research design and procedure are disclosed. The narrative again begins to broaden in the Results section (see Figure 12.1), widening once more as the findings' implications are put in proper context within the Discussion.

The hourglass model is an essential organizing principle for prose in psychology. Keep the shape in mind as you write a summary of your research efforts. Always begin a paper in a broad and inviting way, one that will convince readers that your research topic, and the background work supporting it, is—and should be—of interest to them. As you describe the underlying logic leading up to your hypothesis and proposed research method, narrow your focus so that you explain in appropriate detail why the question being investigated—and the operationalization you designed to test it (see chapters 4, 7, and 8)—make sense. Your writing will be the most detailed (and perhaps least creative) when you disclose the research procedure in the Method section. You will again broaden your scope in the Results section, however, as you explain how you analyzed the dependent measure and why, as well as what was found; and in the Discussion, when you consider how it all points to certain broader conclusions about social life.

Table 12.2 contains a detailed outline of the annotated, APA-style student paper appearing in Appendix C. As you can see, only the four core sections are represented in Table 12.2, yet essential details, including facts, findings, key references, and the like are listed therein. The student author used this outline to plan and then to write the paper appearing in Appendix C. As you plan to draft and then to write up the results of your research, I encourage you not to skip creating an outline, which is the most helpful roadmap for the writing process. Mastering APA style and creating a research summary conforming to it will be much easier if you plan before you write.

Now that you are familiar with the superstructure underlying any APA-style paper, we turn to how to craft each of the individual sections listed in Table 12.1. All of the rules and requirements I describe are discussed in depth in the *Publication Manual* (APA, 2001).

Title

The title of a paper is a reader's first contact with a piece of research, so it should be designed to inform and to attract attention. The title of a social psychological paper should never be dry or dull—after all, people's actions and thoughts are inherently fascinating; on the other hand, it should never be overly cute or clever, either. A good title conveys information about some social psychological phenomenon in an inviting but descriptive way. In doing so, a title should highlight key words implicating particular topics, theories, independent and dependent variables, the nature of some behavior or event, or even characterize research participants. As we learned in chapter 2, key words promote effective searches of databases, including PsycINFO. Thus a paper's title should be conceived in a way that will help readers navigate the social psychological literature. Here are a few example titles gleaned from the January 2006 issue of the *Journal of Personality and Social Psychology*:

Not All Stereotyping Is Created Equal: Differential Consequences of Thoughtful Versus Nonthoughtful Stereotyping (Wegener, Clark, & Petty, 2006)

When Fiends Become Friends: The Need to Belong and Perceptions of Personal and Group Discrimination (Carvallo & Pelham, 2006)

What Is the Relation Between Cultural Orientation and Socially Desirable Responding? (Lalwani, Shavitt, & Johnson, 2006)

Positive Affect and the Experience of Meaning in Life (King, Hicks, Krull, & Del Gaiso, 2006)

Table 12.2   A Detailed Outline of an APA-Style Empirical Paper

Introduction
  1   Overview of research
      Impartial juries should not be biased by defendant traits
  2   Issue being examined
      Physical attractiveness influences perceiver's judgments
  3   Review of the literature
      Example studies: Dion, Bersheid, & Walster (1972); Sigall & Ostrove (1975)
  4   Specific hypothesis
      ALE theory: Attractive individuals will be sentenced for crimes less severely than unattractive people except when the crime is violent.

Method
  1   Participants (number, sex, source)
      45 (15 men, 30 women); ages 18 to 26 (*M* = 20.4); convenience sample
  2   Materials and measures
      Defendant photographs (attractive vs. unattractive), crime scenarios (violent vs. nonviolent), questionnaires (attractiveness, recommended sentence time for crime)
  3   Step-by-step procedure
      Run in groups; viewed photo and scenario, completed two questionnaires
  4   Informed consent and debriefing
      Consent obtained at start of experiment; debriefing conducted at conclusion

Results
  1   Conceptual recap of hypothesis
      Did a violent crime reduce the ALE bias in the case of an attractive defendant?
  2   Review of main results, highlighting statistical analyses
      No significant main effects (attractiveness, crime) or an interaction were obtained (*p* > .05); manipulation checks were supported

Discussion
  1   Meaning of the results and how well they support the hypothesis
      Anticipated results were not confirmed
  2   Shortcomings, if any, to this study
      Stimulus materials and design should be reconsidered
  3   Future directions
      Lack of results in this study has no effect on established knowledge

Note: This outline is based on the annotated APA-style student paper appearing in Appendix C. The information appearing in **boldface** identifies relevant content from this paper.

If you glance through any social psychology journal in the library or by searching through the PsycINFO database, you will find other worthy examples of titles.

On occasion, a title can appear to be highly technical or aimed at a very narrow audience within social psychology. There is nothing inherently wrong with these sorts of titles; however, if you are a student, I encourage you not to emulate them. Instead, write titles that appeal to a broader rather than a more specialized audience (you can focus on the latter if and when you attend graduate school).

APA style requires that article titles be relatively brief, preferably no more than 10 to 12 words in length (you need not necessarily count articles and prepositions, such as "a," "the," "of"); thus, a title's necessarily spare nature should spark an author's creativity. How can you convey the most meaning about social behavior using relatively few words? When writing a title, then, avoid relying on extra words or redundant phrases, such as "An Experimental Investigation of," "A Study Concerning," or the all-too-common "The Effects of." Unless absolutely necessary, a title should not contain abbreviations (e.g., instead of IAT, use "Implicit Association Test").

Formatting the title page. When drafting a paper (by the way, all APA style papers are typed and double-spaced throughout), the title is centered in the upper half of the first page of the manuscript. Immediately below the title lies the author's name, and beneath that is his or her institutional affiliation. Here is an example:

Political Preferences Predict Judgments about Candidates
Bennett J. Todd
Moravian College

Consult the annotated manuscript in Appendix C for a complete example of a title page.

Abstract

Where a good title will capture attention, a well-written Abstract helps individuals decide whether to bother reading the article or paper. To borrow from the language of real estate, a good Abstract provides "curb appeal"—will you stop to look or just keep on driving?

What goes into writing an Abstract? An Abstract is a concise summary of an article's content, and it generally notes what was done to whom, when and why, as well as what was found and how it relates to what is already known about some issue in social psychology. Writing an informative, clear Abstract is a minor art form; too many of them are mechanical or overly detailed, doing little to provoke further curiosity on the part of readers. The main goals of any Abstract are to inform readers who already know about the research topic and to attract those who could become motivated to learn more about it.

An APA-style Abstract describing a social psychology experiment or set of studies is a pithy, unindented paragraph that is between 100 and 120 words long. Abstracts written for theory or review papers are shorter, averaging between 75 to 100 words in length. Despite its brevity, to be useful, an Abstract must be easy to understand. Any reader, not only a social or personality psychologist, should be able to understand a paper's purpose. Here is an example of a well-written Abstract from an article by

Wegener, Clark, and Petty (2006) that appeared in the *Journal of Personality and Social Psychology*:

> Much research emphasizes heuristic use of stereotypes, though stereotypes have long been considered as capable of influencing more thoughtful processing of social informa-tion. Direct comparisons between thoughtful and nonthoughtful stereotyping are lacking in the literature. Recent research in attitude change emphasizes the different conse-quences of judgments arising from relatively thoughtful versus nonthoughtful processes. Therefore, increased thought could not only fail to decrease stereotyping but might also create stereotypic perceptions that are more likely to have lasting impact. The current studies demonstrate thoughtful and nonthoughtful stereotyping within the same setting. More thoughtful stereotyping is more resistant to future attempts at change and to warn-ings of possible bias. Implications are discussed for the typical research questions asked after observing stereotypic judgments.

Formatting an Abstract. An Abstract always appears on page 2 of any APA style manuscript. The word "Abstract" is centered at the top of the page and the summary itself is double-spaced beneath it. A sample Abstract and its format in a manuscript can be found in Appendix C.

Introduction

An APA-style introduction provides an author with the opportunity to explain why some social phenomenon is worthy of empirical scrutiny. The opening paragraphs of an introduction set the tone for the rest of the work. Whether expert or novice, why should a reader care about the topic? Does the topic encourage us to look at people's lives or experiences (including our own) in new or different ways? Besides charting a course for the rest of the paper, a manuscript's introduction contains a thorough review of the literature characterizing what is already known about the topic being examined. This literature review proceeds in a logical progression from the broad issue of interest to the rationale for the current work (remember Bem's hourglass; see Figure 12.1). Specific issues discussed in an APA-style introduction include:

- Why is this social psychological investigation being done?
- What specific question—the hypothesis—is being tested? How was it operation-alized? Why?
- What independent variables are being manipulated? What dependent variables are being measured?
- How will the results expand what we already know about the topic?
- How does the current study fill in existing gaps or address unanswered questions in the existing literature?

For an introduction to be effective, the writing should involve the reader in the first few sentences. Here is a short but compelling opening paragraph from an article on social contagion—how social interaction can move our thoughts and feelings towards consensus with others—and its influence on the perception of time:

> People influence each other, and that influence often leads to the emergence of consensus (Crandall, 1988; Hardin & Higgins, 1996; Latané, 1996; Schaller & Conway, 2001). This simple fact can have consequences for virtually every aspect of human existence. One of those aspects is both central and universal to the human experience—the passage of time. (Conway, 2004, p. 113)

The literature review in an introduction should be comprehensive yet still selective—what studies are *most* relevant to the current investigation? The goal is not to be exhaustive. Some topics (e.g., prejudice and stereotyping, attitudes, gender, aggression) have been so thoroughly examined that writers often choose to review only relatively recent publications (say, those appearing in the last few years). More commonly, of course, an author informs readers early on in the introduction about the specific issue or subtopic being explored in the article. When reviewing issues concerning prior research, only the most pertinent details (e.g., main hypothesis, research design or method, results, conclusions, or unusual techniques) should be presented. Minor details, such as where the research was conducted, how many people took part, and the like, should not be noted (motivated readers can always look up the original citation in the References section and eventually the library to obtain such details). Remember, you are building a case for your research effort, not one for research that already appeared in the literature.

As you discuss prior research, you will feel the need to critique it, to identify and describe the drawbacks you see in earlier work. Your critique should be constructive and scholarly, not negative and picky. No experiment is ever perfect, and no study, however well-conceived, can sufficiently answer all questions of interest. Science is incremental. We honor earlier efforts by using their substantive findings to help us think through our own work. You must raise questions about earlier efforts and you are free to cast doubt on some findings (just be sure that you have searched to be sure that other studies do not demonstrate the same result you are casting doubt on in your review).

As the review winds down and the introduction draws to a close, the hypothesis and the expected results must be clearly stated. When doing so, be sure to provide a brief description—an outline, really—of the methodology used to test the hypothesis. This description need not be long or overly detailed. A few sentences or possibly a paragraph are fine.

Why bother with this when the reader will soon become acquainted with the research procedure in the Results section? For two good reasons, actually. First, one of the nonobvious requirements of APA style is for each section of a manuscript to "stand alone." By that I mean that it should be possible to read any section of the paper—the Method or Discussion, for instance—and still be able to get a complete sense of the whole work, if not all the details and the particulars. The second, related reason is that when readers scour the literature and locate an article, they do not necessarily read it from start to finish. Some readers want to know what statistical test was used to test a hypothesis, so they will focus their time on the Results section. Others will be interested in the "big picture" posed by the research, so they will concentrate on the Discussion, and so on. Thus the writer of an APA-style paper can never assume that his or her work will be consumed from start to finish—readers skip around, so each section must fulfill its intended purpose while still possessing an encapsulated summary of the larger article (see Appendix B).

Here is the closing paragraph from the introduction of Conway's social contagion and time perception experiment—note how clearly the author states the hypotheses, thereby alerting the reader about what follows in the remainder of the journal article:

> In the following experiment, some people were instructed to do a "word puzzles" task while interacting in groups (Interactive Condition). Other people did the same task without interacting, but also in groups (Control Condition). The task was unexpectedly interrupted after awhile, and then the measures of time perception (including both an "objective" time estimate and a measure of "subjective" speed of time's passage) and mood were completed. There were three basic predictions: (1) participants in the Interactive Condition should demonstrate more within-group consensus in time perception than participants in the Control Condition; (2) participants in the Interactive Condition should demonstrate more within-group consensus in mood than participants in the Control Condition; and (3) the effect of the interaction manipulation on time perception consensus should be mediated by the participants' mood consensus. (Conway, 2004, pp. 114–115)

Formatting an introduction. The introduction is never labeled as such. Instead, the paper's title is repeated at the top of page 3. The opening and indented paragraph of the introduction begins two spaces below the title. Much of the introduction appears in the past tense because the research being reviewed (including your own project) has been conducted. A sample introduction can be found in Appendix C.

Method

The Method section outlines the architecture for any research project. Ideally, any reader should be able to take "the plans" from a Method section and use them to replicate the study from start to finish. A Method section contains many details—it is like a script for a play, including the staging directions for the actors (participants) and the director (the experimenter—in other words, you; Dunn, 2008). Pulling together the disparate elements of an experiment into a coherent narrative is not difficult if you follow one organizing principle: a time line. Who did what to whom, when, in what order, and with what, if any, consequence? Almost every study begins with some form of greeting and then instructions to the participant, and all research efforts conclude with a debriefing (see chapter 10). A writer-experimenter's responsibility to readers is to fill in all the details between these two endpoints. In fact, the best way to draft a Method section is by writing down exactly what you, as an experimenter, did from the moment participants arrived until they left following the debriefing.

Besides the implicit time line, Method sections explain how independent variables were manipulated and how dependent variables were measured. Any surveys, questionnaires, rating scales, and the like are presented (almost always in verbatim form) or where they can be found is cited (e.g., in another article or book). If any materials are too long to be reproduced in the Method, simply select some representative examples that can give readers a sense of the whole and refer them to a source where the rest can be viewed.

A Method section is organized by a collection of subheadings appearing in a relatively fixed order. There are three main subsections found in papers summarizing social psychological research—*Participants, Materials* (sometimes labeled *Stimuli*), and the *Procedure*. Additional subsections with unique labels are created as necessary (again, look to the published literature in social psychology for examples).

Participants. This subsection describes the people who took part in the research (Were they men or women, children or adults? How many? What system was used to recruit them? Were they somehow compensated for participating?). Depending on the nature of the experiment, some Participants subsections will be much more detailed than others. Here is a typical subsection which appeared in the Conway time perception study:

> *Participants*
>   Thirty-eight undergraduate students (15 female, 14 male, and nine unreported) at the University of Montana participated for research credit. Participants signed up to participate in a "Word Puzzles" study session. Each session contained only one group. Groups were comprised of four to six members (the average group size was 4.75). Groups were randomly assigned to one of the two experimental conditions. Four groups participated in each condition. Participant gender (and the gender composition of groups) were included as variables in all key analyses, but yielded no effects, so they will not be discussed further. (Conway, 2004, p. 115)

Materials. A Materials subsection provides readers with clear descriptions of what specific equipment, supplies, or other resources were used in the experiment. Sometimes researchers create novel materials for an experiment, whereas on other occasions they borrow or adapt existing materials (e.g., personality measures, questionnaires, software, pictures or other images used as stimuli). When writing this section, your goal should be to give readers sufficient information so that they could either track down the materials or recreate them themselves. What follows is a relatively detailed subsection from a study on social inference:

Materials

Participants gave self-responses and prevalence estimates for items in a computer-based survey. The survey began with initial similarity measures for both Columbia (in-group) and UC Berkeley (out-group) student targets (two items for each target: "I think I'm very similar to most Berkeley [Columbia] students," "The people I identify with are a lot different from most Berkeley [Columbia] students" [reversed]; participants indicated their agreement with these items on a 6-point scale ranging from 1 [*very strongly disagree*] to 6 [*very strongly agree*]).

Participants then gave three responses for 16 items: self-response (yes–no), Columbia estimate (percentage of Columbia students that would say "yes"), and UC Berkeley estimate (percentage of UC Berkeley students that would say "yes"). Eight of the items were consistent with a widely held stereotype of UC Berkeley students (e.g., "Do you engage in political protests at least once a year?" and "Do you have at least one body piercing somewhere other than your ears?"). An additional 8 items were inconsistent with or antithetical to the stereotype (e.g., "Do you think capital punishment is ever an acceptable policy?" and "Do you regularly eat meat?"). Pilot testing confirmed that the 8 "consistent" items were more consistent with the UC Berkeley stereotype than the Columbia one and that the 8 "inconsistent" items were more inconsistent with the UC Berkeley stereotype than the Columbia one. Five participants did not complete the entire estimation task and their partial responses were omitted. (Ames, 2004, Study 1, p. 576)

Procedure. Within the larger Method section, the Procedure subsection supplies a step-by-step chronology of what the participants and the experimenters did behaviorally. Most procedures will present the research design and any particular tasks participants performed; an account of how the participants were assigned to an experimental or control condition (if either); key instructions, usually in verbatim form; a careful description of all independent and dependent variables; and an (often) explicit mention that APA's ethical guidelines for research were followed and that all participants were debriefed.

Procedure subsections for social psychology experiments are often quite long and detailed. On occasion, however, a detailed Materials subsection will cover much of the information that might normally appear in a Procedure. That was the case with the Procedure from the Ames's study on social inference. The information provided in the Materials subsection negated the need for a lengthy description of what participants did once the study began:

Procedure

Participants volunteered as part of an exercise for an introductory psychology course. Participants completed the materials via the Internet outside of class. After reading an informed consent statement, participants completed the materials described above [in the Materials subsection]. Participants were subsequently debriefed through an in-class discussion of the exercise results. (Ames, 2004, Study 1, p. 576)

When writing your first Method section, spend some time in the library leafing through social psychology journals to look for illustrative examples like these that will help you craft a thorough procedure.

Formatting a Method section. Unlike the introduction, the Method section is titled as such; the word "Method" appears centered and double-spaced below the last line of the previous section. The Method section need not begin at the top of a new page unless the introduction ended at the bottom of the previous page. Consult Appendix C for a sample Method section and its formatting requirements.

Results

The Results section represents the broadening of the rhetorical hourglass (see Figure 12.1); thus the content focuses on specific findings linked to the hypothesis, as well as the statistical analyses used to uncover those findings. This broadening should be accomplished by focusing on two main issues: writing about results in a way that will be accessible to most, if not all, readers, and organizing how the findings are presented in the Results section.

In the first place, the meaning of a project's results matters much more than any numbers associated with statistical analyses. Chapter 11 offers specific guidance about putting statistical results into words. Before you begin to write up your project's results using APA style, be sure to review Active Learning Exercise 11A, which is devoted to explaining statistical findings in clear, understandable prose. That being said, numbers do serve an essential if supporting role in any Results section. As discussed in chapter 11, descriptive statistics (e.g., ranges, means, standard deviations)—which characterize behavior in measurable terms (e.g., a mean rating of 5.3 on a 7-point scale)—are used to support inferential statistics (e.g., Was the average rating in one group different from that observed in another?). Ideally, of course, any numerical information is presented from the perspective of what participants *did* behaviorally (e.g., "Members of the experimental group rated the stranger more favorably [$M = 5.2$] than those in the control group [$M = 3.7$], $t(48) = 4.3$, $p < .05$.").

What about the second issue? The key here is having an implicit organization structure for the Results section. Recall that the section focuses both on your findings related to the hypothesis and to the statistical analyses you used to reveal them. How should this be accomplished? Simply inform the reader about what you did and why you did it. Here is a basic framework to give a Results section such an implicit structure:

- Open the Results section by briefly reminding the reader about the study's main hypothesis, the method used to test it, and the nature of the independent and dependent variables (remember, each section of an APA style paper should be able to stand alone). This "top-down" approach—what was done, for what reason, and what comes next—will organize the Results section for the reader.
- Describe the project's most important finding first, highlighting what the research participants did behaviorally. The content of the Results section is results—the actions people performed and whether those acts were consistent with the hypothesis. Speculations concerning the psychological meaning of

participants' responses, or the implications thereof, are reserved for consideration in the Discussion.

- The meaning of the results should arrange the narrative, not the statistical tests or any numbers. Explaining the choice of a statistical test is usually a good idea ("A one-way analysis of variance [ANOVA] was used to test for differences among the average number of negative comments made in each of the three team meetings.").
- Where necessary, supplement the prose summary of findings with a carefully selected table or figure (discussed below). The contents of these visual aids must be referred to ("See Table 3") and explained in the Results.

Formatting the Results section. As shown in Appendix C's model manuscript, the Results section immediately follows the Method section and opens with the centered heading "Results." For further advice on writing about results, see Abelson (1995), Salovey (2000), and Sternberg (2003).

Discussion

The Discussion section is the last core section of the APA style paper. As the closing section, the Discussion provides authors with an opportunity to consider the implications of the findings for current and future research on the topic. Following Bem's (1987) hourglass model, the Discussion section is wider than the Results section, as it makes connections to broader issues of social behavior (recall Figure 12.1). A solid Discussion section provides needed direction for social psychological research on the topic of interest. In contrast, a mediocre Discussion will do little more than restate what is known, claim the importance of the topic, and encourage future research in the area. Why does this happen? Too often authors assume that the Discussion is little more than a perfunctory exercise, a review of what the reader already knows from reading the earlier sections of the manuscript, notably the Results. How can you go about writing an interesting, informative, and yet directive Discussion?

Oddly, there is precious little available guidance regarding how to write a quality Discussion section. The usually detailed and prescriptive *Publication Manual* (APA, 2001), for example, spares little space on how to craft this section. Calfee (2000) suggests that four main issues be included in any Discussion section:

- *Review the hypothesis and findings.* Recap what was done, what was found, and whether the two match up. When results vary from expectation, the thoughtful social psychologist speculates why this might have happened. In some cases, unanticipated results can help a researcher look at specific social behaviors in a new light.
- *Point out problems or flaws.* No experiment is ideal and no set of results is flawless—honestly alluding to a study's drawbacks is the responsibility of any conscientious social psychologist. The Discussion section is the place where major

glitches can be named, where the effect of any shortcoming can be considered. Focus on methodological problems that can be corrected in the future or procedural issues that unduly distracted participants. Note that this is not an invitation to complain about minor or trivial matters (e.g., "Perhaps participants did not take the experiment seriously"); rather it is an opportunity to express concerns about the participant sample, the operationalization of the hypothesis, whether randomization (if any) was flawed, and the like.

- *Reflect on the implications of the research.* What, if anything, do we now know about social behavior that we did not prior to your study? When things go as planned—your experiment reveals what you expected—then a writer carefully considers how the findings might account for some wider range of behavior (e.g., apologies not only restore social relationships, perhaps they also deepen them by causing friends to share positive and negative emotions). Thus a review of a study's implications can lead to theory development. When findings fail to confirm a hypothesis, a researcher has an opportunity to speculate whether the research design, the operationalization of the independent variable, the measurement of the dependent variable, or even the guiding theory could be the problem.

- *Plan future research.* Social psychological research never ends. The findings of one good study suggest the content and scope of subsequent research efforts. When pointing to the need for future research, a writer should err on the side of specificity: More detail is more helpful to readers and would-be researchers than is vague sophistry. Ideally, some readers of a Discussion section will actually be moved to continue a line of research you urged them to consider (just as you may have chosen to conduct your study based on a suggestion encountered at the end of a journal article). Avoid offering the simplistic observation that "more research on this important topic is necessary" unless you concretely explain why it is needed and make concrete suggestions about how to actually do it.

Beyond addressing these four points, I encourage you to personalize your paper's Discussion section by emphasizing what made the topic of interest to you. Why did you design a project on this topic and not another? Why should readers care about your research? How does your work and your ideas fit into the discipline of social psychology? As you think about how to personalize the Discussion, consult the published literature to learn how other authors made their work stand out. Consider emulating the style of this very thoughtful conclusion to a research article on why people of different races have so little contact with one another:

Contact among people of different racial groups continues to be a serious social issue in America. Making the first move to establish intergroup contact and form intergroup relationships can be a daunting task. Fears and anxieties about how they will be treated can prevent people from moving forward. In addition, (mis)perceptions about out-group members' thoughts, feelings, and motives can exaggerate tensions. Recognizing that

's' behavior may reflect motives similar to one's own may be an impor-
ncing the anxiety and frustration associated with intergroup encoun-
son, 2005, p. 106)

g the Discussion section. Where formatting is concerned, the Discussion
.ion is placed right after the Results. The section name is centered and double-
spaced below the end of the Results section. A sample Discussion section may be found
in Appendix C.

References

Like all areas of science, social psychology develops incrementally, relying on earlier
research to guide current or future efforts. The citations appearing in the References
section build the scientific case for a research project (see chapter 2). Only those sources
that really and truly relate to your research should be cited in the References section of
your paper. Reporting them accurately is important, as your search of the social psychological literature for your project probably revealed to you. There is little more frustrating
for readers than trying to find a source when the available reference contains errors.
Whether student or professional, a serious social psychologist makes certain that all references are cited accurately and thoroughly, and formatted according to APA style.

Readers rely on references sections a great deal. Some readers use citations for
reading purposes. If a paper's research topic genuinely interests them, they will obtain
and read key references cited therein. Readers already familiar with a topic expect that
recent articles will cite current scholarship. Thus an up-to-date references section
serves an educative function, alerting interested readers, especially students, about new
developments in social psychology. Finally, a references section serves a scholarly function. Social psychologists will put more faith in a piece of research if it is clear that the
investigator is well-versed in the relevant literature (your instructor is likely to have a
similar reaction). For all of these reasons, then, you should approach the development
and maintenance of your References section with care.

If there is a downside to APA-style references, here it is: Learning the formatting
requirements takes patience and practice. Students often find doing so to be a tiresome
exercise. The truth of the matter is that there is really no way to learn the formatting
requirements except to follow general examples drawn from conventional sources
(e.g., articles, chapters, books) and to consult the *Publication Manual* for guidelines
for more esoteric sources (e.g., letters to the Editor, unpublished sources). As a coun-
terweight to the "but this is so tedious to learn" argument, keep the need for accuracy
in mind; reference errors undermine scientific and educational progress.

Table 12.3 illustrates samples of the most common citation types used in social
psychology papers, whether written by professionals or students. The citation format
for less common sorts of references may be found in the *Publication Manual* (APA,
2001). Other examples of common as well as rare citation types may be found in the
References section of this book. Naturally, when you locate a new source while reading,

Table 12.3 APA-Style Citations for Common Research Sources

Journal articles

Fiedler, K., Nickel, S., Muehlfriedel, T., & Unkelbach, C. (2001). Is mood congruency an effect of genuine memory or response bias? *Journal of Experimental Social Psychology, 37,* 201–214.

Hazan, C., & Shaver, P. R. (1990). Love and work: An attachment theoretical perspective. *Journal of Personality and Social Psychology, 59,* 270–280.

Matthews, K. A. (1982). Psychological perspectives on the Type A behavior pattern. *Psychological Bulletin, 91,* 293–323.

Books

Fiske, S. T., & Taylor, S. E. (1991). *Social cognition* (2nd ed.). New York: McGraw-Hill.

Kasser, T. (2002). *The high price of materialism.* Cambridge, MA: MIT Press.

Edited book

Clark, M. S. (Ed.). (1991). *Prosocial behavior.* Newbury Park, CA: Sage.

Chapter in an edited book

Blair, I. V. (2001). Implicit stereotypes and prejudice. In G. R. Moskowitz (Ed.), *Cognitive social psychology: The Princeton Symposium on the legacy and future of social cognition* (pp. 359–374). Mahwah, NJ: Erlbaum.

Conference presentation

Kruglanski, A. W. (2006, January). *The psychology of terrorism: "Syndrome" versus "tool" perspectives.* Annual meeting of the Society for Personality and Social Psychology, Palm Springs CA.

Electronic (online) sources

Roediger, H. L., III. (2006). E-mail onslaught: What can we do? *Observer, 19,* 35–37. Retrieved January 31, 2006, from http://www.psychologicalscience.org/observer/getArticle. cfm?id=1921

---

be sure to jot down the APA-style reference from the References section of the source in your research notebook (see Active Learning Activity 1A in chapter 1). When it comes time to add the new source to your paper's References, you will be glad that you recorded it completely and accurately. Tracking down lost or forgotten references consumes an enormous amount of time that could be better spent refining or revising the rest of a manuscript.

Formatting the References section. The References section in APA style papers begins on the page immediately following the end of the Discussion section. The heading "References" is centered at the top of the page, and the alphabetized list (by first author surname, first and middle initial) of references is double-spaced underneath. Take careful note of the capitalization used in titles and subtitles (besides the first words in each one, only proper nouns are capitalized). APA style urges the use of what is called a "hanging" indentation, which means that the first line of each reference begins at the left margin of the page and any subsequent lines of text are indented beneath it (see examples in Table 12.3, the manuscript in Appendix C, or the References section at the end of this book).

Tables and figures

Tables and figures serve two main purposes: to illustrate numerical or graphic representations of data and to break up text for the reader. Technical information like unfamiliar statistical analyses can sometimes be overwhelming to read in text form. Tables and figures can clarify, simplify, and highlight key findings for readers, especially students.

Tables are organized displays of statistical information—usually summary or descriptive statistics, occasionally inferential statistics—but not raw data. The content of a table is precise, encouraging readers to carefully examine the relationships among numbers representing behavior. Student researchers like you are apt to need to create tables of means and standard deviations representing observed behavioral differences between the conditions in an experiment.

Where tables emphasize numbers, figures focus on some apparent effect derived from but not dependent on numbers. A figure is a quick and clear visual summary of some relationship among variables found in some data. When numbers are present in a figure, they are usually much less precise than those found in a table. A figure usually discloses one main finding; thus it should be designed so that readers can, with one glance, quickly discern what was found. Common figures include line and bar graphs, and scatter plots.

Tables and figures appear in a variety of forms; however, I urge you to rely on simple rather than complex data displays in any APA-style paper you write. Your work—and your words—should be the focus of a paper, not excessive visual aids. A sample table can be found in the manuscript in Appendix C. For additional guidelines, see the *Publication Manual* (APA, 2001) and two works by Nicol and Pexman (1999, 2003). Let me discourage you from overreliance on software when creating tables and figures. Too many visual "bells and whistles" is distracting in a data display, just as use of multiple colors can be overwhelming; APA style encourages black and white displays. Let me also suggest that you be very conservative where the number of tables or figures in a paper is concerned. I would opt for one or two tables, and perhaps one figure; too many examples of either reduces the reader's interest and willingness to take the time to examine them.

Formatting tables and figures. When creating a table or a figure, be certain to:

- Try to fit the table or figure on one double-spaced page.
- Label each table or figure with a concise, descriptive title and a number (e.g., Table 3, Figure 1).

- Avoid redundancy: No table should repeat information found in any figure (and vice versa).
- Make certain that the written text explains the content of the table or figure.
- Verify the accuracy of the numbers appearing in all tables and the relationships displayed by all figures.
- Place any table(s) and figure(s), respectively, at the end of the APA style manuscript and not in the actual text.

Appendix

An appendix is the place to store information that is not suitable for other sections of the APA style paper. Adding an appendix is useful when certain novel research materials, such as unusual stimuli or a modified or unique questionnaire or rating scale, are unavailable elsewhere. Student writers often find an appendix to be a convenient place to show an instructor many of the materials generated for social psychology experiments (i.e., a description of a study's materials appears in the Materials subsection of the Method, but a copy of what was actually used appear in the Appendix).

Formatting an appendix. An appendix begins on a separate page under a centered heading ("Appendix") at the end of a manuscript. If you created a questionnaire, for example, simply attach a copy of it to the end of your paper.

Author note

Besides the Abstract, the author note is the shortest section of text in the APA-style paper. Appearing at the top of the page immediately following the last page of the Reference section, the author note lists each author and his or her department affiliation, acknowledges any funding or assistance, and indicates whom to contact about the research. Student papers rarely have author notes, but if individuals helped you with your project—perhaps with running the experiment, reading a draft of your paper, or the like—you should thank them in this public way.

Formatting an author note. A typical student author note looks like this:

Author Notes

Doris Jones, Department of Psychology.

I thank Kyle Lanning for his help creating the stereotype images used in this study and the Psychology Club for paying to have the images copied. Dr. Albert and the students in Research Methods 201 gave me helpful comments on several drafts of this paper.

Correspondence concerning this research should be sent to: Doris Jones, 345 Jennings Dorm, Ohio College, Smithville, OH, 22222 or via e-mail: djones@oc.edu.

Table 12.4　Additional Guidelines for Formatting APA-Style Papers

Do not use any binder or folder for your paper—simply staple the pages together.

Type or print on one side of clean, $8^1/_2$ by 11-inch white paper.

Use a simple, readable 12-point font or typescript.

Have at least a 1-inch margin around the four sides of each page.

Use a left-justified margin (the left margin of each page should be flush, i.e., with an even edge).

Do not use a right-justified margin (the right margin should be ragged, i.e., with an uneven edge).

Except for the Abstract, each paragraph should be indented $^1/_2$ inch or 5 spaces from the left margin.

Page numbering starts on the title page; numbers are placed in the upper right corner of each page (except for figures).

Each page has a "page header," usually the first few words of the title, which is placed to the left of the page number (see Appendix C).

The title page lists a "running head," a shortened title meant to appear at the top of each page of a printed article (the placement of a formatted sample may be found on the title page in Appendix C).

Avoid footnotes: Either put the material in the text or leave it out.

Don't forget: Use only double-spacing throughout the paper.

Additional formatting guidelines

Now that you have a working understanding of the order, structure, and function of the various sections of the typical APA-style paper, we need to consider the overall formatting guidelines when pulling a paper together. One guideline has already been mentioned: Never using single spacing. APA-style papers are double-spaced throughout, which makes both reading the work and making written comments on it much easier. Table 12.4 lists other basic formatting guidelines. Besides reviewing this list, be sure to rely on the sample paper in Appendix C as a model when formatting your own paper.

ACTIVE LEARNING EXERCISE　**12A**

Drafting an APA-Style Lab Report of Your Social Psychology Project

You now know how to develop an outline for your paper and have a good idea of how to go about filling in the content for each of the sections appearing in the typical APA-style paper. So now it's time to write, to get down to it. Where should you begin—with the title? Or would it be best to start with the Abstract or the introduction? Some people do adopt a linear approach, working their way from the beginning to the end of a manuscript. I recommend an alternative approach, one that allows you to optimally use what you already know and what you learned by conducting your social psychological research.

Allow me to explain. Table 12.5 proposes that you follow a nonlinear writing plan, one that allows you to begin drafting your paper at the same time you are running the experiment and collecting data. Instead of starting with the beginning of the paper, I suggest that you begin in the middle. As shown by Step 1 in Table 12.5, begin by drafting the Method section—and be sure to do so while you are still collecting data. Why then? For the simple reason that all the details about the research procedure, including the script you are following—literally what you say—when interacting with the participants, are still fresh in your mind.

Once the data are collected, you can move on to Step 2 in Table 12.5 by writing up the Results section (you will need to organize and analyze the data, of course, as advocated in chapter 11). The author of any APA-style paper should know what the results are before taking pen to paper (or, more likely, finger to keyboard). Your goal is to tell a compelling story about what you discovered rather than to write an incremental history of what led you from the glimmer of a project idea to the full-blown research effort (see Bem, 1987). In fact, knowing what happened

Table 12.5 A Recommended Order for Drafting an APA-Style Empirical Paper

Step 1:	Draft the Method section.
Step 2:	Draft the Results section.
	Revisit Step 1 for revising and editing.
Step 3:	Draft the introduction.
	When a reference is cited, add it to the References section.
	Revisit Steps 1 and 2 for revising and editing.
Step 4:	Draft the Discussion.
	Revisit Steps 1, 2, and 3 for revising and editing.
Step 5:	Draft the Abstract.
	Create the Title page.
	Write the Author Notes (if any).
	Create tables and/or figures (if any).
	Verify references for accuracy.
	Create Appendix (if needed).
	Revisit Steps 1, 2, 3, and 4 for revising and editing.
Step 6:	Seek peer comments on the complete draft of the paper.
	Revise and edit based on peer suggestions.
	Revisit Steps 1–6 as needed.
Step 7:	Submit the paper.

Source: Adapted from Dunn (1999, Table 3.6, page 98).

Continued

and whether the findings were as anticipated will absolutely influence how you write the rest of the paper.

After you have completed Steps 1 and 2 in Table 12.5, then you can revise and edit the content of the two section drafts. Revising as you write—taking a meaningful break between drafting sections—will help you to shape the manuscript as it grows and improve the clarity of your writing. Indeed, ongoing editing will ensure that each section can be read independently of the others, an important quality associated with APA style.

After this final round of editing, Step 3 in Table 12.5 suggests that you begin to draft the introduction. Doing so should be an easier process because you already have the results firmly in mind, having completed Step 2. An important part of Step 3 is keeping careful track of references—as you cite one in the introduction (or anywhere in your manuscript, for that matter), be sure to add the complete citation to the References section at the end of the paper. Don't wait—add references the moment you cite them—otherwise you will become wrapped up in the writing process and have to add them later, which inevitably proves to be tiresome. After you have a draft of the introduction, revisit Steps 1 and 2 in Table 12.5. Are there any changes you now want to make to improve the flow or content of the Method or Results?

The next step in Table 12.5 entails drafting the Discussion section (see Step 4). Writing the paper's closing section, mulling over the implications of the findings, should be a smooth process once the Method, Results, and introduction are written (revisiting each is also a part of Step 4). Step 5 involves performing a variety of activities, including drafting the Abstract, creating the title page, author notes (if any), tables and figures (if any), among other activities (see Table 12.5).

Despite the fact that the APA style paper is more or less completed by the end of Step 5, do not neglect Step 6. This next to the last step encourages you to seek peer feedback on the working draft of your manuscript. I will give you concrete advice about seeking comments on writing in the next section of this chapter. For now, consider how useful it will be to have a "fresh pair" of eyes read and comment your work. Sharing your paper with another person will also give you a break from it so that when you receive comments, you can accept them with a fresh perspective, revisit the first six steps in Table 12.5, and then submit the work (see Step 7).

Seeking feedback on your writing

Writing a draft of an APA-style paper is an important part of the writing process, but it is only one part of that process. An equally important part of the process is asking for feedback on your writing. Whom should you ask? You probably have three choices: your instructor, someone in your institution's Writing Center, or a peer. Asking for comments from all three is actually the best approach, but I will focus on peer feedback. Social psychologists routinely share drafts of articles and chapters with col-

Table 12.6   Some Questions for Peer Reviewers of APA-Style Papers

1	What is the purpose of my research? Did I use enough examples to illustrate or demonstrate my arguments?
2	Did I explain the hypothesis clearly? Did the review of the literature in the introduction logically lead to the hypothesis?
3	Was the research methodology clear? Did the experiment appropriately test the hypothesis?
4	Was the Method clear? Do you think you could recreate my project based on what you read in the Method?
5	Were the results clear? What was the main finding? Did it support the hypothesis?
6	Was the Discussion focused? Did the Discussion go beyond the Results section?
7	Do any parts of the manuscript need to be expanded? Do any parts need to be shortened?
8	Which parts of the paper were the easiest to follow? Which were difficult to understand?
9	Do you have any suggestions for improving this paper?
10	Did you notice any spelling, grammar, or punctuation errors? If so, where?

leagues, using these peer comments to revise their work before submitting it to the intended professional outlet. Asking for candid comments from your colleagues is a great way to improve your writing and to learn to more thoroughly revise papers.

Your peer reviewer can be a fellow social psychological researcher from your class or someone whose opinion on writing you trust. (Hint: Avoid asking a romantic partner or a best pal—you are after honesty and rigor, not uncritical or gushing praise.) Whomever you ask, just be certain to keep an open mind about what they tell you. View their criticism as constructive, not destructive. If a peer identifies a problem area in your writing, you can be certain that your instructor (i.e., the person grading your work) is likely to focus on the same issue. The best approach is to tell your peer reviewer what kinds of information will be most helpful to you before he or she reads the paper (e.g., "I want to be sure my hypothesis is clearly stated early on," "Is the Method clear?", "Do the findings make sense to you?"). Table 12.6 lists some questions for you to ask your peer once he or she is finished with the paper. One more thing: Whatever the feedback is like, be sure to be courteous and thank your peer sincerely for helping you improve your work (and to hone your own critical faculties, offer to read and comment on one of your peer's papers).

Preparing a Poster Summary

APA-style papers are not the only way to share research in social psychology. An increasingly common alternative is to create a poster—a mounted, eye-catching display summarizing what was done and found in a piece of research. Poster sessions are now routine events at psychology conferences. A poster session is a public event held in a relatively large space, such as a conference room, a hall, or even a ballroom. Various types of empirical studies—everything from experiments to observational efforts—are presented individually as posters. Unlike the papers from which they often emerge, posters emphasize visual aids (tables, graphs) over text.

Posters describing psychological research tend to follow the structure of APA-style papers, thus there is a title, an introduction, a Method, and so on. Due to space constraints—most posters are accommodated in a 4 by 6 foot area—the text found in each section is brief and to the point. Where an introduction might be 3 or 4 pages long in a student paper, it appears as no more than 3 or so paragraphs, if that, in a poster. Some sections, such as an Abstract, can be superfluous, as the written content of the typical poster really comprises an extended Abstract. Some posters avoid paragraphs altogether, relying instead on a "bullet" style where main points are listed as a few pithy sentences under the traditional APA-style headings.

Tables and figures, however, play a special role in posters. Carefully constructed and judiciously chosen, a table or figure should produce a rapid, visual sense of what was found in the course of the research. The text of the poster is there to explain the tables and graphs (and there should not be too many of them, either—neither readers of papers or posters should be overwhelmed with supporting materials). Both the text and the visual aids should emphasize the nature of the social behavior under examination: What did people do *behaviorally*? Thus a table of means should allow viewers to get a quick sense of the average level of behavior within each experimental condition. Similarly, a bar graph can illustrate the relative frequency of a given behavior in one experimental condition compared to another.

Given the emphasis on visual aids, how can a poster provide as much information as an APA-style paper? In the first place, creating a poster is an opportunity to pull out the essential points from a research project. An investigator is forced to make choices—information that truly matters for purposes of quick summary must be highlighted. Information that is extraneous can be dropped; after all, a poster is a snapshot of a piece of research and not a traditional APA-style paper.

Second, posters have an interactive component. During most poster sessions, the author of each poster stands by it, waiting to have a conversation about the research with interested passers-by. This intentional informality allows interested attendees to read a brief summary, get a visual sense of what was found, and to then talk with the researcher about the findings and their implications for social psychology. Not every one who happens by will want to discuss a poster, of course. Some people will want to read it; others will glance at it and decide that the topic does not interest them. A few people will stop and want to have an extended chat about the work. These differing levels of engagement mimic the behavior of journal readers who flip quickly past some articles while carefully reading others. Thus no participant in a poster session should be upset if only a few people express interest in a research topic—after all, that's the norm.

Table 12.7 outlines possible content for the typical sections found in a poster.

Figure 12.2 illustrates a common layout for a poster. Most posters will need to be designed to fit in a space of 4 by 6 foot or so, either a wall or a portable bulletin board on wheels.

Table 12.7   Suggested Content for Main Sections of a Typical Poster

Introduction (1 to 3 paragraphs maximum): Introduce the research area, identify key past
  research, and present the hypothesis, including the operational definitions of the variables.
Method (3 to 4 paragraph maximum): Characterize the participants (demographic
  information can be summarized in a table); describe the research design (e.g.,
  observational, correlational, experimental) independent and dependent variables (focus on
  behavior), and whether a control group was used. The procedure should be very brief and
  focused.
Results (1 to 3 paragraphs maximum): Indicate how the hypothesis was tested, identify any
  statistical analyses used, and provide behavioral descriptions of the results supported by
  summary statistics. Use tables or figures to illustrate relationships found during the data
  analysis.
Discussion (1 to 3 paragraph maximum): Focus on the finding and infer what it means
  about social behavior. Such speculations must be brief; however, further implications of
  the results can be explored through a 2–3-minute prepared speech.

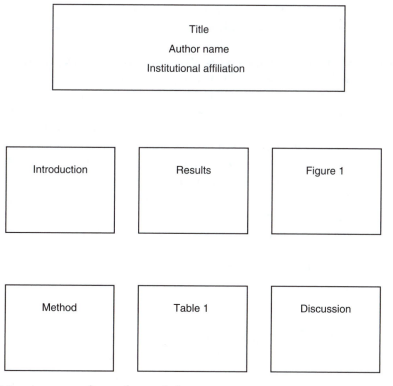

Figure 12.2.   A common layout for psychology posters

ACTIVE LEARNING EXERCISE   **12B**

Making a Poster

There are two basic options for making a poster. You can make one from scratch, which can mean taping or gluing sections of your paper onto colored construction paper or poster board. Appearance counts—be as neat as you can when constructing the poster. The alternative approach is to rely on poster-making technology. Many colleges and universities now own printers that can create large, professional looking posters containing text, graphics, photographs, tables, and often several colors, with ease. Whether you make one by hand or by machine, however, consider following these steps:

Step 1   Edit each section of your APA-style paper down to a manageable length (i.e., from pages to paragraphs or summary "bullets"). A 20-page paper, for example, should be edited down to a handout of between 5 and 10 pages (see Active Learning Exercise 12C below).

Step 2   Use the guidelines in Table 12.7 to make certain that the main sections of the poster are brief and to the point. Retain only the most essential information for these main sections of the poster, remembering that such text will be supplemented by visual aids (tables, graphs), a 2-minute or so verbal summary, and a handout.

Step 3   Create tables or graphs that directly pertain to the poster's text. Make certain that these visual aids are clearly labeled so that a viewer can discern what they mean relatively quickly after looking at the poster.

Step 4   Plan the layout of the poster using Figure 12.2 as a guide or starting point. There is no right or wrong way to lay out a poster as long as you remember that most viewers will expect it to adhere somewhat to APA style and that the content reflects a logical progression of ideas (i.e., from question to execution to interpretation of results).

Step 5   Share a draft of your poster's content and layout with one or two peers. Take a few minutes to discuss the poster's information and layout, as their perspectives will let you know whether your original intentions are understood.

Step 6   Create the poster by hand or by using a large poster printer.

Enter Talking: Preparing and Delivering Oral Research Presentations

This chapter opened with social psychological evidence concerning how and when people are influenced by persuasive communications. We now close with a related topic: how to deliver an informative, professional presentation in social psychology. Will you be trying to persuade your audience? Yes, to a certain extent, if only to convince your listeners that the topic should help them to think more deeply or critically about the nature of some social behavior.

Social psychologists usually refer to these presentations as "talks," not lectures. A good talk contains the following qualities:

- *Substance.* What is the presentation's purpose? Is the talk pitched appropriately? Giving a presentation on a social psychology experiment to the students in one's class is different than speaking to an audience of nonpsychology students, for example. Is technical information clearly explained? Are examples abundant? Why should the audience be interested in the topic?
- *Organization.* Does the presentation have a clear beginning, middle, and end? Does the material flow or is it disjointed? Do visual aids (e.g., slides, transparencies, PowerPoint) help or hinder the audience's understanding of the talk? Is a length for the talk established (e.g., 20 minutes talking time with another 10 minutes for questions) and followed? Or does the talk begin too slowly and end abruptly or, worse still, does it go on far too long?
- *Speaker's style.* As we learned earlier, people trust experts. That being said, conveying enthusiasm, vigor, and curiosity help considerably. Confident speakers are perceived to be convincing and engaging. Appearance matters, too. You need not splurge on a new wardrobe, but you should avoid looking overly casual or sloppy.
- *Connection.* Good speakers engage the audience. They do not lecture or pontificate; they speak as naturally as possible, asking the occasional question and answering whatever queries may come from the audience. A good speaker makes a nonverbal connection, as well, by making eye contact with individuals in the audience.
- *A take-home message.* Effective speakers inform the audience early on what the main message of the talk is, deliver that message in the body of the talk, and mention it again at the end.

Preparing a talk

There is one major rule for giving a talk: Don't read to the audience. Instead, rehearse your talk over and over, and commit it to memory. There is also a second, equally important rule: Talk about what you know and know it well. By now, you should be well versed on the topic of your research project, so crafting a talk based upon it should not be difficult. Thus if you are preparing a talk based on library research or your project paper, then much of the work is already done. What you need to do is to condense what you know into a brief talk that you should be able to deliver to a group of interested people (e.g., fellow students, instructors). Most professional talks are 45

Table 12.8   Steps for Planning a Psychology Talk

Step 1:	Select a talk topic and be sure it is not too broad.
Step 2:	Choose the main point of the talk and summarize it in one or two sentences.
Step 3:	Think about the audience: What do they know about your topic?
Step 4:	Draft an outline of the talk (overview with background and hypothesis, sample and research methods, findings and implications).
Step 5:	Create visual materials (e.g., overheads or computer-based slides) supporting the outline from Step 4.
Step 6:	Rehearse and time your talk (practice in front of a mirror, then a friend); return to steps 4 and 5 as needed.
Step 7:	Give the talk to the intended audience.

minutes long with another 15 minutes for questions from the audience. Student talks, which can be delivered in class or at student-oriented psychology conferences, tend to be 15 minutes long with 5 or so additional minutes for questions. Now, 20 minutes sounds like a long time—in reality, however, it isn't much time at all, especially when you consider that 15 minutes allows you (at most) 5 minutes each on introducing the research problem and hypothesis, describing the sample and the research methods used, and then relating the results and their implications. As anyone who routinely gives presentations will tell you, time flies when you are the one doing the talking.

Table 12.8 lists some steps you can follow to prepare an informal psychology talk. If your talk is based on your research project, then you already have the information for Steps 1 and 2. Step 3 is the one novice speakers usually neglect: What does the audience know (or not know) about the topic? Preparing a talk on a social psychology experiment and presenting it to your classmates is very different than talking to an audience who knows nothing about social psychology, let alone research methods. You must tailor your talk to the needs of listeners (e.g., an un-informed audience will need to have social psychology defined or the concept of random assignment explained—such explanations would be skipped for an informed audience).

Many first-time speakers find Step 4 difficult because it requires them to really edit down their project paper, from many pages to a few sentences or paragraphs. You cannot cover all that you know about your project or the larger topical area in a single presentation. You should only present that information that provides context and an interesting rationale for your project or areas of interest (again, 15 minutes is not much time—be ruthless about including only the most pertinent information in your talk).

The fifth step is one where you should avoid overdoing it: Create and use only a few overheads or computer slides that will illustrate the most important issues in your project. You might, for example, have one slide with the hypothesis; one with information about the participant sample (e.g., demographic information); one with the research design, and the independent and dependent variables; and a few slides for the main results (use tables and figures as needed). Some speakers add another slide listing future directions or implications—and that's all. Remember, although visual aids provide support for your talk, the audience came to hear you, not to look at slides. You must still be the focus of attention.

Steps 6 and 7 get to the heart of the matter—rehearsing and then finally giving the talk. People who are not used to speaking in front of groups often find practicing in front of a mirror to be very helpful. Once they become comfortable "hearing" themselves think out loud, speaking to a practice audience composed of a friend or two is a good idea. In my experience, good public speakers are always a little nervous, and such jitters encourage them to take the task seriously and to work hard at doing a good job. I wish you luck on any talk you have the good fortune to give. One last suggestion: Time yourself. You don't want your 15 minute talk to take 25 minutes—professionals finish on time!

ACTIVE LEARNING EXERCISE   12C

Giving Social Psychology Away via Audience Handouts

Whenever they attend a performance or presentation, most people like to walk away with something from it. They want to have something to remind them about what they heard and saw. At psychology presentations, many speakers will prepare a helpful handout that summarizes their main points, often displays the key findings, lists related and recent publications, and provides contact information regarding the speaker. Such handouts are not difficult to prepare and should be brief, no more than a page or so. If you give a talk, consider creating a summary handout to share when you are finished speaking (if you pass it out earlier, people will read it and pay less attention to you).

Is there a standard format for an audience handout? Not really—however, you may want to follow the standard (but abbreviated) outline of an APA-style paper (recall Table 12.1). List a title, your name, institutional affiliation, and then one paragraph describing the study's purpose and hypothesis, one outlining the Method (briefly), and a final one describing the results and identifying implications and future directions. Given the brevity of the summary, no Abstract is necessary. Add a few key references in a References section—you will be surprised at how many people really want to learn more and will look up your suggested readings. Just keep your summary to one page (and single spacing is fine for these handouts).

ACTIVE LEARNING EXERCISE   12D

Host a Paper or Poster Session

If you have gone to the trouble of conducting a piece of social psychological research, then I do think you should make an effort to share it with others. If your institution or a neighboring one does not currently sponsor a student psychology conference, then you and the members of your class should consider hosting a paper or a poster session.

Paper sessions require some attention to detail. Minimally, you need to have some students willing to speak, as well as an audience willing to listen. Table 12.9 lists some of the logistical issues you should consider when planning a paper session. Someone, perhaps an instructor, needs to be certain each presentation begins and ends on time, and that any question and answer time does not run over into a subsequent talk. Other logistical issues include reserving space for the talks, and ensuring that advertising occurs so that members of the campus community know to attend. Having a modest reception with refreshments after the last talk adds a celebratory element and will encourage further interaction between speakers and audience members.

Poster sessions are easier to organize than paper sessions. Choose a date and time, invite your classmates to create posters based on their research project (see the instructions for poster construction provided above), and then advertise the event on campus and in the psychology department. Be sure to invite your friends and the department faculty to come. The ideal venue is a well-lit, large space with plenty of room for posters (hung on walls or propped on portable stands) and people (speakers and those milling about the posters). As always, a table with some modest refreshments is a good idea—the availability of food and drink encourages people to talk with one another. Allow at least an hour to an hour and a half for the poster session.

Table 12.9   Planning a Paper Session

1   Who will present papers? Class members? How many?
2   When will the paper session be held (date and time)? Will the time of day affect attendance? Where will the paper session be held? In a classroom, a seminar room, or a lecture hall?
3   Who will reserve the room and organize other necessary materials? Are a podium and a projector available? Is the room a "smart" classroom? Will there be refreshments? Who will introduce the speakers? What other issues need to be considered?
4   Who will attend the paper session? Faculty members? Students from other classes? Off-campus guests? Should people be invited directly?
5   How will the event be advertised? Can posters be created? Can email invitations be sent? An ad in the campus newspaper?
6   Will refreshments be available? Water for the speakers? Food and drink afterwards for the speakers and audience?

Parting Thoughts

I very much hope this book has taught you a great deal about research methods in social psychology. You now have a collection of tools, techniques, and advice at your disposal. You are able to conduct a piece of research, experimental or otherwise, from conception to completion, from a promising idea to an engaging paper summarizing your efforts. People—their thoughts, feelings, and behaviors—are indeed endlessly fascinating. I hope this book helped you to understand how to understand them better, and that you found your social psychological research experience to be challenging and rewarding.

Exercises

1 Go to the library and locate journal titles and opening paragraphs that you believe are especially attention-getting and well crafted.
2 Review the guidelines for peer review of written work. Swap draft copies of APA-style papers with a group of classmates. Read and evaluate the drafts according to APA style where content and formatting requirements are concerned.
3 Create a poster based on your project paper.
4 Outline and prepare a talk based upon your project paper.
5 Plan a paper or a poster session involving the members of your research methods in social psychology class.

Appendix A
Major Journals in Social Psychology

Asian Journal of Social Psychology
Basic and Applied Social Psychology
British Journal of Social Psychology
European Journal of Social Psychology
European Review of Social Psychology
Journal of Applied Social Psychology
Journal of Experimental Social Psychology
Journal of Personality
Journal of Personality and Social Psychology
Journal of Research in Personality
Journal of Social and Clinical Psychology
Journal of Social and Personal Relationships
Personality and Social Psychology Bulletin
Personality and Social Psychology Review
Representative Research in Social Psychology
Social Behavior and Personality
Social Cognition
Social Psychology Quarterly
The Journal of Social Psychology

Appendix B
Reading Journal Articles in
Social Psychology

The primary mode of scientific communication in social psychology is the scholarly journal article. Social and personality psychologists who publish tend to do so in such journals (a list of major journals in social and personality psychology is provided in Appendix A). Guidelines for searching for journal articles are provided in chapter 2 and the rationale for their structure and content is discussed in chapter 12. My purpose in this appendix is to suggest how best to approach the task of reading and learning from journal articles in social psychology. A more general discussion of reading appears in chapter 2.

Social psychology journals are professional, topically focused scientific periodicals that are usually published monthly, bimonthly, or quarterly. Similar to any high-quality journal, most are subject to peer review; that is, professionals from the discipline anonymously and constructively review colleagues' submissions to determine whether and in what form articles will be accepted for publication. Prestigious journals often have a rejection rate that reaches 80 or 90% of the submissions received.

In social as well as all other areas of psychology, journal articles come in three basic types:

Empirical article. A summary of one or more laboratory or field-based investigations which are often experimental. The basic or traditional APA-style article (see Table 12.1 for an outline of the sections) is the empirical article, which adheres to the hourglass structure (Bem, 1987, 2000).

Review article. Review articles summarize and synthesize findings from empirical articles and other sources pertaining to a theme, topic, or psychological effect. Besides organizing what is known about a topic, review papers often offer direction toward questions for future research.

Theory article. A theoretical article focuses on a new way to answer a research question, or to construe or interpret a behavior (e.g., a new theory to explain altruism). While empirical articles present new knowledge, and review papers condense what is already known, theory articles offer new perspectives on how to explain a topic.

Reading Empirical Articles

Due to their ubiquity as research resources for student projects, I will focus on empirical articles. There are really two distinct approaches to reading a journal article: reading for depth or skimming for key points.

Reading for depth

Reading for depth involves reading an entire article. Note, however, that you do not necessarily need to begin with the Abstract and the introduction, working your way steadily to the Discussion and References. Of course, you can read any article from beginning to end and, in fact, most students do. But you can also read the sections in an APA-style article out of order. You might begin with the Discussion—the section that really summarizes the entire work—and move on to the Results, then the introduction, and end with the Method.

As you progress through a journal article, you can improve your understanding and retention of information by asking yourself questions about each section.

- *Title and Abstract.* Is the title informative? Does the Abstract help you understand the purpose and nature of the research? Is the hypothesis clear? What other information would you like to know?
- *Introduction.* Why did the investigator decide to study this topic? How does the present research relate to prior efforts in the area? Is the hypothesis under investigation novel or a variation on prior research efforts? What were the main questions the researcher sought to answer?
- *Method.* Who took part in the study? How was the hypothesis operationalized? Do you believe the operationalization was reasonable? What were the independent and dependent variables? How were these variables manipulated and measured, respectively? Was the procedure clear? Do you see any problems with the research design or its execution?
- *Results.* What were the findings? Did the results support the hypothesis? If the predicted results were not obtained, how did the researcher account for what was found?
- *Discussion.* What new information do the research results add to social psychological knowledge? Did the research answer some questions while posing others for the future? Are there practical as well as theoretical implications of the findings? Where should research on this topic proceed next?

Skimming an article for key points

Naturally, the best way to learn about a research effort is to read an entire article describing it. Sometimes, however, you will want a quick sense of some aspect of the research. The information you need can be acquired in a shorter amount of time by "skimming" an article in a particular way. Skimming is preliminary or prereading to learn some fact or particular piece of information. Many researchers skim articles to decide whether the research discussed therein is relevant to their own efforts. Keep in mind that each section of a well-written APA-style article can "stand alone" so that a reader can get a sense of the whole work (if not every detail) by reading only the introduction, the Results, or the Discussion (by itself, a Method section is usually too procedural to provide sufficient context for a study's purpose).

When you skim a section or sections of a journal article, examine any headings or subheadings. These words and phrases often identify key themes or concepts that will help you understand the article. Similarly, watch for transitional phrases (e.g., "First," "Second," "Most importantly,") that highlight supporting information. These phrases highlight the logic underlying the rationale, design, and execution of a study. Careful scrutiny of transitions will help you locate a researcher's main arguments.

I will suggest three ways to skim, looking for particular information in a social psychology article.

Skimming to learn the purpose of the research. The main reason to skim any article is to learn the purpose of some piece of research. Read the Abstract and then the introduction (focus especially on the last few paragraphs) to learn why an experiment or other study was conceived and conducted.

Skimming to learn what was done. You might want to know how a hypothesis or the variables related to it were operationalized. Read the Abstract and then turn to the Method section in order to get a quick sense of how an experiment or other study was performed. Be certain to identify all independent and dependent variables. You should also read the last few paragraphs of the introduction so that you have the study's hypothesis firmly in mind and can relate it to key variables.

Skimming to learn what was found. You might believe the best course of action here is to read the Results. This is certainly not a bad idea, but the Discussion section actually provides the "forest" where findings are concerned—the main findings and their implications, as well as an overview of the experiment(s)—whereas most Results sections tend to be overly focused on particular and occasionally esoteric details, the "trees." To learn what was found, read the Abstract and then turn to consider the content of the Discussion section. If the findings are not apparent from the Discussion, then flip back a few pages and skim the Results.

Read On

Empirical journal articles are the lifeblood of social and personality psychology. Journal articles represent the science of psychology at work. Researchers, teachers, and students like you all depend on the discoveries disclosed in these scientific communications. As you read more articles and do so with greater frequency, you will draw and retain meaning from them that can inform your own research efforts.

Appendix C
Student Research Paper

The running head identifies a brief title, which is capitalized and fewer than 50 letter long.

Running head: ATTRACTIVENESS AND SENTENCING

A running head appears at the top of all pages. Page numbering begins with the title page.

Double spacing is used throughout the paper

Exploring the Effects of Defendant Attractiveness and the Seriousness
of a Crime on Sentencing

Laura Sahlender

Moravian College

A title, author name(s), and affiliation appear in the upper portion of the title page. The title is centered and main words are capitalized. The author name is centered under the title, and the affiliation is centered under the author name.

Abstract

The American jury system prides itself on granting citizens speedy, public trials by impartial juries. Certain characteristics can influence jury members' sentencing recommendations, thereby compromising their impartiality. I hypothesized that attractive defendants would be sentenced less severely by participants than unattractive defendants, and that this attractiveness–leniency effect (ALE) would only occur for nonviolent crimes. Forty-five participants examined a defendant photo, read a mock crime scenario, completed a survey, and sentenced the defendant. Sentencing did not vary due to defendant attractiveness or the nature of the crime; however, recommendations for refining the research design are discussed.

Abstracts appear on p. 2. A centered heading labels the abstract.

Abstracts are not indented. Left justification is used throughout APA-style papers.

Abstracts are 120 words or less in length.

The title from page 1 is repeated and centered at the top of page 3.

The introduction always begins on page 3.

Parenthetic citations use the ampersand (&) for "and."

Several parenthetic citations are listed alphabetically, separated by semicolons.

Exploring the Effects of Defendant Attractiveness and the Seriousness of
a Crime on Sentencing

Under the American judicial system, all citizens are granted the right to a speedy and public trial by an impartial jury when resolving legal disputes. An impartial jury should not allow any factors to bias their judgments when reaching a verdict; however, defendant traits could bias jurors' decisions regarding crime severity and the sentence lengths guilty parties will serve. There is much at stake in jury trials and it is imperative that we know if the accused are being judged accurately and fairly (e.g., Bubnis, 1995).

Physical attractiveness plays an important role in society, influencing how people act and respond towards others. When making judgments about others, people routinely apply stereotypes based on appearance, so that "what is beautiful is good" (Dion, Bersheid & Walster, 1972) and attractiveness suggests higher skills (Sigall & Ostrove, 1975). Such spontaneous judgments are effortless but often lack substantive merit; physical appearance is presumed to predict character traits. Although jury trials are supposed to be free of bias where verdicts are concerned, many studies (e.g., Darby & Jeffers, 1988; Deitz & Byrnes, 1981; McKelvie & Coley, 1993; Sigall & Ostrove, 1975) show that physical attractiveness impacts the length and severity of sentencing, creating serious disadvantages for those people who are perceived to be less attractive (Efran, 1974; Stewart, 1980).

The attractiveness–leniency effect (ALE) is the theory that individuals who are found to be more attractive will be sentenced less severely than those who are viewed as unattractive. Juror characteristics have also been examined in some studies to determine what perceiver qualities predict sentencing decisions. Darby and Jeffers (1988), for example, had participants rate defendant attractiveness and the participants' own attractiveness. The researchers found that participants who rated themselves as attractive behaved according to the ALE theory, while those who rated themselves as lower in attractiveness were more lenient when sentencing defendants.

Defendant attractiveness is not the only variable that can bias juror decision making. Gray and Ashmore (1976), for example, explored the length and severity of sentencing as a function of the defendants' race, religious belief, and socioeconomic class. Other studies have found substantive differences in defendant sentencing due to the race of defendants and jurors (Abwender & Hough, 2001), participant gender (Deitz & Byrnes, 1981), and the seriousness of the crime (McKelvie & Coley, 1993).

One potentially important variable—whether the crime is a violent one—receives little attention in the relevant literature. One reasonable prediction is that the ALE bias operates in situations where the crime is nonviolent (e.g., theft of property). When the crime is judged to be violent (i.e., a victim is intentionally, physically harmed by a perpetrator), however, perhaps the ALE bias dissipates. In other words, jurors will judge defendants more harshly and suggest more severe legal penalties when crimes are violent rather than nonviolent.

Prior research did not sufficiently address how violent crimes influence sentence severity and whether the degree of violence reduces the biasing influence of defendant attractiveness. Relying on the basic ALE theory, I hypothesized that defendants who were rated as more attractive would be sentenced less severely by the jurors (research participants) than a defendant rated as unattractive. Despite this attractiveness bias, however, I anticipated that in the case of violent crimes, both the attractive and unattractive defendants would receive equally harsh sentences. To test this hypothesis, participants took part in a scenario-based experiment where they saw a photograph of either an attractive or unattractive defendant who was convicted of committing either a violent or a nonviolent crime. Participants indicated whether they believed the defendant was guilty of the crime and then recommended how long the defendant should be incarcerated (number of months) for the crime.

Method

Participants

Forty-five participants (15 men, 30 women) who ranged in age from 18 to 26 yrs (M = 20.4) took part in this study. All participants were undergraduate students, most of who signed up to earn extra credit for an introductory psychology class. The remaining members of this convenience sample were recruited by word of mouth and personal emails.

Design and Materials

This study used a 2 (attractive vs. unattractive defendant) x 2 (violent vs. nonviolent crime) factorial design. Participants were assigned to one of four groups to view a photograph and to evaluate a crime scenario. The relative attractiveness of the two defendant photos was determined by pilot testing. Pilot participants rated six photographs on a scale ranging from 1 (very unattractive) to 7 (very attractive). The highest and lowest scoring photos were selected as stimulus photos for the study.

Second-level headings are italicized and appear at the left margin.

Statistical symbols appear in italics.

The materials subsection describes any resources used in the experiment.

Writing in the first person is permitted by APA style.

The hypothesis is always presented before the Method section.

First-level headings are centered but not italicized.

Participant information discloses demographic details and reasons for participation.

Method sections are written in the past tense.

The violent and categorically very serious crime related to an assault and robbery of a nurse while walking back to her car after her shift, whereas the mildly serious, nonviolent crime involved a defendant selling pirated music over the Internet. A brief questionnaire asked participants about the defendant's responsibility for the crime (i.e., a manipulation check to verify the defendant's perceived guilt for the crime) and to sentence the defendant to some number of months (if any) incarceration (the dependent measure). A second questionnaire asked them to rate the attractiveness of the defendant (a second manipulation check to confirm that the defendant photos received ratings similar to the pilot sample), and to complete some demographic questions (e.g., participants' age, sex).

Procedure

Participants began by reading and signing an Informed Consent form. Participant groups were shown the photograph of either the attractive or unattractive defendant and then read the scenario describing the very serious or mildly serious crime. Participants in the serious crime condition read this scenario:

> The defendant, a 30-year-old male, was convicted of assaulting and robbing a 34-year-old female on November 5, 2004. The victim, a nurse, was walking to her car after her shift to return home. When she left the hospital, the nurse did not have time to wait for the security escort service to take her to her car. As the victim was getting into her car, she was jumped from behind by the defendant, who tried to grab her purse. The nurse managed to set off the panic button in her car. As she did so, the defendant began to beat her about the head and neck, so she gave up her purse. The defendant then fled from the scene. Because the defendant was not wearing any type of mask, the victim was able to describe him and subsequently identify him in a lineup.

Those participants who received the nonviolent scenario read about a 30-year-old defendant male who sold CDs of pirated music downloaded from the Internet. The nonviolent scenario was of equal length and had the same level of detail found in the violent scenario (copies of all materials can be obtained from the author).

Participants then completed the questionnaire assessing the defendant's guilt and recommended how long the defendant should be incarcerated (number of months). Once the manipulation check and dependent measure were collected, participants were then handed the second short questionnaire. After finishing

---

Quotations of 40 words or more should be indented.

the second questionnaire, participants were given a debriefing in accordance with the American Psychological Association's Ethical Principles when using human research participants (American Psychological Association, 2003). Participants were asked not to discuss the experiment with other individuals until data collection was complete.

Results

Preliminary analyses indicated there were no effects due to participants' sex. Thus this variable will not be considered further. Regardless of whether they read about the violent or the nonviolent scenario, all participants believed that both the attractive and less attractive defendants were guilty of their crimes.

Did the presence of a violent crime reduce or eliminate the ALE bias toward the attractive defendant? A two-way factorial analysis of variance (ANOVA) was conducted to evaluate the effect of defendant attractiveness and seriousness of the crime on length of the sentences recommended by the participants. Table 1 presents the mean recommended sentence by condition. Despite the fact that the means in Table 1 appear to confirm the prediction, neither of the two main effects or the interaction reached statistical significance, Fs $(1, 41) < 1.0$, $p =$ ns. An examination of the standard deviations associated with the means reveals a great deal of variation in participant responses in each of the four conditions (see Table 1).

[Insert Table 1 about here]

To verify that the attractive defendant was perceived as more attractive than his unattractive counterpart, the second manipulation check was analyzed. Confirming the pretest findings, the attractive defendant ($M = 4.2$) was rated as more attractive than the less attractive target ($M = 1.8$), t (43) = 2.64, $p < .05$.

Discussion

This study explored whether a defendant's perceived level of attractiveness and the nature of a crime (violent or nonviolent) influenced sentencing recommendations. I hypothesized that a defendant who was more attractive would be sentenced less severely than a less attractive defendant. This ALE bias, however, was expected to occur only in the case of a nonviolent crime. When a crime was violent, an attractive defendant would be judged as harshly as an unattractive defendant.

Unlike previous studies that have found significant links between the attractiveness of a defendant and the (shorter) length of his sentence (Darby & Jeffers, 1988; Sigall & Ostrove, 1975), the present study was not able to support the influence of the ALE bias. Possibly different types of data collection (e.g.,

---

Main sections of APA-style papers follow one another with no page breaks.

Abbreviations are identified the first time they are used.

APA style does not require a "call out" for a table's placement but such directions are helpful in student papers.

The Discussion section reviews what was or was not found in the experiment.

A study's shortcomings are identified and discussed in the Discussion section.

individual rather than group sessions) and larger sample sizes affected the findings in prior studies. Perhaps the defendant scenarios in this study should have received the same rigorous pilot testing that was used to verify the attractiveness of the defendant photographs. More systematic pilot testing might have suggested appropriate changes to the crime scenarios or even the study's procedure. Unfortunately, neither time nor a sufficient number of extra participants were available.

Fitting the Crime to Campus Audiences

Future researchers may want to choose different crime scenarios which will better capture the perceived differences between violent and nonviolent crimes in the minds of college-age research participants. Staging the violent crime scenario in a campus setting and making the victim a traditional-aged student could elicit stronger, more consistent opinions regarding sentencing. What about the nonviolent crime scenario? Perhaps pirated software, a common problem on college campuses, is not taken very seriously by participants who are college students. Many college students routinely swap downloaded music from the Internet with their friends. Such trades may not be viewed as questionable or illegal activities. A more typical campus crime, such as the theft of a bicycle, a backpack, or a wallet, might trigger a different reaction from college-aged participants. Altering the research design in order to be reliant on fewer participants is another possibility. Researchers might consider using a within-subjects design so that participants can serve in both conditions, rating both the violent and nonviolent crimes and both the attractive and unattractive defendants. However, careful planning would be necessary to omit any carryover effects.

Conclusion

The absence of anticipated effects in this experiment does not undo the many studies demonstrating that attractive people get bigger breaks than less attractive people in our society. Further research into this field may come to show that the defendant characteristics do, in fact, have a bearing on how they are sentenced. With time, the jury system may have to be changed accordingly in order to accommodate all types of people, so as to really be impartial to the influence of personal characteristics.

Possible refinements to future research efforts are suggested.

APA-style references appear in alphabetical order and use a "hanging indent" style.

References

Abwender, D. A., & Hough, K. (2001). Interactive effects of characteristics of defendant and mock juror on U.S. participants' judgment and sentencing recommendations. *The Journal of Social Psychology, 141*, 603–615.

American Psychological Association. (2002). *Ethical principles of psychologists and code of conduct.* Retrieved November 19, 2004, from http://www.apa.org/ethics/code2002.html

Bubnis, C. (1995). *The effects of expert testimony and gender on juror decision making.* Unpublished honors thesis, Moravian College, Bethlehem, PA.

Darby, B. W., & Jeffers, D. (1988). The effects of defendant and juror attractiveness on simulated courtroom trial decisions. *Social Behavior and Personality, 16*, 39–50.

Deitz, S. R., & Byrnes, L. E. (1981). Attribution of responsibility for sexual assault: The influence of observer empathy and defendant occupation and attractiveness. *The Journal of Psychology, 108*, 17–29.

Dion, K., Bersheid, E., & Walster, E. (1972). What is beautiful is good. *Journal of Personality and Social Psychology, 24*, 285–290.

Efran, M. G. (1974). The effect of physical appearance on judgments of guilt, interpersonal attractiveness, and severity of recommended punishment in a simulated jury task. *Journal of Research in Personality, 8*, 45–54.

Gray, D. B., & Ashmore, R. D. (1976). Biasing influence of defendants' characteristics on simulated sentencing. *Psychological Reports, 38(3, Pt. 1)*, 727–738.

McKelvie, S. J., & Coley, J. (1993). Effects of crime seriousness and offender facial attractiveness on recommended treatment. *Social Behavior and Personality, 21*, 265–277.

Sigall, H., & Ostrove, N. (1975). Beautiful but dangerous: Effects of offender attractiveness and nature of the crime on juridical judgment. *Journal of Personality and Social Psychology, 31*, 410–414.

Stewart, J. E. (1980). Defendant's attractiveness as a factor in the outcome of criminal trials: An observational study. *Journal of Applied Social Psychology, 10*, 348–361.

The References section always begins on a new page.

Journal names, book titles, and volume numbers are italicized.

References use an ampersand (&) rather than "and" between author names.

The initial letter of the first word of any title or subtitle, as well as any proper nouns, is capitalized.

An Author Note appears on a separate page after the References.

The second paragraph is reserved for acknowledgments and notes to readers.

The third paragraph lists contact information.

The first paragraph identifies the author and any departmental affiliation.

Attractiveness and Sentencing   9

Author Notes

Laura Sahlender, Department of Psychology.

I thank the six members of my lab group for allowing me to use their photographs during pilot testing of the stimulus materials. Copies of all the materials used in this experiment are available from the author.

Correspondence concerning this research should be sent to Laura Sahlender, c/o the Department of Psychology, Moravian College, 1200 Main Street, Bethlehem, PA 18018-6650 or by e-mail to lss05@mc.edu.

Table 1

Mean Scores in Sentencing by Defendant Attractiveness and Violence of Crime

Scenario	Mean sentence	(Standard deviation)	*n* per cell
Attractive defendant			
Violent crime	52.55	(22.95)	11
Nonviolent crime	12.00	(10.98)	11
Unattractive defendant			
Violent crime	54.70	(16.25)	10
Nonviolent crime	15.31	(9.93)	13

Note: Higher numbers refer to longer recommended time (in months) incarceration.

References

Abrams, D., Viki, G. T., Masser, B., & Bohner, G. (2003). Perceptions of stranger and acquaintance rape: The role of benevolent and hostile sexism in victim blame and rape proclivity. *Journal of Personality and Social Psychology, 84*, 111–125.

Abelson, R. P. (1995). *Statistics as principled argument.* Hillsdale, NJ: Erlbaum.

Abramson, L. Y., Metalsky, F. I., & Alloy, L. B. (1989). Hopelessness depression: A theory-based subtype of depression. *Psychological Review, 96*(2), 358–372.

Adair, J. G. (1984). The Hawthorne Effect: A reconsideration of the methodological artifact. *Journal of Applied Psychology, 69*, 334–345.

Adair, J. G., Dushenko, T. W., & Lindsay, R. C. L. (1985). Ethical regulations and their impact on research practice. *American Psychologist, 40*, 59–72.

Adorno, T. W., Frenkel-Brunswik, E., Levinson, D. J., & Sanford, R. N. (1950). *The authoritarian personality.* New York: Harper and Row.

Albarracin, D., Johnson, B. T., & Zanna, M. P. (Eds.). (2005). *The handbook of attitudes.* Mahwah, NJ: Erlbaum.

Allen, M. (1991). Meta-analysis comparing the persuasiveness of one-sided and two-sided messages. *Western Journal of Speech Communication, 55*, 390–404.

Allport, G. W. (1985). The historical background of modern social psychology. In G. Lindzey & E. Aronson (Eds.), *The handbook of social psychology* (Vol. 1, 1–46). New York: Random House.

American Psychological Association. (1982). *Ethical principles in the conduct of research with human participants.* Washington, DC: Author.

American Psychological Association. (1993). *Guidelines for ethical conduct in the care and use of animals.* Washington, DC: Author.

American Psychological Association. (2001). *Publication manual of the American Psychological Association* (5th ed.). Washington, DC: Author.

American Psychological Association. (2002). *Ethical principles of psychologists and the code of conduct.* Retrieved May 9, 2007, from www.apa.org/ethics/code2002.html#8

American Psychological Association. (2004). *Thesaurus of psychological index terms* (10th ed.). Washington, DC: Author.

Ames, D. R. (2004). Strategies for social inference: A similarity contingency model of projection and stereotyping in attribute prevalence estimates. *Journal of Personality and Social Psychology, 87*, 573–585.

Anastasi, A., & Urbina, S. (1996). *Psychological testing* (7th ed.). New York: Prentice Hall.

Anderson, C. A. (1989). Temperature and aggression: Ubiquitous effects of heat on occurrence of human violence. *Psychological Bulletin, 106,* 74–96.

Anderson, C. A., & Anderson, D. C. (1984). Ambient temperature and violent crime: Tests of the linear and curvilinear hypothesis. *Journal of Personality and Social Psychology, 46,* 91–97.

Arkin, R. M., & Burger, J. M. (1980). Effects of unit relation tendencies on interpersonal attractions. *Social Psychology Quarterly, 43,* 380–391.

Aronson, E., Brewer, M., & Carlsmith, J. M. (1985). Experimentation in social psychology. In G. Lindzey & E. Aronson (Eds.), *Handbook of social psychology* (3rd ed., Vol. 1, pp. 441–486). New York: Random House.

Aronson, E., & Carlsmith, J. M. (1968). Experimentation in social psychology. In G. Lindzey & E. Aronson (Eds.), *The handbook of social psychology* (2nd ed., Vol. 2, pp. 1–79). Reading, MA: Addison-Wesley.

Aronson, E., Ellsworth, P. C., Carlsmith, J. M., & Gonzales, M. H. (1990). *Methods of research in social psychology* (2nd ed.). New York: McGraw-Hill.

Aronson, E., & Linder, D. (1965). Gain and loss of esteem as determinants of interpersonal attraction. *Journal of Experimental Social Psychology, 1,* 156–171.

Aronson, E., & Mills, J. (1959). The effects of severity of initiation on liking for a group. *Journal of Abnormal and Social Psychology, 59,* 177–181.

Aronson, E., Wilson, T. D., & Akert, R. M. (1994). *Social psychology: The heart and the mind.* New York: Harper Collins.

Aronson, E., Wilson, T. D., & Brewer, M. B. (1998). Experimentation in social psychology. In D. T. Gilbert, S. T. Fiske, & G. Lindzey (Eds.), *The handbook of social psychology* (pp. 99–142). New York: McGraw-Hill.

Asch, S. (1951). Effects of group pressure upon the modification and distortion of judgment. In H. Guetzkow (Ed.), *Groups, leadership, and men* (pp. 177–190). Pittsburgh, PA: Carnegie Press.

Asch, S. E. (1955). Opinions and social pressure. *Scientific American, 193*(5), 31–35.

Asch, S. E. (1956). Studies of independence and conformity: A minority of one against a unanimous majority. *Psychological Monographs, 70*(9, Whole No. 416).

Asch, S. E. (1961). Issues in the study of social influences on judgment. In I. A. Berg & B. M Bass (Eds.), *Conformity and deviation* (pp. 143–158). New York: Harper.

Babyak, M., Snyder, C. R., & Yoshinobu, L. (1993). Psychometric properties of the Hope Scale: A confirmatory factor analysis. *Journal of Research in Personality, 27,* 154–169.

Baron, R. A., & Richardson, D. R. (1994). *Human aggression.* New York: Plenum Press.

Baron, R. M., & Kenny, D. A. (1986). The moderator–mediator variable distinction in social psychological research: Conceptual, strategic, and statistical considerations. *Journal of Personality and Social Psychology, 51,* 1173–1182.

Baron, R. S., Moore, D., & Sanders, G. S. (1978). Distraction as a source of drive in social facilitation research. *Journal of Personality and Social Psychology, 36,* 816–824.

Bar-Tal, D., & Saxe, L. (1976). Perceptions of similarly and dissimilarly attractive couples and individuals. *Journal of Personality and Social Psychology, 33,* 772–781.

Batson, C. D. (1987). Prosocial motivation: Is it ever truly altruism? In L. Berkowitz (Ed.), *Advances in experimental social psychology* (Vol. 20, pp. 65–122). New York: Academic Press.

Batson, C. D. (1991). *The altruistic question: Toward a social-psychological answer.* Hillsdale, NJ: Erlbaum.

Batson, C. D. (1995). Prosocial motivation: Why do we help others? In A. Tesser (Ed.), *Advanced social psychology* (pp. 332–381). New York: McGraw-Hill.

Batson, C. D., Ahmad, N., Lishner, D. A., & Tsang, J.-A. (2002). Empathy and altruism. In C. R. Snyder & S. J. Lopez (Eds.), *Handbook of positive psychology* (pp. 485–498). New York: Oxford University Press.

Baum, A., Gatchel, R. J., & Schaeffer, M. A. (1983). Emotional, behavioral, and physiological effects of chronic stress at Three Mile Island. *Journal of Consulting and Clinical Psychology*, *51*, 565–572.

Baumeister, R. F. (1982). A self-presentational view of social interaction. *Psychological Bulletin*, *91*, 3–26.

Baumeister, R. F., Vohs, K. D., & Funder, D. C. (2007). Psychology as the science of self-reports and finger movements: Whatever happened to actual behaviour? *Perspectives on Psychological Science*, *2*, 396–403.

Baumrind, D. (1964). Some thoughts on the ethics of research: After reading Milgram's "Behavioral study of obedience." *American Psychologist*, *19*, 421–423.

Baumrind, D. (1985). Research using intention deception: Ethical issues revisited. *American Psychologist*, *40*, 165–174.

Beals, W. B., Sebring, H. L., & Crawford, J. T. (1946–1949). Judgment of the Nuremberg Doctors Trial Tribunal. *Trials of war criminals before the Nuremberg Military Tribunals*. Washington, DC: U.S. Government Printing Office.

Beaman, A. L., Barnes, P. J., Klentz, B., & McQuirk, B. (1978). Increasing helping rates through information dissemination: Teaching pays. *Personality and Social Psychology Bulletin*, *4*, 406–411.

Bem, D. J. (1972). Self-perception theory. In L. Berkowitz (Ed.), *Advances in experimental social psychology* (Vol. 6, pp. 1–62). New York: Academic Press.

Bem, D. J. (1987). Writing the empirical journal article. In M. P. Zanna & J. M. Darley (Eds.), *The compleat academic: A practical guide for the beginning social scientist* (pp. 171–201). New York: Random House.

Bem, D. J. (1995). Writing a review article for *Psychological Bulletin*. *Psychological Bulletin*, *118*, 172–177.

Bem, D. J. (2000). Writing an empirical article. In R. J. Sternberg (Ed.), *Guide to publishing in psychology journals* (pp. 3–16). Cambridge, UK: Cambridge University Press.

Bennett, D. J. (1998). *Randomness*. Cambridge, MA: Harvard University Press.

Benoit, W. L., & Strathman, A. (2004). Source credibility and the Elaboration Likelihood Model. In J. S. Seiter & R. H. Gass (Eds.), *Perspectives on persuasion, social influence, and compliance gaining* (pp. 95–111). Boston, MA: Pearson Education.

Berkowitz, L. (1993). *Aggression: Its causes, consequences, and control*. New York: McGraw-Hill.

Berkowitz, L., & LePage, A. (1967). Weapons as aggression-eliciting stimuli. *Journal of Personality and Social Psychology*, *7*, 202–207.

Bickman, L. (1981). Some distinctions between basic and applied approaches. In L. Bickman (Ed.), *Applied social psychology annual* (Vol. 2, pp. 23–44). Newbury Park, CA: Sage.

Birnbaum, M. H. (2001). *Introduction to behavioral research on the Internet*. Upper Saddle River, NJ: Prentice Hall.

Blass, T. (Ed.). (2000). *Obedience to authority: Current perspectives on the Milgram paradigm*. Mahwah, NJ: Erlbaum.

Blass, T. (2004). *The man who shocked the world: The life and legacy of Stanley Milgram.* New York: Basic Books.

Bond, C. F., & Titus, L. J. (1983). Social facilitation: A meta-analysis of 241 studies. *Psychological Bulletin, 94,* 265–292.

Borgida, E., & Nisbett, R. E. (1977). The differential impact of abstract vs. concrete information on decisions. *Journal of Applied Social Psychology, 7,* 258–271.

Breckler, S. J. (1990). Applications of covariance structure modeling in psychology: Cause for concern? *Psychological Bulletin, 107,* 260–273.

Brendl, C. M., Markman, A. B., & Messner, C. (2001). How do indirect measures of evaluation work? Evaluating the inference of prejudice in the Implicit Association Test. *Journal of Personality and Social Psychology, 81,* 760–773.

Brickman, P., Coates, D., & Janoff-Bulman, R. J. (1978). Lottery winners and accident victims: Is happiness relative? *Journal of Personality and Social Psychology, 36,* 917–927.

Burke, P. J. (Ed.). (2006). *Contemporary social psychological theories.* Stanford, CA: Stanford University Press.

Buss, D. M. (2000). *The dangerous passion: Why jealous is as necessary as love and sex.* New York: The Free Press.

Byrne, D. (1971). *The attraction paradigm.* New York: Academic Press.

Cacioppo, J. T., & Berntson, G. G. (Eds.). (2004). *Essays in social neuroscience.* Cambridge, MA: MIT Press.

Cacioppo, J. T., Harkins, S. G., & Petty, R. E. (1981). The nature of attitudes and cognitive responses and their relationship to behavior. In R. Petty, T. Ostrom, & T. Brock (Eds.), *Cognitive responses in persuasion* (pp. 31–54). Hillsdale, NJ: Erlbaum.

Cacioppo, J. T., & Petty, R. E. (1981). Social psychological procedures for cognitive response assessment: The thought-listing techniques. In T. V. Merluzzi, C. R. Glass, & M. Genest (Eds.), *Cognitive assessment* (pp. 309–342). New York: New York University Press.

Cacioppo, J. T., & Petty, R. E. (1986). Social processes. In M. G. H. Coles, E. Donchin, & S. W. Porges (Eds.), *Psychophysiology* (pp. 646–679). New York: Guilford.

Cacioppo, J. T., & Tassinary, L. G. (Eds.). (1990). *Handbook of psychophysiology: Physical, social, and inferential elements.* New York: Cambridge University Press.

Cacioppo, J. T., Tassinary, L. G., & Berntson, G. (Eds.). (2000). *Handbook of psychophysiology.* New York: Cambridge University Press.

Cacioppo, J. T., Visser, P. S., & Pickett, C. L. (Eds.). (2005). *Social neuroscience: People thinking about people.* Cambridge, MA: MIT Press.

Calfee, R. (2000). What does it all mean: The discussion. In R. J. Sternberg (Ed.), *Guide to publishing in psychology journals* (pp. 133–145). New York: Cambridge University Press.

Campbell, D. T. (1957). Factors relevant to validity of experiments in social settings. *Psychological Bulletin, 54,* 297–312.

Campbell, D. T. (1969). Reforms as experiments. *American Psychologist, 24,* 409–429.

Campbell, D. T., & Fiske, D. W. (1959). Convergent and discriminant validation by the multitrait-multimethod matrix. *Psychological Bulletin, 56,* 81–105.

Campbell, D. T., & Stanley, J. C. (1966). *Experimental and quasi-experimental designs for research.* Skokie, IL: Rand McNally.

Canter, M. B., Bennett, B. E., Jones, S. E., & Nagy, T. F. (1994). *Ethics for psychologists: A commentary on the APA Ethics Code.* Washington, DC: American Psychological Association.

Caplan, B. (1995). Division 22 presidential address: Choose your words! *Rehabilitation Psychology, 40,* 233–240.

Carey, B. (2006, September 12). Lady Macbeth not alone in her quest for spotlessness. *The New York Times,* F5.

Carlsmith, J. M., & Anderson, C. A. (1979). Ambient temperature and the occurrence of collective violence: A new analysis. *Journal of Personality and Social Psychology, 37,* 337–344.

Carvallo, M., & Pelham, B. W. (2006). When fiends become friends: The need to belong and perceptions of personal and group discrimination. *Journal of Personality and Social Psychology, 90,* 94–108.

Cassell, E. J. (2002). Compassion. In C. R. Snyder & S. J. Lopez (Eds.), *Handbook of positive psychology* (pp. 434–445). New York: Oxford University Press.

Chalfonte, B. L., & Johnson, M. K. (1996). Feature memory and binding in young and older adults. *Memory and Cognition, 24,* 403–416.

Chastain, G., & Landrum, R. E. (Eds.). (1999). *Protecting human subjects: Departmental subject pools and institutional review boards.* Washington, DC: American Psychological Association.

Christensen, L. (1988). Deception in psychological research: When is its use justified? *Personality and Social Psychology Bulletin, 14,* 664–675.

Cialdini, R. B. (2000). *Influence: Science and practice* (4th ed.). New York: Allyn & Bacon.

Cialdini, R. B., & Ascani, K. (1976). Test of a concession procedure for inducing verbal, behavioral, and further compliance with a request to give blood. *Journal of Applied Psychology, 61,* 295–300.

Cialdini, R. B., Borden, R., Thorne, A., Walker, M., Freeman, S., & Sloan, L. T. (1976). Basking in reflected glory: Three (football) field studies. *Journal of Personality and Social Psychology, 34,* 366–375.

Cialdini, R. B., & Richardson, K. D. (1980). Two indirect tactics of image management: Basking and blasting. *Journal of Personality and Social Psychology, 39,* 406–415.

Cialdini, R. B., Vincent, J. E., Lewis, S. K., Catalan, J. Wheeler, D., & Darby, B. L. (1975). Reciprocal concessions procedure for inducing compliance: The door-in-the-face technique. *Journal of Personality and Social Psychology, 31,* 206–215.

Clark, M. S., & Mills, J. (1993). The difference between people in communal and exchange relationships: What it is and is not. *Journal of Personality and Social Psychology, 19,* 684–691.

Clark, R. D., & Word, L. E. (1972). Why don't bystanders help? Because of ambiguity? *Journal of Personality and Social Psychology, 24,* 392–401.

Clary, E. G., Snyder, M., Ridge, R. D., Miene, P., & Haugen, J. (1994). Matching messages to motives in persuasion: A functional approach to promoting volunteerism. *Journal of Applied Social Psychology, 24,* 1129–1149.

Clore, G. L. (1992). Cognitive phenomenology: Feelings and the construction of judgment. In L. I. Martin & A. Tesser (Eds.), *The construction of social judgments* (pp. 133–163). Hillsdale, NJ: Erlbaum.

Cohen, D., Nisbett, R. E., Bowdle, B., & Schwartz, N. (1996). Insult, aggression, and the southern culture of honor: An "experimental ethnography." *Journal of Personality and Social Psychology, 70,* 945–960.

Cohen, G. L., Garcia, J., Apfel, N., & Master, A. (2006). Reducing the racial achievement gap: A social-psychological intervention. *Science, 313,* 1307–1310.

Cohen, J. (1988). *Statistical power analysis for the behavioral sciences* (2nd ed.). Hillsdale, NJ: Erlbaum.

Cohen, J., & Cohen, C. (1983). *Applied multiple regression/correlation analysis for the behavioral sciences* (2nd ed.). Hillsdale, NJ: Erlbaum.

Connor Snibbe, A., & Markus, H. R. (2005). You can't always get what you want: Educational attainment, agency, and choice. *Journal of Personality and Social Psychology, 88,* 703–720.

Conway, L. G., III. (2004). Social contagion of time perception. *Journal of Experimental Social Psychology, 40,* 113–120.

Cook, T. D., & Campbell, D. T. (1979). *Quasi-experimentation: Design and analysis issues for field settings.* Skokie, IL: Randy McNally.

Converse, J. M., & Presser, S. (1986). *Survey questions: Handcrafting the standardized questionnaire.* Newbury Park, CA: Sage.

Cooper, H. M., & Hedges, L. V. (Eds.). (1994). *The handbook of research synthesis.* New York: Russell Sage.

Cooper, J. (2007). *Cognitive dissonance: Fifty years of a classic theory.* Newbury Park, CA: Sage.

Cooper, W. H. (1981). Ubiquitous halo. *Psychological Bulletin, 90,* 218–244.

Cozby, P. C. (1997). *Methods of behavioral research* (6th ed.). Mountain View, CA: Mayfield.

Cronbach, L. J. (1951). Coefficient alpha and the internal structure of tests. *Psychometricka, 16,* 297–334.

Crowne, D. P., & Marlowe, D. (1960). A new scale of social desirability independent of psychopathology. *Journal of Consulting Psychology, 24,* 349–354.

Croyle, R. T., & Cooper, J. (1983). Dissonance arousal: Physiological evidence. *Journal of Personality and Social Psychology, 45,* 782–791.

Csikszentmihalyi, M. (1997). *Finding flow: The psychology of engagement with everyday life.* New York: Basic Books.

Csikszentmihalyi, M., & Larson, R. (1984). *Being adolescent.* New York: Basic Books.

Csikszentmihalyi, M., & Larson, R. (1987). Validity and reliability of the experience sampling method. *Journal of Nervous and Mental Disease, 175,* 526–536.

Csikszentmihalyi, M., & LeFevre, J. (1989). Optimal experience in work and leisure. *Journal of Personality and Social Psychology, 56,* 815–822.

Danner, D. D., Snowdon, D. A., & Friesen, W. V. (2001). Positive emotions in early life and longevity: Findings from the nun study. *Journal of Personality and Social Psychology, 80,* 804–813.

Darley, J. M., & Latané, B. (1968). Bystander intervention in emergencies: Diffusion of responsibility. *Journal of Personality and Social Psychology, 8,* 377–383.

Darley, J. M., Teger, A., & Lewis, L. (1973). Do groups always inhibit individuals' responses to potential emergencies? *Journal of Personality and Social Psychology, 26,* 395–399.

Dawes, R. M. (1972). *Fundamentals of attitude measurement.* New York: Wiley.

Dawes, R. M. (1980). Social dilemmas. *Annual Review of Psychology, 31,* 169–193.

Dawes, R. M. (1991, June). *Discovering "human nature" versus discovering how people cope with the task of getting through college: An extension of Sears's argument.* Paper presented at the Third Annual Convention of the American Psychological Society, Washington, DC.

DePaulo, B. M., & Friedman, H. S. (1998). Nonverbal communication. In D. T. Gilbert, S. T. Fiske, & G. Lindzey (Eds.), *The handbook of social psychology* (Vol. 2, pp. 3–40). New York: McGraw-Hill.

DePaulo, B. M., Lanier, K., & Davis, T. (1983). Detecting the deceit of the motivated liar. *Journal of Personality and Social Psychology, 45,* 1096–1103.

Derlega, V., Metts, S., Petronio, S., & Margulis, S. T. (1993). *Self-disclosure.* Newbury Park, CA: Sage.

Derryberry, D., & Tucker, D. M. (1994). Motivating the focus of attention. In P. M. Neidenthal & S. Kitayama (Eds.), *The heart's eye: Emotional influences in perception and attention* (pp. 167–196). San Diego, CA: Academic Press.

Devine, P. G. (1989). Stereotypes and prejudice: Their automatic and controlled components. *Journal of Personality and Social Psychology, 56,* 5–18.

Diener, E. (1976). Effects of prior destructive behavior, anonymity, and group presence on deindividuation and aggression. *Journal of Personality and Social Psychology, 33,* 497–507.

Diener, E., & Crandall, R. (1978). *Ethics in social and behavioral research.* Chicago: University of Chicago Press.

DiLalla, D. L., & Dollinger, S. J. (2006). Cleaning up data and running preliminary analyses. In F. T. L. Leong & J. Austin (Eds.), *The psychology research handbook* (2nd ed., pp. 241–253). Thousand Oaks, CA: Sage.

Dillman, D. A. (1978). *Mail and telephone surveys: The total design method.* New York: Wiley.

Dillman, D. A. (2000). *Mail and Internet surveys: The tailored design method.* New York: Wiley.

Dion, K. K., Berscheid, E., & Walster, E. (1972). What is beautiful is good. *Journal of Personality and Social Psychology, 24,* 285–290.

Dollard, J., Doob, L. W., Miller, N. E., Mowrer, O. H., & Sears, R. R. (1939). *Frustration and aggression.* New Haven, CT: Yale University Press.

Dovidio, J., Kwakami, K., Johnson, C., Johnson, B., & Howard, A. (1997). On the nature of prejudice: Automatic and controlled processes. *Journal of Experimental Social Psychology, 33,* 510–540.

Duncker, K. (1945). On problem solving. *Psychological Monographs, 58*(5, Whole No. 270).

Dunn, D. S. (1999). *The practical researcher: A student guide to conducting psychological research.* New York: McGraw-Hill.

Dunn, D. S. (2001). *Statistics and data analysis for the behavioral sciences.* New York: McGraw-Hill.

Dunn, D. S. (2008). *A short guide to writing about psychology* (2nd ed.). New York: Longman.

Dunn, D. S., & Elliott, T. R. (2005). Revisiting a constructive classic: Wright's *Physical Disability: A Psychosocial Approach. Rehabilitation Psychology, 50,* 183–189.

Dunn, D. S., & Wilson, T. D. (1990). When the stakes are high: A limit to the illusion of control effect. *Social Cognition, 8,* 305–323.

Duval, S., & Wicklund, R. A. (1972). *A theory of objective self awareness.* Oxford: Academic Press.

Eagly, A. H., Ashmore, R. D., Makhijani, M. G., & Longo, L. C. (1991). What is beautiful is good, but . . . : A meta-analytic review of research on the physical attractiveness stereotype. *Psychological Bulletin, 110,* 109–128.

Eagly, A., H., & Chaiken, S. (1975). An attributional analysis of communicator characteristics on opinion change: The case of communicator attractiveness. *Journal of Personality and Social Psychology, 32*, 136–144.

Easterbrook, J. A. (1959). The effect of emotion on cue utilization and the organization of behavior. *Psychological Review, 66*, 183–201.

Ebbesen, E. B., Kjos, G. L., & Konecni, V. (1976). Spatial ecology: Its effects on the choice of friends and enemies. *Journal of Experimental Social Psychology, 12*, 505–518.

Eckland, B. (1968). Theories of mate selection. *Social Biology, 15*, 71–84.

Edwards, A. L., & Thurstone, L. L. (1952). An internal consistency check for scale values determined by the method of successive intervals. *Psychometrika, 17*, 169–180.

Ekman, P., & Friesen, W. V. (1969). Nonverbal leakage clues to deception. *Psychiatry, 32*, 290–292.

Ekman, P., & Friesen, W. V. (1978). *Facial Action Coding System: A technique for the measurement of facial movement.* Palo Alto, CA: Consulting Psychologists Press.

Eisenberger, N. I., Lieberman, M. D., & Williams, K. D. (2003). Does rejection hurt? An fMRI study of social exclusion. *Science, 302*, 290–292.

Ellsworth, P. C., Carlsmith, J. M., & Henson, A. (1972). Staring as a stimulus to flight in humans: A series of field experiments. *Journal of Personality and Social Psychology, 21*, 302–311.

Ellsworth, P. C., & Smith, C. A. (1988). Shades of joy: Patterns of appraisal differentiating pleasant emotions. *Cognition and Emotion, 2*, 301–331.

Epley, N., & Huff, C. W. (1998). Suspicion, affective response, and educational benefit as a result of deception in psychology research. *Personality and Social Psychology Bulletin, 24*, 759–768.

Ericsson, K. A., & Simon, H. A. (1980). Verbal reports as data. *Psychological Review, 87*, 215–251.

Ericsson, K. A., & Simon, H. A. (1993). *Protocol analysis: Verbal reports as data* (Rev. ed.). Cambridge, MA: MIT Press.

Estrada, C. A., Isen, A. M., & Young, M. J. (1994). Positive affect improves creative problem solving and influences reported source of practice satisfaction in physicians. *Motivation and Emotion, 18*, 285–299.

Exline, R. V. (1971). Visual interaction: The glance of power and preference. *Nebraska Symposium on Motivation* (pp. 163–206). Lincoln: University of Nebraska Press.

Feingold, A. (1992). Good looking people are not what we think. *Psychological Bulletin, 111*, 304–341.

Fenigstein, A. (1984). Self-consciousness and the overperception of self as a target. *Journal of Personality and Social Psychology, 47*, 860–870.

Ferguson, E., & Bibby, P. (2004). The design and analysis of quasi-experimental field research. In G. M. Breakwell (Ed.), *Doing social psychology research* (pp. 93–127). Oxford: Blackwell.

Festinger, L. (1957). *A theory of cognitive dissonance.* Stanford, CA: Stanford University Press.

Festinger, L., & Carlsmith, J. M. (1959). Cognitive consequences of forced compliance. *Journal of Abnormal and Social Psychology, 58*, 203–210.

Festinger, L., Schachter, S., & Back, K. (1950). *Social pressures in informal groups.* Stanford, CA: Stanford University Press.

Fillenbaum, S. (1966). Prior deception and subsequent experimental performance: The "faithful" subject. *Journal of Personality and Social Psychology, 4,* 532–537.

Fischoff, B. (1975). Hindsight is not equal to foresight: The effect of outcome knowledge on judgment under uncertainty. *Journal of Experimental Psychology: Human Perception and Performance, 1,* 288–299.

Fischoff, B. (1982). For those condemned to study the past: Heuristics and biases in hindsight. In D. Kahneman, P. Slovic, & A. Tversky (Eds.), *Judgment under uncertainty: Heuristics and biases* (pp. 201–208). Cambridge, UK: Cambridge University Press.

Fiske, S. T. (2004). *Social beings: A core motives approach to social psychology.* New York: Wiley.

Flick, U. (1998). *An introduction to qualitative research.* London: Sage.

Fraley, R. C. (2004). *How to conduct behavioral research over the Internet: A beginner's guide to HTML and CGI/Perl.* New York: Guilford.

Frank, M. G., Ekman, P., & Friesen, W. V. (1993). Behavioral markers and recognizability of the smile of enjoyment. *Journal of Personality and Social Psychology, 64,* 83–93.

Frankl, V. (1985). *Man's search for meaning* (Rev. & updated). New York: Washington Square Press.

Fredrickson, B. L. (1998). What good are positive emotions? *Review of General Psychology, 2,* 300–319.

Frick, A., Bachtiger, M. T., & Reips, U.-D. (2001). Financial incentives, personal information and drop-out in online studies. In U.-D. Reips & M. Bosnjak (Eds.), *Dimensions of Internet science* (pp. 209–219). Lengerich, Germany: Pabst Science Publishers.

Funder, D. C. (1999). *Personality judgment: A realistic approach to person perception.* New York: Academic Press.

Funder, D. C. (2004). *The personality puzzle* (3rd ed.). New York: Norton.

Gaertner, S. L., & Dovidio, J. F. (1986). The aversive form of racism. In J. F. Dovidio & S. L. Gaertner (Eds.), *Prejudice, discrimination, and racism* (pp. 61–89). Orlando, FL: Academic Press.

Gardner, M. (1975). *Mathematical carnival.* New York: Knopf.

Garner, W. R., Hake, H. W., & Eriksen, C. W. (1956). Operationism and the concept of perception. *Psychological Review, 63,* 149–159.

Gergen, K. E. (1973). Social psychology as history. *Journal of Personality and Social Psychology, 26,* 309–320.

Gergen, K. E. (1976). Social psychology, science and history. *Personality and Social Psychology Bulletin, 2,* 373–383.

Gergen, K. E. (1982). *Toward transformation in social knowledge.* New York: Springer-Verlag.

Gigerenzer, G., Swijtink, Z., Porter, T., Daston, L., Beatty, J., & Kruger, L. (1989). *The empire of chance: How probability changes science and everyday life.* Cambridge, UK: Cambridge University Press.

Gilbert, D. T. (1998). Ordinary personology. In D. T. Gilbert, S. T. Fiske, & G. Lindzey (Eds.), *The handbook of social psychology* (4th ed., Vol. II, pp. 89–150). New York: McGraw-Hill.

Gilbert, D. T. (2006). *Stumbling on happiness.* New York: Knopf.

Gilbert, D. T., Fiske, S. T., & Lindzey, G. (Eds). (1998). *Handbook of social psychology* (Vols I and II). New York: McGraw-Hill.

Gilbert, D. T., & Hixon, J. G. (1991). The trouble of thinking: Activation and application of stereotypic beliefs. *Journal of Personality and Social Psychology, 60*, 509–517.

Gilbert, D. T., Pinel, E. C., Wilson, T. D., Blumberg, S. J., & Wheatley, T. P. (1998). Immune neglect: A source of durability bias in affective forecasting. *Journal of Personality and Social Psychology, 75*, 617–638.

Gillis, J. S. (1976). Participants instead of subjects. *American Psychologist, 31*, 95–97.

Gilovich, T., Griffin, D., & Kahneman, D. T. (Eds.). (2002). *Heuristics and biases: The psychology of intuitive judgment.* New York: Cambridge University Press.

Glass, G. V. (1976). Primary, secondary, and meta-analysis of research. *Educational Researcher, 5*, 3–8.

Gortner, E.-M., & Pennebaker, J. W. (2003). The archival anatomy of a disaster: Media coverage and community-wide health effects of the Texas A&M bonfire tragedy. *Journal of Social and Clinical Psychology, 22*, 580–603.

Gould, S. J. (1996). *The mismeasure of man* (Rev. ed.). New York: Norton.

Greenwald, A. G., & Banaji, M. R. (1995). Implicit social cognition: Attitudes, self-esteem, and stereotypes. *Psychological Review, 102*, 4–27.

Greenwald, A. G., McGhee, D. E., & Schwartz, J. L. K. (1998). Measuring individual differences in implicit cognition: The Implicit Associations Test. *Journal of Personality and Social Psychology, 74*, 1464–1480.

Gregory, R. J. (2003). *Psychological testing: History, principles, and applications* (4th ed.). Boston: Allyn & Bacon.

Gubrium, J. F., & Holstein, J. A. (Eds.). (2002). *Handbook of interview research: Context & method.* Thousand Oaks, CA: Sage.

Guttman, L. (1944). A basis for scaling quantitative data. *American Sociological Review, 9*, 139–150.

Hacking, I. (1975). *The emergence of probability.* London: Cambridge University Press.

Hall, E. T. (1966). *The hidden dimension.* Garden City, NJ: Doubleday.

Hansen, D. E., Vandenberg, B., & Patterson, M. L. (1995). The effects of religious orientation on spontaneous and nonspontaneous helping behaviors. *Personality and Individual Differences, 19*, 101–104.

Harker, L.A., & Keltner, D. (2001). Expressions of positive emotion in women's college yearbook pictures and their relationship to personality and life outcomes across adulthood. *Journal of Personality and Social Psychology, 80*, 112–124.

Harmon-Jones, E., & Mills, J. (Eds.). (1999). *Cognitive dissonance: Progress on a pivotal theory in social psychology.* Washington, DC: American Psychological Association.

Harris, M. B. (1998). *Basic statistics for behavioral science research* (2nd ed.). Boston: Allyn and Bacon.

Hassin, R. R., Uleman, J. S., & Bargh, J. A. (Eds.). (2005). *The new unconscious.* New York: Oxford University Press.

Haugtvedt, C. P., & Wegener, D. T. (1994). Message order effects in persuasion: An attitude strength perspective. *Journal of Consumer Research, 21*, 205–218.

Hayes, J. R. (1981). *The complete problem solver.* Philadelphia, PA: Franklin Institute.

Hazlewood, J. D., & Olson, J. M. (1986). Covariation information, causal questioning, and interpersonal behavior. *Journal of Experimental Social Psychology, 22*, 276–291.

Hedrick, T. E., Bickman, L., & Rog, D. J. (1993). *Applied research design: A practical guide.* Newbury Park, CA: Sage.

Hektner, J. M., & Csikszentmihalyi, M. (2002). The experience sampling method: Measuring the context and the content of lives. In R. B. Bechtel & A. Churchman (Eds.), *Handbook of environmental psychology* (pp. 233–243). Hoboken, NJ: Wiley.

Helson, R. (1967). Personality characteristics and developmental history of creative college women. *Genetic Psychology Monographs, 76,* 205–256.

Henderson, B. B. (2000). The reader's guide as an integrative writing experience. *Teaching of Psychology, 28,* 257–259.

Higbee, K. L., Millard, R. J., & Folkman, J. R. (1982). Social psychology research during the 1970s: Predominance of experimentation and college students. *Personality and Social Psychology Bulletin, 8,* 180–183.

Horowitz, M. J. (1976). *Stress response syndromes.* New York: Jason Aronson.

Houtkoop, H. (2000). *Interaction and the standardized survey interview: The living questionnaire.* New York: Cambridge University Press.

Hovland, C. J., Janis, I. L., & Kelley, H. H. (1953). *Communication and persuasion: Psychological studies of opinion change.* New Haven, CT: Yale University Press.

Hovland, C. J., & Weiss, W. (1951). The influence of source credibility on communication effectiveness. *Public Opinion Quarterly, 15,* 635–660.

Hoyle, R. H., Harris, M. J., & Judd, C. M. (2002). *Research methods in social relations* (7th ed.). Belmont, CA: Wadsworth.

Hoyle, R. H., & Robinson, J. C. (2004). Mediated and moderated effects in social psychological research: Measurement, design, and analysis issues. In C. Sansone, C. C. Morf, & A. T. Panter (Eds.), *The Sage handbook of methods in social psychology* (pp. 213–233). Thousand Oaks, CA: Sage.

Isen, A. M. (1987). Positive affect, cognitive processes, and social behavior. In L. Berkowitz (Ed.), *Advances in experimental social psychology* (Vol. 20, pp. 203–253). San Diego, CA: Academic Press.

Isen, A. M. (1999). Positive affect. In T. Dalgleish & M. J. Power (Eds.), *Handbook of cognition and emotion* (pp. 521–539). New York: Wiley.

Isen, A. M. (2002). Missing in action in the AIM: Positive affect's facilitation of cognitive flexibility, innovation, and problem solving. *Psychological Inquiry, 13,* 57–65.

Isen, A. M. (2004). Some perspectives on positive feelings and emotions: Positive affect facilitates thinking and problem solving. In A. S. R. Manstead, N. Frijda, & A. Fischer (Ed.), *Feelings and emotions: The Amsterdam symposium* (pp. 263–281). New York: Cambridge University Press.

Isen, A. M., Daubman, K. A., & Nowicki, G. P. (1987). Positive affect facilitates creative problem solving. *Journal of Personality and Social Psychology, 52,* 1121–1131.

Isen, A. M., & Levin, P. F. (1972). Effect of feeling good on helping: Cookies and kindness. *Journal of Personality and Social Psychology, 21,* 384–388.

Janoff-Bulman, R. (1992). *Shattered assumptions: Towards a new psychology of trauma.* New York: Free Press.

Jennings, D., Amabile, T. M., & Ross, L. (1982). Informal covariation assessment: Data-based vs. theory-based judgments. In A. Tversky, D. Kahneman, & P. Slovic (Eds.), *Judgment under uncertainty: Heuristics and biases* (pp. 211–230). New York: Cambridge University Press.

Joiner, T. E., Jr., Hollar, D., & Van Orden, K. (2006). On Buckeyes, Gators, Super Bowl Sunday, and the Miracle on Ice: "Pulling together" is associated with lower suicide rates. *Journal of Social and Clinical Psychology, 25,* 179–195.

Jones, A. C., & Josephs, R. A. (2006). Interspecies hormonal interactions between man and the domestic dog *(Canis familiaris)*. *Hormones and Behavior, 50,* 393–400.

Jones, E. E., & Harris, V. A. (1967). The attribution of attitudes. *Journal of Experimental Social Psychology, 3,* 1–24.

Jones, E. E., & Sigall, H. (1971). The bogus pipeline: A new paradigm for measuring affect and attitude. *Psychological Bulletin, 76,* 349–364.

Jones, S. R. G. (1992). Was there a Hawthorne Effect? *The American Journal of Sociology, 98,* 451–468.

Jones, W. H., Briggs, S. R., & Smith, T. G. (1986). Shyness: Conceptualization and measurement. *Journal of Personality and Social Psychology, 51,* 629–639.

Josselson, R., Lieblich, A., & McAdams, D. P. (Eds.). (2002). *Up close and personal: The teaching and learning of narrative research.* Washington, DC: American Psychological Association.

Judd, C. M., & Kenny, D. A. (1981). *Estimating the effects of social interventions.* Cambridge, UK: Cambridge University Press.

Katz, I. (1996). The Nuremberg Code and the Nuremberg Trial. *JAMA, 276,* 1662–1666.

Kelman, H. C. (1968). *A time to speak: On human values and social research.* San Francisco: Jossey-Bass.

Kenny, D. A., Kashy, D. A., & Bolger, N. (1998). Data analysis in social psychology. In D. T. Gilbert, S. T. Fiske, & G. Lindzey (Eds.), *The handbook of social psychology* (pp. 233–265). New York: McGraw-Hill.

Kiesler, S., & Sproull, L. (1986). Response effects in the electronic survey. *Public Opinion Quarterly, 50,* 402–413.

Kim, H. J., & Drolet, A. (2003). Choice and self-expression: A cultural analysis of variety seeking. *Journal of Personality and Social Psychology, 85,* 373–382.

Kim, H., & Markus, H. R. (1999). Deviance or uniqueness, harmony or conformity? A cultural analysis. *Journal of Personality and Social Psychology, 77,* 785–800.

Kimmel, A. J. (2004). Ethical issues in social psychology research. In C. Sansone, C. C. Morf, & A. T. Panter (Eds.), *The Sage handbook of methods in social psychology* (pp. 45–70). Thousand Oaks, CA: Sage.

King, L. A., Hicks, J. A., Krull, J. L., & Del Gaiso, A. K. (2006) Positive affect and the experience of meaning in life. *Journal of Personality and Social Psychology, 90,* 179–196.

Kitts, J. A. (2003). Egocentric bias or information management? Selective disclosure and the social roots of norm misperception. *Social Psychology Quarterly, 66,* 222–238.

Klinesmith, J., Kasser, T., & McAndrew, F. T. (2006). Guns, testosterone, and aggression: An experimental test of a mediational hypothesis. *Psychological Science, 17,* 568–571.

Knapp, F., & Heidingsfelder, M. (2001). Drop-out analysis: Effects of the survey design. In U.-D. Reips & M. Bosnjak (Eds.), *Dimensions of Internet science* (pp. 221–230). Lengerich, Germany: Pabst Science Publishers.

Krosnick, J. A., & Alwin, D. F. (1989). Aging and susceptibility to attitude change. *Journal of Personality and Social Psychology, 57,* 416–425.

LaFrance, M., & Banaji, M. (1992). Toward a reconsideration of the gender–emotion relationship. *Review of Personality and Social Psychology, 14,* 178–201.

Lalwani, A. K., Shavitt, S., & Johnson, T. (2006) What is the relation between cultural orientation and socially desirable responding? *Journal of Personality and Social Psychology, 90,* 165–178.

Langer, E. J. (1975). The illusion of control. *Journal of Personality and Social Psychology, 32,* 311–328.

Langer, E. J. (1983). *The psychology of control.* Beverly Hills, CA: Sage.

Langer, E. J. (1989). Minding matters: The consequences of mindlessness–mindfulness. In L. Berkowitz (Ed.), *Advances in experimental social psychology* (Vol. 22, pp. 137–174). San Diego, CA: Academic Press.

Langer, E. J., & Rodin, J. (1976). The effects of enhanced personal responsibility for the aged. *Journal of Personality and Social Psychology, 34,* 191–198.

Langer, E. J., & Roth, J. (1975). Heads I win, tails it's chance. *Journal of Personality and Social Psychology, 32,* 951–955.

LaPiere, R. T. (1934). Attitudes vs. actions. *Social Forces, 13,* 230–237.

Larson, R., & Richards, M. H. (1994). *Divergent realities: The emotional lives of mothers, fathers, and adolescents.* New York: Basic Books.

Latané, B., & Darley, J. M. (1968). Group inhibition of bystander intervention. *Journal of Personality and Social Psychology, 10,* 215–221.

Latané, B., & Darley, J. M. (1969). Bystander "apathy." *American Scientist, 57,* 218–250.

Latané, B., & Darley, J. M. (1970). *The unresponsive bystander: Why doesn't he help?* New York: Appleton-Century-Crofts.

Latané, B., & Rodin, J. A. (1969). A lady in distress: Inhibiting effects of friends and strangers on bystander intervention. *Journal of Experimental Social Psychology, 5,* 189–202.

Lau, R. R. (1984). Dynamics of the attribution process. *Journal of Personality and Social Psychology, 46,* 1017–1028.

Lau, R. R., & Russell, D. (1980). Attributions in the sports pages. *Journal of Personality and Social Psychology, 39,* 29–38.

Lazarsfeld, P. F. (1949). *The American soldier*—an expository review. *Public Opinion Quarterly, 13,* 377–404.

Lazarus, R. S., & Folkman, S. (1984). *Stress, appraisal, and coping.* New York: Springer.

Leahey, T. H. (2004). *A history of psychology: Main currents in psychological thought* (6th ed.). Upper Saddle River, NJ: Pearson.

Liberman, V., Samuels, S. M., & Ross, L. (2002). The name of the game: Predictive power of reputations vs. situational labels in determining Prisoner's Dilemma game moves. *Personality and Social Psychology Bulletin, 30,* 1175–1185.

Lincoln, Y. S., & Guba, E. G. (1985). *Naturalistic inquiry.* Newbury Park, CA: Sage.

Ling, P. M. (2004). *Preparing literature reviews: Qualitative and quantitative approaches.* Glendale, CA: Pryczak Publishing.

Lipsey, M. W. (2001). *Practical meta-analysis.* Thousand Oaks, CA: Sage.

Lopez, S. J. (2006a, May). *Giving positive psychology away: Ten strategies that promote student engagement.* Invited presentation at the 18th Annual Meeting of the Association for Psychological Science, New York.

Lopez, S. J. (2006b). C. R. (Rick) Snyder (1944–2006) [Obituary]. *American Psychologist, 61,* 719.

Losch, M. E., & Cacioppo, J. T. (1990). Cognitive dissonance may enhance sympathetic tonus, but attitudes are changed to reduce negative affect rather than arousal. *Journal of Experimental Social Psychology, 26,* 289–304.

Lykken, D., & Tellegen, A. (1996). Happiness is a stochastic phenomenon. *Psychological Science, 7,* 186–189.

Malle, B. F. (2004). *How the mind explains behavior: Folk explanations, meaning, and social interaction.* Cambridge, MA: MIT Press.

Manning, R., Levine, M., & Collins, A. (2007). The Kitty Genovese murder and the social psychology of helping: The parable of the 38 witnesses. *American Psychologist, 62,* 555–562.

Mark, M. M., & Reichardt, C. S. (2004). Quasi-experimental and correlational designs: Methods for the real world when random assignment isn't feasible. In C. Sansone, C. C. Morf, & A. T. Panter (Eds.), *The Sage handbook of methods in social psychology* (pp. 265–286). Thousand Oaks, CA: Sage.

Markus, H. R., & Kitayama, S. (2004). Models of agency: Sociocultural diversity in the construction of action. In V. Murphy-Berman & J. Berman (Eds.), *Nebraska Symposium on Motivation. Cross-cultural differences in perspectives on the self* (pp. 1–57). Lincoln: University of Nebraska Press.

Masuda, T., & Nisbett, R. E. (2001). Attending holistically vs. analytically: Comparing the context sensitivity of Japanese and Americans. *Journal of Personality and Social Psychology, 81,* 922–934.

McAdams, D. P. (1993). *The stories we live by: Personal myths and the making of the self.* New York: Morrow.

McAdams, D. P., Josselson, R., & Lieblich, A. (Eds.). (2001). *Turns in the road: Narrative studies of lives in transition.* Washington, DC: American Psychological Association.

McCarthy, M., & Pusateri, T. P. (2006). Teaching students to use electronic databases. In W. Buskist & S. F. Davis (Eds.), *Handbook of the teaching of psychology* (pp. 107–111). Malden, MA: Blackwell.

McConahay, J. B., & Hough, J. C. J. (1976). Symbolic racism. *Journal of Social Issues, 32,* 23–45.

McKenna, R. J. (1995). *The undergraduate researcher's handbook: Creative experimentation in social psychology.* Boston: Allyn and Bacon.

McSweeny, A. J. (1978). The effects of response cost on the behavior of a million persons: Charging for directory assistance in Cincinnati. *Journal of Applied Behavioral Analysis, 11,* 47–51.

Mednick, M. T., Mednick, S. A., & Mednick, E. V. (1964). Incubation of creative performance and specific associative priming. *Journal of Abnormal and Social Psychology, 69,* 84–88.

Mehl, M. R., & Pennebaker, J. W. (2003). The social dynamics of a cultural upheaval: Social interactions surrounding September 11, 2001. *Psychological Science, 14,* 579–585.

Miles, M. B., & Huberman, A. M. (1984). *Qualitative data analysis: A sourcebook of new methods.* Newbury Park, CA: Sage.

Milgram, S. (1963). Behavioral study of obedience. *Journal of Abnormal and Social Psychology, 67,* 371–378.

Milgram. S. (1964). Issues in the study of obedience: A reply to Baumrind. *American Psychologist, 19,* 848–852.

Milgram, S. (1972). Interpreting obedience: Error and evidence. In A. G. Miller (Ed.), *The social psychology of psychological research* (pp. 139–154). New York: The Free Press.

Milgram, S. (1974). *Obedience to authority: An experimental view.* New York: Harper Torchbooks.

Milgram, S. (1977). *The individual in a social world.* Reading, MA: Addison-Wesley.

Millar, M., & Tesser, A. (1986). Effects of affective and cognitive focus on the attitude–behavior relation. *Journal of Personality and Social Psychology, 51,* 270–276.

Miller, A. G. (2004). What can the Milgram obedience experiments tell us about the holocaust?: Generalizing from the social psychology laboratory. In A. G. Miller (Ed.), *The social psychology of good and evil* (pp. 193–239). New York: Guilford.

Miller, D. T., & McFarland, C. (1987). Pluralistic ignorance: When similarity is interpreted as dissimilarity. *Journal of Personality and Social Psychology, 53*, 298–305.

Miller, D. T., & Ross, M. (1975). Self-serving biases in the attribution of causality: Fact or fiction? *Psychological Bulletin, 82*, 213–225.

Miller, G. A. (1969a). Psychology as a means of promoting human welfare. *American Psychologist, 24*, 1063–1075.

Miller, G. A. (1969b, December). On turning over psychology to the unwashed. *Psychology Today, 3*(7), 53–54, 66–68, 70, 72, 74.

Mishler, E. G. (1986). *Research interviewing: Context and narrative.* Cambridge, MA: Harvard University Press.

Mitchell, J. (1972). You turn me on, I'm a radio [Recorded by J. Mitchell]. On *For the roses* [CD]. Los Angeles, CA: Electra. (1990).

Moneta, G. B., & Csikszentmihalyi, M. (1996). The effect of perceived challenges and skills on the quality of subjective experience. *Journal of Personality, 64*, 275–310.

Monson, T. C., & Snyder, M. (1977). Actors, observers, and the attribution process: Towards a reconceptualization. *Journal of Experimental Social Psychology, 13*, 89–111.

Mook, D. G. (1983). In defense of external invalidity. *American Psychologist, 38*, 379–387.

Moore, J. S., Graziano, W. G., & Millar, M. G. (1987). Physical attractiveness, sex role orientation, and the evaluation of adults and children. *Personality and Social Psychology Bulletin, 13*, 95–102.

Moskowitz, G. B. (2005). *Social cognition: Understanding self and others.* New York: Guilford Press.

Murchison, C. (Ed.). (1935). *A handbook of social psychology.* Worcester, MA: Clark University Press.

Myers, D. G. (2005). *Social psychology* (8th ed.). New York: McGraw-Hill.

Nagy, T. F (2005). *Ethics in plain English: An illustrative casebook for psychologists* (2nd ed.). Washington, DC: American Psychological Association.

Newell, A., & Simon, H. A. (1972). *Human problem solving.* Englewood Cliffs, NJ: Prentice-Hall.

Nicholson, C. (2006, August). Freedom and choice, culture and class. *Observer, 19*(8), 31, 45.

Nicks, S. D., Korn, J. H., & Mainieri, T. (1997). The rise and fall of deception in social psychology and personality research, 1921 to 1994. *Ethics & Behavior, 7*, 69–77.

Nicol, A. A. M., & Pexman, P. M. (1999). *Presenting your findings: A practical guide for creating tables.* Washington, DC: American Psychological Association.

Nicol, A. A. M., & Pexman, P. M. (2003). *Displaying your findings: A practical guide for creating figures, posters, and presentations.* Washington, DC: American Psychological Association.

Nisbett, R. E., & Cohen, D. (1996). *Culture of honor: The psychology of violence in the south.* Boulder, CO: Westview Press.

Nisbett, R., & Ross, L. (1980). *Human inference: Strategies and shortcomings of social judgment.* Englewood Cliffs, NJ: Prentice-Hall.

Nisbett, R. E., & Wilson, T. D. (1977). Telling more than we can know: Verbal reports on mental processes. *Psychological Review, 84*, 231–259.

Nosek, B. A., Banaji, M. R., & Greenwald, A. G. (2002). Harvesting implicit group attitudes and beliefs from a demonstration web site. *Group Dynamics: Theory, Research, and Practice, 6,* 101–115.

Nosek, B. A., Greenwald, A. G., & Banaji, M. R. (2007). The Implicit Association Test at age 7: A methodological and conceptual review. In J. A. Bargh (Ed.), *Automatic processes in social thinking and behavior* (pp. 265–92). Philadelphia, PA: Psychology Press.

Observer Forum. (2004, June). [Letters to the editor]. *APS Observer, 17*(6), 8–13.

Omoto, A. M., & Snyder, M. (1993). AIDS volunteers and their motivations: Theoretical issues and practical concerns. *Nonprofit Management and Leadership, 4,* 157–176.

Orne, M. T. (1962). On the social psychology of the psychological experiment: With particular reference to demand characteristics and their implications. *American Psychologist, 17,* 776–783.

Orne, M. T. (1981). The why and how of a contribution to the literature: A brief communication. *International Journal of Clinical and Experimental Hypnosis, 29,* 1–4.

Orne, M. T., & Holland, C. C. (1968). On the ecological validity of laboratory deception. *International Journal of Psychiatry, 6,* 282–293.

Panksepp, J. (2003). Feeling the pain of social loss. *Science, 302,* 237–239.

Parsons, H. M. (1974). What happened at Hawthorne? *Science, 183,* 922–932.

Paulhus, D. L. (1991). Measurement and control of response bias. In J. P. Robinson, P. R. Shaver, & L. S. Wrightsman (Eds.), *Measures of personality and social psychological attitudes* (Vol. 1, pp. 17–59). San Diego, CA: Academic Press.

Pavlov, I. P. (1957). *Experimental psychology and other essays.* New York: Philosophical Library.

Peerenboom, C. A., Hodge, F. W., Passano, E. B., Warren, H. C., Washburn, M. F., & Bentley, M. (1929). Instructions in regard to preparation of manuscript. *Psychological Bulletin, 26*(2), 57–63.

Pelham, B. W. (1999). *Conducting experiments in psychology: Measuring the weight of smoke.* Pacific Grove, CA: Brooks/Cole.

Pennebaker, J. W. (1989). Confession, inhibition, and disease. In L. Berkowitz (Ed.), *Advances in experimental social psychology* (Vol. 22, pp. 211–244). New York: Academic Press.

Pennebaker, J. W. (1993). Mechanisms of social constraint. In D. M Wegner & J. W. Pennebaker (Eds.), *Handbook of mental control* (pp. 200–219). Englewood Cliffs, NJ: Prentice-Hall.

Pennebaker, J. W. (1997). *Opening up: The healing power of expressing emotions.* New York: Guilford.

Pennebaker, J. W., Barger, S. D., & Tiebout, J. (1989). Disclosure of traumas and health among holocaust survivors. *Psychosomatic Medicine, 51,* 577–589.

Pennebaker, J. W., & Harber, K. D. (1993). A social stage model of collective coping: The Loma Prieta Earthquake and the Persian Gulf War. *Journal of Social Issues, 49*(4), 125–145.

Pennebaker, J. W., & Newtson, D. (1983). Observations of a unique event: The psychological impact of the Mount Saint Helens Volcano. *New Directions for Methodology of Social and Behavioral Science, 15,* 93–109.

Penner, L. A. (2002). Dispositional and organizational influences on sustained volunteerism: An interactionist perspective. *Journal of Social Issues, 58,* 447–467.

Peterson, C., & Seligman, M. E. P. (2003). Character strengths before and after September 11. *Psychological Science, 14,* 381–384.

Peterson, C., & Seligman, M. E. P. (2004). *Character strengths and virtues: A handbook and classification.* New York: Oxford University Press.

Peterson, C., Seligman, M. E. P., Yurko, K. H., Martin, L. R., & Friedman, H. S. (1998). Catastrophizing and untimely death. *Psychological Science, 9,* 127–130.

Petty, R. E. (1983). *Social psychophysiology: A sourcebook.* New York: Guilford.

Petty R. E., & Cacioppo, J. T. (1981). *Attitudes and persuasion: Contemporary approaches.* Dubuque, IA: Wm. C. Brown.

Petty, R. E., & Cacioppo, J. T. (1986). *Communication and persuasion: Central and peripheral routes to attitude change.* New York: Springer-Verlag.

Petty, R. E., Cacioppo, J. T., & Goldman, R. (1981). Personal involvement as a determinant of argument-based persuasion. *Journal of Personality and Social Psychology, 41,* 847–855.

Pratkanis, A. R. (1992). *Age of propaganda: The use and abuse of persuasion.* New York: W. H. Freeman.

Pratkanis, A. R., Greenwald, A., G., Leippe, M. R., & Baumgardner, M. H. (1988). In search of reliable persuasion effects: III. The sleeper effect is dead: Long live the sleeper effect. *Journal of Personality and Social Psychology, 52,* 203–218.

Pratto, F., Sidanius, J., Stallworth, K., & Malle, B. (1994). Social dominance orientation: A personality variable predicting social and political attributes. *Journal of Personality and Social Psychology, 67,* 741–763.

Prentice-Dunn S., & Rogers, R. (1980). Effects of deindividuating situational cues and aggressive models on subjective deindividuation and aggression. *Journal of Personality and Social Psychology, 39,* 235–244.

Punzo, V. A., & Miller, E. (2002). Investigating conscious experience through the beeper project. *Teaching of Psychology, 29,* 295–297.

Rand Corporation. (1955). *A million random digits.* Glencoe, IL: Free Press.

Reips, U.-D. (2000). The Web experiment method: Advantages, disadvantages, and solutions. In M. H. Birnbaum (Ed.), *Psychological experiments on the Internet* (pp. 89–117). San Diego, CA: Academic Press.

Reis, H. T., & Gable, S. L. (2000). Event-sampling and other methods for studying everyday experience. In H. T. Reis and C. M. Judd (Eds.), *Handbook of research methods in social and personality psychology* (pp. 190–222). Cambridge, UK: Cambridge University Press.

Rhodes, N., & Wood, W. (1992). Self-esteem and intelligence affect influenceability: The mediating role of message reception. *Psychological Bulletin, 111,* 156–171.

Robinson, J. P., Shaver, P. R., & Wrightsman, L. S. (Eds.). (1991). *Measures of personality and social psychological attitudes* (Vol. 1). San Diego: Academic Press.

Rodin, J., & Langer, E. J. (1977). Long-term effects of a control relevant intervention. *Journal of Personality and Social Psychology, 35,* 897–902.

Roediger, R. (2004, April). What should they be called? *APS Observer, 17*(4), 5, 46–48.

Roese, N., & Jamieson, D. W. (1993). Twenty years of bogus pipeline research: A critical review and meta-analysis. *Psychological Bulletin, 114,* 363–375.

Roethlisberger, F. J., & Dickson, W. J. (1939). *Management and the worker.* Cambridge, MA: Harvard University Press.

Rosenthal, R. (1966). *Experimenter effects in behavioral research.* New York: Appleton-Century-Crofts.

Rosenthal, R. (1967). Covert communication in the psychology experiment. *Psychological Bulletin, 67,* 356–367.

Rosenthal, R. (1969). Interpersonal expectations: Effects of the experimenter's hypothesis. In R. Rosenthal & R. Rosnow (Eds.), *Artifact in behavioral research* (pp. 181–277). New York: Academic Press.

Rosenthal, R. (1976). *Experimenter effects in behavioral research* (Enlarged ed.). New York: Irvington.

Rosenthal, R. (1991). *Meta-analytic procedures for social research* (Rev. ed.). Newbury Park, CA: Sage.

Rosenthal, R. (1993). Cumulating evidence. In G. Keren & C. Lewis (Eds.), *A handbook for data analysis in the behavioral sciences: Methodological issues* (pp. 519–559). Hillsdale, NJ: Erlbaum.

Rosenthal, R. (1994a). Interpersonal expectancy effects: A 30-year perspective. *Current Directions in Psychological Science, 36*, 176–179.

Rosenthal, R. (1994b). Science and ethics in conducting, analyzing, and reporting psychological research. *Psychological Science, 5*, 127–134.

Rosenthal, R. (1995a). Methodology. In A. Tesser (Ed.), *Advanced social psychology* (pp. 17–49). New York: McGraw-Hill.

Rosenthal, R. (1995b). Writing meta-analytic reviews. *Psychological Bulletin, 118*, 183–192.

Rosenthal, R., & Fode, K. L. (1963). The effects of experimenter bias on the performance of the albino rat. *Behavioral Science, 8*, 183–189.

Rosenthal, R., & Jacobson, L. (1968). *Pygmalion in the classroom.* New York: Holt, Rhinehart, & Winston.

Rosenthal, R., & Rosnow, R. L. (1984). Applying Hamlet's question to the ethical conduct of research: A conceptual addendum. *American Psychologist, 39*, 561–563.

Rosenthal, R., & Rosnow, R. L. (1991). *Essentials of behavioral research: Methods and data analysis* (2nd ed.). New York: McGraw-Hill.

Rosenthal, R., & Rubin, D. B. (1978). Interpersonal expectancy effects: The first 345 studies. *The Behavioral and Brain Sciences, 3*, 377–415.

Rosenthal, R., & Rubin, D. R. (1980). Summarizing 345 studies of interpersonal expectancy effects. In R. Rosenthal (Ed.), *New directions for methodology of social and behavioral sciences: Quantitative assessment of research domains* (pp. 79–95). San Francisco: Jossey-Bass.

Rosnow, R. L., & Rosenthal, R. (1996). *Beginning behavioral research: A conceptual primer* (2nd ed.). Englewood Cliffs, NJ: Prentice-Hall.

Ross, A. S., & Braband, J. (1973). Effects of increased responsibility on bystander intervention II: The cue value of a blind person. *Journal of Personality and Social Psychology, 25*, 254–258.

Ross, L. (1977). The intuitive psychologist and his shortcomings: Distortions in the attribution process. In L. Berkowitz (Ed.), *Advances in experimental social psychology* (Vol. 10, pp. 174–221). New York: Academic Press.

Ross, L., Lepper, M. R., & Hubbard, M. (1975). Perseverance in self-perception and social perception: Biased attributional processes in the debriefing paradigm. *Journal of Personality and Social Psychology, 32*, 880–892.

Ross, L., & Nisbett, R. E. (1991). *The person and the situation: Perspectives of social psychology.* New York: McGraw-Hill.

Ross, M., & Sicoly, F. (1979). Egocentric biases in availability and attribution. *Journal of Personality and Social Psychology, 32*, 880–892.

Salant, P., & Dillman, D. A. (1994). *How to conduct your own survey.* New York: Wiley.

Sales, B. D., & Folkman, S. (Eds.). (2000). *Ethics in research with human participants.* Washington, DC: American Psychological Association.

Salovey, P. (2000). Results that get results: Telling a good story. In R. J. Sternberg (Ed.), *Guide to publishing in psychology journals* (pp. 121–132). New York: Cambridge University Press.

Sapir, E. (1951). *Selected writings in language, culture, and personality* (D. G. Mandelbaum, Ed.). Berkeley: University of California Press.

Schachter, S. (1959). *The psychology of affiliation: Experimental studies of the sources of gregariousness.* Stanford, CA: Stanford University Press.

Schachter, S., & Singer, J. E. (1962). Cognitive, social and physiological determinants of emotional state. *Psychological Review, 69,* 379–399.

Scheier, M. F., & Carver, C. S. (1985). The Self-Consciousness Scale: A revised version for use with general populations. *Journal of Applied Social Psychology, 15,* 687–699.

Schelling, T. C. (1978). *Micromotives and macrobehavior.* New York: Norton.

Scherbaum, C. A. (2006). A basic guide to statistical research and discovery: Planning and selecting statistical analysis. In F. T. L. Leong & J. Austin (Eds.), *The psychology research handbook* (2nd ed., pp. 275–292). Thousand Oaks, CA: Sage.

Schimmack, U. (2003). Affect measurement in experience sampling research. *Journal of Happiness Studies, 4,* 79–106.

Schkade, D. A., & Kahneman, D. (1998). Does living in California make people happy? A focusing illusion in judgments of life satisfaction. *Psychological Science, 9,* 340–346.

Schlenker, B. R. (1974). Social psychology and science. *Journal of Personality and Social Psychology, 29,* 1–15.

Schlenker, B. R. (1976). Social psychology and science: Another look. *Personality and Social Psychology Bulletin, 2,* 384–390.

Schultz, D. P. (1969). The human subject in psychological research. *Psychological Bulletin, 72,* 214–228.

Schulz, R. (1976). Effects of control and predictability on the psychological well-being of the institutionalized aged. *Journal of Personality and Social Psychology, 33,* 563–573.

Schuman, H. (1981). *Questions and answers in attitude surveys: Experiments on question form, wording, and context.* New York: Academic Press.

Schuman, H. (1996). *Questions and answers in attitude surveys: Experiments on question form, wording, and context.* Thousand Oaks, CA: Sage.

Schuman, H., & Presser, S. (1979). The open and closed question. *American Sociological Review, 44,* 692–712.

Schuman, H., & Presser, S. (1981). *Questions and answers in attitude surveys.* New York: Academic Press.

Schuman, H., & Presser, S. (1996). *Questions and answers in attitude surveys: Experiments on form, wording, & context.* Thousand Oaks, CA: Sage.

Schwartz, N., & Clore, G. L. (1983). Mood, misattribution, and judgments of well-being: Informative and directive functions of attributional states. *Journal of Personality and Social Psychology, 45,* 513–523.

Schwartz, N., Groves, R. M., & Schuman, H. (1998). Survey methods. In D. T. Gilbert, S. T. Fiske, & G. Lindzey (Eds.), *The handbook of social psychology* (Vol. 1, pp. 143–179). New York: McGraw-Hill.

Schwartz, S. H., & Gottlieb, A. (1981). Participants' post-experimental reactions and the ethics of bystander research. *Journal of Personality and Social Psychology, 17*, 396–407.

Scollon, C. N., Diener, E., Oishi, S., & Biswas-Diener, R. (2004). Emotion across cultures and methods. *Journal of Cross-Cultural Psychology, 35*, 304–326.

Sears, D. O. (1986). College sophomores in the laboratory: Influences of a narrow data base on social psychology's view of human nature. *Journal of Personality and Social Psychology, 51*, 515–539.

Sechrest, L. (1971). Situational sampling and contrived situations in assessment of behaviour. *Pakistan Journal of Psychology, 4*, 3–19.

Segal, M. W. (1974). Alphabet and attraction: An unobtrusive measure of the effect of propinquity in a field setting. *Journal of Personality and Social Psychology, 30*, 654–657.

Seidman, I. (1998). *Interviewing as qualitative research: A guide for researchers in education and the social sciences.* New York: Teachers College Press.

Severson, K. (2006, October 11). Seduced by snacks? No, not you. *The New York Times*, F1, F5.

Shadish, W. R., Cook, T. D., & Campbell, D. T. (2001). *Experimental and quasi-experimental designs for generalized causal inference.* Boston: Houghton Mifflin.

Sharpe, D., Adair, J. G., & Roese, N. J. (1992). Twenty years of deception research: A decline in subjects' trust? *Personality and Social Psychology Bulletin, 18*, 585–590.

Shelton, J. N., & Richeson, J. A. (2005). Intergroup contact and pluralistic ignorance. *Journal of Personality and Social Psychology, 88*, 91–107.

Sidanius, J., & Pratto, F. (1999). *Social dominance: An intergroup theory of social hierarchy and oppression.* Cambridge, UK: Cambridge University Press.

Siegel, S., & Castellan, N. J., Jr. (1988). *Nonparametric statistics for the behavioral sciences.* New York: McGraw-Hill.

Sirken, M. G., Herrmann, D. J., Schechter, S., Schwartz, N., Tanur, J. M., & Tourangeau, R. (Eds.). (1999). *Cognition and survey research.* New York: Wiley.

Slovic, P., & Fischoff, B. (1977). On the psychology of experimental surprises. *Journal of Experimental Psychology: Human Perception and Performance, 3*, 455–551.

Smith, E. R. (1998). Mental representation and memory. In D. T. Gilbert, S. T. Fiske, & G. Lindzey (Eds.), *Handbook of social psychology* (Vol. 1, pp. 391–445). New York: McGraw-Hill.

Smith, S. S., & Richardson, D. (1983). Amelioration of deception and harm in psychological research: The important role of debriefing. *Journal of Personality and Social Psychology, 44*, 1075–1082.

Snedecor, G. W., & Cochran, W. G. (1980). *Statistical methods* (7th ed.). Ames: Iowa State University Press.

Snowdon, D. A. (1997). Aging and Alzheimer's disease: Lessons from the Nun Study. *Gerontologist, 37*, 150–156.

Snyder, C. R. (1994). *The psychology of hope: You can get there from here.* New York: Free Press.

Snyder, C. R., Harris, C., Anderson, J. R., Holleran, S. A., Irving, L. M., Sigmon, S. T., et al. (1991). The will and the ways: Development and validation of an individual-differences measure of hope. *Journal of Personality and Social Psychology, 60*, 570–585.

Snyder. C. R., & Lopez, S. J. (2007). *Positive psychology: The scientific and practical explorations of human strengths.* Thousand Oaks, CA: Sage.

Snyder, M., Omoto, A. M., & Lindsay, J. J. (2004). Sacrificing time and effort for the good of others: The benefits and costs of volunteerism. In A. G. Miller (Ed.), *The social psychology of good and evil* (pp. 444–468). New York: Guilford Press.

Snyder, M., Tanke, E. D., & Berscheid, E. (1977). Social perception and interpersonal behavior: On the self-fulfilling nature of social stereotypes. *Journal of Personality and Social Psychology, 35,* 656–666.

Sommer, R. (1968). The Hawthorne dogma. *Psychological Bulletin, 70,* 592–595.

Spencer, S. J., Steele, C. M., & Quinn, D. M. (1999). Stereotype threat and women's math performance. *Journal of Experimental Social Psychology, 35,* 4–28.

Steele, C. M. (1997). A threat in the air: How stereotypes shape intellectual identity and performance. *American Psychologist, 52,* 613–629.

Stephens, N. M., Markus, H. R., & Townsend, S. S. M. (2007). Choice as an act of meaning: The case of social class. *Journal of Personality and Social Psychology, 93,* 814–830.

Sternberg, R. J. (2003). *The psychologist's companion: A guide to scientific writing for students and researchers* (4th ed.). New York: Cambridge University Press.

Sternberg. R. J. (Ed.). (2006). *Reviewing scientific works in psychology.* Washington, DC: American Psychological Association.

Stone, A. A., Kessler, R. C., & Haythornthwaite, J. A. (1991). Measuring daily events and experiences: Decisions for the researcher. *Journal of Personality, 59,* 575–607.

Stone, L. D., & Pennebaker, J. W. (2002). Trauma in real time: Talking and avoiding online conversations about the death of Princess Diana. *Basic and Applied Social Psychology, 24,* 173–183.

Strube, M. J. (2005). What did Triplett really find? A contemporary analysis of the first experiment in social psychology. *American Journal of Psychology, 118,* 271–286.

Taylor, S. E. (1983). Adjustment to threatening events: A theory of cognitive adaptation. *American Psychologist, 38,* 1161–1173.

Taylor, S. E. (1989). *Positive illusions: Creative self-deception and the healthy mind.* New York: Basic Books.

Taylor, S. E., & Brown, J. D. (1988). Illusions and well-being: A social psychological perspective on mental health. *Psychological Bulletin, 103,* 193–210.

Taylor, S. E., & Brown, J. D. (1994). Positive illusions and well-being revisited: Separating fact from fiction. *Psychological Bulletin, 116,* 21–27.

Taylor, S. E., & Fiske, S. T. (1975). Point of view and perceptions of causality. *Journal of Personality and Social Psychology, 32,* 439–445.

Taylor, S. J., & Bogdan, R. (1998). *Introduction to qualitative research methods: A guidebook and resource* (3rd ed.). New York: Wiley.

Thorndike, E. L. (1920). A constant error in psychological ratings. *Journal of Applied Psychology, 4,* 25–29.

Thurstone, L. L. (1929). Theory of attitude measurement. *Psychological Bulletin, 36,* 222–241.

Tourangeau, R., & Rasinski, K. A. (1988). Cognitive processes underlying context effects in attitude measurement. *Psychological Bulletin, 103,* 299–314.

Tourangeau, R., Rasinski, K. A., Bradburn, N., & D'Andrade, R. (1989). Carryover effects in attitude surveys. *Public Opinion Quarterly, 53,* 495–524.

Tourangeau, R., Rips, L. J., & Rasinski, K. (2000). *The psychology of survey response.* New York: Cambridge University Press.

Triplett, N. (1898). The dynamogenic factors in pacemaking and competition. *American Journal of Psychology, 9,* 507–533.

Tulving, E., & Craik, F. I. M. (Eds.). (2000). *The Oxford handbook of memory.* New York: Oxford.

Uleman, J. S., & Bargh, J. A. (Eds.). (1989). *Unintended thought.* New York: Guilford.

U. S. Census. (2007). *Historical income tables-families.* Retrieved February 27, 2007, from http://www.census.gov/hhes/www/income/histinc/f06ar.html

Vaux, A., & Briggs, C. S. (2006). Conducting mail and Internet surveys. In F. T. L. Leong & J. T. Austin (Eds.), *The psychology research handbook: A guide for graduate students and research assistants* (2nd ed., pp. 186–209). Thousand Oaks, CA: Sage.

Vitelli, R. (1988). The crisis issue addressed: An empirical analysis. *Basic and Applied Social Psychology, 9,* 301–309.

Wagner, H. L., & Manstead, A. S. R. (Eds.). (1989). *Handbook of social psychophysiology.* New York: John Wiley & Sons.

Wampold, B. E. (2006). Designing a research study. In F. T. L. Leong & J. T. Austin (Eds.), *The psychology research handbook: A guide for students and research assistants* (2nd ed., pp. 93–103). Thousand Oaks, CA: Sage.

Wansink, B. (2006). *Mindless eating: Why we eat more than we think.* New York: Bantam.

Webb, E. J., Campbell, D. T., Schwartz, R. D., & Sechrest, L. (1999). *Unobtrusive measures* (Revised ed.). Thousand Oaks, CA: Sage.

Webb, E. J., Campbell, D. T., Schwartz, R. D., Sechrest, L., & Grove, J. B. (1981). *Nonreactive measures in the social sciences* (2nd ed.). Boston: Houghton Mifflin.

Weber, S. J., & Cook, T. D. (1972). Subject effects in laboratory research: An examination of subject roles, demand characteristics, and valid inference. *Psychological Bulletin, 77,* 273–295.

Wegner, D. M. (1994). *White bears and other unwanted thoughts: Suppression, obsession, and the psychology of mental control.* New York: Guilford Press.

Wegner, D. M., Schneider, D. J., Carter, S., III, & White, T. (1987). Paradoxical effects of thought suppression. *Journal of Personality and Social Psychology, 53,* 5–13.

Wegner, D. M., Wenzlaff, R., Kerker, R. M., & Beattie, A. E. (1981). Incrimination through innuendo: Can media questions become public answers? *Journal of Personality and Social Psychology, 40,* 822–832.

Wegener, D. T., Clark, J. K., & Petty, R. E. (2006). Not all stereotyping is created equal: Differential consequences of thoughtful versus nonthoughtful stereotyping. *Journal of Personality and Social Psychology, 90,* 42–59.

Whitley, B. E., Jr., & Kite, M. E. (2006). *The psychology of prejudice and discrimination.* Belmont, CA: Thompson.

Whorf, B. L. (1964). *Language, thought, and reality: Selected writings* (J. B. Carroll, Ed.). Cambridge, MA: MIT Press.

Wicker, A. W. (1969). Attitudes versus actions: the relationships of verbal and overt behavioral responses to attitude objects. *Journal of Social Issues, 25,* 41–78.

Williams, K. D. (2002). *Ostracism: The power of silence.* New York: Guilford.

Wilson, T. D. (2002). *Strangers to ourselves: Discovering the adaptive unconscious.* Cambridge, MA: Harvard University Press.

Wilson, T. D. (2005). The message is the method: Celebrating and exporting the experimental approach. *Psychological Inquiry, 16,* 185–193.

Wilson, T. D. (2006). The power of social psychological interventions. *Science, 313,* 1251–1252.

Wilson, T. D., & Dunn, E. W. (2004). Self-knowledge: Its limits, value, and potential for improvement. *Annual Review of Psychology, 55,* 493–518.

Wilson, T. D., Dunn, D. S., Bybee, J. A., Hyman, D. B., & Rotondo, J. A. (1984). Effects of analyzing reasons on attitude–behavior consistency. *Journal of Personality and Social Psychology, 47,* 5–16.

Wilson, T. D., Dunn, D. S., Kraft, D., & Lisle, D. J. (1989). Introspection, attitude change, and attitude–behavior consistency: The disruptive effects of explaining why we feel the way we do. In L. Berkowitz (Ed.), *Advances in experimental social psychology* (Vol. 22, pp. 287–343). San Diego, CA: Academic.

Wilson, T. D., & Gilbert, D. T. (2003). Affective forecasting. In M. P. Zanna (Ed.), *Advances in experimental social psychology* (Vol. 35, pp. 346–413). New York: Academic Press.

Wilson, T. D., & Gilbert, D. T. (2005). Affective forecasting: Knowing what to want. *Current Directions in Psychological Science, 14*(3), 131–134.

Wilson, T. D., & Schooler, J. W. (1991). Thinking too much: Introspection can reduce the quality of preferences and decisions. *Journal of Personality and Social Psychology, 60,* 181–192.

Wilson, T. D., & Stone, J. I. (1985). Limitations on self-knowledge: More on telling more than we can know. In P. Shaver (Ed.), *Review of Personality and Social Psychology* (Vol. 6, pp. 167–183). Beverly Hills, CA: Sage.

Winer, B. J., Brown, D. R., & Michels, K. M. (1991). *Statistical principles in experimental design* (3rd ed.). New York: McGraw-Hill.

Wong, M. M., & Csikszentmihalyi, M. (1991). Affiliation motivation and daily experience: Some issues on gender differences. *Journal of Personality and Social Psychology, 60,* 154–164.

Woodzicka, J. A., & LaFrance, M. (2001). Real versus imagined gender harassment. *Journal of Social Issues, 57*(1), 15–30.

Wortman, C. B. (1975). Some determinants of perceived control. *Journal of Personality and Social Psychology, 31,* 282–294.

Wright, B. A. (1983). *Physical disability: A psychosocial approach* (2nd ed.). New York: Harper & Row.

Wright, B. A. (1991). Labeling: The need for greater person–environment individuation. In C. R. Snyder & D. R. Forsyth (Eds.), *Handbook of social and clinical psychology: The health perspective* (pp. 469–487). New York: Pergamon.

Wright, B. A., & Lopez, S. J. (2002). Widening the diagnostic focus: A case for including human strengths and environmental resources. In C. R. Snyder & S. J. Lopez (Eds.), *Handbook of positive psychology* (pp. 26–44). New York: Oxford.

Wright, D. B. (1997). *Understanding statistics: An introduction for the social sciences.* London: Sage Publications.

Zajonc, R. B. (1965). Social facilitation. *Science, 149,* 269–274.

Zajonc, R. B., Heingartner, A., & Herman, E. M. (1969). Social enhancement and impairment of performance in the cockroach. *Journal of Personality and Social Psychology, 13,* 83–92.

Zhong, C. B., & Liljenquist, K. (2006). Washing away your sins: Threatened morality and physical cleansing. *Science, 313,* 1451–1452.

Zimbardo, P. G. (1969). The human choice: Individuation, reason, and order versus deindividuation, impulse, and chaos. In W. J. Arnold & N. Levine (Eds.), *Nebraska symposium on motivation, 1969* (pp. 237–307). Lincoln: University of Nebraska Press.

Zullow, H. M., & Seligman, M. E. P. (1990). Pessimistic rumination predicts defeat of presidential candidates, 1900 to 1984. *Psychological Inquiry, 1*, 52–61.

Author Index

Larson, R. 130, 131, 132
Latané, B. 25–6, 186, 194, 211, 241
Lau, R. R. 141–2
Lazarsfeld, P. F. 28
Lazarus, R. S. 30
Leahey, T. H. 187
LeFevre, J. 130
Leippe, M. R. 300
LePage, A. 189
Lepper, M. R. 55, 274
Levin, P. F. 56
Levine, M. 25
Levinson, D. J. 8
Lewis, L. 25
Lewis, S. K. 214–15
Liberman, V. 250
Lieberman, M. D. 226
Lieblich, A. 227
Liljenquist, K. 213, 215
Lincoln, Y. S. 281
Lindsay, J. J. 16
Lindsay, R. C. L. 13, 53
Lindzey, G. 40
Ling, P. M. 144
Lipsey, M. W. 144
Lishner, D. A. 30
Lisle, D. J. 151
Longo, L. C. 178
Lopez, S. J. 60, 279, 280
Losch, M. E. 254
Lykken, D. 89

Mainieri, T. 53
Makhijani, M. G. 178
Malle, B. F. 8, 119–20, 121
Manning, R. 25
Manstead, A. S. R. 226
Margulis, S. T. 37
Mark, M. M. 146
Markman, A. B. 225
Markus, H. R. 207, 208, 242
Marlowe, D. 176–7
Martin, L. R. 133
Masser, B. 186
Master, A. 213, 214
Masuda, T. 186

McAdams, D. P. 227
McAndrew, F. T. 4–5, 14, 189
McCarthy, M. 38, 39
McConahay, J. B. 219
McFarland, C. 25
McGhee, D. E. 225, 251
McKenna, R. J. 116, 289, 290
McQuirk, B. 26
McSweeny, A. J. 126–7
Mednick, E. V. 83
Mednick, M. T. 83
Mednick, S. A. 83
Mehl, M. R. 114
Messner, C. 225
Metalsky, F. I. 184
Metts, S. 37
Michels, K. M. 107
Miene, P. 16
Miles, M. B. 281
Milgram, S. 49–52, 53, 55, 56, 57, 58–9, 74, 186, 193, 195, 212, 244, 245, 250, 251, 257, 282
Millar, M. 151
Millar, M. G. 178
Millard, R. J. 13
Miller, A. G. 52
Miller, D. T. 25, 141
Miller, E. 131, 132
Miller, G. A. 276
Miller, N. E. 189
Mills, J. 37, 186, 234
Mishler, E. G. 223
Mitchell, J. 75
Moneta, G. B. 130
Monson, T. C. 142
Mook, D. G. 245–6, 250
Moore, D. 22
Moore, J. S. 178
Moskowitz, G. B. 221
Mowrer, O. H. 189
Myers, D. G. 28

Nagy, T. F. 73
Newell, A. 223
Newtson, D. 114, 139
Nicholson, C. 207, 242

Subject Index

cell phones
  delivery of independent variables 195
  in experience sampling method research 132
census 153–4, 156
chance, games of 183, 212
chance situations: mimicking skill situations 183–5
character traits: changed by September 11 137–9
chi-square tests 290–1
children: informed consent 68
choices 150–1, 207–8
  as exerting control 184
  observation of participant 213
citation types 316–17
citations 35, 44, 45, 229
  in references 316
  in social psychology logs 42
clarity
  of APA style 302
  of questions 164–73
class, social: and personal agency 208, 242–3
codeability, behavioral measures 209
cognition, social 12, 26
cognitive dissonance, theory of 234–5, 254, 257
cognitive psychology, field of 6
cold pressor test 279–81
collaborators *see* confederates
collective behavior: after Loma Prieta earthquake 111–12
collective coping, model of 112–13
collective events: data collection at 260
collective focus: in disciplines 5, 6
college sophomore problem 92, 248
  reduced in Internet-based research 134
  as threat to external validity 242–3
combination designs 109
commitments, future: measurement 214–15
communication
  one-sided 301
  persuasive 299–302
  two-sided 301
communities: as source for research topic ideas 29

community, sense of 207–8
comparison groups
  lack of: in time series designs 126
  nonequivalent 124–5
competition, interpersonal 21–2
compliance: of research participants 257–8
computers
  delivery of independent variables 196
  used to reduce experimenter bias 267
  working bibliographies on 42
  see also Internet; web searches; web sites
conclusions
  avoiding unnecessary conclusions in questions 169–70
  drawing conclusions 11
concrete, behavioral measures as 209
conditions 4
  aggression experiment 4
confederates
  delivery of independent variables 193–4
  to reduce experimenter bias 266
  role of 58–9
  scripts for 269
  use of 55
confidentiality 274
  maintenance of 67, 71, 72
  in questionnaires and surveys 177
  see also anonymity
conflict 13
conformity study 47, 48, 194, 257
confounded variable 106
consciousness 157
  in experience sampling methods 130
consistency
  of APA style 302
  in behavior 233–5
  of independent variables 192
  internal 230–1
construct validity 236, 252–3
consumer behavior study 249
contamination effects *see* carryover effects
content: of questions 165, 221
context effects: in questionnaires and surveys 171–2
contexts
  of behavior: in judgment study 186